CONTEMPORARY
Black
Biography

ISSN-1058-1316

CONTEMPORARY

Black

Biography

Profiles from the International Black Community

Volume 47

THOMSON

GALE

Detroit • New York • San Francisco • San Diego • New Haven, Conn. • Waterville, Maine • London • Munich

Contemporary Black Biography, Volume 47
Sara and Tom Pendergast

Project Editor
Pamela M. Kalte

Image Research and Acquisitions
Robyn V. Young

Editorial Support Services
Nataliya Mikheyeva

Rights and Permissions
Denise Buckley, Shalice Shah-Caldwell, Margaret Chamberlain

Manufacturing
Dorothy Maki, Rhonda Williams

Composition and Prepress
Mary Beth Trimper, Gary Leach

Imaging
Lezlie Light, Mike Logusz

ISBN 0-7876-6735-8
ISSN 1058-1316

Printed in the United States of America
10 9 8 7 6 5 4 3 2 1

Contemporary Black Biography Advisory Board

Contents

Introduction

Contemporary Black Biography provides informative biographical profiles of the important and influential persons of African heritage who form the international black community: men and women who have changed today's world and are shaping tomorrow's. *Contemporary Black Biography* covers persons of various nationalities in a wide variety of fields, including architecture, art, business, dance, education, fashion, film, industry, journalism, law, literature, medicine, music, politics and government, publishing, religion, science and technology, social issues, sports, television, theater, and others. In addition to in-depth coverage of names found in today's headlines, *Contemporary Black Biography* provides coverage of selected individuals from earlier in this century whose influence continues to impact on contemporary life. *Contemporary Black Biography* also provides coverage of important and influential persons who are not yet household names and are therefore likely to be ignored by other biographical reference series. Each volume also includes listee updates on names previously appearing in *CBB*.

Designed for Quick Research and Interesting Reading

- *Attractive page design* incorporates textual subheads, making it easy to find the information you're looking for.

- *Easy-to-locate data sections* provide quick access to vital personal statistics, career information, major awards, and mailing addresses, when available.

- *Informative biographical essays* trace the subject's personal and professional life with the kind of in-depth analysis you need.

- *To further enhance your appreciation* of the subject, most entries include photographic portraits.

- *Sources for additional information* direct the user to selected books, magazines, and newspapers where more information on the individuals can be obtained.

Helpful Indexes Make It Easy to Find the Information You Need

Contemporary Black Biography includes cumulative Nationality, Occupation, Subject, and Name indexes that make it easy to locate entries in a variety of useful ways.

Available in Electronic Formats

Diskette/Magnetic Tape. *Contemporary Black Biography* is available for licensing on magnetic tape or diskette in a fielded format. Either the complete database or a custom selection of entries may be ordered. The database is available for internal data processing and nonpublishing purposes only. For more information, call (800) 877-GALE. **On-line.** *Contemporary Black Biography* is available online through Mead Data Central's NEXIS Service in the NEXIS, PEOPLE and SPORTS Libraries in the GALBIO file and Gale's Biography Resource Center.

Disclaimer

Contemporary Black Biography uses and lists websites as sources and these websites may become obsolete.

We Welcome Your Suggestions

The editors welcome your comments and suggestions for enhancing and improving **Contemporary Black Biography.** If you would like to suggest persons for inclusion in the series, please submit these names to the editors. Mail comments or suggestions to:

The Editor
Contemporary Black Biography
Thomson Gale
27500 Drake Rd.
Farmington Hills, MI 48331-3535
Phone: (800) 347-4253

Maurice Ashley

1966—

Chess player

Maurice Ashley helped shatter stereotypes by becoming the top-ranked black chess player in the world, as well as by coaching championship school teams made up mostly of minority children. "For kids, it's what they see," he said in the *New Yorker.* "And they don't see black chess players—no blacks in intellectual fields at all. It's when the kids start seeing these paths that they become possibilities in their minds, and then it's not a shock to them that Harlem kids can be national chess champions." Ashley has also startled traditional chess aficionados and attracted new fans to the game with his rousing commentating of chess matches that make chess seem like a contact sport.

Ashley was born on March 6, 1966, in Jamaica, where he spent the first 12 years of his life before his family moved to Brooklyn, New York. He feels that his early experience saved him from the poor self-image of many blacks born in American inner cities. "I didn't have the word 'disadvantaged' pummeled into my brain," Ashley told Hugh Pearson of the *Wall Street Journal.* As Pearson added in the same article, Ashley "had a firm enough grounding to keep himself focused on his studies, even though drug dealers plied their trade nearby."

Stayed Focused through Chess

Also helping Ashley stay on a straight path was his discovery of chess. He became keenly interested in the game after watching his brother play with his friends, and was soon reading chess books so he could play better. As a teenager he played often with other African Americans in Brooklyn's Prospect Park while continuing to study game strategy on his own. "I grew up like a lot of these kids, playing ball in the streets, listening to hip-hop," said Ashley in the *New Yorker* of the children he has taught to love chess. "Not really having anything to do—that was a big theme in my life. And then I discovered chess. It was like a light, and I just kept moving in that direction."

A key mentor for the young Ashley was Willie Johnson, a friend of a friend who was an Expert level player, one step below the Masters level in the chess world. "He helped keep me from being frustrated when I lost to some of the better players," said Ashley when interviewed by *Contemporary Black Biography* (*CBB*). "He was instrumental in helping me stay focused and in supporting me in ways not just emotionally but financially. He helped me out whenever he could so I could to buy chess books or enter tournaments."

Since no African Americans were top tournament chess players during his formative years, Ashley found his roles models elsewhere. "I tended to look outside the chess world for my heroes, at people who were blazing the trail in professions that were not, so to speak, black-oriented," he claimed during an interview with *CBB*. A number of these "heroes" were women—such as Zina Garrison and Lori McNeil in tennis and Debi Thomas in ice skating—who were among the first blacks to make a mark in their respective sports.

Coached a New Generation

After graduating from City College, Ashley soon got

At a Glance . . .

Born on March 6, 1966, in Kingston, Jamaica; married Michele Ashley; children: Nia. *Education:* City College of New York.

Career: Moved from Jamaica to Brooklyn, NY, 1978; achieved rank of International Master as chess player; became highest-ranked black chess player in the world; began coaching Raging Rooks chess team at Adam Clayton Powell, Jr., Junior High School, New York, NY, 1989; led Raging Rooks to National Junior High School Championship, 1991; started up Dark Knights chess team at Mott Hall School, New York, NY, 1992; began commentating televised chess events on ESPN, 1993; coached Dark Knights to National Junior High School Championship, 1994; became commentator for Professional Chess Association's Intel World Chess Grand Prix, 1990s; served as online chess mentor for public schools around U.S., 1990s; released interactive CD-ROM chess program entitled Maurice Ashley Teaches Chess, 1996; participated in the Chess-in-the- Schools International Chess Festival, 1997.

Addresses: *Home*—Brooklyn, New York; *Web*—www.mauriceashley.com.

the opportunity to bring his love of the game to young people in New York City. The American Chess Foundation, which later became the Chess-in-the Schools Program, asked Ashley to go out to different schools to help promote chess in minority neighborhoods. By 1989, he was coaching the Raging Rooks, the chess team of Adam Clayton Powell, Jr., Junior High School. Before long, he had created one of the most successful chess programs for kids in the United States. He led the Rooks to the National Championships in Salt Lake City in 1990, where one of his players, Kasaun Henry, won the top unrated title in the varsity section.

Ashley followed up that success by leading his team to a tie for first-place in the Nationals held in Dearborn, Michigan, in 1991. His team's showing that year resulted in a barrage of media attention, making the Raging Rooks front-page news in the *New York Times*. Ashley was fully aware that much of the hoopla was due to the racial factor. "I look upon a lot of the attention we got in much the same way as I view articles that characterize me as the best black chess player in the world," he told the *New Yorker*. "It's degrading in a way, but it has its uses, and I'm happy to use it to bring attention to the game and prestige to our pro-

gram."

Proving his success as a coach was no fluke, Ashley revealed his winning ways once again after becoming the coach of the Dark Knights team at Harlem's Mott Hall Middle School in 1992. Two years later, he led a team made up of seven Hispanic players and three Asians to the National Junior High School Chess Team Championship. Key to Ashley's coaching success with the Raging Rooks and Dark Knights was his understanding of the mindset of inner-city children and his use of sports metaphors to reach kids at their level to generate enthusiasm for the game. "Maurice's coaching sessions are sometimes like meetings of the Joint Chiefs [U.S. political leaders] in wartime, sometimes like pickup basketball games, and sometimes like abusive comedy routines," noted the *New Yorker*.

Helped Promote Chess as a Sport

A self-proclaimed sports fanatic, Ashley treats the chessboard like a playing field and the players like real-life athletes. "Chess is a sport," he told *CBB*. "It's competitive, it's work, it's pressure, it's tension, it's pain, it's guts and glory, and disappointment and defeat. All the classic sports metaphors are in chess, so it was very easy for me to transfer many of the ideas that I found in the sports world to the chessboard."

Ashley later became an online chess mentor for public schools around the country, which allowed him to present problems and answer questions via e-mail with young players. By the mid 1990s, he was also gaining exposure as a new breed of commentator for chess tournaments. "Ashley is loud," commented Richard Sandomir in the *New York Times* about Ashley's announcing at the Professional Chess Association's Intel World Chess Grand Prix tournament in New York City in 1994. "Not obnoxious. Just louder than a voice is expected to be for noise-free chess." Ashley has often proclaimed his eagerness to overcome the quiet and reserved reputation of chess, in order to make people realize how rewarding the game is. At the Grand Prix Tournament he stunned other commentators by his use of phrases usually reserved for sports announcers, and by discussing players' emotional states in addition to their playing skill.

Ashley's style and his success as a coach caught the attention of ESPN, which hired him to be their play-by-play announcer for televised chess events. He was an enthusiastic commentator for the well-publicized 1997 tournament of world-champion Garry Kasparov versus Deep Blue, the IBM computer. Ashley feels that Deep Blue's victory was mostly due to a lapse of will and concentration by Kasparov. "I still think we need another match to really confirm for us what level of play the computer has truly attained," he said.

The previous year, Ashley released an acclaimed interactive CD-ROM chess instruction program for beginning to intermediate players called Maurice Ashley Teaches Chess that became the only software endorsed by the Professional Chess Association. According to a press release from CD-ROM co-publisher Davidson & Associates, the program "combines Ashley's inspiring teaching style with extensive video coaching, thousands of fast-paced interactive challenges, chess strategies, and video annotated Master Games." Ashley's CD-ROM featured many analogies from football and other sports to explain the rules and strategies of chess, even using a video chalkboard like those used by sports commentators.

Newsweek called the CD-ROM "excellent," while *Home Education Review* said "It's great for people just learning to play, or those who need some help improving their game." Ashley's goal with the CD-ROM was to make the game accessible to virtually anyone. "My CD-ROM is for people who don't know anything about the game," he told *VIBE*. "It's for those who think it's too complicated, too crazy."

Achieved Grandmaster Status

Ashley placed 21st in the 1997 U.S. Open Chess Tournament in New York City, and also participated in the Chess-in-the-Schools International Chess Festival at New York City's Downtown Athletic Club. In April of 1997, he was ranked #41 in the United States by the U.S. Chess Federation and was still the highest-ranked black chess player in the world. But Ashley was not satisfied with his performance. He told *Ebony* that "I felt the frustration of seeing my future behind me, and I decided I had to focus on one thing–playing."

In the summer of 1997, he stopped coaching to concentrate fully on achieving the rank of grandmaster. The rank of grandmaster is difficult to achieve. A player must score "norms," or excellent performance ratings, in three tournaments against other top-rated chess players. In 1999 Ashley became the first black grandmaster. At the time there were only 470 grandmasters in the world.

As he recaptured his skill as a player, Ashley did not lose sight of those he had mentored. He is proud to see the accomplishments of some of his former students who are now graduating from some of the country's most prestigious colleges. Ashley firmly believes that chess sharpens the mind in ways that help in all parts of life. He returned to mentoring and coaching in 1999 when he became the director of the chess program at the Harlem Educational Activities Fund. The Fund opened a chess center in Harlem in 1999 to promote chess in the community. In order to make chess a more exciting game to play and watch, Ashley organized a company called Generation Chess in 2003 to create competitive chess tournaments that penalized players for agreeing to a draw before 50 moves. Ashley also serves as chess commentator for ESPN2 and travels throughout the country to inspire others to take up

chess. In 2003 the U.S. Chess Federation named Ashley Grandmaster of the Year.

Selected works

Maurice Ashley Teaches Chess (CD-ROM), Simon and Schuster, 1995.

Sources

Periodicals

Ebony, July 1999, p. 30.
Home Education Review, September/October 1996.
Jet, March 22, 2004, p. 25.
New York Times, June 30, 1994, p. B16; July 11, 1996, sec. 13, p. 9; April 19, 1996, p. B1; May 6, 1996, p. A10; February 11, 1996, sec. 13, p. 9.
New Yorker, February 24, 1992, p. 29.
Newsweek, July 8, 1996, p. 8.
VIBE, November 1996, p. 132.
Wall Street Journal, February 17, 1995, p. A10.

On-line

Maurice Ashley, www.mauriceashley.com (August 19, 2004).

Television

America Beyond the Color Line with Henry Louis Gates Jr., PBS, 2004.

Other

Additional information for this profile was obtained from a Davidson & Associates press release and through an interview with Maurice Ashley.

—Ed Decker and Sara Pendergast

Arnold A. Auguste

1946—

Publisher

When Arnold A. Auguste left his native Trinidad for Canada, he planned on pursuing a journalism career. Unfortunately, he couldn't find a place to work that matched his ideals. "I didn't originally set out to own a paper, I just wanted to write," he told *The Eye Opener.* Steeped in equal doses of debt and optimism, Auguste began publishing *Share,* a weekly paper aimed at Toronto's black and Caribbean communities. That was in 1978, and Auguste could afford to publish no more than 2,000 copies per week. But by 2004, *Share* was pumping out 50,000 copies a week and reaching an estimated 150,000 readers. *Share* is now Canada's largest ethnic newspaper and a vital component of Canada's media industry.

Founded 'Share' in His Apartment

Born and raised in Trinidad, West Indies, Arnold A. Auguste left the Caribbean nation when he was 23 years old. He arrived in Toronto, Canada, in 1970 and began to contribute columns to *Contrast,* a politically aggressive paper that had its roots in the black power movement of the 1960s. Eventually he enrolled in Ryerson University's journalism program. After graduating in 1976 he was hired as an editor at *Spirit,* a paper targeting the black community. The paper soon released him, however, due to budget cuts. He next landed an editorial position at *Contrast,* another paper serving the black community, but his moderate ideals clashed with the paper's hard-line stance. He was fired within a year.

Just two years out of journalism school and with two lost jobs on his fledgling resume, Auguste decided to do something radical. Unable to find the type of paper he wanted to write for, he decided to create it. In 1978 Auguste formed Arnold A. Auguste Associates Limited and launched *Share,* a weekly newspaper dedicated to the black and Carribean community of Toronto. The name of the paper captured the tone of the reporting; Auguste wanted his community to share its good news, to share with each other. "*Share* is not just about news, where as main-stream news is, news only," Auguste told *African Canadian Online.* "*Share*'s focus is on Toronto. It is a community newspaper which covers our community, what we are doing here, in Toronto. *Share* is connected to the community at large."

Auguste produced the first three issues out of his apartment. Though initial reaction to the paper was positive, someone did not like what he was doing. Shortly after the third edition hit the streets, Auguste's apartment was firebombed. He lost everything he owned. Though it was a major personal and financial setback, Auguste remained undeterred. He found a new place to live and work and continued producing *Share* almost without a hitch.

Produced Positively Different Paper

Share was a different publication in a lot of ways. It was the first ethnic paper to be distributed for free in Toronto. Anywhere blacks and Caribbean people congregated, *Share* could be found—Caribbean and African markets, hair salons, restaurants. The paper also looked different. The front page folded open to reveal a glossy magazine-style cover. In addition *Share* proved to be the first colorblind black paper. More concerned

At a Glance . . .

Born in 1957(?) in Trinidad, West Indies. *Education:* Ryerson University, Journalism, 1976.

Career: *Spirit,* Toronto, Canada, editor, 1976; *Contrast,* Toronto, Canada, editor, 1977; *Share,* Auguste A. Arnold Associates Limited, Toronto, Canada, publisher and editor-in-chief, 1978–.

Memberships: Ethnic Press Council of Canada, board of directors.

Awards: Black Business and Professional Association, Harry Jerome Business Award, 1993; Ethnic Press Council of Canada, Excellence in Journalism.

Addresses: *Office*—Share, 658 Vaughan Rd., Toronto, Ontario, M6E-2Y5, Canada.

with quality reporting and writing than any status quo, Auguste did not hesitate to hire writers of any ethnicity. One white writer, hired in 1980, told *The Eye Opener* that "I think mostly what [Auguste] wanted was to see his community covered thoroughly, and it didn't matter to him what color the reporter was, so long as they could do that for him."

However, what really made *Share* stand out was its positive spin on the news. "If I want to read about crime in the black community, I'd read the *Toronto Sun,*" Auguste told *The Eye Opener.* "I'd much rather print a story about a young black man winning an award, than a young black man committing a crime." He continued emphasizing that he wanted immigrants, Carribeans, and Africans in particular "to see that they didn't make a mistake in coming here. There's a lot of good things going on in this community." To that end *Share* has always focused on positive or neutral stories about the black and Caribbean communities in Toronto. The *Share* Web site noted, "Our team of qualified journalists, including the publisher, gives our readers a comprehensive view of what our community is all about every week, 52 weeks of the year, together with analyses and commentaries from our community's point of view, in addition to news from the Caribbean and Africa, sports, entertainment, business, religion, etc." The only thing blatantly missing from the paper's extensive coverage was crime, and in a large city like Toronto where crime—particularly black-on-black crime, is high—Auguste's refusal to cover the issue drew criticism from other papers as well as the public. Auguste dismissed the criticism, insisting that the purpose of the paper was to inspire the community to do better.

Forged Success His Way

Auguste himself spoke out against crime and wrote editorials in efforts to stop violence. But as his editorial on *Share*'s 26th anniversary stated: "We believed that positive news would encourage members of our community to excel. We believed that, as we shared our good experiences and ideas; as we shared our successes; as we shared the successes of our children, we would encourage each other, not so much to ignore the negatives that were placed in our paths, but to focus on the potential this city, this province and this country offered." Auguste has remained consistent on these points since he founded the paper.

Auguste has also been quick to point out that his feel-good paper has struck a chord with the public. As of 2002 the paper had a weekly print run of 50,000 and was reaching over 150,000 readers. Though many advertiser-supported papers struggle to stay afloat, *Share* has never lost money. Advertisers with products aimed at the black and Carribean communities vie for prime ad space. Meanwhile, other papers falter alongside *Share*. Both of Auguste's former employers, *Contrast* and *Spirit,* have long been shut down. Other black-focused publications such as *Pride* and *Caribbean Camera* are too small to infringe on *Share*'s market.

Further proof of the power of Auguste's positive approach occurred when long-time editor Jules Elder quit *Share*. The two men had drifted apart philosophically over the years and Elder finally left in 1998 to work for the *Toronto Sun*. At that time Auguste took over editorial duties, reinforced his positive approach, and launched an extensive Web site for the paper. As a result, circulation rose by more than 50 percent over the next four years. Auguste was also able to increase the size of the paper from 20 to 32 pages, allowing for more advertisers. *Share*'s success gave Auguste a kind of validation for his approach to the news. As he told *The Eye Opener*: "We're successful, and we keep growing, so that ought to tell you we're on the right track."

Sources

On-line

"About Share News," *Share,* www.sharenews.com (August 14, 2004).
"The Black Press in Canada," *African Canadian On-line,* www.yorku.ca/aconline/literature/press.html (August 14, 2004).
"Negative News Doesn't Get Its Share," *The Eye Opener,* www.theeyeopener.com/storydetail.cfm?storyid=71 (August 14, 2004).

—Candace LaBalle

Barry C. Black

1948—

U.S. Senate Chaplain, Chief Navy Chaplain

Black, Barry C., photograph. Courtesy of Barry C. Black.

In June of 2003 Rear Admiral Barry C. Black was appointed the 62nd Chaplain to the United States Senate. His nomination by then-President Bill Clinton and the Secretary of the Navy during Black's tenure as Chief of Navy Chaplains was acknowledgement of a long and illustrious military career and indeed a special relationship with God. The appointment makes Black the first military chaplain, the first Seventh-day Adventist, and the first African American to fill the position, ministering to a flock of 6,000, comprising senators, spouses, Chiefs of Staff, and Capitol Hill employees. Black is advisor to the most powerful people in the United States government on moral, spiritual, and ethical issues that affect the lives of millions in the United Sates and abroad.

Studied Bible and Oratory

Chaplain Barry C. Black was born on November 1, 1948, in the inner city of Baltimore, Maryland, to Pearline and Lester Black. "My mother was a beautiful person who connected with all her children and made each of us feel special," Chaplain Black said in an interview with *Contemporary Black Biography* (*CBB*). "She was a storyteller with the ability to find allies and build networks, and she was athletic. I inherited these skills from my mother." Sensing his destiny, Pearline told her son, "You will have a special destination in life and a life with God." This she believed because when she was baptized and pregnant with the chaplain she had asked God to do something special with his life.

Pearline taught her eight children the importance of God and education as the way to a better life without poverty. Raising a large family alone, Pearline, a Seventh-day Adventist, found church to be the supportive environment she needed to accomplish this. At Berea Temple and its Baltimore Junior Academy her children found a thriving community of helping hands, a quality education, and much needed tuition assistance. Black's mother found friends like Albertha Brown, who shared her home with young Barry after school, providing him a haven from the mean streets of Baltimore.

During church services Black heard the best preachers in the community and began to develop his language skills. "Mother supplemented this by giving us a nickel

Born on November 1, 1948, in Baltimore, MD; married Brenda Pearsall Black, 1973; children: Barry II, Brendan, Bradford. *Education:* Oakwood College, BA, theology, 1970; Andrews Theological Seminary, MDiv, 1973; North Carolina Central University, MA, counseling, 1978; Eastern Baptist Seminary, DMin, theology, 1982; Salve Regina University, MA, management, 1989; United States International University, PhD, psychology, 1996; La Sierra University, Honorary DD, 2004. *Military Service:* United States Navy Chaplain Corps, United States and Okinawa, Japan, 1976-2003. *Religion:* Seventh-day Adventist.

Career: United States Navy, Norfolk, VA, Philadelphia, PA, Okinawa, Japan, Annapolis, MD, Chaplain, 1976-83; U.S. Navy Training Center, San Diego, CA, Recruit Training Command Chaplain, 1983-85; USS Belleau Wood, Long Beach, CA, Command Chaplain, 1985-88; Marine Aircraft Group 31, Beaufort, SC, Group Chaplain, 1989-91; Naval Education and Training Command, Pensacola, FL, Deputy Command Chaplain, 1991-94; U.S. Atlantic Fleet, Norfolk, VA, Fleet Chaplain, 1994-97; U.S. Navy, Washington, DC, Deputy Chief of Chaplains, 1997-2000; U.S. Navy, Washington, DC, Chief of Chaplains, 2000-03; US Senate, Washington, DC, Chaplain of the United States Senate, 2003–.

Awards: U.S. Navy, Navy and Marine Corps Commendation Medals, 1985; U.S. Navy, Meritorious Service Medal, 1994 and 1988; U.S. Navy, Defense Meritorious Service Medal, 2001 and 1996; U.S. Navy, Legion of Merit Award, 1997; U.S. Navy, Distinguished Service Medal, 2002.

Addresses: *Office*—U.S. Capitol, E. Capitol Street at First Street, Washington, DC 20011.

for scriptures we memorized. She had to put me on a flat rate; I was breaking the bank," Black remembered. At school young Barry would study the prose of Longfellow, Emerson, Milton, and Thoreau. "I entered poetry readings and oratorical contests. I had a love for the music of language," explained Black. Hearing his oratory skills, the congregation and school provided affirmation that oratory was also his gift.

Heeded His Calling

Black felt from an early age that he wanted to be a minister and knew he had a "special feeling for God," but he resisted. "I wanted to pursue God, but most ministers in the inner city seemed poor. In my junior year of college I decided to go with the desire of my heart and pursue the ministry even if it meant poverty."

First Black received his bachelor of theology degree in 1970, from Oakwood College in Huntsville, Alabama. He entered Andrews Theological Seminary at Berrien Springs, Michigan, earning a master of divinity degree in 1973. There he enjoyed the focus on theology. Next Black moved to Durham, North Carolina, to pastor seven churches in South Carolina and North Carolina. Preaching two or three times each week allowed Black to learn quickly; within two years he was sent to pastor three other churches in North Carolina.

By this time Black had married Brenda Pearsall, who he met during his junior year at Oakwood College, and he began work on a master's degree in counseling, completing it in 1978. Brenda was an English major; her skills would become a valuable asset as Black developed his language skills. In 1982 Black completed a doctorate in theology, and received a master's degree in management in 1989. In 1996 he was awarded a doctorate in psychology.

One day in North Carolina, while speaking with three young servicemen from Norfolk, Virginia, Black wondered why they did not worship back on base. When asked, they said they had never heard of a black Navy Chaplain. "It planted a seed," says Black. The Navy needed African-American chaplains, and Black wanted to work with young people. "Also I didn't want to minister to just people from my own race," he told *CBB*. "I wanted a broader challenge."

Found His Place and Mission

Black was just 25 years old and, citing his young age, church leaders would not grant Black approval to minister to the young people of his church. Subsequently he did find what he was searching for with the United States Navy in 1976. At the time his church was seeking individuals interested in providing ministry in the military, so Black joined the Navy. Intending initially to stay three years, Black knew after his first day he had found his niche. "The variety of denominations, the improved salary, the appreciation on the part of a diverse group of people for my particular talents and gifts, the additional challenge of being physically fit, the joy of working with young people, all those factors I recognized very quickly and thought this is too good to be true. The experience was a protracted honeymoon for 27 years that went by very quickly," said Black.

Black found that his own skill set was exactly what the Navy sought. He had always been athletic, excelling in sports in college, and many years of counseling, preaching, and Bible studies had made him an effective communicator. "Also, I enjoyed leading, setting goals, establishing objectives. I enjoyed achieving these shared objectives and teaching people in areas that relate to how to be ethically fit." Black also welcomed the structure and having others being accountable to him.

Black knew if he worked hard he could count on the Navy to compensate him for his abilities. "I felt it was a level playing field and I would not be a victim of discrimination," he said. "I could compete like an athlete and if I'm good enough and that is documented on paper then I knew I could go to the top. I sought to excel."

The Chaplain knew that traveling with the Navy and meeting new people would excite his passion for diverse cultures and languages. Here was a way to "spread my wings in many directions," the Chaplain said. With his love of language he would develop a practical familiarity with Spanish, German, Italian, French, Japanese, and Korean.

Appointed to Top Posts

Black held several posts during his 27-year career in the Navy, eventually becoming Deputy Chief of Chaplains in 1997, and in 2000 he became Chief of Navy Chaplains. As chief he held responsibility for the spiritual care of servicemen from 190 religious traditions. He advised and provided ministry to the Chief of Naval Operations, the Secretaries of the Navy and Defense, and the Commandants of the Marine Corps and Coast Guard.

Black's Naval career prepared him well for his appointment in 2003 to Chaplain of the United States Senate. Once again he would advise and minister to very powerful people. He opens each Senate session with prayer and provides ministry to all levels of personnel on Capitol Hill. Senators and spouses, Chiefs of Staff, chefs, janitors, and the police officers all look to the Chaplain for guidance. "You must have a comfort level working with people from a broad variety of traditions," says the Chaplain. "You have to be comfortable meeting the press and discussing issues such as the nature of church and state relations and the ethical dimensions of various issues that come before the Senate, such as stem cell research and the Defense of Marriage Act."

Chaplain Black spends his days visiting the Senate chamber and cloakrooms, advising on ethical matters, conducting Bible studies, and counseling staff. He interacts with various groups regarding their concerns, prepares speeches and sermons, and officiates at funerals and memorial services. Often he represents the Senate in matters away from Capitol Hill and occasionally speaks at Camp David, the President's retreat.

Through the years Chaplain Black's dedication as a spiritual leader has earned him a position of influence at the top levels of government and the military. Black heeded his calling and advises others to do the same. He said we should each "discover the purpose for which we were created. Ask 'Who am I and why am I here?' If you don't ask yourself these questions of identity and mission you will probably lead a life, as Thoreau says, 'of quiet desperation.'"

Sources

Periodicals

Adventist News Network, June 17, 2003, p. 1.

On-line

"Rear Admiral Barry Black Appointed U.S. Senate Chaplain U.S. Dream Academy Board Member," *U.S. Dream Academy,* www.usdreamacademy.com (July 16, 2004).

"Chaplain Office," *U.S. Senate,* www.senate.gov/reference/office/chaplain (July 15, 2004).

"Senate Chaplain Pays a Visit," *FreeRepublic.com,* www.freerepublic.com (July 17, 2004).

Other

Additional information for this profile was obtained through an interview with Chaplain Barry C. Black on August 31, 2004.

—Sharon Melson Fletcher

Homer S. Brown

1896-1977

Judge, attorney, civil rights activist

Considered the father of the Pennsylvania state Fair Employment Practices Act and the first African-American judge in Pittsburgh, Pennsylvania, Homer S. Brown was a civil and political rights activist for most of his life. For over fifty years, from the time he received his law degree in 1923 until illness forced him to retire two years before his death in 1975, Judge Brown worked to facilitate positive change within the black community in the areas of employment, education, and civil rights. His passion and activism for the promotion of civil rights and his numerous contributions to his local and statewide community secured him a place of honor and integrity in the history of Pennsylvania.

Homer Sylvester Brown was born in Huntington, West Virginia, on September 23, 1896, to the Reverend William Roderick Brown and Maria Wiggins Rowlett Brown. He was educated at Virginia Union University in Richmond, Virginia, and received his law degree from the University of Pittsburgh in 1923, graduating third in a class of 22. During his lifetime, Brown also received honorary doctor of law degrees from Lincoln University, Virginia Union University, University of Pittsburgh, and Virginia State College. He married Wilhelmina Byrd in 1927 and had one son, Byrd Rowlett Brown.

Homer Brown's legacy continued on through his son Byrd Brown, who was also a noted Pittsburgh attorney and civil rights activist in Pittsburgh. Byrd held his father's legacy in highest respect, taking up the torch where he had left off. According to the *Pittsburgh Post-Gazette*, Mayor Tom Murphy of Pittsburgh said upon Byrd's death in 2001, "Pittsburghers, especially

younger African-Americans, need to know Byrd Brown for something more than that he was a successful and talented attorney. Byrd Brown was an African-American who stood in the front lines of the civil rights movement and faced down enormous hatred and prejudice. It takes a rare kind of courage to be able to do that." This courage, talent, and motivation came from a father who had modeled success and practiced greatness in a time of oppression.

Homer S. Brown became a member of the Allegheny County Bar Association on October 26, 1923, shortly after getting his law degree. As a young attorney, Brown began working to improve his community. During the Great Depression of the 1930s, there was a dramatic increase in Pittsburgh crime. Brown chaired a committee, called the Friendly Service Bureau, to promote crime reduction within the Hill City District of Pittsburgh. With the help of the city's mayor at the time, Cornelius D. Scully, the crime reduction program drastically reduced crime and improved the quality of life for the youth of the Hill District.

In 1934, Brown was elected to the Pennsylvania House of Representatives and served seven consecutive terms until 1950. In 1937, he began to question the hiring practices of the Pittsburgh Board of Education. He organized state hearings to investigate, and the results paved the way for a major lawsuit. Although Pittsburgh had desegregated its schools in 1875, the Pittsburgh Board of Education had refused to hire black teachers. The lawsuit, argued by black attorneys Richard F. Jones and Joseph Givens, changed the practices of the Board; it hired the school's first black music instructor,

Lawrence Peeler, within a year of the court case. Homer Brown scored one of numerous victories in this important lawsuit. In 1943 he was voted the most able member of the House by the Capital News Correspondents' Association and also named the most outstanding legislator.

While he was a member of the House of Representatives, Brown faced one of his greatest struggles—to secure human rights protection for working class residents of Pennsylvania. He authored a bill to prohibit discrimination in employment in Pennsylvania in 1945, giving him the famous title "Father of the State Fair Employment Practices Act" (FEPC). After extensive research was conducted on discrimination practices in Pennsylvania, it was found that nine out of ten firms discriminated against race, religion, or national origin in the hiring of workers. The result of this research proved that there was a need for Brown's FEPC. Its establishment in Pennsylvania was another major victory for Brown and for the working class in Pennsylvania.

Brown might also be called the "father of firsts." He was the founder and first President of the Pittsburgh branch of the National Association for the Advancement of Colored Persons (NAACP), a position that he served for 24 years. In 1943, he was the first African-American appointed to the Pittsburgh Board of Education, and in 1949 he became the first African-American to hold the position of Allegheny County Judge. He was elected to the Court of Common Pleas in 1956 and remained until 1975 when poor health forced his retirement.

On the bench Brown was known well for his decision in 1968 that the City of Pittsburgh's tax on hospitals, known as the "sick tax," was unconstitutional. Another historic decision came in 1973 when he ruled that prayers could be offered at graduation ceremonies. The United States Supreme Court upheld both of these decisions. He was also instrumental in the passage of several bills, known as the "Pittsburgh Package," which created the Housing Authority, of which Brown served as a charter member, and the Pittsburgh Renaissance.

But Brown was not only active in the judicial arena. He was also the member of numerous other organizations, such as Chair of the Board of Directors of the YMCA; the White House Commission on Education in 1955, and the Pennsylvania Governor's Committee on Education in 1960. He also served on the advisory board of the United Nations Educational, Scientific, and Cultural Organization and served one year in the U.S. Army. Because of his tireless work to improve life for those in and around his community, Brown was well known and highly respected in Pennsylvania. As a matter of fact, when Thurgood Marshall, the future U.S. Supreme Court justice, came to town, he dined in the prominent home of Homer and Wilhelmina Brown.

The Homer S. Brown Law Association, founded in 1969 in Pittsburgh in honor of Brown, is the only African-American law association in the city, representing the interests of approximately 200 African-American attorneys and jurists. The goal of the organization is to protect political and civil rights, increase the legal knowledge of the community, assist local law students, and benefit members by providing employment information. The membership group supports minority lawyers and tracks hiring progress in Pittsburgh and continues to be extremely active in the Pittsburgh community. Judge Homer S. Brown's legacy lives on.

Twenty-three volumes of photocopies of material belonging to Homer Brown are on deposit at Virginia Union University in Richmond. Material in these volumes were collected and compiled by his wife, Wilhelmina Byrd Brown, and gifted to the university in 1978 and 1980. This collection signifies the prolific work of Brown during his activities as judge, lawyer, and civil rights activist. Materials related to Brown's fight against Governor Earle's bill to change the Pennsylvania Grand Jury System in 1938 and 1939 documents regarding charges of discrimination against the City of Pittsburgh in hiring of African-Americans as teachers, are of particular interest in the collection. The collection also includes a number of judicial opinions written by Judge Brown between 1961 and 1974. Judge Brown died at his home in Pittsburgh on May 22, 1977.

Sources

On-line

"Byrd Brown Feted by Peers: Father's Group Honors Son's Leadership and Work," *Pittsburgh Post-Gazette,* www.post-gazette.com/businessnews/200 00118brown3.asp (September 2, 2004).

"The Civil Rights Movement in Pittsburgh: To Make This City 'Some Place Special,'" *Freedom Corner,* www.freedomcorner.org/downloads/glasco.pdf (September 23, 2004).

"Fallen Heroes," *Freedom Corner,* www.freedomcorner.org/fallen_heros.html (September 2, 2004).

"Lawyer Byrd Brown Dies; Giant in Civil Rights Struggle," www.post-gazette.com/obituaries/2001 0504brown2.asp (August 26, 2004).

"Pittsburghers of the Century," *Pittsburgh Magazine,* www.wqed.org/mag/articles/12_99/100pgh_1. html#b (August 26, 2004).

—Cheryl A. Dudley

Nick Cannon

1980—

Actor, writer, musician

A promising young actor who has demonstrated box-office appeal to both black and white audiences, Nick Cannon has been called the Tom Cruise of his generation. In addition to performing, he has also written and produced material for television and film and has written and recorded an album. Attractive, charming, and a self-described workaholic, Cannon "has the looks, talent and intelligence to be a star for as long as he wants," according to *Jet*.

Started as Stand-up Comic

Born on October 17, 1980, in San Diego, California, Cannon was raised there by his mother and his paternal grandmother. He also spent time with his father in North Carolina. A natural performer, he auditioned for the television program *It's Showtime at the Apollo* when he was 11 years old. Soon afterward he made his first appearance as a stand-up comic on his father's religion program on public access television. "People probably though I was cute more than they thought my jokes were funny," he recalled to *Los Angeles Times* writer Soren Baker.

During his teens Cannon lived in California with his mother. Though he was attracted to show business, his mother insisted that he finish high school before trying to launch his entertainment career. He graduated from Monte Vista High School in 1998, and began to appear in comedy clubs in Los Angeles. An agent discovered him there and got him a job with the Nickelodeon television channel, where he appeared as a warm-up act on the hit series *All That*. Cannon was

such a success that Nickelodeon gave him his own comedy show in 2002. The comic wrote material and served as executive producer for *The Nick Cannon Show*, and also wrote for such programs as *Keenan & Kel* and *Cousin Skeeter*.

Cannon's stand-up appearances had also caught the eye of actor and producer Will Smith, who got the young performer a small role in the hit movie *Men in Black II*. Smith also produced a TV pilot starring Cannon for the WB network.

Earned Acclaim as Actor

Soon after, Cannon landed his first starring role in the film *Drumline*. Cannon played Devon Miles, a drummer from Harlem who receives a scholarship to the fictitious Atlanta A&T University, a historically black university with a marching band that needs some new energy. Devon is a bright talent, but resists the authority of the band director and provokes a fierce competition with the team's lead drummer. He also develops a romantic interest in the head cheerleader. "Obviously, he's kicked off the team," wrote Wesley Morris in the *Boston Globe*, "and obviously, he'll be redeemed in time for the Classic."

Despite *Drumline*'s predictable plot, critics enjoyed the film, particularly because of its focus on African-American college life—a subject rarely seen in contemporary cinema. Critics also appreciated Cannon's performance. *New York Times* writer A.O. Scott called him an "engaging lead actor," and Kenneth Turan in

At a Glance . . .

Born on October 17, 1980, in San Diego, CA.

Career: Actor; Nick Cannon Youth Foundation, founder and director.

Addresses: *Agent*—c/o Miramax, 375 Greenwich St., New York, NY 10013.

the *Los Angeles Times* noted that the filmmakers were "smart in picking its lively, likable cast, starting with Nick Cannon."

Drumline proved Cannon's potential as an actor, but also proved his crossover appeal. The film, which grossed $13 million in its opening weekend and totaled more than $55 million domestically, drew an audience that was about 60 percent black and 40 percent non-black. According to Baker in the *Los Angeles Times*, the film was part of a "seismic shift in the way young black men are portrayed in cinema" and "helped show that young black men could carry a drama that focused on driven college kids rather than gangs and guns."

Cannon again played a wholesome character in his next film, *Love Don't Cost a Thing*. He portrayed Alvin Johnson, a gifted student from a supportive family, who pays a popular girl to let him date her so that he can gain friends and status at his high school. Reviewers admired Cannon's ability to show how Alvin changes from an awkward and earnest young man to an obnoxious showoff once he becomes popular. The actor, wrote Baker in the *Los Angeles Times*, "brings a good deal of charm to both Johnson incarnations, making it hard to dislike the guy who abandons his lifelong friends, disobeys his supportive mother and even turns on [the girl] once his popularity swells." Cannon explained to Baker that he enjoyed finding depth in this character: "I always try to figure out, even if he's a bad character or a jerk: What can you love about this character? If you can find that good, innocent side within that character, then that's where the money is."

Added Music to His Career

Cannon, who plays drums, drum machine, synthesizer, and harmonica, has also incorporated his music into his many of his creative ventures. He composed the theme song to his self-titled TV series, and also wrote "Shorty Put It to the Floor" for *Love Don't Cost a Thing*. In 2003 he released his first compact disc, *Nick Cannon*. Singles from the album, including "You Pops Don't Like Me" and "Feelin' Freaky," received considerable airplay on music cable channels, as did the hit song and video "Gigolo." That summer, Cannon was part of the popular "Scream 3" tour.

Easily bored by routine, Cannon told *New York Times* writer Linda Lee that "If I stay in one place too long or do one thing too long, my bones ache." Though he enjoyed partying in his teens, he now prefers sharper focus on his work. "I can't go out anymore," he explained. "Now I'm a workaholic." With roles in several upcoming films, including *Shall We Dance?* and *Roll Bounce*, Cannon shows no signs of slowing his performing pace.

In addition to his music and acting, Cannon is branching out into film producing and screenwriting. He executive-produced and wrote the treatment for *The Underclassman*, an action-comedy in which he also starred. He also served as executive producer for *The Beltway*, a political thriller that provided him a change of pace from his usual comedic roles. He is working on his first screenplay and has begun work on a memoir.

With the help of his father, a motivational speaker, Cannon has created the Nick Cannon Youth Foundation, which hosts inspirational conventions for young men. The actor hopes to inspire young people to aim for creative success while maintaining a positive life. "I'm taking my career into my own hands," he told *Ebony*. "I have a focus and a vision [now] that nobody can bring to pass but me."

Selected works

Films

Whatever It Takes, Columbia Tri-Star, 2000.
Men in Black II, Columbia Tri-Star, 2002.
Drumline, 20th Century Fox, 2002.
Love Don't Cost a Thing, Alcon Entertainment, 2003.
Shall We Dance?, Miramax, 2004.
The Underclassman, Miramax, 2005.
Roll Bounce, Fox Searchlight/Fox 2000, 2005.
The Beltway, Miramax. 2005.

Television

All That, Nickelodeon, 1998-2000.
The Nick Cannon Show, Nickelodeon, 2002.

Recordings

Nick Cannon, Jive Records, 2003.

Sources

Periodicals

Boston Globe, December 13, 2002, p. E7; December 12, 2003, p. E5.

Ebony, February 2004, p. 22.
Jet, January 12, 2004, p. 65.
Los Angeles Times, January 19, 2002, p. F30; December 13, 2002, p. E12; December 16, 2002, p. E1; December 11, 2003, p. E20.
New York Times, December 13, 2002; December 22, 2002; December 12, 2003.

On-line

"Hard-Working Nick Cannon on Life, Work, and Staying Grounded," *About.com,* http://romanticmovies.about.com (September 13, 2004).
"Nick Cannon," *Internet Movie Database*, www.imdb.com (September 8, 2004).

—E. Shostak

Wilfred Cartey

1931-1992

Educator, author, poet

Wilfred George Onslow Cartey is remembered for his work as an author, editor, compiler, and critic of African and Caribbean literature. Blind since he was a young adult, Cartey had a distinguished career as a scholar and lecturer, spending the majority of his career as a professor at the City University of New York (CUNY) and publishing extensively.

Cartey was born on July 19, 1931 in Port-of-Spain, Trinidad, British West Indies, to Samuel and Ada Cartey. He grew up in the West Indies. After graduating with a bachelor's degree from the University of the West Indies, in St. Augustine, in 1955, Cartey was awarded a fellowship from the Bernard Van Leer Foundation and a Fulbright travel grant for 1955 to 1959. He moved to New York and enrolled in Columbia University, earning his master's degree there in 1956. The following year he became an instructor in Spanish at Columbia University, a position he held from 1957 to 1962. During the summer of 1959 Cartey taught at the University of Puerto Rico as a visiting scholar and lecturer.

In 1963 Cartey was awarded a position as an associate professor of comparative literature at Columbia. There, he began his long career as a leading lecturer, educator, and literary critic of African and Caribbean literature. While fulfilling his teaching duties, he also continued his postgraduate studies and was awarded his doctoral degree in 1964 from Columbia University. His dissertation, which analyzed the writings of three black poets of the West Indies, was entitled "Three Antillian Poets: Emilio Ballagas, Luis Pales Matos, and Nicolas Guillen:

Literary Development of the Negro Theme in Relation to the Making of Modern Afro-Antillian Poetry and the Historic Evolution of the Negro." In that same year, Cartey published his first work, *Some Aspects of African Literature*, put out by the University of Vermont after Cartey had spent the summer at the university as a visiting professor. He spent the following summer as a visiting professor at his alma mater, the University of the West Indies. In 1967 he published a children's book, *The West Indies: Islands in the Sun,* before once again turning his attention to literary criticism. During the 1967-68 academic year, Cartey taught at the University of Ghana as a visiting professor.

In 1969 Cartey became an adjunct professor at Columbia University and joined the faculty of the City College of CUNY as a professor of comparative literature. He maintained a professional and academic relationship with both universities until his death in 1992. Also in 1969 Cartey published his most widely acclaimed work, *Whispers from a Continent: The Literature of Contemporary Black Africa*. Not only was Cartey's analysis of African literature well-received, but the book was published at a time when interest in African cultural themes was emerging in the United States and the critical literary response had not yet caught up to the growing interest. As a result, *Whispers from a Continent* was seen as an important, groundbreaking introduction to African literature.

Throughout his career Cartey published extensively. During the late 1960s and early 1970s, he contributed to, edited, compiled, and wrote an impressive amount of material. In 1970, with the support of an urban center grant, he contributed to *The Human Uses of the University: Planning a Curriculum in Urban and Ethnic Affairs at Columbia University,* co-edited by Joseph Colmen and Barbara Wheeler. He also partnered with Marlin Kilson to publish the two-volume *African Reader.* This documentary-style reader presented selections from an array of writers, including African political leaders, authors, civil servants, historians, journalists, as well as selections from African and European governmental documents. The first volume covered colonial Africa, from the last third of the eighteenth century through the first half of the twentieth century, and the second volume addressed independent Africa. He edited an anthology of African literature titled *Palaver* and compiled a selection of poetry as *Black Images,* which had the comprehensive subtitle of *The Evolution of the Image of the Black Man in the Poetry of Spanish-English-French-Speaking Caribbean, the United States, Latin America, and West Africa.* He also published the journal article "The Reality of Four Negro Writers," a critique of Ezekiel Mphahlele, George Lamming, Carolina Maria de Jesus, and James Baldwin, which appeared in *Roots,* one of numerous contributions he made to academic journals.

During the 1972-73 school year Cartey served as the Martin Luther King Distinguished Professor of Comparative Literature at Brooklyn College of CUNY. In 1973 he was elevated to the position of distinguished professor at CUNY and spent a second summer that year as a visiting professor at the University of the West Indies. He also served as a visiting professor at Howard University in 1976 and at the University of California at Berkeley in 1979. In 1979 he was awarded the title of distinguished professor of black studies by CUNY, a position which he held until his death.

During the last half of the 1970s and into the 1980s Cartey continued to write extensively. Some of Cartey's works, including his poetry, were self-published, such as *Waters of My Soul* (1975), *Red Rain* (1977), *Embryos* (1982), and *Black Velvet Time* (1984), although *The House of Blue Lighting* (1973), *Children of Lalibela* (1985), and *Choreographers of the Dawn* (1989) were professionally published.

In 1991 Cartey published his final work of literary criticism, *Whispers from the Caribbean: I Going Away, I Going Home,* in which he addresses the unique community of the West Indies that has been created by its politics, economics, and history of colonialism and diaspora. According to Cartey, Caribbean literature acknowledges this fragmented and despondent history of the area yet molds from this despair and bleakness a vibrant and vivid community that creates its own cultural value, which he terms "unique communality." He also plays on themes, familiar to the Caribbean literary community, of exile or migration and subsequent return. In *Whispers from the Caribbean* Cartey introduces readers to an array of indigenous writers and includes several of his own poems.

On March 28, 1992, Cartey died in New York after a short illness. During his career, Cartey made significant contributions to the advancement of African and Caribbean literature as an author, editor, and critic. He was eulogized by his brother John during a ceremony hosted by the Caribbean Writer's Summer Institute at the University of Miami in July 1992.

Selected writings

Nonfiction

Some Aspects of African Literature, University of Vermont, 1964.

Whispers from a Continent: The Literature of Contemporary Black Africa, Random House, 1969.

(With Joseph Colmen and Barbara Wheeler) *The Human Uses of the University: Planning a Curriculum in Urban and Ethnic Affairs at Columbia University,* Praeger, 1970.

(With Marlin Kilson) *The African Reader: Volume 1. Colonial Africa; Volume 2. Independent Africa* (editor), Random House, 1970.

Palaver (editor), T. Nelson, 1970.

Whispers from the Caribbean: I Going Away, I Going Home, Center for Afro-American Studies, University of California, 1991.

Poetry

The House of Blue Lightning, Emerson Hall, 1973.
Waters of My Soul, self-published, 1975.
Red Rain, self-published, 1977.
Suns and Shadows, Emerson Hall, 1978.
Embryos, self-published, 1982.
Black Velvet Time, self-published, 1984.
Children of Lalibela, Printed Word, 1985.
Choreographers of the Dawn, Printed Word, 1989.

Other

The West Indies: Islands in the Sun (for children), Nelson, 1967.

Black Images (anthology), Teachers College Press, 1970.

Sources

Periodicals

Journal of Black Studies, December, 1984.
New York Times, March 25, 1992, p. D22.
Research in African Literatures, Summer 1993, p. 148.
Times Literary Supplement, October 1, 1971.

On-line

Brannigan, John, "'The Regions Caesar Never Knew': Cultural Nationalism and the Caribbean Literary Renaissance in England," http://social.chass.ncsu.edu/jouvert/v5i1/bran.htm (September 13, 2004).

"Wilfred Cartey," *Biography Resource Center,* www.galenet.com/servlet/BioRC (September 13, 2004).

Cartey, John, "A Whisper from the Caribbean: A Program to Honor the Memory of Wilfred Cartey," *Caribbean Writer's Summer Institute, Archival Video Collection,* http://scholar.library.miami.edu/cls/speakersDisplay.php (September 13, 2004).

—Kari Bethel

Wilt Chamberlain

1936-1999

Basketball player

Few individual athletes have ever excelled at a sport as spectacularly as Wilt Chamberlain, the 7' 1" center who dominated professional basketball for more than 14 seasons beginning in 1959. Chamberlain, or "Wilt the Stilt" as he was often known, is enshrined in record books and memories for a legendary 1962 performance in which he scored 100 points in a single game, a record no other player has come close to matching.

Chamberlain set records and led the National Basketball Association (NBA) in many statistical categories during all phases of his long career. Toward the end of his playing days, responding to criticism that his individual scoring exploits came at the expense of his team's performance, he demonstrated his all-around skills by beginning to win awards for defensive play and to notch impressive numbers of assists—passes that enabled another player to score. "When I think of pro basketball, I think of Wilt Chamberlain," basketball Hall of Famer Jerry West was quoted as saying in *African-American Sports Greats*. "He just stood out."

Excelled in High School and College

Born Wilton Norman Chamberlain on August 21, 1936, in Philadelphia, he was one of eight siblings. His father was a custodian and handyman, and his mother a housecleaner and laundress; both were of normal height. Chamberlain grew rapidly during his teenage years and began to play basketball seriously during junior high school. His three years on the basketball team at Philadelphia's Overbrook High School were a

portent of his career to come: he scored 2,252 points (90 of them in one game), and led the team to two city championships. Some considered him the nation's top high-school player. The NBA's Philadelphia Warriors, anticipating the heavy recruitment of phenomenal young players that would become commonplace in later decades, claimed the rights to his future professional services, and many dozens of colleges dangled lures Chamberlain's way in hopes of persuading him to enroll. Chamberlain settled on the University of Kansas, making his varsity debut as a sophomore in 1956.

His college career was likewise spectacular. Named an All-American in both his sophomore and junior years, Chamberlain led Kansas to the National Collegiate Athletic Association (NCAA) finals in the spring of 1957. Several of the rules of college basketball had to be changed as a result of Chamberlain's talents, which simply dwarfed those of previous players. Opposing players double-and triple-teamed him and played a slowed-down game rather than attempt to confront Chamberlain's offensive skills head-on. These techniques helped the University of North Carolina defeat Kansas 54-53 in triple overtime in the 1957 championship game.

Such tactics also frustrated the rapidly developing Chamberlain, who startled the basketball world by turning professional rather than returning to Kansas for his senior year. NBA rules forbade him from joining the league until the year in which he would have graduated from college, so Chamberlain played for the razzle-

At a Glance . . .

Born Wilton Norman Chamberlain on August 21, 1936, in Philadelphia; son of William (a handyman) and Olivia (a housecleaner); died October 12, 1999, in Los Angeles, CA *Education:* University of Kansas, 1954-58.

Career: Harlem Globetrotters, professional basketball player, 1958-59; Philadelphia Warriors (team became Golden State Warriors in 1965), professional basketball player, 1959-65; Philadelphia 76ers, professional basketball player, 1965-68; Los Angeles Lakers, professional basketball player, 1968-73). San Diego Conquistadors, American Basketball Association, coach, 1973-74; appeared in television commercials and films, 1970s-1980s; Wilt Chamberlain Restaurants, Inc., owner, 1992-99.

Selected Awards: NCAA Tournament Most Valuable Player (MVP), 1957; NBA Rookie of the Year, 1960; NBA MVP, 1960, 1966, 1967, 1968; inducted into Basketball Hall of Fame, 1979; Philadelphia Sports Writers Association Living Legend Award, 1991; number retired by Philadelphia 76ers, 1991.

dazzle touring professional team the Harlem Globetrotters during the 1958-59 season. He joined the Philadelphia Warriors in 1959, having already collected a large bonus for signing.

Individual Triumphs in NBA

Chamberlain was an NBA star from the beginning, leading the league in scoring and rebounding, and taking home honors not only for Rookie of the Year but also for Most Valuable Player. Frustrated by defensive tactics similar to those he had faced in college, and by what he considered biased officiating, he threatened to leave the league and return to the Globetrotters in 1960. But he did not follow through on his threat, and soon learned to outmaneuver his tormentors through sheer size, speed, and skill. In the 1960-61 season he led the league in scoring once again; he would not relinquish his position atop the league's scoring lists for another five seasons.

The 1961-62 season took Chamberlain beyond stardom into the realm of legend. For an ordinary basketball player, scoring 35 or 40 points in a game is considered an exceptional performance. Chamberlain averaged 50.4 points per game that year. The apex of

his scoring binge came on March 2, 1962, when Chamberlain scored 100 points in a game against the New York Knicks—one of those sports records that seem to defy the inevitable advance of human physical capabilities, promising to remain unattainable by any other player.

Moving with the Warriors to San Francisco, and then returning to his hometown as a result of a 1965 trade in which he was sent to the Philadelphia 76ers, Chamberlain continued to dominate the pro basketball scene. The one accomplishment that remained out of his grasp was that of playing on a team that won the league championship. When Chamberlain faced off against Boston Celtics center Bill Russell, it was Chamberlain who came out on top statistically, outscoring and outrebounding his Boston nemesis. But the Celtics' balance and superb teamwork often made them the winners at game's end.

Won Titles with 76ers, Lakers

Chamberlain reacted with true sportsmanship to this situation, reining in his high-scoring style and concentrating on defensive skills and on the fortunes of his team as a whole. His efforts bore fruit: the 76ers won a then-unprecedented 68 regular-season games and cruised past strong Boston and San Francisco to win the NBA championship. Traded to the Los Angeles Lakers in 1968, Chamberlain continued to hone his defensive skills. He led the league in assists in the 1967-68 season, and played a crucial role in propelling the Lakers to the 1971-72 NBA title. The Lakers erased the 76ers' record of 68 regular-season wins, winning 69 times, including a string of 33 consecutive wins.

When he finally retired from the NBA in 1973, Chamberlain was the holder or co-holder of no fewer than 43 NBA records. The first player to score over 30,000 points in a career (he finished with 31,419), he set career records for average game scoring (30.1 points per game), average rebounds per game, total career rebounds, most complete games played, and in many other categories. He scored 50 points or more on 118 separate occasions. Despite the physicality of his opponents' attempts to cope with him, Chamberlain never "fouled out" of a game—he was never ejected from a game for committing more than a certain number of prohibited personal fouls. Flamboyant and flashy as he could sometimes be, Chamberlain was also one of the most reliable players in basketball history.

Chamberlain faded from the limelight somewhat after the end of his professional career. A one-year stint as coach of the San Diego Conquistadors in the failed American Basketball Association was followed by various non-basketball ventures: Chamberlain invested in and even played on teams in such sports as volleyball, racquetball, and track and field. Inducted into the

Basketball Hall of Fame in 1978, Chamberlain in the 1980s made some film and television appearances and built a mansion in the foothills above Los Angeles. He also started a chain of restaurants in the early 1990s.

Another venture gained more attention. Chamberlain's 1991 autobiography *A View from Above,* written without the aid of a co- author, caused a stir and sold well, largely as a result of Chamberlain's claim that he had slept with 20,000 women over the course of his life. Coming as it did nearly simultaneously with basketball star Magic Johnson's announcement that he was suffering from the AIDS virus, the resulting controversy hurt Chamberlain's image for a time. But Chamberlain was no stranger to criticism, and outlasted the storm. Known to brush off negative publicity, he countered with the pithy comment that "nobody roots for Goliath."

Chamberlain passed away on October 12, 1999, a victim of congestive heart failure. He was widely remembered not only as one of the greatest basketball players of the century, but as a kind, warmhearted man. Former rival Bill Russell remarked to *Sports Illustrated* that "if Wilt had possessed a mean streak, there would have been no stopping him." Chamberlain's legacy lives on, in endowed scholarships at his alma mater, the University of Kansas; in an 18-foot tall bronze sculpture outside Philadelphia's Wachovia Center basketball arena; and in the memories of all those who saw his epic battles with Russell to determine who was the best big man in basketball.

Selected writings

A View from Above, Villard Books, 1991.

Sources

Books

Chamberlain, Wilt, *A View from Above*, Villard Books, 1991.

Estell, Kenneth, ed., *The African-American Almanac*, Gale, 1994.

Libby, Bill, *Goliath: The Wilt Chamberlain Story*, Dodd, Mead, 1977.

Porter, David L. ed., *African-American Sports Greats*, Greenwood, 1995.

Periodicals

Boston Globe, February 9, 1997, p. C7.

Jet, January 30, 1995, p. 50.

Maclean's, November 18, 1991, p. 84.

Sporting News, February 17, 1997, p. 31; October 25, 1999, p. 12.

Sports Illustrated, December 9, 1991, p. 22; October 25, 1999, p. 80.

—James M. Manheim and Tom Pendergast

Maurice Cheeks

1956—

Professional basketball player and coach

Cheeks, Maurice, photograph. AP/Wide World Photos.

Maurice Cheeks played point guard in the National Basketball Association (NBA) for 15 years. During his long career, the 6-foot, 1-inch tall Cheeks was known for his speed, his ability to handle the ball, his consistent play, and his work ethic. Never one to seek out the spotlight, he was, and continues to be, admired as a person of high integrity. After spending 11 years as member of the Philadelphia 76ers, Cheeks spent the last four years of his playing career traded among numerous teams. After he retired, he coached one season in the Continental Basketball Association (CBA) before returning to Philadelphia as an assistant coach. In 2001 he accepted the job as head coach of the Portland Trail Blazers. His contract extends through the 2005-06 season.

College Days

Cheeks was born on September 8, 1956, in Chicago, Illinois. He grew up in the Robert Taylor housing projects on the city's South Side and attended DuSable High School. In 1974 he enrolled at West Texas State University (now West Texas A&M University), one of the few schools that offered him a basketball scholarship. The small city of Canyon, Texas, located near Amarillo, was foreign terrain to a kid from the South Side, and Cheeks became lonely for home. During his freshman year, he became intent on leaving school and returning to Chicago. However, his mother, Marjorie, was adamant. "She said, 'Maurice, you quit school and you better not come home,'" Cheeks later recounted with a smile to the *New York Times*. "I stayed in school. I don't know what would have happened to me if I hadn't."

At West Texas State, Cheeks was a four-year starter and three-time most valuable player on the Buffaloes basketball team. During his senior year, he averaged 16.8 points per game and shot 56.8 percent from the field. Over his entire college career, he averaged 11.8 points per game and finished fourth on the school's all-time scoring list with 1,227 points. During his sophomore and junior years, the Buffaloes posted winning records of 19-7 and 18-12, but in his senior year the team slipped to an unimpressive 8-19. (Eventually, West Texas dropped to the Division II level.) Cheeks graduated in 1978.

At a Glance . . .

Born on September 8, 1956, in Chicago, IL; married; two children. *Education:* Attended West Texas State University (now West Texas A&M University), 1974-78.

Career: Philadelphia 76ers, professional basketball player, 1978-89; San Antonio Spurs, professional basketball player, 1990; New York Knicks, professional basketball player, 1990-91; Atlanta Hawks, professional basketball player, 1991-93; New Jersey Nets, professional basketball player, 1993. Quad City Thunder, CBA, assistant coach, 1993-94; Philadelphia 76ers, NBA, assistant coach, 1994-2001; Portland Trail Blazers, NBA, head coach, 2001–.

Selected Awards: NBA All-Star Team Selection, 1983, 1986-88.

Addresses: *Office*—c/o Portland Trail Blazers, One Center Court, Suite 200, Portland, OR 97227.

Having played four years nestled away in a small Texas town and on a losing team, Cheeks did not have high expectations for the NBA draft. However, unbeknownst to him, he had caught the attention of Jack McMahon, a talent scout and assistant coach for the Philadelphia 76ers. Cheeks, who knew McMahon had been in the stands for several of his games, just assumed he was there to scout other players from the Missouri Valley Conference, such as Indiana State's Larry Bird. However, during his senior year Cheeks was invited to Cincinnati to play with other NBA hopefuls in front of scouts and management. As a result of his performance, McMahon's interest spread to others in the Philly organization, and the 76ers became intent on drafting the young point guard. Cheeks was the 14th selection in the second round, 36th overall, in the 1978 NBA draft. For the next 11 years, he wore a 76ers uniform.

Little Mo

During his rookie year of 1978-79, Cheeks averaged almost 30 minutes of playing time, with 8.4 points and 5.3 assists per game. In his second season in the NBA, he increased his averages to 11.4 points and 7 assists per game. The 76ers made it to the NBA finals in 1980 but were defeated by the Los Angeles Lakers, losing the series 4-2. Although his points-per-game average

dropped slightly to 9.4 during 1980-81, Cheeks maintained nearly seven assists per game, increased his steals, and decreased his turnovers. In the 1981-82 season, Cheeks had a career-high 209 steals, and the 76ers returned to the NBA finals, but once again fell to the Lakers in the series final, 4-2.

By the 1982-83 season, with the help of legendary players Julius "Dr. J" Irving and Moses Malone, the 76ers were nearly unstoppable. Cheeks became known as "Little Mo" to parallel Malone's title of "Big Mo." They won 50 of their first 57 games, finished the season with a league-best 65-17 record, and went on to win the 1983 NBA championship, this time sweeping the Lakers in four games. That year Cheeks earned his first of four trips to the NBA All-Star Game.

Throughout the 1980s, Cheeks was a solid performer for the 76ers. During the 1985-86 season he averaged 15.4 points and a career-high 9.2 assists per game and had 207 steals. The following year, he posted a career-best 15.6 points per game, with 7.9 assists per game and 180 steals. He played in almost all the 76ers' games, averaging over 38 minutes per game from 1985 to 1988. During the 1988-89 season Cheeks appeared in a career-low 71 games and averaged 11.6 points per game, his lowest since the 1981-82 season. He continued to average nearly eight assists per game.

Philadelphia: Gone and Back

In August 1989, as Cheeks pulled out of his driveway in suburban Philadelphia, a television crew with cameras and microphones descended on him to get his reaction to the fact that the 76ers had traded him to San Antonio. It was the first Cheeks had heard of the trade. Stunned, he rolled up his window and drove away. After the 11 years—the entirety of his adult life—Cheeks left Philadelphia. Along with teammates Christian Welp and David Wingate, he was went to the San Antonio Spurs for Johnny Dawkins and Jay Vincent. On February 21, 1990, the Spurs made a midseason change, trading Cheeks straight-up for the New York Knicks' Rod Strickland. After finishing the 1990-91 season, he was traded to the Atlanta Hawks for Tim McCormick. After one season with the Hawks, Cheeks was sent to the New Jersey Nets, where he finished out his last year in a player in the NBA.

Overall, during the 15 years of his NBA playing career, Cheeks averaged 11.1 points and 6.7 assists per game. He played in 1,101 games, scored a total of 12,195 points, and had 7,392 assists. He retired as the NBA's all-time leader in steals (since surpassed) with 2,310. One of seven 76ers who have had their number retired, his number 10 hangs from the rafters of the Wachovia Center.

After his retirement as a player, Cheeks landed his first coaching job as an assistant coach for the CBA's Quad

City Thunder in Rock Island, Illinois. Cheeks spent the 1993-94 season with the Thunder, who won the CBA championship at the end of the season. In 1994 the 76ers offered Cheeks a place on the bench as an assistant coach, which he gladly accepted. Always a fan favorite, Cheeks was welcomed back to Philadelphia with enthusiasm. He spent the next seven years as an assistant with the 76ers and is credited with being a calm and soothing influence in the volatile relationship that developed between head coach Larry Brown and star point guard Allen Iverson.

Became Head Coach

In 2001 the Portland Trail Blazers took a chance on Cheeks, hiring him as their head coach after finishing the previous season with a slide into fourth place in the division and suffering a humiliating first-round playoff defeat at the hands of the Lakers. By all accounts, Cheeks inherited a highly talented (and highly paid) but underachieving and dysfunctional team. Hot topics in the Portland press were the litany of charges filed against Portland's players, including marijuana possession, driving without licenses or insurance, domestic abuse, rape, assault, and general misconduct both on and off the basketball court. Star forward Rasheed Wallace had led the league in technical fouls the prior year. Whether Cheeks could salvage the team was a question open for debate. Phil Taylor of *Sports Illustrated* noted prior to the beginning of the 2001 season: "Maurice Cheeks was a quiet guy who wasn't considered head coach material, but he's paid his dues, and maybe he's the guy to turn this team around. It won't be surprising if they went in the tank again, though."

The Blazers started off the 2001-02 season on shaky legs, going just 11-11, and both fans and players began to grumble. Yet, once again, Cheeks proved that one does not need to shout to be heard. Technical fouls went down, performance went up, and the Blazers finished the season a respectable 49-33. However, they were again knocked out by the Lakers in the first round of the playoffs in three games. In his second season the Blazers won 50 games and faced the Dallas Mavericks in the first round of the playoffs. After going down three games to none (in what was now a seven-game series), the Blazers battled back to win the next three to tie the series. However, the Mavericks, who had home court advantage, took the final game 107-95.

Following the 2002-03 season, Larry Brown left Philadelphia and his feud with Allen Iverson behind, and rumors were rampant that Cheeks was the top choice to take his place. However, with Cheeks still bound by his contract, the Trail Blazers, who did not want to risk losing their head coach, refused Philadelphia's request to speak with Cheeks about the job. He was out of the

running before he ever joined the race. According to the *Philadelphia Daily News*, Cheeks responded by saying, "As head coach of the Blazers, my allegiance to and focus is on this organization and our fans." Although he readily acknowledges his debt to Portland for giving him a chance to coach, Cheeks has nonetheless retained a deep emotional attachment to Philadelphia, and the feeling is mutual. "He was the glue for that championship team," Dawn Staley, a top point guard in the women's NBA who was originally from Philadelphia, told the *Sunday Oregonian*. "People here know he was the guy who kept everyone on that team involved and together. He's a blue-collar guy, a simple guy who likes simplicity. We have an appreciation for that, and that's why he's been so embraced."

A Redemptive Moment

If Cheeks is appreciated in Philadelphia and Portland, that feeling extended across the entire nation during the 2003 playoffs when Natalie Gilbert, a 13-year-old eighth grader who had won a contest to sing the national anthem before Game 3, lost track of the words. As she struggled along, suddenly Cheeks appeared beside her, put a fatherly arm around her shoulder, and whispered the words to her. As she recovered and began to sing once again, Cheeks joined in, lifting his other arm to encourage the 20,000 fans present to join in, which they did. The moment was replayed in the media all over the country, and the *Philadelphia Inquirer* said, "Rarely has the national anthem…been rendered with such heartfelt gusto. It was a glorious, redemptive moment." Cheeks later told CNN, "I just started walking. I had no idea what I was going to do, what I was going to say. But as I approached her, I just wanted to help her, and I didn't know if I even knew the words."

During the 2003-04 season the Trail Blazers struggled as management made some significant changes in the team's makeup during the year. After beginning the season with a 0-10 road trip, several trades were made, and in February 2004, Wallace and Wesley Person were traded to Atlanta for Shareef Adbur-Rahim, Theo Ratliff, and Dan Dickau. Although the new players began to gel by the close of the season, the team posted a record of 41-41, the first non-winning record for the team since 1988-89. The Trail Blazers also failed to make the playoffs, ending a 21-year playoff streak, just one short of the NBA record of 22. Despite the mediocre record, with a season of rebuilding now behind them, the Trail Blazers extended Cheeks' contract through the 2005-06 season.

Cheeks knows that his role as coach extends beyond understanding the fundamentals of basketball. He is role model, father figure, mentor, taskmaster, and leader. In 2002 he told the *Chicago Sun-Times*, "Maybe I won't win 55 games and a championship, but

I may help someone's life in that locker room, and that may be why I'm here.... I've been through rough times, and I've always stayed my course of who I am—which is a pretty good person—and I pride myself on that." Cheeks lives in Portland with his wife; they have two children.

Sources

Periodicals

Associated Press, April 13, 2004; April 15, 2004.
Chicago Sun-Times, December 30, 2002, p. 73.
Columbian (Vancouver, WA), July 22, 2001, p. B1; December 17, 2002, p. B1; March 10, 2003, p. B6.
Jet, July 16, 2001, p. 50.
Knight Ridder/Tribune News Service, April 30, 2003; May 30, 2003; April 21, 2004.
New York Times, May 11, 2003, p. SP2; June 4, 2003, p. D5.

San Antonio Express-News, December 10, 2003, p. C1.
Sporting News, November 5, 2001, p. 34-35.
Sports Illustrated, May 23, 1983, p. 28-31; May 14, 1990, p. 28-31; October 29, 2001, p. 166; October 28, 2002, p. 140.
Sunday Oregonian, April 4, 2004, p. C1.
USA Today, April 28, 2003, p. C3.

On-line

Blazers.com: Official Website of the Portland Trail Blazers, www.nba.com/blazers (August 17, 2004).
"Maurice Cheeks," *Basketball Reference,* www.basketballreference.com/players/playerpage.htm?ilkid=CHEEKMA01 (July 12, 2004).
"Vocal Support," *CNN,* http://cnnstudentnews.cnn.com/TRANSCRIPTS/0304/28/ltm.17.html (August 17, 2004).

—Kari Bethel

Nathaniel "Sweetwater" Clifton

1922(?)-1990

Professional basketball player

One of the first three African-American players in the National Basketball Association (NBA), Nat "Sweetwater" Clifton was actually the first under official contract to play in the league. He was a "first" in another way as well: he might be considered the NBA's first black star. While Chuck Cooper and Earl Lloyd, Clifton's African-American contemporaries who integrated the NBA in the year 1950, were low-key, low-profile players, Clifton was a popular figure and a born entertainer who delighted fans with his feats on the court. Some said that had he come of age in the era of multimillion-dollar endorsement deals, he would have scored big with his public-friendly personality and become a rich man.

A player who spent some years in all-black leagues before coming to the NBA, Clifton avoided divulging his age. He is reported to have been born in England, Arkansas, on October 13, 1922. Clifton's family moved to Chicago when he was eight. His birth name was Clifton Nathaniel, but after he became a high school star in Chicago he reversed the two names when sportswriters complained that the last name Nathaniel was too long to fit in a headline. The nickname "Sweetwater" (or "Sweets") is often reported to have derived from his fondness for soft drinks, but the truth revealed more about the life of Southern black migrants in Chicago: since the family often couldn't afford soft drinks, Clifton would fill bottles with water and then pour sugar into them.

Standing over 6-foot, 7-inches tall and weighing 235 pounds, Clifton dominated his opponents while playing on the basketball team at Chicago's DuSable High School. His hands spanned ten inches, and he could pick up and palm a basketball as easily as others might handle a tennis ball. In the city championship semifinals in his senior year of 1942, he scored 45 points, blowing away the former tournament record of 24. The *Chicago Daily News* called him one of the two greatest high school basketball players in Illinois history. He also played softball on a team called the Gas House Gang.

Clifton played one season at Xavier University in New Orleans before being drafted into the U.S. Army in 1944. He served for three years in Europe and then turned professional on his return home, becoming the first black player to join the Dayton Metropolitans and then playing for the all-black New York Rens. In July of 1948 Clifton signed with the Harlem Globetrotters, the legendary African-American masters of razzle-dazzle basketball. The Globetrotters were at the peak of their fame and influence, touring the world and drawing thousands for exhibition games at which they often defeated all-white NBA squads. Clifton was signed for a reported annual salary of $10,000—said to be the highest salary paid to a black basketball player up to

At a Glance . . .

Born Clifton Nathaniel on October 13, 1922(?), in England, AR; died August 31, 1990, in Chicago, IL; married. *Education:*Attended Xavier University, New Orleans, LA. *Military Service:* U.S. Army, 1944-47.

Career: Dayton Metropolitans and New York Rens, basketball player, late 1940s; Harlem Globetrotters, basketball player, 1948; New York Knickerbockers, professional basketball player, 1950-57; Detroit Pistons, professional basketball player, 1957-58; Harlem Magicians, Harlem Globetrotters, and Chicago Majors, basketball player, 1958-early 1960s; taxi driver, Chicago, 1960s–1990.

Awards: NBA All-Star Game Selection, 1957.

that time.

For a while it wasn't clear which major-league sport Clifton would play in first. Baseball scouts were well aware of the power he had shown on Chicago softball diamonds, and while he was with the Globetrotters he played for three seasons in major league baseball's farm system. In 1950, playing for the AA-level team in Wilkes-Barre, Pennsylvania, he hit .304 with an impressive 86 runs batted in. Globetrotters owner Abe Saperstein began looking for chances to unload his restless star property.

That chance came in the summer of 1950, after the Boston Celtics had drafted Chuck Cooper and officially broken the NBA's color line. After a stretch of negotiations, Saperstein sold Clifton's contract to the New York Knickerbockers for $12,500, of which Clifton pocketed $2,500. In today's world of stratospheric salaries this would be considered a raw deal, and Clifton had questions even at the time. He was also upset after discovering that the white all-stars against whom the Globetrotters played exhibition games were paid better than the 'Trotters themselves. But he remained on good enough terms with Saperstein to continue to play for the Globetrotters during the NBA off-season.

Clifton made his Knicks debut on November 3, 1950 and quickly became an integral part of the newly powerful squad. Playing at forward, he was often assigned to guard opposing centers. The Knicks made the NBA finals during each of Clifton's first three years, and he averaged 8.6 points per game as a rookie and cracked double digits in his second year. Clifton "had the body of a power forward of today but he never

looked much to score," former Knickerbocker Al McGuire told the *St. Louis Post-Dispatch.* "He was the first guy to really cuff a ball without the stickum. He even cleared his rebounds with one hand most of the time."

In fact, Clifton felt hamstrung by the conservative style of Knicks coach Joe Lapchick, who favored a game very different from the fast, high-scoring contests Clifton had been used to with the Globetrotters. Nevertheless, his career with the Knicks was a solid one. He got along well with his white teammates. "Around Chicago and in the army, I was used to playing with white players, and I could get along," Clifton was quoted as saying by *They Cleared the Lane* author Ron Thomas. "I figured everybody had to make a living and nobody gave me any dirt. They [the Knicks] were a great bunch of guys." Clifton joined other Knicks players at card games and in church. Only once did an opposing player, Bob Harris of the Celtics, insult Clifton with a racial slur, and Clifton knocked him out cold with a one-two punch combination. Normally, Clifton was known as a genial man with a taste for sharp clothing.

Clifton's best year was his last with the Knicks, the 1956-57 season, when he averaged over 13 points a game and played in the NBA All-Star Game. After that year he was traded to the Detroit Pistons and, after his first year there, in which he was frustrated with his lack of playing time, he left the NBA. He played for a startup pro team, the Harlem Magicians, and then spent several seasons with the still-popular Globetrotters and another startup, the Chicago Majors. After a knee injury in the mid-1960s, he retired.

Immensely popular in Chicago, Clifton had continued to live in his home neighborhood. Married, and with no pension coming from the NBA, he had to find a job. Though he had many contacts near home and probably could have landed a city government job, he settled on driving a taxi and continued to do so for the rest of his life. "He had a lot of avenues open to him, but he would never [have] been comfortable in a shirt and tie in an office; the worst thing in the world for him would be a 9-to-5." Inducted into the Black Athletes Hall of Fame in 1978, Clifton died at the wheel of his cab near Chicago's Union Station on August 31, 1990.

Sources

Books

Thomas, Ron, *They Cleared the Lane: The NBA's Black Pioneers,* University of Nebraska Press, 2002.

Periodicals

New York Times, September 2, 1990, Section 1, p. 41; September 4, 1990, p. D13.

St. Louis Post-Dispatch, September 23, 1990, p. D10.

On-line

"Globetrotters Go for Legitimacy," *CNN/Sports Illustrated,* http://sportsillustrated.cnn.com/inside_game/alexander_wolff/news/2000/11/16/hoop_life (August 2, 2004).
"Nat Clifton," *Basketball Reference,* www.basketball reference.com (August 17, 2004).

—James M. Manheim

Charles "Chuck" Cooper

1926-1984

Professional basketball pioneer

The man who officially integrated professional basketball when he was drafted by the Boston Celtics of the National Basketball Association (NBA) in April of 1950, Chuck Cooper was a modest figure who specialized in offensive team play and generally stayed away from the spotlight. Like other early African-American players in the NBA, his experiences in the league were marred, though not overshadowed, by a series of racist incidents. In later life, however, Cooper revealed many negative reactions he had felt regarding the way he was treated by NBA coaches and administrators. After leaving the NBA in the late 1950s he made a complete break with the game of basketball. "I think that even though he was the first trailblazer, I don't think he enjoyed that experience," Cooper's wife Irva was quoted as saying by author Ron Thomas in *They Cleared the Lane*. "I think it was painful, and nobody likes pain."

Charles Henry Cooper was born on September 29, 1926, in Pittsburgh, Pennsylvania, to a mailman father and a former schoolteacher mother. Pittsburgh at the time was a thoroughly segregated city, and young Chuck Cooper faced numerous restrictions on where he could go and what he could do. After trying out for the basketball team at Westinghouse High School, he almost quit when he realized that he was being forced to do what basketball players sometimes call "dirty work:" struggling in tight defensive quarters and opening up space for other players, but rarely being given the chance to shoot the ball himself. Coach Ralph Zahnhiser, however, told Cooper he had a strong future in basketball, and Cooper returned to the team.

Played for West Virginia State College and Duquesne

As a senior at Westinghouse, Cooper averaged over 13 points per game, paced the school to Pittsburgh's city championship, and was chose as the All-City first team's center. Like several other talented young African-American players, Cooper headed for historically black West Virginia State College, whose program also produced the early black NBA pioneer Earl Lloyd. He played a promising semester there but left the school to enter the military in the winter of 1944-45, during the late stages of World War II. After a tour of duty on the West Coast, Cooper was drawn back home to Pittsburgh and enrolled at Duquesne University.

It was Cooper's solid career at very mainstream Duquesne that attracted the attention of professional scouts and began to give rise to his dreams of a basketball career. Over four years as a starter, Cooper amassed a school-record total of 990 points. He received several All-American honors during his successful senior year and led the Duquesne squad to two appearances in the then high-profile National Invitational Tournament (NIT). Cooper encountered some racial hostility, at one point responding (in an interview quoted by Thomas) to an opposing player who had shouted "I got the nigger" with the retort "And I got your mother in my jockstrap." Duquesne backed Cooper's right to participate, canceling games with Southern schools that refused to play in integrated contests.

As he approached his graduation from Duquesne in 1950 with a bachelor's degree in education, Cooper signed on with the famed touring all-black Harlem Globetrotters team. His agile defensive skills and shot-blocking ability inspired the nickname of Tarzan. At least one sportswriter had speculated that Cooper, the cream of the 1950 college crop, might be the player to duplicate baseballer Jackie Robinson's achievement and break the NBA's color line. On April 25, 1950, Cooper was selected in the second round of the NBA draft by Boston Celtics owner Walter Brown. When an associate pointed out that Cooper was black, Brown answered that (according to the *HoopHall: Basketball Hall of Fame* Web site) he didn't care whether Cooper

was "striped, plaid, or polka dot." Other black players, including Lloyd and Cooper's fellow Globetrotters center Nat "Sweetwater" Clifton, also joined the NBA for the 1950 season, but Cooper was the first one drafted.

Formed Friendly Relationships with Celtics Players

The 6-foot, 4-inch, 200-lb. Cooper made his debut with the Celtics on November 1, 1950, and he went on to notch a strong rookie season. He played in 66 games, averaging 9.5 points and 8.5 rebounds per game and sparking a renaissance in the Celtics' drooping fortunes. Cooper formed bonds with his teammates, including future Celtics great Bob Cousy, with whom he would sometimes go out in the evening to listen to jazz concerts in Boston. The NBA, largely stocked with college graduates who had encountered diverse environments, was a setting different from the world of predominantly rural-born white baseball players that Jackie Robinson had encountered, and Cooper was not a solo wall-breaker but shared the spotlight with the NBA's other new black players.

All this meant that overt racist harassment did not become a constant plague on Cooper's career. "I wasn't alone," Cooper told *Jet*. "I didn't have to take all the race-baiting and heat on my shoulders like Jackie Robinson." There were, however, segregated Southern hotels that refused Cooper admittance, and Cooper did face racial slurs on the court. Only once, in 1952, did he come to blows over them, in a game against the Milwaukee Hawks.

Discrimination, however, also comes in subtler forms. Cooper's scoring production declined in his next three seasons after his rookie year, reaching a low of 3.3 points per game in the 1953-54 season. Although Cooper at first had expressed delight at the fast-moving, offense-heavy game practiced in the NBA, he later came to believe that he was being marginalized as a defensive, "in-the-trenches" style player, and that the NBA wasn't ready for a high-scoring black star. Though both Cousy and Celtics coach Red Auerbach later disputed this idea, Cooper felt that he was once again doing the "dirty work."

Played in NBA Championships

Cooper was traded to the Milwaukee Hawks for the 1954-55 season and to the Fort Wayne (Indiana) Pistons the following year. These moves rejuvenated Cooper's career temporarily. He played for Fort Wayne in the 1956 NBA championships but remained frustrated. He then played for a year with the all-black Harlem Magicians squad before leaving basketball for good after suffering a back injury in a car crash. Reflecting on his career in the NBA, and on his frustrations with the role he was asked to play, Cooper said in an interview quoted by Thomas: "People say I look pretty good for 50. But all the damage done to me is inside. That's where it hurts…. My difficulties were internal, inside of me and inside the system that prevailed in basketball."

Cooper's life after basketball was notable for his level of commitment to social activism and for his resolutely maintained distance from the basketball world. He married twice, first in 1951 and again in 1957; the second marriage, to Irva Lee, produced four children, one of whom played basketball and later expressed the wish that his father had pushed him harder. Cooper himself enrolled in social work classes at the University of Minnesota and earned a master's degree in 1961.

Returning to Pittsburgh, he worked for and eventually rose to the position of director in several neighborhood antipoverty organizations. He was named head of the city's parks and recreation department in 1970, becoming Pittsburgh's first black department director. Later he moved into an urban affairs post at Pittsburgh National Bank, where he spearheaded development and affirmative action programs. Pittsburgh residents of the 1970s and 1980s knew Chuck Cooper mostly as a member of numerous high-profile boards and civic organizations. He was inducted into the Pennsylvania Sports Hall of Fame in 1974, and in 1983 Duquesne established a Chuck Cooper Award to honor talented basketball underclassmen. The basketball career of the player who blazed the way for all the sport's numerous African-American stars, however, was largely forgotten when he died of liver cancer on May 2, 1984, in Pittsburgh.

Sources

Books

Thomas, Ron, *They Cleared the Lane: The NBA's Black Pioneers,* University of Nebraska Press, 2002.

Periodicals

Jet, November 18, 1996, p. 48.

On-line

Brown, Clifton, "True Trail Blazers," *NBA History,* www.nba.com/history/true_trailblazers_moments.html (July 28, 2004).
"Charles Henry Cooper," *Biography Resource Center,* www.galenet.com/servlet/BioRC (August 16, 2004).
"The NBA: Integration Happens," *HoopHall: Basketball Hall of Fame,* www.hoophall.com/exhibits/freedom_nba.htm (July 28, 2004).

—James M. Manheim

Michael Copeland

1954—

Martial arts master and teacher

Through a lifetime of hard work, Michael Copeland has become both an example and a teacher of what can be accomplished when desire is combined with determination. Beginning as a young boy trying to find a way to protect himself from the attacks of older boys, Copeland devoted his life to the study of Asian arts of self-defense. In the process, he not only developed a physical skill that would protect him from attack, but he also learned a clear and focused mental philosophy which would give him maturity and inner calm. Since martial arts training is in many ways an inner journey, Copeland was both surprised and honored when he became the first African American inducted into the World Karate Union's Hall of Fame in 2002.

Copeland was born on May 21, 1954, in Brooklyn, New York. His father, John Copeland, worked as a cement contractor, and his mother Lilly was a nurse's aid. John and Lilly Copeland had a difficult marriage. When Copeland was eight years old, his parents sent him to a Catholic boarding school in Riverhead on Long Island. Our Lady of the Little Flower removed Copeland from the conflict he had experienced at home, but he soon found himself bullied by older boys. He promised himself that he would learn to fight, so that he could defend himself in the future.

Introduced to Martial Arts

Copeland attended Our Lady of the Little Flower for almost four years. When he returned to home, his parents had separated. Though he continued to see both his parents, Copeland lived at his father's home. Life on the Brooklyn streets was not easy for a twelve-year-old boy, but Copeland was determined not to be bullied again. When an older boy punched him in the face, his reaction was to run and get his father's machete, a large heavy knife. John Copeland stopped the fight and decided that his son needed a different way to defend himself. He took young Mike to a martial arts demonstration at a local church.

Martial arts are self-defense techniques developed in various parts of Asia. While martial arts teach students how to fight, an important characteristic of the training involves a spiritual and mental discipline that teaches students a way of thinking about the world.

As Michael Copeland watched his first martial arts demonstration, he made a decision. He would master this way of fighting, and he would be better than the teacher who performed the demonstration. However, he had little money to pay for training. He solved this problem at first by going to the library. He read every book he could find about karate, a Japanese martial art which means "empty hand," because no weapons are used. Using the pictures in the books, he practiced on his own. Word spread in the neighborhood that Mike Copeland was a karate expert. Though this rumor did provide him with some protection, since it caused the bullies to fear him, Copeland knew that he would need some real training to become the expert he wished to be.

At a Glance . . .

Born on May 21, 1954, in Brooklyn, New York; married Helen Hazard, September 8, 1984; children: Miesha and Michael Jr. *Education:* attended Morrisville Community College, 1972-73, attended Long Island University, 1974.

Career: Trained in Isshinryu Karate, 1970-74; trained in Kung Fu, 1974-76; trained in Tang Soo Do, 1976-78; trained in Tae Kwan Do, 1979-89; earned Fourth Degree Black Belt Tae Kwan Do, 1989; trained in Kuden Jutsu, 1989–; operated Karate school, 1998-2001; Kuden Jutsu instructor, Ocean City Fitness Center, 2001–.

Selected memberships: World Karate Union; Worldwide Martial Arts Union; U.S. Tae Kwon Do Union; Kuden Jutsu America.

Selected awards: World Karate Union Hall of Fame Inductee, 2002; Action Magazine Hall of Fame Inductee, 2004; Worldwide Martial Arts Union Hall of Fame Inductee as Instructor of the Year, 2004.

Addresses: *Office*—1200 Southwest Boulevard, Building 5C, Vineland, New Jersey, 08360

Exploring Different Styles

In 1970 Copeland moved to Queens and took his first part-time job. From 11 p.m. to 4 a.m., several nights a week, he loaded trucks. Many mornings, he went directly from work to school, where a sympathetic gym teacher allowed him to shower and change. Though he found himself sleepy during classes, he was finally earning enough money to pay for karate training. He found a local studio that taught Isshinryu, a style of Karate that was developed during the mid-1950s in Okinawa, Japan. Copeland studied Isshinryu Karate for four years, earning a brown belt. Different color belts are awarded as students pass tests for different levels of training. Though each martial art has its own belt system, usually white belts are worn by beginners and black belts by masters. Brown belts often represent a high level of expertise, just below black belt.

As he began to experience the positive effects of the discipline of martial arts training, Copeland explored other styles. In 1974 he met a Kung Fu master and began to study the Chinese style of martial arts that had recently been brought into public awareness by a popular television show of the same name. He studied the Tiger Claw style of Kung Fu for two years. Later, he met and studied with Lawrence Clark, a New York master of Tang Soo Do, a Korean style of martial art.

In 1979 Lilly Copeland died, and a grieving Michael moved to Atlantic City, New Jersey, to live near his aunt. Gambling had become legal in Atlantic City, and casinos were opening around the city. Copeland found a job working in the kitchen in a casino restaurant. Lonely, with little to do in the evenings except run along the beach and sip beer in the bars, he began once again to seek out martial arts training. His search led him to Master Li, a teacher of a newly popular style of Korean martial art called Tae Kwan Do.

Tae Kwan Do, a later version of Tang Soo Do, means "the study of punching and kicking," and is characterized by high, spinning kicks. Some historians believe that Tae Kwan Do can be traced back to a military fight training and honor code used in Korea as early as 50 BCE. The style began to gain its modern popularity during the 1960s, and by 1980 was recognized by the International Olympic Committee. In 2000 Tae Kwon Do became an official sport of the Olympics.

As Copeland began once again to study a new type of martial arts, he had to learn how to set aside the things he already knew and open his mind to learning new forms. Master Li told him it would take ten years to become a master of Tae Kwan Do, and Copeland immediately set himself to the task. He trained seriously and began to enter competitions. When he lost his bout at his first State Championship tournament in 1983, he asked Master Li the secret to winning. His teacher simply said, "Go practice."

Copeland took this lesson to heart and never again practiced "just enough to get by." He trained early in the morning and late at night, improving his skills while others slept. He married and started a family, and he worked at various jobs to earn his living, but Tae Kwon Do became his true career. Between 1984 and 1989 he won several state competitions and competed in the national championships. By 1989 he had earned his fourth degree black belt in Tae Kwon Do, becoming a master as he had determined to do ten years before.

New Challenges Lead to Recognition

Though proud of his success, Copeland soon began to seek other challenges. He met Frank Romano, a martial arts teacher who had developed Kuden Jutsu, a new style of martial arts that combines several styles of fighting along with use of several types of weapons. Kuden Jutsu means "the art passed on by oral tradition." First developed by Romano, it is a combination of six different styles of fighting: freestyle, traditional forms, use of weapons, hand techniques, Polynesian ground fighting, and joint manipulation. Copeland was especially interested in the use and history of martial arts weapons, many of which had evolved from the farm tools that peasants had once used to defend themselves from invading soldiers.

In June of 1996 Copeland once again removed the black belt of the expert and replaced it with the white belt of the beginner. He threw himself into learning the newly developing style of Kuden Jutsu with his usual energy and determination. Soon he was skilled in the use of several weapons along with the many different styles of hand and footwork used by Kuden Jutsu. In 1998 he opened his own studio to teach his skills to others. He ran his studio for three years, then opted to close it and teach his art through the Ocean City Fitness Center.

In early 2001 personal tragedy struck the Copeland family. His wife's parents, Shirley and Richard Hazard, were murdered during a robbery at their house. Copeland had been close to his mother- and father-in-law. The loss of his loved ones in such a violent way shook him deeply, but reinforced his belief in self defense and strengthened his devotion to the spiritual aspect of his martial arts. In 2002 when his commitment to his work was rewarded with entry in the World Karate Union Hall of Fame, he dedicated his achievement to the Hazards.

Copeland's recognition by the WKU was followed quickly by two more marks of success. In 2004 he was inducted into the Action Magazine Hall of Fame and the Worldwide Martial Arts Union Hall of Fame. The Worldwide Martial Arts Union named him Instructor of the Year.

Copeland's response to his international recognition has been quiet pride and continued hard work. He has tried to lead an upright life in accordance with the teachings of many martial arts, which stress persistence and practice, along with taking good care of the body. "Through all the years, I never thought this would happen for me," he told *Contemporary Black Biography* with some wonder, "but I never gave up on myself."

While often working more than one job to support himself and his family, Copeland has continued to teach the disciplines of the martial art philosophy. He takes special pride in having trained his own children, who both gained a solid knowledge of martial arts before moving on to follow their own goals in life. In 2004 he was pleased to have the distinction of training the first female student in the world to earn a black belt in Kuden Jutsu.

Sources

Periodicals

Jet, August 18, 2003, p.55.

On-line

"Kuden Jutsu: A Self Defense Oriented Art Comprising 6 Styles." *Romatron: Kuden Jutsu Enterprises,* www.romatron.com (September 17, 2004)

Other

Information for this profile was obtained through an interview with Michael Copeland on September 19, 2004.

—Tina Gianoulis

Leon Dash

1944—

Journalist

Dash, Leon, photograph. Brian Johnson, Department of Journalism, University of Illinois

Leon Dash won American journalism's top honor, a Pulitzer Prize, for his 1994 series about a District of Columbia grandmother and her family, "Rosa Lee's Story." The series appeared in the *Washington Post,* where Dash had been an investigative reporter for a number of years, and chronicled one woman's impoverished, crime-filled life in the nation's capital over the years. Dash's reportage later appeared in book form as *Rosa Lee: A Mother and Her Family in Urban America.*

Other stories written by Dash had also won acclaim, including his 1989 book *When Children Want Children: The Urban Crisis of Teenage Childbearing.* Though sometimes criticized for depicting the sadder side of African-American life in big cities, Dash has argued that he simply tries to show both sides of the story. The "why" behind his subjects' choices is what he tries to illuminate. "I'm trying to make people understand the motivations of those around them," he told Guy Friddell, a reporter for the *Virginian Pilot,* "because there's a lot of confusion about the circumstances that produce particular behavior."

Hired as Journalism Intern

Dash was born in 1944 in New Bedford, Massachusetts, but grew up in New York City's Harlem and Bronx neighborhoods. Following an early ambition to become a lawyer, he enrolled at Howard University in Washington, D.C., in the early 1960s. Struggling to make ends meet, he took a night-shift job for a company that steam-cleaned building exteriors, but he was not cut out for the work. "It got cold, so I looked for an indoor job," he recalled in the interview with Friddell for the *Virginian Pilot.* He found his calling at one of the city's leading newspapers, the *Washington Post,* beginning as a copy person on what was called the "lobster" or overnight shift, from 6:30 p.m. to 2:30 a.m. A year later, in 1966, he was hired as a journalism intern and cub reporter.

After graduating from Howard in 1968, Dash joined the U.S. Peace Corps for two years. This volunteer organization brought young American professionals to some of the neediest corners of the globe, and Dash was sent to teach school in Kenya. He then returned to

At a Glance . . .

Born Leon DeCosta Dash Jr. on March 16, 1944, in New Bedford, MA; son of Leon Sr. and Ruth Dash; children: Darla, Destiny. *Education:* Howard University, BA, 1968.

Career: *Washington Post,* Washington, D.C., copy person, 1965, *Washington Post,* intern and reporter, 1966; U.S. Peace Corps, Kenya, volunteer, 1968-70; *Washington Post,* reporter, 1971; *Washington Post,* West African bureau chief, 1979-84; *Washington Post,* investigative reporter, 1984-98; University of Illinois at Urbana-Champaign, Departments of Journalism and African American Studies, professor, 1998–.

Memberships: National Association of Black Journalists.

Awards: Pulitzer Prize, 1995, for "Rosa Lee's Story;" National Association of Black Journalists, general news award, 1986; Investigative Reporters and Editors Organization, first place award, 1987; PEN/Martha Albrand Nonfiction, ; special citation, 1989, for *When Children Want Children.*

Addresses: *Office*—University of Illinois, College of Communications, Professor, Department of Journalism, 119 Gregory Hall, 810 S. Wright St., Urbana, IL 61801.

the *Washington Post* to work as a reporter. In part, he was drawn to a career in journalism because of his social conscience. Young and idealistic, at a time when the recently enacted civil rights laws seemed to portend such promise, he believed he could spur further change through his articles. He quickly grew disillusioned. "Within a decade I started doing the same stories over, particularly on the dilapidated conditions of public housing in Washington," he told Friddell in the 1997 *Virginian Pilot* story. "And those conditions had not changed. And up to this day it hasn't changed."

Nevertheless, Dash did publish important stories as well as his first book, written with Ben Bagdikian, 1972's *The Shame of the Prisons.* He became the newspaper's West African bureau chief in 1979, and returned five years later to carry on his investigative work in Washington. The first story that bore his new byline was "A Question of Justice: Cellmates' Word Sent Woman to Jail," but Dash soon turned his attentions to

the rising number of teenage parents in the District of Columbia. Stories such as "Young Black Pregnancies: Truth Is the First Answer" led to the publication of his second book, *When Children Want Children: The Urban Crisis of Teenage Childbearing,* in 1989.

Traced One Woman's Life Story

Dash then decided to delve into just one family in Washington and chronicle a tale of how poverty and substandard schools, combined with a lack of parenting skills and the lingering effects of slavery, seemed to beget generation after generation of the urban underclass. The woman he chose, Rosa Lee Cunningham, had eight children by six different fathers, and had been jailed repeatedly for theft and drug dealing by the time he met her. She was also a heroin addict, as were some of her children. Dash's 1994 series on Cunningham and her family won the 1995 Pulitzer Prize for explanatory journalism, which he shared with *Post* photographer Lucian Perkins. It appeared in book form as *Rosa Lee: A Mother and Her Family in Urban America* in 1996.

Dash had spent four years with Cunningham and her family. She was born in 1936, one of eleven children of North Carolina sharecroppers. Her mother, a domestic, was prone to violence, and though her father had a job as a cement-layer, he drank heavily. Growing up in the poorest section of Washington, Cunningham had never lived in a house with electricity as a child. She was expelled from school before the age of 14 because she was pregnant. At the time, she had not yet learned to read or write. Cunningham subsisted several years as a nightclub waitress who sold heroin to her customers on the side. She moved on to working in a strip club, and then became a prostitute.

Along the way, Cunningham became an expert shoplifter, which she did to both feed and clothe her own children and to satisfy her taste for stylish items. She was jailed eight times for stealing. "She wasn't ashamed of what she did," Dash explained to a writer for London's *Observer,* Nicci Gerrard. "She was amoral. She didn't see that she had any other options. What else could she do to survive? This is modern America. If you are born into the underclass, you have two ways to go: you can sink into dire and desperate straits, or you can join the criminal classes."

Cunningham's life took a bad turn in the mid-1970s when she finally became heroin user herself; needle use and prostitution eventually brought a diagnosis of human inmmuno-deficiency virus (HIV), which causes Acquired Immune Deficiency Syndrome, or AIDS, for Cunningham. Some of her children would also test positive for HIV, and her oldest son, who had been sexually abused at a very early age by the male babysitter Cunningham had hired to look after the children while she waited tables, was released from prison weighing 70 pounds in order to die at home. An almost equally horrific fate befell her oldest daughter, Patty, who had witnessed the transactions when Cunningham became a prostitute and brought her customers home. When Patty was eleven years old, one of the men asked Cunningham if her daughter was also available. Dash writes that this was the only episode in her life for which Cunningham was ashamed.

Defended Story's Message

Not surprisingly, Cunningham was a grandmother before she was 30, and the third generation grew up in even more desperate circumstances, now armed with guns and prone to crack-dealing and addiction. When Dash's series on the family ran, the *Post* logged over four thousand calls in response. Many of the paper's African-American readers were outraged that the *Post* had chosen to run a story that played into the worst stereotypes about the urban black underclass. There were far more positive stories it might have chose to tell, Dash's detractors claimed.

In response, Dash pointed to two of Cunningham's children, Alvin and Eric, who had grown into responsible parents, homeowners, and civil-service employees. Both had been able to transcend their home life with the help of mentors—in one case, a social worker, and the other a teacher. Each of the adults taught the boys to read. "People say I should understand less and condemn more," Dash reflected in the interview with the *Observer*'s Gerrard. "Condemn! How can we condemn human beings who have been given the short straw from birth? Sure, Rosa Lee made bad choices, she did dreadful things. What would you or I do, in her life?"

Dash took a dying Cunningham back to the North Carolina area where her family had lived in the years after slavery. She met cousins, and mesmerized an audience when she spoke at a church service. One of the more interesting points that Dash made in his series was the reason why blacks in the District of Columbia had not seemed to fare as well as others who had left the South in the Great Migration northward after the First World War. In other cities, they found decent-paying factory jobs or post-office work—but many of the blacks from the South who came to Washington found a long-entrenched black population who already held many of the good jobs, and who treated the newcomers with disdain. Cunningham's parents, moreover, were from a part of North Carolina that was deeply rural and isolated. Called "swamp blacks" even

by other African Americans in the area, families like Cunningham's parents were descended from slaves who had worked the plantations deep in the heart of Roanoke River country. As a result, they were nearly untouched by twentieth-century progress by the time she was born, when the Great Depression had caused cotton prices to plummet and sent families like hers to the cities in search of a better life than sharecropping.

In 1998, Dash retired from the *Washington Post* to take a professorship at the University of Illinois at Urbana-Champaign, where he teaches journalism and African-American studies. Cunningham had died in 1996, the same year his book about her family was published. As he reflected in the *Observer* interview with Gerrard, though to those who never met her Cunningham seemed a tragically flawed character, "she was my friend. She was an extraordinary woman… monstrous, wonderful, brave. She had no idea. When she died I missed her. I keep in touch with some of the children. And witnessing her life made me unable to judge any longer. After all, I am black. It could have been me."

Selected writings

(With Ben Bagdikian) *The Shame of the Prisons,* Simon & Schuster, 1972.
When Children Want Children: The Urban Crisis of Teenage Childbearing, William Morrow, 1989.
Rosa Lee: A Mother and Her Family in Urban America, Harper Collins, 1996.

Sources

Periodicals

Austin American-Statesman (TX), September 29, 1996, p. E6.
Commonwealth, November 4, 1994, p. 9.
Guardian (London), August 16, 1997, p. 18.
Observer (London), August 24, 1997, p. 6.
People, June 8, 1992, p. 40.
Time, September 30, 1996, p. 75.
Virginian Pilot, April 5, 1997, p. B1.

On-line

"Leon Dash," *Inside Medill News,* www.medill.north-western.edu/inside/2002/leondash.html (August 3, 2004).

—Carol Brennan

Frank Marshall Davis

1905-1987

Poet, journalist

A central figure in African-American literary history, Frank Marshall Davis was a poet whose work drew on and put a personal stamp on many of the trends in black poetry of the 1930s and 1940s. He was influenced by jazz and tried to evoke its rhythms in words. He drew detailed portraits of urban African-American life. And like Langston Hughes and many of his other contemporaries, he was a social activist who used literature to illustrate injustice in no uncertain terms.

Davis was also a pioneering figure in the field of African-American journalism. Insufficient recognition of the role Chicago writers played in African-American cultural life contributed to a long-lasting underestimation of Davis's work, as did his move to Hawaii in midlife, under threat from a growing wave of anticommunist repression. Davis was rediscovered enthusiastically, however, by politically oriented black writers of the later twentieth century.

Victim of Attempted Lynching

Frank Marshall Davis was born on December 31, 1905, in Arkansas City, Kansas. The violence of small-town Midwestern life was unrelenting; Davis was told by teachers and townspeople that blacks were inferior, and when he was five a group of white boys tried to lynch him. He took heart, though, when he first heard a new music that was spreading across the South. "The blues? We were formally introduced when I was eight; even then I had the feeling we weren't strangers," Davis wrote in his autobiographical *Livin'*

the Blues: Memoirs of a Black Journalist and Poet. "So when the blues grabbed me and held on, it was like meeting a long-lost brother."

Davis graduated from Arkansas City High School and moved to Wichita, Kansas, around 1924, taking journalism classes at Friends College and at Kansas State Agricultural College (now Kansas State University of Agricultural and Applied Science). As a freshman there, he faced the option of writing either an essay or a poem for an English class and took what he thought was the easy way out. The professor liked his poem, and Davis ran off to the library to write more. Hooked on writing, Davis moved to Chicago in January of 1927 and soon had some stories published in *National Magazine.* Some of his work is published under his pen name Frank Boganey—the last name of his mother's second husband. In April of 1927 Davis began his journalism career as an editor and columnist with the *Chicago Evening Bulletin.*

Working for the *Chicago Whip,* the *Gary* (Indiana) *American,* the Associated Negro Press, and (from 1931 to 1934) the *Atlanta World,* Davis became a jack-of-all-trades. "I served not only as straight news reporter but as rewrite man, editor, editorial writer, political commentator, theatrical and jazz columnist, sports writer, and occasionally news photographer," Davis wrote in his autobiography. As managing editor of the *Atlanta World* he transformed the paper from a weekly to a thrice-weekly and finally to a daily publication. All the while, he was writing poetry, and in 1934 he moved back to Chicago from Atlanta. The year 1935 saw the publication of Davis's first book, *Black Man's Verse,* by Black Cat Press. Davis followed up that volume with *I Am the American Negro* two years later.

Worked for Associated Negro Press

Those books made Davis's reputation and cemented his relationships with Langston Hughes, Richard Wright, and other leading black writers whom he met while participating in the federal Works Progress Administration Writers' Project and other organizations. In 1937 Davis received a Julius Rosenwald Fellowship, and through World War II he continued to earn a living as a journalist and editor with the Associated Negro Press. His poetry involved itself with various subjects and sources; two series of poems set in a graveyard and describing its occupants (one in each of his first two books) seemed influenced by a parallel section of Edgar Lee Masters's *Spoon River Anthology.* He depicted urban scenes and wrote occasional lyric poems of great beauty. "Peddling/From door to door/Night sells/ Black bags of peppermint stars/Heaping cones of vanilla moon," he wrote in one poem.

Most often, though, Davis was identified with militant poems. His works dealt with lynching, poverty, and the other grinding conditions under which African Americans live, and he indicted the hypocrisy of white America repeatedly. Several poems, including "'On-

ward Christian Soldiers,'" took direct aim at white violence on a global scale; "Day by day // Black folk learn // Rather than with // A heathen spear // 'Tis holier to die // By a Christian gun." These works made a strong impression, but some critics shied away from them; Hughes (as quoted by Davis biographer John Edgar Tidwell) offered the even-handed but cautionary assessment that "when [Davis's] poems are poetry, they are powerful."

Davis broadened his activities into many areas of black culture and society in the 1930s and 1940s. He used his newspaper platform to call for integration of the sports world, and he began to engage himself with community organizing efforts, starting a Chicago labor newspaper (the *Star*) toward the end of World War II. In 1945 he taught one of the first jazz history courses in the United States at the Abraham Lincoln School in Chicago. He briefly joined the Communist Party, although he had disparaged the efforts of Communist organizers while living in the South in the 1930s and later downplayed the extent of his involvement.

Moved to Hawaii

Still, Davis's leftist associations were strong enough to attract unwelcome attention from the government after the war, and by the time his third book, *47th Street: Poems,* was published in 1948, he was under pressure from the Un-American Activities Committee of the House of Representatives. That book, often considered Davis's best, aimed at a readership that extended beyond African-American circles and offered portraits of a broad range of Chicagoans. On vacation that summer in Hawaii with his second wife, Chicago socialite Helen Canfield Davis, he decided to stay on in Honolulu and remained there for the rest of his life. The interracial marriage lasted 24 years but finally ended in divorce. Davis first became a father at age 44, and the couple raised five children.

Davis said that he was drawn to life in Hawaii because of the islands' multiethnic culture. He wrote some poetry in Hawaii and worked on his autobiography beginning in the early 1960s. He penned a column for a Honolulu labor newspaper. But mostly he dropped off the literary radar, starting a paper-supplies company, Oahu Papers, which mysteriously burned to the ground in March of 1951. In 1959 he started another similar firm, the Paradise Paper Company. Several times he was questioned about his leftist affiliations by congressional investigators, but by the late 1950s the anticommunist hysteria had died down.

In the late 1960s and early 1970s, young African-American writers (especially those affiliated with the Black Arts Movement) began to rediscover Davis's work. He visited Howard University in Washington to give a poetry reading in 1973, marking the first time he had seen the U.S. mainland in 25 years. His work began to show up in anthologies, and in the late 1970s he published two more small volumes of poetry, *Jazz Interludes: Seven Musical Poems* and *Awakening and Other Poems*. Davis died in Honolulu on July 26, 1987, just before a group of young scholars became interested in documenting his life and work. *Livin' the Blues* was published posthumously in 1992. It was assembled from Davis's notes by John Edgar Tidwell, who in 2002 edited a publication of Davis's collected works, *Black Moods*.

Selected works

Black Man's Verse, Black Cat, 1935.
I Am the American Negro, Black Cat, 1937.
Through Sepia Eyes, Black Cat, 1938.
47th Street: Poems, Decker (Prairie City, IL), 1948.
Livin' the Blues: Memoirs of a Black Journalist and Poet, ed. John Edgar Tidwell, University of Wisconsin Press, 1992.
Black Moods: Collected Poems, ed. John Edgar Tidwell, University of Illinois Press, 2002.

Sources

Books

Davis, Frank Marshall, *Black Moods: Collected Poems,* University of Illinois Press, 2002.
King, Woodie, Jr., ed., *The Forerunners: Black Poets in America,* Howard University Press, 1975.

Periodicals

African American Review, Summer-Fall 2003, p. 466.
Black Scholar, Summer 1996, p. 17.
Western Journal of Black Studies, Winter 2002, p. 215.

On-line

"Black Poet's Works Reflected Fire, Love, Strength," *University of Kansas Office of University Relations,* www.ur.ku.edu/News/02NSeptNews/Sept13/martin.html (August 2, 2004).
"Frank Marshall Davis," *Contemporary Authors Online,* www.galenet.galegroup.com/servlet/BioRC (August 2, 2004).

—James M. Manheim

Mary Pearl Dougherty

1915-2003

U.S. Foreign Service employee

Mary Pearl Dougherty had few African-American contemporaries, and fewer still who were women, when she began her career with the United States Foreign Service in the 1940s. She was not an ambassador but a secretary, and histories of the U.S. State Department and diplomatic corps have little to say about her. But her knowledge of the diplomatic world was deep, and she lived on after her retirement in the memories of younger African-American Foreign Service officers, who looked to her as a mentor and fondly referred to her as "Mother Pearl." Although her training was of an indirect sort, she may be numbered among a generation of influential African Americans who were shaped by the pioneering historian Carter G. Woodson, "the father of black history."

Dougherty was born in Alabama in 1915. Her early years were spent partly in Cleveland, Ohio, where she attended a business college and trained to be a secretary. In the 1930s she moved to Washington, D.C. and studied psychology at American University. But times were difficult for black Washingtonians in the later years of the Great Depression, and Dougherty jumped at the chance to take a prestigious secretarial job with Carter G. Woodson, the scholar and former Howard University professor who pioneered the whole field of black history.

"Dr. Woodson was a disciplinarian," Dougherty told *American Visions*. "You were to be at your desk, your coat off and ready to work, at 9 a.m. sharp." Local young commercial school graduates who had heard of his reputation looked for jobs elsewhere. "But I was very well trained at the leading commercial school in Ohio, so it didn't bother me," Dougherty recalled. "Besides, back in the '30s, you needed a damn job." She started out as a typist in the fall of 1938, mailing out membership materials for Woodson's Association for the Study of Afro-American Life and History (ASNLH). But she caught Woodson's attention, and six months later she became the great scholar's personal assistant.

She had never heard of Woodson before coming to Washington, and nothing in Dougherty's education in Cleveland had given her any idea of the riches of African-American history. But she learned a great deal. She got an education in precise speech and grammar as well, one that laid important groundwork for her career in the diplomatic world. Woodson would dictate entire chapters of his books, without even looking at notes. "Then, when I would show him the transcript, he would say, 'Mrs. D., you split an infinitive!'" she told *American Visions*.

In the first years of World War II Dougherty worked as a real estate secretary and did a stint at the U.S. War Department (now the Department of Defense). In 1944 she joined the Foreign Service. At the time, black State Department employees were a small minority, and those working in the overseas offices of the Foreign Service were even scarcer. By 1953, nine years after Dougherty began her career, only 55 of the State Department's 8,231 overseas employees were African American, and many of those were sent, by tradition, to black-ruled countries such as Liberia and

At a Glance . . .

Born in 1915 in Alabama; raise in Cleveland, OH; died on November 13, 2003, in Washington, DC. *Education:* Attended business college in Cleveland, OH; attended American University, Washington, DC. *Religion:* Baptist.

Career: Personal secretary to historian Carter G. Woodson, 1938-41; real estate secretary; U.S. Department of War, early 1940s; secretary, U.S. Foreign Service, 1944-74; volunteer escort, U.S. Foreign Service, 1974-79; personal assistant to vice president for academic affairs, Howard University, 1970s; consultant, National Association of Negro Business and Professional Women's Clubs.

Memberships: Phyllis Wheatley YMCA (vice president); African American Women's Association (president); Thursday Luncheon Group, U.S. State Department.

Haiti. The situation didn't begin to change substantially until the civil rights reforms of the 1960s.

Dougherty's talents broke color barriers. She held posts in African nations: Liberia, the Central African Republic, and Zaire. But later she was assigned as well to South Vietnam and to European countries on both sides of the Iron Curtain: France, Germany, and Romania. Nominally she was a secretary, but she was one of those secretaries who grease the wheels for the smooth functioning of important events, and who shepherd the careers of those they choose to aid. She traveled around Europe and the world, and she became familiar with the ways of people from many different cultures.

In her later years with the agency, Dougherty was a role model and confidant for young black Foreign Service officers; they in turn bestowed upon her the sobriquets of "Aunt Mary," "Ms. D," and "Mother Pearl." She could be counted on for advice on anything from homesickness to the proper glasses in which to serve different drinks at an embassy dinner party. After Dougherty retired from the Foreign Service in 1974, the State Department continued to make unofficial use of her knowledge; she escorted, on a volunteer basis, high-ranking guests from countries such as South Africa, Egypt, Korea, the Ivory Coast, and India as they visited the United States and traveled around the country.

Dougherty never really retired. She worked as an assistant to Howard University vice president Lorraine Williams in the 1970s, and in 1977, working as a consultant to the National Association of Negro Business and Professional Women's Clubs, she resumed her international travels, assembling and leading a delegation that visited the West African countries of Senegal, Cameroon, Sierra Leone, the Gambia, and Malawi. She kept in touch with State Department doings as a member (and co-founder) of the department's Thursday Luncheon Group, and she served as vice president of Washington's Phyllis Wheatley YWCA and as president of the African-American Women's Association. For over 50 years she was a member of Washington's Shiloh Baptist Church, close to Woodson's home, and she was pained to see the building's decay toward the twentieth century's end.

Honors that came to Dougherty at the end of her life were of a personal rather than an official kind. In 1990 she was the subject of a surprise "roast" at a suburban Washington restaurant, organized by friends and fellow Foreign Service veterans and attended by more than 100 people. "Mary deserved it," future U.S. ambassador to Senegal Harriet Elam told the *Washington Post*. "She worked over half a century helping other people." Elam herself had first met Dougherty in Paris in the 1960s and was one of many young diplomats who benefited from her advice early in their careers. Dougherty, who left no closely related survivors at her death, lived in the Washington neighborhood of Cleveland Park in her retirement. She was diagnosed with cancer and died at age 88 on November 13, 2003, at Washington's Methodist Home.

Sources

Periodicals

American Visions, February/March 2000, p. 45.
Jet, December 15, 2003, p. 18.
Washington Post, July 5, 1990, p. J3; November 18, 2003, p. B5.
Sun Reporter (San Francisco, CA), September 14, 1978, p. 20.

—James M. Manheim

Julius "Dr. J" Erving

1950—

Basketball player, basketball executive

So much has been written and said about Julius Erving over the years that it is difficult to say what is most important about him. He will go down in history as one of the basketball pioneers who took a sport that had been traditionally played on a wooden floor and changed it so that it was played in mid-air, and he popularized a form of scoring known as the dunk. He was a legendary figure that very few people saw play in his early professional years in the American Basketball Association, and his reputation probably forced the more established National Basketball Association to merge with that league. He was the consummate team player, who won championships in both professional leagues. He was a perfect gentleman and an ambassador for the game at a time when its popularity was at a low ebb, and he will be remembered forever as "Dr. J."

Julius Winfield Erving II was born February 22, 1950, in Roosevelt, New York. He and his brother were raised by their mother, Callie. His father, Julius, was absent much of the time, and when young Julius was seven his dad was hit and killed by a car. "I never really had a father, but then the possibility that I ever would was removed," he told *Esquire*. He attended Roosevelt High School, where he was a fine student and an even better basketball player. He made the all-county and All-Long Island teams in high school.

A Natural Basketball Player

Julius was a natural at basketball as a youngster, both in school and on the playground. Erving told *Esquire*,

"I've never felt particularly unique. Even within the context of basketball, I honestly never imagined myself as anything special. I remember back home, when I first started playing, at nine, ten, I had a two-hand shot. Then by twelve-and-a-half, thirteen, I had a one-hand shot. Always went to the basket, that was my way, that pattern was set by then." "Actually, I don't think I've changed much as a player since then," he continued. "Back then, before I was physically able, I felt these different things within me, certain moves, ways to dunk. I realized all I had to do was be patient and they would come. So I wasn't particularly surprised when they did, they were part of me for so long. I didn't find anything particularly special about them. It wasn't that I didn't think I was a good player, that I could play, I just assumed everyone could do these things if they tried."

Erving parlayed his good grades and basketball success into a college career at the University of Massachusetts. He planned on becoming a doctor, and it wasn't until he found himself among the nation's scoring leaders that it occurred to him that he could make the move from the traditionally weak basketball school to a pro career. He got a break when he was invited to play some exhibition games for an Olympic development squad—those being the days when a college All-Star team also comprised the U.S. Olympic basketball team—and his reputation began to grow among pro scouts. His mother suffered some medical problems during Julius' college days, and he skipped his senior season to play in the American Basketball Association (ABA), which had a hardship rule that allowed college

At a Glance . . .

Born Julius Winfield Erving II on February 22, 1950, in Roosevelt, New York; son of Julius Erving and Callie (Erving) Lindsey; married Turquoise, 1972 (divorced, 2003); children: Cheo, Julius III, Jazmin, and Cory (with Turquoise); Alexandra Stevenson. *Education:* Attended University of Massachusetts.

Career: Virginia Squires (ABA), professional basketball player, 1971-73; New York Nets (ABA), professional basketball player, 1973-76; Philadelphia 76ers (NBA), professional basketball player, 1976-87. Coca-Cola Bottling Company, Philadelphia, co-owner, 1987–; Orlando Magic, executive vice-president, 1997-2003; NBC-TV, television commentator; JDREGI (management and marketing firm), president.

Memberships: Meridian Bancorp, board of directors.

Awards: ABA Most Valuable Player, 1974, 1975 (shared), 1976; ABA All-Star First Team, 1973-76; NBA Most Valuable Player, 1981; All-NBA First Team, 1978, 1980-83; Jackie Robinson Award, 1983; American Express Man of the Year, 1985; named to Naismith Memorial Basketball Hall of Fame, 1993.

Addresses: *Agent*—c/o The Allen Agency, 23852 Pacific Coast Hwy. Suite £401, Malibu, CA 90265.

Became ABA All-Star

In 1972-73 Erving had another strong season, leading the league with 31.9 points-per-game (PPG). That year he also made the league's All-Star First Team, but he still faced the problem of his budding career being played in obscurity. The ABA was almost never on television, and the Squires hardly played in a major market. Erving had tried to jump to the NBA, signing a contract with the Atlanta Hawks after his rookie season, but a judge ruled that he was the property of the Squires and had to return to that team. At the end of his second season the Squires gave Erving a bit of a boost toward the big-time when they traded him to the league's Big Apple franchise, the New York Nets.

In his first season with the Nets Erving helped that team to the league championship, leading the league with a 27.4 scoring average and increasing that average to 27.9 over 14 playoff games. He was named both the league's regular season most valuable player (MVP) and the playoff MVP. Erving had now won a league championship in the biggest market in the country, but still relatively few people had seen him play. The league still didn't have a network television contract, and the Nets were low in the pecking order of New York Sports teams, never selling out a regular season game.

In his second season with the Nets Erving won the league's Most Valuable Player award with a 27.9 PPG average and 10.9 rebounds per game. Despite his averaging 27.4 points in the playoffs, the Nets lost in the first round. The following year, however, Erving again led the league with 29.3 points per game, and led the Nets in a charmed season all the way to the league championship series.

During this season Erving's reputation grew dramatically. It cannot be said that he invented the airborne style of basketball, often referred to as "playing above the rim." Others had preceded him in that style, most notably Connie Hawkins and Elgin Baylor. But Erving, while not really reinventing the sport, had upped the ante by being just a little bit faster, jumping just a little bit further, being just a little bit more spectacular than anyone ever had before. While the ABA's games still were not often broadcast for a national audience, the media began to do more features on the amazing basketball player playing for the New York team in that other league. Another key point came during the ABA's 1976 All-Star Game, when the first-ever slam-dunk contest was held. Erving won it, due in large part to his final dunk, on which he gripped the ball in one hand, ran the length of the floor, took off in flight at the free throw line and dunked before coming down. Several other players have done the identical dunk since, but at the time it seemed as if Erving had done the impossible. Footage of the dunk received widespread television exposure, and Erving became a national phenomenon.

underclassmen to enter the league. Erving signed with the Virginia Squires as a free agent in 1971.

Erving enjoyed immediate success in the ABA. During his rookie season he played 84 games, averaged over 27 points and 15 rebounds a game, and led the Squires on a strong playoff run. He was named to the league's All-Rookie Team and the All-Star Second Team. It was also during Erving's rookie year with Virginia that a strong part of his identity was born. "The Doctor" had been a handle placed on Erving since grade school, when he announced in front of his class he wanted to be a doctor when he grew up. It became a playground moniker when his high school teammate, Leon Saunders, and Erving began referring to each other as "The Doctor" and "The Professor." During that season in Virginia, Squire Fatty Taylor began sticking the "J" onto Erving's name, and the nickname "Dr. J" was born.

That season Erving capped his ABA career, and the history of the league, with a sensational final series against the Denver Nuggets. The Nets beat the Nuggets four games to two, and Erving was so instrumental and spectacular in both the wins and the losses, that it was sometimes easy to forget there were nine other players on the floor. Erving scored 45, 48, 31, 34, 37, and 31 points in the six games, and led the Nets back from 22 points down in the final game at Nassau Coliseum. It was the last game in the history of the ABA.

Leaped to NBA Stardom

Before the 1976-77 basketball season, the ABA folded in triumph, with four of its teams, including the Nets, being accepted into the older, more established, more conservative NBA. Although history has not recorded definitively that Julius Erving was the primary or possibly even only reason the NBA agreed to the merger, that likelihood has been suggested and a strong case can be made that Erving had proven that world-class basketball was played in the ABA. At any rate, Julius Erving was finally about to showcase his talents on the biggest basketball stage in the world.

As some had predicted, Erving found a bit more resistance to his freewheeling style of play in the older league. The day before his first season in that league was to begin, the Nets traded him to the Philadelphia 76ers. His scoring average dropped about 25 percent with Philadelphia compared to what it been in New York, to about 21.8 points per game his first season. He did help the Sixers to the league championship series that year, but their loss to the Portland Trailblazers was considered such a disappointment that the team felt it had to live down the loss for years afterward. The highlight of the season for Dr. J may have been the All-Star Game, in which he had 30 points and 12 rebounds, and won the game's Most Valuable Player award.

That started a long string of seasons in which Erving was considered the best player in the league who had never won a championship. Through the late 1970s and early 1980s his image was that of a spectacular player, certainly one of the best in the league. Yet the question remained as to whether he would ever win a NBA championship. He didn't dominate the NBA as he had the ABA, although he played in the All-Star Game every year, was named to either the league's post-season first or second All-Star team every year except 1979, and even won the league's Most Valuable Player award in 1981. But it seemed every year either the Boston Celtics or Los Angeles Lakers beat the 76ers and left them waiting.

The year Erving and the 76ers were waiting for finally came during the 1982-83 season. That year Erving won the All-Star Game MVP for the second time, even though his scoring that season was at its second-lowest point since he came into the NBA, only 21.4 points per game. But the 76ers had acquired a strong inside force that season in Moses Malone and they proved unstoppable in the playoffs, steamrolling into the finals, where they met the Lakers, to whom they had lost tough final series in 1980 and 1982. Erving's scoring average was down for the playoffs as well, to under 20 points per game, and Malone was the standout as the 76ers won the first three games from the Lakers. Dr. J saved his magic for the final game, making a shot from the top of the key in the closing seconds to give Philadelphia a three-point lead and clinch the championship. It was also during this series that Erving made a shot that will probably be repeated on highlight reels forever, a reverse windmill layup from behind the backboard. Dr. J, who by this was wearing his trademark Afro short and with some flecks of gray, had his most memorable shot and his first NBA championship.

It also turned out to be his last NBA championship. Although the 76ers continued to be a strong team, and made the playoffs every year—Erving never missed the playoffs in his ABA or NBA careers—they never made it back to the NBA finals. Erving still averaged over 20 points a game for the 1983-84 and 1984-85 seasons, then saw his PPG drop below that mark for the first time in his professional career for his last two seasons.

Became Game's Elder Statesman

But while Dr. J's game may have fallen off a bit in his late 30s, he had another reputation that became even stronger in those late seasons. He was known as one of the true gentlemen of professional basketball, and was universally admired by opponents, sportswriters, broadcasters, and fans. He was never seen to be short-tempered or rude with reporters or fans, a difficult task considering the constant demands placed on a basketball star of his stature. Erving had entered the league at a time when its popularity was at a low ebb, with two-thirds of the league's teams in serious financial trouble. While the subsequent arrival of Magic Johnson, Larry Bird, and later Michael Jordan, had more to do with the ascent of the game's stature in the 1980s, Erving served an important role in keeping the game afloat and bolstering its reputation. "I've never heard anybody knock him or express jealousy," Dominique Wilkins of the Atlanta Hawks said during Erving's final season. "Never one negative word. I can't name you one other player who has that status."

Also in those final seasons, Erving began to make the transition from his playing days to his retirement years by making shrewd business investments. In 1983 he purchased shares in the New York Coca-Cola Bottling Company, and three years later he turned that investment into an outright purchase of the larger Philadelphia Coca-Cola Bottling Company, the 15th largest bottling facility in the world. As a result, he and his partner, Bruce Llewellyn, shared ownership one of the largest black-owned businesses in the world. He also started up a shoe store—dress shoes, not basketball shoes—which failed, and a television station and a cable television company in New York State.

When Erving announced that 1986-87 would be his last NBA season, he received an honor that is reserved for only the elite athletes: he was honored with special ceremonies not just in Philadelphia, but in each of the other arenas on his last visit. Accolades and souvenirs were showered on him on his farewell tour, as the league thanked Erving for what he had done for the game. In Los Angeles, Lakers coach Pat Riley told the crowd, "There may have been some better people off the court. Like a few mothers and the pope. But there was only one Dr. J the player."

Awards continued to be bestowed on Erving even after his playing days were over. In 1993 he was elected to the Basketball Hall of Fame, and in 1994, as part of its 40th anniversary, Sports Illustrated named him to a list of its 40 most important athletes. In 1996, as the NBA celebrated its 50th anniversary, Erving was an easy choice for one of the top 50 players in the history of the league.

Retired a Legend

Erving found plenty to keep him busy in his retirement. He continued to work with his business enterprises and charitable causes, and did some work in the 1990s for NBC TV's NBA broadcasts. In 1997 the Orlando Magic hired Erving as its executive vice- president, widely defining his duties as concerning both basketball and business aspects of the operation. Erving left the Magic after the 2002-03 season to pursue other business opportunities. Also in 1997 the legend of Dr. J was revived when Converse, a sneaker company which had seen its market share fall off dramatically since the mid-1980s, made Erving, along with Larry Bird and Magic Johnson, the staple of a new marketing campaign. Although Erving had by then not played basketball professionally in a decade, the company saw a dramatic turn in its fortunes, with sales up substantially.

Though Erving had enjoyed a squeaky clean public image for many years, events and press coverage in the late 1990s and early 2000s were not so positive. In 1999 it was revealed that Dr. J was the father of rising tennis star Alexandra Stevenson, the product of an adulterous liaison with a Philadelphia sportswriter. Tragedy struck the Erving family in 2000 when their youngest son, 19-year-old Cory, came up missing. After a 39-day search, it was discovered that his car had run off the road and into a swamp near the family's Florida home, drowning Cory. Though Erving was quoted in People saying that "we will be a stronger family as a result" of the tragedy, by 2003 his 31-year marriage to his wife, Turquoise, disintegrated in messy divorce proceedings that revealed a second child born out of wedlock.

While history may remember Erving for his statistics, or the championships he won, or the leagues he made profitable, it is more likely that most of the people who watched him play will remember him for other reasons. Long after he played, fans still swapped stories about the spectacular dunks and other moves they saw Erving make. Upon Erving's retirement, Frank DeFord of *Sports Illustrated* wrote, "More than any single player, Erving transformed what had been a horizontal game (with occasional parabolas) into a vertical exercise. Basketball is now a much more artistic game than it was before—than any game was before—because of Julius Erving. The slam, before the Doctor, was essentially an act of power—a stuff is what it was usually called—as great giants jammed the ball through the hoop. Erving transformed the stuff into the dunk, and made what had been brutal and the product of size into something beautiful and a measure of creativity."

Sources

Books

Haskins, James, *Doctor J.: A Biography of Julius Erving,* Doubleday, 1975.
Porter, David L., ed., *African-American Sports Greats: A Biographical Dictionary,* Greenwood Press, 1995.
Wilker, Josh, *Julius Erving,* Chelsea House, 1995.

Periodicals

Basketball Digest, February 2002, pp. 30-35; March 2002, pp. 18-20; May-June 2004, pp. 20-22.
Black Enterprise, March 1986, p. 13.
Esquire, February 1985, p. 112.
Investor's Business Daily, April 16, 2002, p. A4.
Jet, June 23, 1997, p. 48; July 26, 1999, p. 34; July 24, 2000, p. 54.
New York Times, March 26, 1997, p, D3.
People Weekly, July 19, 1999, p. 73; July 24, 2000, p. 67.
Sports Illustrated, May 4, 1987, p. 74; September 19, 1994, p. 146; May 31, 2004, p. 39.
Time, July 12, 1999.

On-line

"Julius Erving," *NBA History,* www.nba.com/history/players/erving_summary.html (August 18, 2004).
"Julius Erving," *Remember the ABA,* www.remember theaba.com/TributeMaterial/Erving.html (August 18, 2004).

—Mike Eggert And Tom Pendergast

Ronald L. Fair

1932—

Fiction writer, poet

Ronald L. Fair's body of work displays contradictory qualities. On one hand, he was a realistic chronicler of the lives of urban African Americans in the 1960s, one who captured the disillusionment of blacks who fled Southern white racism only to discover that Northern cities brought oppression and dislocation of a different kind. On the other, he was a literary experimenter, one who wrote in economical, clipped, often ironic and satirical styles quite distinct from the expansive, preacherly prose of some of his African-American contemporaries. Audiences of the 1960s and 1970s never knew quite what to make of Fair's writing; he remained less well known than other African-American writers of the period, and he eventually left the United States for Europe, never to return. Yet he had several strong advocates in the literary world, and his output, with several finished but unpublished works, seemed ripe for rediscovery in the new millennium.

Born in Chicago on October 27, 1932, Fair was the son of Herbert and Beulah Hunt Fair, Mississippi farmworkers who took pride in their African heritage. Fair attended public schools in Chicago. He started writing as a teenager as a way of questioning the world in which he found himself and of expressing angry feelings. He was inspired by the example of Richard Wright, one of his prime influences, and a black English teacher encouraged him to keep writing. Fair joined the U.S. Navy in 1950 and served for three years as a hospital worker. He married while he was in the Navy and had two children, but that marriage ended in divorce.

Back home, Fair attended a business college, the Stenotype School of Chicago. He got a job as a court reporter after finishing school in 1955 and remained in that profession for 12 years. Fair kept writing outside of work hours, and he published various short writings in the *Chicago Defender, Ebony, Chat Noir,* and other publications. His first novel, *Many Thousand Gone: An American Fable,* was issued by Harcourt in 1965.

Fair's first novel covered a span of a century, from the Civil War to the 1960s, in 120 terse pages. It presented a fictional town called Jacobsville, Mississippi, whose residents remained unaware that slavery was no longer in existence. Against this backdrop, Fair unfolded the various forms of governmental and extralegal horrors that befell African Americans beginning in the Reconstruction era. Reviewers praised the unique bitter tone of Fair's descriptions of rape and lynching, but many failed to appreciate the symbolism of the novel's plot, which was directed toward the idea that African Americans had to wake up to the repression under which they lived.

Fair worked as a writer for a year as an *Encyclopedia Britannica* writer while readying his second novel, *Hog Butcher,* for publication. *Hog Butcher* remains perhaps the best known of Fair's writings. In 1975 it was made into a film called *Cornbread, Earl and Me,* featuring future superstar Laurence Fishburne as the ten-year-old protagonist and narrator, and it was published in paperback under that title. The book tells the story of a police coverup intended to conceal a mis-

At a Glance . . .

Born on October 27, 1932, in Chicago, IL; son of Herbert and Beulah Fair; married Lucy Margaret Jones, November 10, 1952 (divorced); married Neva June Keres, June 19, 1968; children (first marriage): Rodney D., Glen A.; (second marriage) Nile. *Education:* Attended Stenotype School of Chicago, 1953-55. *Military service:* U.S. Naval Reserve, 1950-53.

Career: City of Chicago, court reporter, 1955-67; *Encyclopedia Britannica,* writer, ca. 1966; writer, 1967–; Columbia College, Chicago, literature instructor, 1967; Northwestern University, literature instructor, 1968; Wesleyan University, Middletown, CT, Center for Advanced Studies, visiting fellow, 1969; Wesleyan University, visiting professor, 1970-71.

Awards: National Institute of Arts and Letters, Arts and Letters Award, 1970, for *World of Nothing;* American Library Association, Best Book Award, 1972, for *We Can't Breathe;* National Education Association fellowship, 1974; Guggenheim Foundation fellowship, 1975.

Addresses: *Publisher*—c/o Lotus Press, P.O. Box 21607, Detroit, MI 48221.

taken fatal shooting of budding basketball star "Cornbread" Maxwell. Rich with detail about the lives of transplanted Southern blacks in Chicago and about the myriad ways in which the city's government and society were stacked against them, *Hog Butcher,* in the words of Bernard W. Bell in *The Contemporary Afro-American Novel,* showed "the continuing appeal of traditional realism and naturalism to some contemporary black novelists."

In 1967, Fair took a job teaching literature at Chicago's Columbia College. He moved on to Northwestern University the following year and also married his second wife, Neva June Keres, with whom he had one more child. With the help of awards and fellowships that included a stint at Wesleyan University's Center for Advanced Studies in 1969 and an Arts and Letters Award the following year, Fair became a full-time writer. He taught at Wesleyan as a visiting professor in the 1970-71 academic year.

Despite his new freedom from a nine-to-five workday, Fair's productivity as a writer slowed down somewhat. His next book, *World of Nothing,* did not appear until 1970. True to form, Fair changed direction and con-

founded expectations yet again with that book, which consisted of two short novellas, both with elements of pointed, edgy satire. The story that gives this book its title is a picturesque but sharp and partly surreal portrait of a group of black Chicagoans whose lives interact, while "Jerome" dealt with sexual abuse in the Catholic church and, like several of Fair's earlier works, featured a youthful central character.

In 1971 Fair went to Europe. Later in life he would bemoan the lack of opportunities available to African-American writers, but he was drawn to Europe while he was still riding high career-wise. Like many black creative figures before him, Fair felt liberated in Europe from American racial tensions. He and his wife spent several months in Sweden with support from that country's government culture ministry, and then enjoyed six months in 1972 in a French villa on an academic house exchange. Fair, according to *From Harlem to Paris* author Michel Fabre, announced a plan to "buy a house over here and return HOME to France." Later, however, despite having disliked Sweden's cold climate, he moved to Finland and remained there.

The book Fair considered his supreme effort, *We Can't Breathe,* was published in 1972. Another realistic tale, it followed five Chicago friends, one of whom becomes a writer by the book's end. Strongly autobiographical, *We Can't Breathe* won the American Library Association's Best Book award in 1972 but was criticized, to use the words of *New York Times* critic George Davis, as "not as well shaped as his previous books." *We Can't Breathe* sold well at first, but sales eventually tailed off.

Fair continued writing after this setback. He won a Guggenheim fellowship in 1975 and worked on an epic novel called *The Migrants,* which traced a large cast of characters through black America's Great Migration from South to North. He published two collections of poetry and several short stories in the late 1970s. *The Migrants* remained unpublished, however, and Fair grew disillusioned. "I'm still writing—seven books looking for a publisher, perhaps that will happen again….Sorry I can't be more helpful, but I don't care to talk about many of these things, …" he told *Dictionary of Literary Biography* contributor R. Baxter Miller in the early 1980s. "[S]orry they haven't published more of my books, but you know…they cut off the Black writer…they really cut him off."

Fair finally dropped completely off the literary radar screen, even disappearing from directories of creative artists. He announced a new commitment to Christianity in 1980, and he was reported to have taken up sculpture. Fair's unusual life and his unique body of work awaited serious consideration by researchers as the importance of Chicago writers in black cultural history became apparent in the early 2000s.

Selected works

Many Thousand Gone: An American Fable (short novel), Harcourt, 1965.
Hog Butcher (novel), Harcourt, 1966; republished as *Cornbread, Earl and Me,* Bantam, 1975.
World of Nothing: Two Novellas, Harper, 1970.
We Can't Breathe (novel), Harper, 1972.
Excerpts (poetry), Paul Breman, 1975.
Rufus (poetry), P. Schlack (Germany), 1977; 2nd ed. Lotus Press, 1980.

Sources

Books

Bell, Bernard W., *The Afro-American Novel and Its Tradition,* University of Massachusetts Press, 1987.
Davis, Thadious M., ed., *Dictionary of Literary Biography, Volume 33: Afro-American Fiction Writers After 1955,* Gale, 1984.
Fabre, Michel, *From Harlem to Paris: Black American Writers in France, 1840-1980,* University of Illinois Press, 1991.

Periodicals

Christian Science Monitor, February 4, 1965, p. 11.
Los Angeles Times, September 4, 1966, p. 129.
New York Times, January 10, 1965, Book Review, p. 27; February 6, 1972, Book Review, p. 6.
Washington Post, February 6, 1972, p. BW8.

On-line

Mootry, Maria K., "Post-World War II African-American Literature in Illinois," *Northern Illinois University Library,* www.lib.niu.edu/ipo/il960136.html (August 6, 2004).
"Ronald L. Fair," *Contemporary Authors Online,* www.galenet.galegroup.com/servlet/BioRC (August 6, 2004).

—James M. Manheim

Tom Feelings

1933-2003

Illustrator

If any man should be regarded as the personification of the "black is beautiful" philosophy, that man is Tom Feelings. Feelings spent a lifetime as a painter, sculptor, and book illustrator underscoring this message. From the dawn of the U.S. civil rights era, when he came of age as an artist, Feelings was passionately committed to the mission of encouraging black children to understand their own spiritual and physical beauty. Feelings remained faithful to that mission for more than 40 years.

While the "black is beautiful" creed admits that support is needed for life's downside, Feelings believes that having great joy is possible in the lives of African Americans. He acknowledges that the sorrow arising from slavery and racism–as it resonates against the joy of surviving such ordeals–expresses the uniqueness of being black in the United States. He summed up this belief in the foreword to his picture book about slavery, *The Middle Passage*: "As the blues, jazz, and the spirituals teach, one must embrace all of life, both its pain and joy, creatively. Knowing this, I, we, may be disappointed, but never destroyed."

Devoted to developing the theme of black equality in a society that does not always practice what it preaches, Feelings left no doubt about how he wishes his work to be understood. In every book he has illustrated, whether written by him or not, he has been faithful to the statement he made in a 1985 interview with *Horn Book* magazine. "I bring to my work a quality which is rooted in the culture of Africa and expanded by the experience of being black in America."

Drawing the Story of a Neighborhood

Thomas Feelings was born in 1933, in the ultra-urban, Bedford- Stuyvesant section of Brooklyn, New York. He began to draw at age four, copying pictures from newspaper comic strips into a book of blank pages sewn together by his mother. He was just a little older when he heard about Thipadeaux, a black artist who was teaching at the Police Athletic Academy in his neighborhood. Feelings showed some of his drawings to Thipadeaux. The teacher suggested that, rather than copying from other people's work, he try to draw some of the real people in his neighborhood. Feelings began at home with oil paintings of his mother and his aunt and went on to draw the adults and the wary, diffident children he saw around him.

At first, learning to draw was difficult. Thipadeaux pushed Feelings to improve, often making him draw things over and over. Nevertheless, Feelings was anxious to improve and enjoyed being treated like a serious student. When he was about nine years old, his eagerness to learn was heightened even further by the magic world of the adult library. Faced with a school assignment involving black educator Booker T. Washington and George Washington Carver, a famed black inventor and scientist, Feelings was dazzled to discover that the achievements of African Americans had merited respect from Americans outside of his realm of experience. He was too young to understand the artistic importance of this discovery—that he was beginning to see his neighborhood with the eyes of the objective observer.

At a Glance . . .

Born Thomas Feelings on May 19, 1933, in Brooklyn, NY; died on August 25, 2003; son of Samuel (a cab driver) and Anna Nash (Morris) Feelings; married Muriel Grey (a school teacher and author), 1968 (divorced, 1974); children: two sons, Zamani and Kamili. *Education:* Cartoonists and Illustrators' School, New York, NY, 1951-53; School of Visual Art, New York, NY, 1957-60. *Military Service:* U.S. Air Force, illustrator in Graphics Division, London, England, 1953-57.

Career: *New York Age,* creator and writer of Tommy Traveler in the World of Black History comic strip, 1958-59; freelance illustrator and contributor to various magazines, 1961-64; Ghanian government, illustrator for *African Review,* 1964-66; illustration instructor, art consultant, Tema, Ghana, 1964-66; Ministry of Education, teacher and consultant, Guyana, 1971-74; University of South Carolina, artist in residence, 1990-95.

Memberships: Schomburg Center for Research.

Awards: Newbery Honor, for *To Be a Slave,* 1969; Caldecott Honor Book, 1972, for *Moja Means One;* Outstanding Achievement Award, School of Visual Arts, 1974; Coretta Scott King Award, for *Something on My Mind,* 1979; Visual Artists Fellowship Grant, National Endowment of the Arts, 1982; National Book Award nomination for *Jambo Means Hello,* 1982; Distinguished Service to Children Through Art award, University of South Carolina, 1991; Coretta Scott King Award, for *Soul Looks Back in Wonder,* 1994; Coretta Scott King Award, for *The Middle Passage,* 1996.

A Mission Born

Feelings's surroundings broadened after he left high school. First, courtesy of a three-year scholarship, came a period of study at the Cartoonists and Illustrators' School in New York City. Next came a four-year hitch in England for the U.S. Air Force. After his return to the United States in 1957, Feelings pursued further study at the School of Visual Arts. While there, Feelings's personal style received an unexpected boost. During a discussion of art history that ranged through the works of many artists, Feelings asked the professor why none of the artists being

studied were African. He was told that African art was regarded as "primitive" rather than innovative art. Clearly, the teacher felt that a painter's method was far more important than what was being expressed. Feelings refused to accept that as a lesson worth studying, so he walked out of the room.

Feelings returned to the world of the comic strip to bring the achievements of black Americans to the world's attention. His creation, *Tommy Traveler in the World of Negro History,* began to appear in *New York Age,* a Harlem newspaper with a black readership. Reproduced in 1991, *Tommy Traveler* told the story of a black boy who read his way through all the library's books on African American history. Referred by the librarian to a book collector named Dr. Gray, an awed Feelings was able to imagine himself back into the lifetimes of Frederick Douglass, Phoebe Fraunces, and other celebrated African Americans. The strip ran for about one year, but Feelings eventually discontinued it because the story form was too restrictive to display his reactions to the world around him.

By 1961 Feelings finished art school with an extensive portfolio. He tried to obtain freelance assignments but was often told by editors that he was limiting his chances by concentrating solely on black subjects. Encouraged by the magazines *Freedomways* and *The Liberator,* both with wide black readerships, he continued to concentrate on African Americans and their lives. In 1962 his determination was rewarded by an assignment that would appear in *Look* magazine.

While on assignment for *Look,* Feelings traveled to New Orleans, Louisiana. Despite the fact that he had to stay in a segregated hotel, he found the children happier and more relaxed as a result of the sunlight and the abundant food. This difference showed in his pictures of the children, who looked far less vigilant and tense than their New York City counterparts. Feelings did not forget to convey the sad truth that went along with these pleasures–blacks in the South seemed to have no more control over their lives than they did in the North.

African is Beautiful

The awakening spirit of African self-worth in the United States—symbolized by Rosa Parks's 1955 refusal to give up her bus seat—appeared even more strongly in Africa, where many former European colonies overthrew their oppressors. In 1957 Ghana gained independence. The new head of state, Kwame Nkrumah, made known his desire for an international cadre of black educators who could take his people by the hand and point them toward a future of profitable self-determination.

In 1964 Tom Feelings went to the Ghanian city of Tema to join other African Americans recruited by the

Nkrumah government. He worked both for the government's magazine, *African Review*, and as a children's book illustrator. Feelings exulted in being among the majority and in achieving his most important goal—to aid in the production of positive images for black children.

As Feelings told *Horn Book* magazine in 1985, "Africa helped make my drawings more fluid and flowing; rhythmic lines started to appear in my work." Some of this new movement appears in illustrations of robed Ghanian women that he painted for his 1972 autobiography *Black Pilgrimage*. Proud and graceful, they often seem to be on the point of swirling off the page. Another picture in the book shows the same state of mind. Against a forest background of gentle greens and beiges, women in Western dress with baskets on their heads actually seem to sway in unison along a path.

Ghana proved an idyllic setting for the developing artist. The entire experience was a spiritual odyssey for Feelings. He knew that Africa was the homeland of his people as well as the cradle of civilization before the European slave-traders had docked there. His closeness to such history strengthened the bond he had always felt. It brought home to him the most enduring lesson about himself that he was ever to share. Feelings explained in *Black Pilgrimage*: "I am an African, and I know now that black people, no matter in what part of the world they may live, are one African people."

New Worlds to Conquer

In 1966 Nkrumah was ousted by a coup d'etat. Feelings returned to the United States to find that the publishing industry had changed significantly. The blossoming civil rights movement had produced an insatiable hunger for African American history, literature, and especially children's books suitable for both recreational reading and teaching purposes. Educators' research had revealed a shameful scarcity of material with accurate representations of black dialogue and black people–stereotypes still dominated the written word. As a result, new emphasis was placed on literature of only the highest quality to be produced with black children in mind. New children's bookshops worked to supply the burgeoning market. Their demand in turn brought a wider scope to publishers, who eagerly produced a growing number of books for and about different cultures. It was a fertile environment for a culturally-oriented artist able to offer authentic visions of Africa.

Buttressed by an overflowing portfolio, Feelings started to illustrate children's picture books immediately. First came *Bola and the Oba's Drummers* from McGraw-Hill; then in 1971 he illustrated *Moja Means One: A Swahili Counting Book*. The book proved to be a turning point. The text, written by his wife Muriel, explained the numbers in Swahili, a language spoken by millions of people in East Africa. Feelings's drawings gave African American children an authentic feel for a different culture by introducing them to Kenyan landmarks and cultural features in particular. Many reviewers agreed that the drawings were beautiful and instructive, so much so that they expanded the book's original marketability.

Praise for the book was not universal, however. Sidney Long, writing in *Horn Book* magazine, noted that the drawing technique sometimes seemed too sophisticated for its intended readers—between six to eight years of age. The sophistication, he claimed, made it difficult to find the objects to be counted. A second reviewer criticized the appropriateness of the muted grey and ocher colorings of most of the pictures. Feelings explained that he simply wanted to make his work stand out in quiet comparison to all the bright reds, blues, and greens other picture-book illustrators used.

Applauded for Cultural Achievement

The following year *Moja Means One* was chosen as a Caldecott Honor selection, marking it as a runner-up for the Caldecott Medal. Named in honor of Randolph Caldecott, an English picture book illustrator who died in 1886, the award has been a mark of excellence in children's literature since it was established in 1938. The accolade to *Moja Means One* ensured that Feelings was on his way to professional success.

Feelings was also on his way to Guyana, a former British colony in South America that had once done a brisk business in slaves from Ghana. The Guyanese government in 1971 intended to instill its own educators and people with pride and patriotism while providing them with the modern education accessible to more industrialized nations. Feelings joined in the effort partly to complete the spiritual quest he had begun with his journey to Ghana.

Feelings headed the Guyanese Ministry of Education's newly-created children's book project while also training young government illustrators. Since the country possessed printing presses capable of reproducing only two-color work, he found the work challenging. He did not quit, however. Instead, he "rediscovered the lesson of improvising within a restrictive form," as he noted in *Horn Book* magazine. Feelings did leave Guyana and the government project there in 1974 in order to return to the United States.

By the mid-1970s Feelings had illustrated six books, including a volume of diary extracts collected by Julius Lester, called *To Be a Slave*. Shortly thereafter, he was asked to do ten color illustrations for a new edition of Booker T. Washington's autobiography, *Up from Slavery*. Despite the tragic subject, Feelings found himself continually painting pictures in warm and radiant colors that were quite inappropriate to such a project. Knowing these pictures would convey a falsely positive image of slavery, he cancelled the contract.

Multi-Generational Picturebooks

If the 1970s had been a time of new experiences, the 1980s found Feelings firmly grasping the themes that had been germinating within his work since his youth in Bedford-Stuyvesant. His autobiography, *Black Pilgrimage*, records a conversation with an eight-year-old girl that proved unforgettable for the artist. Feelings tried to explain to her that his drawings were of "pretty little black children, like you." The young girl expressed her refusal to see anything beautiful about the black children, replying, "Ain't nothin' black pretty." Feelings's lifelong dedication to the beauty of African people and their descendants graphically illustrated his inability to accept such a hateful attitude.

In 1981 Feelings's urge to show readers the potential and the intelligence of black children blossomed into *Daydreamers*, a book filled with the drawings of 20 years accompanying a poem by Eloise Greenfield. *Daydreamers* marked the beginning of a conscious effort by Feelings to appeal to adults as well as to the elementary- school-age children for whom the book was intended. This appeal to adult/junior readership came across even more strongly in *Now Sheba Sings the Song*, published in 1987, in which Feelings collaborated with poet laureate of the United States, Maya Angelou.

Warming to the idea of a multi-generational readership, Feelings used short poems about children by several black authors for his 1993 publication, *Soul Looks Back in Wonder*. In addition to another Maya Angelou poem, there was a never-before published poem by Langston Hughes, who had died in 1967. Margaret Walker, whose 1966 novel *Jubilee* had become a classical description of American life under slavery, also contributed text. Though publishers and reviewers considered *Soul Looks Back in Wonder* most appropriate for children in grades three through six, one reviewer noted that several of the poems in the collection probably would appeal more to adults than to children. This divided readership is purely intentional, reflecting Feelings's profound belief that adults must help smooth the way for children. "Young black kids really are having a hard time nowadays," he said in *Sandlapper* magazine. "That's why I made this book [*Soul Looks Back in Wonder*]."

The Middle Passage

Feelings's 1995 masterpiece, *The Middle Passage*, is illustrated in his trademark style of understated color tones ranging from cream to storm-cloud charcoal to black. The book depicts the journey on slave ships from Africa through the middle passage to the Caribbean and North America. With realistic details and no text to explicate his drawings, Feelings shows the terror and horror of slavery. The slaves were shackled together between decks, many were killed by sharks while trying to escape, and torture and starvation were used to force submission to the ships' overseers. In *The Middle Passage* Feelings tried to tell the whole truth about slavery. He won a Coretta Scott King Award for the book's illustrations in 1996.

Though the Guyanese Ministry of Education was emphatic about the need for children to know the truth in their history books, Feelings found it impossible to work on *The Middle Passage* while he worked for them. His return to the United States allowed him to fathom the reason. "I had to be in a place that constantly reminded me of what I was working on and why I was working on it," he wrote in the introduction to *The Middle Passage*. "For me that was New York City. That's where the pain was."

Despite the grim visions of inhumanity that are illuminated in *The Middle Passage*, in the book's introduction, Feelings encourages African Americans not to feel depressed by them. "They should be uplifted and say to themselves: 'You mean we survived this? We made it through all this and we are still here today?'" After retiring from the University of South Carolina, where he taught book illustration, Feelings continued to caution black children never to waste their own potential. He died of cancer in 2003 in Mexico.

Selected writings

(Illustrator) *Bola and the Oba's Drummers*, McGraw, 1967.
(Illustrator) *To Be A Slave*, Dial, 1968.
(Illustrator) *Zamani Goes to Market*, Seabury, 1970.
(Illustrator) *Jambo Means Hello*, Dial, 1971.
Black Pilgrimage, Lothrop, 1972.
(Illustrator) *Moja Means One: A Swahili Counting Book*, Dial, 1974.
(Illustrator) *Something on My Mind*, Dial, 1978.
(Illustrator) *Daydreamers*, Dial, 1981.
(Illustrator) *Now Sheba Sings the Song*, Dial, 1987.
Tommy Traveler in the World of Negro History, Black Butterfly Books, 1991.
Soul Looks Back in Wonder, Dial, 1993.
The Middle Passage: White Ships/Black Cargo, Dial, 1995.

Sources

Books

Hearne, Betsy, and Roger Sutton, eds., *Evaluating Children's Books: A Critical Look,* University of Illinois, 1992, pp. 106-15.

Kingman, Lee, et al, *Illustrators of Children's Books, 1967-1976*, Horn Book, 1978.

Rollock, Barbara, *Black Authors & Illustrators of Children's Books,* 2nd ed., Garland Publishing, 1992, p. 70.

Smith, Irene, *The History of the Newbery and Caldecott Medals,* Viking, 1957, pp. 25-28.

Something About the Author, vol. 8, Gale Research, 1976, pp. 56-57.

Periodicals

American Visions, August 2000.

Horn Book, November/December 1985, pp. 685-95.

New York Times, August 30, 2003, p. A15.

Sandlapper, Summer, 1994, pp. 46-47.

School Library Journal, February 1992.

Washington Post, August 29, 2003, p. B6.

—Gillian Wolf and Sara Pendergast

Al Green

1946—

Singer, Songwriter, Minister

Considered by music writers as the last true successor of Sam Cooke and Otis Redding, Al Green has enjoyed a long and rewarding career as a pop and gospel singer. His pop and religious works have earned consistent praise from musicians and critics alike. Unlike the great R&B shouters and early soul singers, Green has a voice that, although capable of rich blues-drenched tone and soaring falsetto cries, delivers plaintive emotion without harsh delivery or guttural technique. His sexy, silken voice landed him a string of million-selling hits in the 1970s. Following his departure from popular music in 1980, he became a member of the ministry and a singer of gospel music. His recent return to pop music, and the appearance of his music in documentaries and film soundtracks, has once again brought him widespread notice. Able to straddle the fence between secular and religious music, he has devoted himself to the universal message of music.

Sang from an Early Age

Albert Green was born on April 13, 1946, in Forrest City, Arkansas. As a teenager Green and his brothers, Walter, William, and Robert, formed a gospel quartet, The Green Brothers. Though he sang in the gospel group, Green had developed an affinity for both religious and popular music. He stated, as quoted in *Black Popular Music* by Arnold Shaw, "Sam Cooke, Jackie Wilson—I didn't make distinctions between spiritual and secular music to any great extent back then. If they sang with feeling, from their hearts, I loved the music."

At age 12 Green moved with his family to Grand Rapids, Michigan, a city about 180 miles west of Detroit. Four years later, he and several school friends formed a pop group, the Creations. In 1967 the group, renamed Al Green and the Soulmates, recorded the pop hit "Back Up Train" for the Hotline label; the song rose to number five on the R&B charts and number 41 on the Billboard charts. Despite the song's success the group did not score a follow-up hit and disbanded soon after.

In 1968 Green performed at a club in Midland, Texas, backed by Memphis bandleader and trumpeter Willie Mitchell (who had scored a hit with a remake of King Curtis's instrumental "Soul Serenade"). Impressed with Green's talent, Mitchell, a part-time talent scout and producer for Hi Records in Memphis, invited the young singer to record on the label with the promise that he could make Green a star in little over a year. About six months later, Green arrived in Memphis. As Arnold Shaw explained in *Black Popular Music*, "Together, Green and Mitchell sought to forge a style that combined the pop-soul of Detroit's Motown with the down home soul of Memphis' Stax [label], aiming for a black-white synthesis that blended black soul with white pop." In the studio Mitchell assembled a stellar line-up of back-up musicians to perform behind Green—musicians that included the family team of guitarist Teenie Hodges, organist Charles Hodges, and bassist Leroy Hodges, as well as veteran members of Booker T. and The MG's and Stax studio drummer Al Jackson Jr. (who had also played with Otis Redding). The music formula put forth by Mitchell and Green proved an outstanding combination. As music writer Peter Guralnick wrote in *Sweet Soul Music*, "Willie Mitchell and Al Green came up with an old idea phrased in a new way, the last eccentric refinement of Sam Cooke's lyrical gospel-edged style as filtered through the fractured vocal approach of Otis Redding and the peculiarly fragmented vision of Al Green himself."

In 1968 the Green-Mitchell collaboration released a cover of the Beatles' "I Want Hold Your Hand" and a commercially unsuccessful rendition of the Hayes-Porter ballad "One Woman." Not until he recorded a remake of the Temptations' hit "I Can't Get Next to You" did Green establish himself as pop singing star. For Green's next single "Tired of Being Alone," Mitchell sought a more subtle sound in Green's voice. "We started working, trying to get him to sing softer," explained Mitchell, as quoted in the *Chicago Tribune*, "We started coming up with jazz chords—retty music on top and heavy on the bottom. And it just clicked." Accompanied by Teenie Hodges' relaxed and tasteful guitar work, "Tired of Being Alone" emerged as Green's first smash hit. These singles appeared on Green's 1971 LP *Al Green Gets Next to You*, which also included Green's gritty number "I'm a Ram" and a cover of blues pianist Roosevelt Sykes' "Driving Wheel" (Green's rendition was inspired by a later remake of the song by blues singer Little Junior Parker). Green's original "You Say It" owes a debt to Green's early Memphis singing mentors Sam and Dave.

Hit Number One

Green's title cut of the 1972 LP *Let's Stay Together* brought him his first number one hit. "This third record," observed Robert Gordon, in the liner notes to the album, "solidified Green's direction. After modeling himself on Sam Cooke and Otis Redding, he established his own style. Writing and co-writing seven of the album's nine tunes, his tendency toward funk is subsumed by his gentle side." In *Sweet Soul Music* Peter Guralnick also noted the impact of the Green-Mitchell collaboration on the black music scene: "Willie Mitchell and Al Green would soon take soul music—real, unabashed, wholehearted soul music—to quiet, luxuriantly appointed places it had never been before."

The year 1972 also saw the release of Green's biggest selling album, *I'm Still in Love with You*, which, with the exception of a token cover of Roy Orbison's "Pretty Woman," is a fine showcase of Green's talent. Green draws upon material from the Doors' "Light My Fire" to Kris Kristofferson's "For the Good Times." On the popular and driving number "Love and Happiness," Green conjures up the dual role of preacher and soul singer to bring forth a pop music classic.

In 1974 Green released the LP *Al Green Explores Your Mind* on the Hi label. That same year, the momentum of his career suffered a severe setback. While he was climbing out of the bathtub at his home, Green's girlfriend poured a pot of boiling grits on him, causing second-degree burns to his back and arms. The young woman then committed suicide. After recovering from the physical and emotional affects of the much-publicized incident with his former girlfriend, Green recorded the 1976 LP *Full Of Fire* for the Hi label. Once again joined by the stellar line-up of Wayne Jackson and the Hodges brothers, Green and producer Willie Mitchell, wrote Bill Adler in a *Down Beat* review, "manage to shuffle around the familiar elements of their formula for success." Though the LP shows signs of disco influence, Green and the Hi studio band maintain a tasteful balance. In 1977 Green, expressing increasing interest in recording gospel music, parted company with Mitchell and without the line-up of the Hi rhythm section recorded the critically acclaimed LP *The Belle Album*. Though it did bring commercial success, the *Belle Album* was noted for Green's playing of acoustic and electric guitar and inventive sound techniques. In 1978 Green cut *Truth N' Time*, an LP that included the gospel songs "Blow Me Down" and "King of All" and a religious treatment of Burt Bacharach's "Say a Little Prayer for Me."

Left Secular Music

In the late 1970s Green purchased his own church, The Full Gospel Tabernacle in Memphis, and became the institution's pastor. In 1980 Green left secular popular music to devote himself to religion. Though he had included at least one religious number on his previous LPs, Green's conversion surprised his former producer Mitchell who stated, as quoted in the *Chicago Tribune*, "I had no idea he was going to become a preacher, but he was always religious." In *Black Gos-*

pel, Green expressed the work involved in his dual role as singer and pastor: "I have to divide my time between my singing and my church in Memphis and well, I do my best to rightly divide it. And I have to devote a sufficient amount of time to do a good job, which is kinda difficult sometimes. I preach every other Sunday in church, and we have so many members."

A new religious direction led Green to a modern gospel recording career. Green's voice is in fine form on the albums *Higher Plane* (1981) and *Precious Lord* (1982). Though recorded for the Hi label, *Precious Lord* is a polished effort which lacked Mitchell's rich production sound. Taking note of Green's gospel career, Tony Heilbut commented in *The Gospel Sound* that Green's voice exhibited "a limber falsetto, a breathless crooner, a growling preacher—in three-way encounter." In 1982 Green also starred in the stage production *Your Arms Too Short to Box with God* with Patti LaBelle. He signed with A&M Records in 1985 and recorded three albums for the label, including the 1987 release *Soul Survivor*. In live performance Green continued to awe audiences. In the *New York Times* Jon Pareles captured Green's on-stage energy in a review of the singers' performance at New York's Radio City in August of 1987: "He would bring a song down to a whisper; he'd break into his clear, agile falsetto, or show off by walking away from the microphone as he sang, projecting his unassisted voice well past the first 20 rows.... Green shifted continually between control and abandon; he skipped and strutted, made faces, stood with seemingly limp arms and then broke into preacherly gesticulations. By the final song he was jumping into the air at musical peaks." The year 1987 also saw the release of his documentary, *The Gospel According to Green*. The 94-minute documentary, co-written and co-produced by Green and Mitchell, featured concert footage and interviews with the two artists. Most noteworthy is Mitchell's recollections of his experience in the studio with this soul singing icon.

In 1988 Green appeared at the Nelson Mandela Birthday Concert in London; two years later he performed at the John Lennon Memorial Concert at Peir Head, Liverpool. Green's 1989 A&M album *I Get Joy* contained the lead track "You're Everything to Me"—a number, as Bill Dahl described in the *Chicago Tribune*, that "could just as easily be construed as an ode to a lover as to the Lord." Green's 1991 release, *One In a Million*, for the Word/Epic label was followed by the LP *Love is Reality*, a religious-based blend of up-tempo numbers immersed in synth-pop and funk rhythms. *Love is Reality* contained a set of numbers that, as Bill Dahl wrote in the *Chicago Tribune*, "are nearly indistinguishable from the standard urban contemporary fare, with slick arrangements and occasionally ambiguous lyrics."

By 1993 Green began to once again record secular material, and in the following year appeared in the music film *Rhythm, Country, and Blues*, a tribute to the musical cultures of Memphis and Nashville. The film's soundtrack, produced by Don Was, featured a number of musical performances by R&B and country stars, including a duet by Green and Lyle Lovett of "(Ain't it Funny) How Time Slips Away." For his 1995 release for MCA Records, *Your Heart's in Good Hands*, Green was backed by the legendary Memphis Horns.

By the late 1990s, Green had overcome diminishing record sales and was enjoying a surge of fan interest. His song "Take to Me the River" had become, as a result of a 1980s cover by the Talking Heads, his most famous composition; his 1970s hit "Let's Stay Together" attracted renewed interest when it was featured in the film soundtrack to the 1994 film *Pulp Fiction*. His career received another boost in 1999 when he made a quest appearance on the popular television series *Ally McBeal,* singing his 1972 song "How Can You Mend a Broken Heart." In 2003, Green worked with his old companion, Willie Mitchell, at his old studio, Hi Records, on the release of *I Can't Stop*. On this well-reviewed album, Green successfully returned to the sound that made him famous in the 1970s on such tracks as "I Can't Stop" and "Not Tonight." At the same time, he was receiving recognition for the broad range of his work, being inducted into both the Gospel Hall of Fame and the Songwriters Hall of Fame in 2004.

Through stardom, religious sojourns, and self-resurrection as a pop music performer, Green has remained a dynamic artist whose ability easily crosses the borders of secular and religious music. Unlike his mentor Sam Cooke who left the church in the late 1950s to embark on a career in pop music, Green left a successful pop recording career to devote himself to God and church. To many, his periodic crossing over between pop and gospel reveals a sign of inward restlessness. In discussing Green's career, Arnold Shaw in *Black Popular Music* related that "there is little indication that his immense success as a popular entertainer has brought the serenity he seeks in his colloquies with God." Dividing his time between church and concert stage, Green, whether singing the praises of God or celebrating the temporal joys of life, remains one of the last of the great soul singers.

Selected works

Albums

Green Is Blues, Hi Records, 1970.
Al Green Gets Next to You, Hi Records, 1971.
Let's Stay Together, Hi Records, 1972.
I'm Still in Love with You, Hi Records, 1972.
Al Green Explores Your Mind, Hi Records, 1974.
Greatest Hits, Hi Records, 1975.
Full of Fire, Hi Records, 1976.
The Belle Album, Hi Records, 1977.

Greatest Hits, Volume 2, Motown, 1977.
Truth N' Time, Hi Records, 1978.
Higher Plane, A&M, 1981.
Precious Lord, 1982.
Soul Survivor, A&M, 1987.
I Get Joy, A&M, 1989.
Trust in God, A&M, 1986.
One in a Million, Word/Epic, 1991.
Love Is Reality, Word/Epic, 1992.
Your Heart's in Good Hands, MCA Records, 1995.
Feel's Like Christmas, Capitol, 2001.
I Can't Stop, Blue Note, 2003.
The Immortal Soul of Al Green, Hi/The Right Stuff, 2004.

Other

(With Davin Seay) *Take Me to the River* (biography), HarperEntertainment, 2000.

Sources

Books

Black Gospel: An Illustrated History of the Gospel Sound, Blanford Press, 1985.

Guralnick, Peter, *Sweet Soul Music: Rhythm & Blues and the Southern Dream of Freedom,* Harper & Row, 1986.
Heilbut, Tony, *The Gospel Sound: Good New and Bad Times,* Limelight edition, 1985.
Shaw, Arnold, *Black Popular Music in America,* Schirmer, 1986.

Periodicals

Chicago Tribune, June 6, 1993.
Down Beat, July 15, 1976.
Ebony, December 2003, p. 32.
Entertainment Weekly, December 5, 2003, p. 44.
Jet, March 1, 2004, p. 14.
New York Times, August 17, 1987; September 9, 1987.

Other

Gordon, Robert, *Lets Stay Together* (liner notes), Hi Records, 1972.

—John Cohassey and Tom Pendergast

Samuel C. Hamilton

19(??)—

International Grand Polemarch, Kappa Alpha Psi, business executive

Samuel C. Hamilton, who became the highest office holder in the historically black fraternity Kappa Alpha Psi in 2003, has also been recognized as a prominent business and community leader. Through his professional and civic affiliations, he helped to implement such programs as small business funding and development, affordable housing, and public health campaigns. As head of one of the "Divine Nine" African-American fraternities and sororities in the United States, which have been recognized for their major role in fostering high standards of black achievement, he has committed himself to increasing the organization's role in community outreach and in promoting individual achievement.

Fraternity Helped Nurture Career Aspirations

Born in Knoxville, Tennessee, Hamilton earned a bachelor of arts degree from Clark/Atlanta University in Atlanta, Georgia. There he became active in the Kappa Alpha Psi fraternity. This fraternity, originally known as Kappa Alpha Nu, was formed in 1911 at Indiana University, where only ten African-American students were enrolled at that time. Realizing that these students were tremendously isolated and were not receiving necessary support from the school administration, Elder Watson Diggs and Byron Kenneth Armstrong led them in organizing a permanent African-American fraternity. From the start, the fraternity provided a necessary means of establishing social bonds among the university's black students. Kappa Alpha Psi also stressed achievement and service.

By the 1920s Kappa Alpha Psi had opened chapters across the United States. It created its first national community service program, which mentored high school students, in 1922. Business leadership has also been a prominent focus for the organization. Its Kappa Instructional Leadership League, developed in the 1960s by the Los Angeles chapter, aims to help young men develop leadership skills across a wide range of professions. In 1981 the fraternity created the Kappa Alpha Psi Foundation for the purpose of fund raising. The fraternity numbers several prominent alumni, including Dr. David Satcher, the sixteenth surgeon-general of the United States, and Carl Stokes, the first black mayor of Cleveland, Ohio.

Interested in a business career, Hamilton found Kappa Alpha Psi a source of friendship and support that proved instrumental in his successful transition from college to the business world. After graduating from Clark/Atlanta University, he began his career in the Hartford, Connecticut, area, working as a partner in a real estate investment office. He later worked as regional director with the Aetna Life and Casualty Company.

Promoted Community-Based Opportunities

In his current position as executive director and chief executive officer of the Hartford Economic Development Corporation (HEDCO) and the Greater Hartford Business Development Center, Inc., Hamilton has be-

At a Glance . . .

Born in Knoxville, TN; married; children: one son. *Education*: Clark/Atlanta University, BA; University of Connecticut, graduate studies; University of Massachusetts, graduate studies; Indiana University, graduate studies.

Career: Real estate investment firm, partner; Aetna Life and Casualty Company, regional director; Hartford Economic Development Corporation, executive director and chief executive officer.

Memberships: United Way of the Capital Area, Hartford, CT, chair, 1998-2001; Kappa Alpha Psi, International Grand Polemarch, 2003–.

Awards: Whitney M. Young, Jr. Service Award, and Boyce Barlow Lifetime Achievement Award, Kappa Alpha Psi; Community Service Award, United Way of the Capital Area, Hartford, CT, 2001.

Addresses: *Office*—15 Lewis St., Suite 204, Hartford, CT 06103.

come widely recognized for community-based business initiatives. HEDCO works to promote economic development in Hartford and 57 neighboring cities and towns by collaborating with public and private organizations to create incentives to aid small businesses in the area. According to its Web site, HEDCO and its partner organizations seek to "foster the community relationships crucial to sustained and broad-based economic growth" by providing start-up assistance, funding, and other services to businesses that might otherwise be forced to close or relocate.

Hamilton has also made significant contributions through his activities in volunteer organizations. He helped form the Hartford Neighborhood Development Support Collaborative, which obtained funding from 20 diverse sources to support affordable housing and neighborhood economic renewal. He has served as a board member of Child and Family Services and TLC, a group shelter for teens, and served on the Institute for Internationals Sport's Task Force for the Development of the Institute for the Black Athlete. Hamilton, whose son is an assistant basketball coach at SUNY-Binghamton, is also a member of the expert panel of the Center for Sports Parenting and is an Elder of the First Presbyterian Church.

His work with the United Way, in which he has been active since 1986, has earned Hamilton particular

recognition. He has served on the organization's executive committee, strategic planning committee, and Hartford neighborhood support collaborative, and he chaired the allocations committee from 1993 to 1995. Hamilton also chaired the *Are You the Missing Piece?* campaign, jointly sponsored by the United Way and the American Red Cross, which aimed to increase awareness of the need for Hispanic and African-American bone marrow donors. Hamilton served as chairman of the board of directors of the United Way of the Capital Area [Hartford] from 1998 to 2001. In 2001, the United Way of the Capital Area presented Hamilton with its annual Community Service Award, which, according to the organization's Web site, recognized his "dedication to the spirit of philanthropy and community service."

Assumed Leadership of Kappa Alpha Psi

Active in Kappa Alpha Psi since his student days, Hamilton held several offices in the organization, including Grand Keeper of Records and Exchequer. He worked throughout his career to promote partnerships between the fraternity and the United Way to benefit community development. He served as Senior Grand Vice Polemarch, the second-highest office of the fraternity, under Grand Polemarch Howard L. Tutman, Jr. When Tutman retired from his post in 2003, Hamilton became Kappa Alpha Psi's thirtieth Grand Polemarch.

As leader of the fraternity, Hamilton has declared his intention to focus on increased outreach and membership, as well as expanded partnerships with businesses and other organizations. He has announced collaborations between the fraternity and public health organizations, including a program in conjunction with the American Cancer Society to promote awareness and treatment of prostate cancer, a disease that disproportionately affects African-American men. He has launched initiatives to prepare for the observation of Kappa Alpha Psi's centennial in 2011, and has promoted the fraternity's Unity '04 Voter Empowerment Campaign, aimed at increasing voter registration and participation in the 2004 national elections. As Hamilton observed in the Grand Polemarch's Message in the *Kappa Alpha Psi Journal*, "Kappa's participation in Unity '04 will help to ensure that in our local communities every eligible person of color is registered to vote, educated on the issues and provided transportation to the Voting place on Election Day. . . . Every generation must take part in the electoral process because the outcome will affect each and every one of us; if not now, at some point in the future."

In recognition of his service to the fraternity, Kappa Alpha Psi presented Hamilton with the Whitney M. Young, Jr. Service Award. Hamilton also received the fraternity's Boyce Barlow Lifetime Achievement Award. Hamilton, who is married and has one son, lives in Manchester, Connecticut.

Sources

Books

Ross, Lawrence C., Jr., *The Divine Nine: The History of African American Fraternities and Sororities*, Kensington Books, 2000, pp. 45-72.

Periodicals

Kappa Alpha Psi Journal, April, 2004, p. 89.

On-line

Center for Sports Parenting, www.sportsparenting. org (September 13, 2004).
Hartford Economic Development Corporation, www.hedco-ghbdc.com (September 13, 2004).
"2001 Community Service Awards," *United Way of the Capital Area*, www.uwcact.org (September 13, 2004).

—E. Shostak

Carla D. Hayden

1952—

Library director

Hayden, Carla, photograph. Courtesy of Dr. Carla Hayden.

Carla D. Hayden served as president of the American Library Association for a one-year term beginning in 2003. A veteran of the Chicago and Baltimore public library systems, Hayden won praise for taking a tough stance against the Patriot Act of 2001, a federal law which forced public libraries to comply with Federal Bureau of Investigation requests about patrons' records.

Born on August 10, 1952, in Tallahassee, Florida, Hayden grew up in Chicago and earned her undergraduate degree from Roosevelt University in the city. She went on to earn two advanced degrees, including a Ph.D., from the University of Chicago's Graduate Library School. She began her career with the Chicago Public Library in 1973 as a library associate and children's librarian. Six years later, she became young adult services coordinator with the Chicago system, one of the largest in the United States.

Between 1982 and 1987, Hayden served as library services coordinator for the Museum of Science and Industry, one of Chicago's leading cultural institutions. She moved on to the University of Pittsburgh, where she became an associate professor at its School of Library and Information Science, but returned to her native city in 1991 when she was offered a second-in-command post at the Chicago Public Library as deputy commissioner and chief librarian. Two years later, she accepted an offer to become executive director of the Enoch Pratt Free Library in Baltimore, Maryland. The Pratt had been a pioneering free library, open to all, and had served the city admirably for nearly a century. Named after the wealthy merchant who established it, the Pratt was anchored by a central branch with four other locations, and its charter stipulated that it should be run by a self-perpetuating board of trustees and remain free of the political fray or city budget constraints. It had its own endowment, and its services served as a model for scores of other urban American library systems over the next several decades.

By the time Hayden arrived, however, the Pratt had fallen on hard times, beset by budget woes and aging buildings. Hayden helped revitalize the system, working with both the board and the city. She updated its technology and had an annex for the central library built thanks to a private fundraising campaign. She also improved its outreach services to the neighborhoods it served, especially with an after-school center open to teens that offered homework assistance as well as college and career counseling. For her work Hayden was honored with the Librarian of the Year Award from *Library Journal* magazine in 1995, becoming the first African American to win the professional accolade.

Hayden's high profile, thanks to her work at Pratt, made her a natural for the candidacy of the American Library Association (ALA) presidency. In 2002, she stood for election for the 2003-2004 year, which would include a 2002 stint as vice president. She was the third African-American librarian to win election to the oldest and largest professional organization of librarians in the world. Headquartered in Chicago, the ALA has 64,000 members from 16,000 public libraries in the United States. Its president sets an agenda for the year that helps public librarians in America focus on the needs of the communities they serve.

Upon winning the election, Hayden announced that "equity of access" was one of her primary goals for the year. As she explained in the ALA journal *American*

Libraries, "equity of access can be defined as people having the right to unlimited library services and materials—no matter their age, ethnicity, physical ability, income, language, geographic location, or the type of library they are using," and urged her colleagues to "rededicate ourselves to maintaining that seamless web that helps our customers reach their dreams. Libraries and librarians are truly lifelines for so many."

Hayden rose to her greatest challenge when she openly challenged the Patriot Act, which had been passed by Congress just weeks after the 9/11 attacks in 2001. Some of its more controversial measures, designed to improve domestic security in the United States and safeguard against further attack, were viewed as violations of protections guaranteed to American citizens under the Constitution. These dealt with the powers of the Federal Bureau of Investigation (FBI) and its interest in monitoring citizens without their knowledge. One section of the Patriot Act allowed the FBI to access library records to look for the names of borrowers who checked out books the Bureau thought could be linked to terrorism. Another section of that law specified that if a librarian informs a patron about the FBI surveillance, they faced punishment that could include jail. "With this act, the government doesn't have to show cause that a crime has been committed to spy on people," *Essence* writer Barbara Reynolds quoted Hayden as saying. "In fighting the war on terrorism, we must ensure that our civil liberties are not the greatest casualty."

Hayden was so vocal in her fight against this part of the Patriot Act that U.S. Attorney General John Ashcroft personally telephoned her and promised to declassify reports related to FBI surveillance. Undaunted, Hayden was instrumental in leading the ALA to team with the American Booksellers Association for a signature drive and petition to Congress to revise this section of the Patriot Act. For this effort, *Ms.* Magazine named her one of its ten Women of the Year for 2003. She remains director of the Pratt Library system.

Sources

Books

Notable Black American Women, Book 3, Gale, 2002.

Periodicals

American Libraries, June-July 2002, p. 10; August 2003, p. 5; January 2004, p. 8; June-July 2004, p. 46.
Essence, July 2004, p. 34.
Jet, March 4, 1996, p. 22.
Library Journal, March 15, 2002, p. 44.
Time for Kids, September 12, 2003, p. 7.

—Carol Brennan

Francis Hendy

195(?)—

Fashion Designer

Since learning the art of sewing at his mother's knee in Trinidad, Francis Hendy has been quietly building a fashion legacy. Known for his innovative mix of materials and skins, Hendy has dressed everyone from fellow Trinidadians to Carnival goers, rap stars to New York fashionistas. All have been seduced by designs described on the Francis Hendy Web site as "… daring and fashion forward, always exploring new horizons in color, fabric and design." At the close of 2004, with a new collection being introduced, four distinct fashion lines, and plans for wholesaling and franchising his brand, Hendy was set to clothe Americans nationwide in his funky, colorful fashions.

Hendy, Francis, photograph. Jeff Vespa/WireImage.com

Born to Sew

Francis Hendy was born in Port of Spain, Trinidad, to a family of five siblings. His father Franklin was a contractor and builder and his mother Elizabeth was a seamstress, deeply involved in the Trinidad fashion scene. "I started out spending time in her sewing room, threading needles, sewing buttons, and hemming," Hendy told *Fashion Mannuscript*. His love of fashion

had started way before his fingers were nimble enough to thread a needle, however. "My mother also tells the story that when I was a small boy, I would always select my own clothes," Hendy told *Fashion Mannuscript*. "She would always have to make sure they were neat and ironed, or I would not wear them. On occasion I was known to pick her clothes as well."

Hendy displayed a nearly equal love of soccer. "He was an avid soccer player," Hendy's sister Charmain Hendy told *Contemporary Black Biography* (*CBB*). In fact it was his love of soccer that drove him to design his first clothes. He couldn't find pants to fit his legs, muscle-carved by years on the soccer field. Hendy was set on pursuing a professional soccer career, but after an injury sidelined that dream, he began to devote more time to designing and sewing clothes. "Eventually he set up his own fashion business in Trinidad working out of our house," Charmain told *CBB*.

In 1972, at about the age of 21, Hendy decided to join an older sister in New York City and seriously pursue a design career. In New York he approached Trinidadian contacts and began designing custom clothes for them.

At a Glance . . .

Born in the early 1950s in Port of Spain, Trinidad; married Gale Hendy; children: Ansis Hendy. *Education:* Attended Fashion Institute of Technology, New York, and Parson's School of Design, New York. *Religion:* Christian.

Career: Francis Hendy, Inc., New York, NY, fashion designer, 1986–.

Awards: National Children's Leukemia Foundation, Michael Award for Menswear Designer of the Year, 2000; City of New York, City Hall Proclamation, 2003; *Caribbean Voice,* Caricom Day Award, 2003.

Addresses: *Office*—Francis Hendy, Inc., 244 West 39th Street, 11th Floor, New York, NY, 10018. *Web site*—www.francishendy.com.

He also began creating elaborate costumes for Brooklyn's annual Caribbean Day Parade. He sharpened his talents with an apprenticeship with a master tailor, and also took courses at the Parson's School of Design and the famed Fashion Institute of Technology. "Although much of what I do is self-taught and heredity, attending classes at FIT and Parsons was valuable to honing my natural skills and inherent capabilities," Hendy told *Fashion Mannuscript.* In 1986 Hendy set up a small storefront shop in the Flatbush district of Brooklyn. Francis Hendy Inc. provided ready-to-wear and custom pieces to a loyal clientele.

Robed Rap Stars

By 1996, Hendy was bringing in $80,000 per year at his tiny shop and he felt he had reached his limit. In 1998 he decided to move into Manhattan's famed garment district and he opened a showroom on West 39th Street. "I wanted to be around the big boys and to get international exposure," Hendy told *Crain's New York Business.* Instead he got MTV exposure, which proved a lot more valuable. Hendy became the designer of choice for rap and R&B artists including Missy "Misdemeanor" Elliot, LL Cool J, Macy Gray, and R. Kelly. His designs—etched leather, patchworked fur, studded vests, second-skin-like lycra—appealed to the musicians who wore the custom-made pieces in videos and on tour. "Rapper and actor DMX also wore our leather jackets in the recent hit action movie *Exit Wounds,*" Hendy told *Fashion Mannuscript.* By 1999 Francis Hendy Inc, had annual sales of $400,000, fueled in large part by his musician clientele.

Hendy entered the high-profile ready-to-wear market in the Spring of 1998 with the debut of his first men's sportswear collection during New York's famed Fashion Week. By 2000 he was getting quite a bit of notice, though his clothes still had rock star leanings. "Francis Hendy is the designer who wants to please everyone—if you're a music celebrity that is," wrote the *Daily News Record* of his 2000 collection. The review concluded on a positive calling his designs, "refreshingly inspired." Fashion insiders agreed and Hendy was awarded the prestigious 2000 Michael Award for Menswear Designer of the Year. Previous winners included fashion heavy-hitters Marc Jacobs for Louis Vuitton, Hugo Boss, and Joseph Abboud. Hendy called receiving the award the proudest moment of his career. "It was a huge surprise. I had not been thinking about any thing like that," he told *Fashion Mannuscript.* "Any designer would like to be honored and appreciated in such a way by their industry peers, but I did not think it would come so soon."

Over the next several years Francis Hendy, Inc. grew. A half-dozen full-time sewers joined the staff as well as all four of Hendy's siblings. Charmain Hendy told *CBB,* "I'm the CEO. Doreen Hendy-Kopingon, manages the company and handles the financial side of things. Noelin Hendy works in marketing, and Ange Hendy does production." As the company expanded, Hendy's designs became more sophisticated, less rock-and-roll. His Fall 2001 collection was inspired by his father, who died that year. "It celebrates his life and times in fashion," Hendy told *Fashion Mannuscript.* He went on to describe the collection as "a retro look, with modern style and sensibilities." That year his sales topped half a million. He was also short-listed for the Rising Star award from the Fashion Group International. Meanwhile, Hendy sharpened his design focus. "His work philosophy is melding color and cut, using unconventional materials to create classic, but not trendy, modern, sexy, designer sportswear. His design philosophy is fashion forward, not following trends, but creating them," Charmain told *CBB.*

Expanded Fashion Offerings

In 2002 Hendy added a women's line to his offerings. "I'm looking forward to dressing women in lots of color," Hendy told *Women's Wear Daily.* "My clothes are about fun and happiness, clothes that are easy to wear and that offer a lot of pieces that interchange." Meanwhile his men's collection for 2002 was received well by the press. A reviewer for the fashion website *Lucire* wrote of the collection, "This was as good as it gets: classic menswear for the widest possible range of customer." The article went on to praise Hendy's use of "leather pieces in diverse colors and animal skins." Hendy had used leather extensively since he debuted as rap's designer du jour and he confessed on his own Web site, "I'm happiest when I'm creating designs with leather and suede." He also became known for his use of ultra suede, a synthetic suede-like material. "It is functional, easy to work with, and very comfortable to wear," Hendy told *Fashion Mannuscript*. "It can feel very luxurious on the body, the lighter weights are cool for summer and the heavier weights are great for winter."

In September of 2002 Hendy opened his first retail shop in the trendy Soho district of New York. He stocked the 1700-square-foot space with clothes from his Hendy Bridge line of moderately priced classics in a wide variety of colors and styles. He also included his FH2Tees line, which featured casual pieces in dark blue and black denim. Luxury pieces from his top-end line, Francis Hendy, were also in stock. As fashion lovers flocked to his slick new shop, his 2003 collection received rave reviews for its textural variation and luxurious materials. "For the woman who is modern, sexy and international, Hendy's clothes are opulent in textures, autumnal colors and individual style," the *Amsterdam News* reported. "[For men] Hendy has designed multiple styles of fashionable funky leather jackets and ultra suede shirts complemented by various textures of fall pants and merino-wool shirts. His pants are tailored in luxurious tweed, colorful pinstriped wool and matte leather."

A deeply spiritual man and a born-again Christian, Hendy credited much of his success to his faith. "I don't know if there is a secret formula, but everything we do is done with much prayer. We put God first in all that we do," he told *Fashion Mannuscript*. Nonetheless, Hendy still struggled. The shaky post 9/11 economy forced Hendy to shut his Soho shop after only a year. Back in the Garment District show room, Hendy and team found it difficult to keep up with customer demand. "I meet a lot of storeowners, but I have to pick and choose because I'm not set up to do big orders," Hendy told *Black Enterprise*. Sister Charmain told *CBB* that they hoped to change that soon. "We are working to build our wholesale business. We have four different lines and we're working to get them into department stores and specialty stores nationwide. We're also working on our brand recognition so we can get our franchising done." With his skill, family, and faith behind him, it seems that Hendy can't miss. Expect to see his clothes hanging in a closet near you soon.

Sources

Periodicals

Black Enterprise, July, 2000.
Crain's New York Business, December 13, 1999.
Daily News Record, September 18, 2000.
Women's Wear Daily, September 12, 2002.

On-line

Francis Hendy, www.francishendy.com/francis.html (August 13, 2004).
"It's A Family Affair: Francis Hendy Interview," *Fashion Mannuscript,* www.fashionartsxchange.com/Articles/FM-06-2001.pdf (August 13, 2004).
"Jason Bunin, R. Scott French, Francis Hendy, Cloal," *Lucire,* www.lucire.com/2002/fall2002/0608fe2.shtml (August 13, 2004).
White, Renee Minus, "Fall/Winter 2003: New York Designers Hit the Runway," *Amsterdam News,* www.amsterdamnews.org/News/article/article.asp?NewsID=22556&sID=24 (August 13, 2004).

Other

Additional information for this profile was obtained through an interview with Charmain Hendy on August 16, 2004.

—Candace LaBalle

Kelly Holmes

1970—

Track athlete, middle distance runner

Holmes, Kelly, photograph. © Reuters/Corbis

Despite problems with injury Kelly Holmes was one of Great Britain's most promising track athletes of the 1990s and the first few years of the twenty-first century. Although she won medals in previous Olympic, Commonwealth, and World Championship competitions, her greatest career success came in the 2004 Athens Olympics when she took gold medals in the women's 800 meters and 1500 meters. Holmes set personal best times in both finals, running against strong opposition. In the 1500m final seven of the athletes set personal best times, while Holmes's winning time of 3 minutes 57.90 seconds in the 1500m final broke her own United Kingdom record, set in June 1997. By winning two gold medals at the Olympic games in Athens in 2004, Holmes became the first British athlete to achieve the Olympic double since Albert Hill in Antwerp in 1920 and became arguably the most successful British track athlete of all time.

Schoolgirl Champion

Kelly Holmes was born on April 19, 1970, in Pembury, Kent, a small town in southeast England. She was raised by her mother, Pam Norman (now Thomson) after her father, Jamaican-born Derrick Holmes, walked out; Holmes was two years old when her mother married Michael Norris. She has two half brothers from this marriage and a half-sister from her mother's second marriage, to Gary Thomson. Holmes had a happy childhood, attending the Hugh Christie School in Tonbridge, Kent, where she was encouraged to take up running. Holmes returns to the school each year to set the students "Kelly's Challenge."

Holmes showed exceptional ability as a young athlete, winning the English Schools' 1500m title at junior and senior levels. With encouragement from her family, she began training with coach Dave Arnold at the age of twelve. By age fourteen, she declared that she wanted to be an Olympic athlete. But in 1988, because of a lack of funding for British sports, Holmes opted for a career outside of athletics and joined the British Army. At first she was a truck driver, but eventually became a PT (Physical Training) instructor, where she reached the rank of sergeant. Holmes had a reputation in the army for being tough and single-minded in everything she did, earning the respect of other recruits and the officers above her. Major Peter Lyons of the Army

Athletic Association told the *Guardian* newspaper: "Nobody got away with anything under her. She was firm and fair...She was very dedicated, very determined."

In 1992 Holmes was beginning to feel frustrated as she watched women she had competed against on the track become successful athletes. It was after watching Lisa York, a former rival, compete in the 3000m at the Barcelona Olympics that she took up serious training again. It soon became clear that she had the talent to compete on a world stage and in her first year she competed in international under-23 competitions. By 1993 she held the United Kingdom and Amateur

Athletic Association of England (AAA) 800m titles and was soon winning medals on a regular basis. She won her first major 800m gold medal in the 1994 Commonwealth Games in Victoria, British Columbia, a title she took again in Manchester in 2002. But despite her success Holmes remained in the army until 1997, sometimes returning from a major athletics competition to go straight on guard duty. In army championships Holmes was allowed to compete in the men's 1500m races because none of the women competitors could match her. She also excelled at volleyball, was the army's female Judo champion, and at one meeting won the 800m, the 3000m, and was a member of a winning relay team.

A Career Blighted by Injury

After success in major competitions there was the promise of more to come. In 1995 Holmes set the British records over 800m and 1000m, and took a bronze in the world championships in Gothenburg. Despite breaking the British 1000m record for a second time and becoming the fastest British woman over 1500m in 1996, Holmes encountered difficulties. A stress fracture meant she could only manage fourth place in the 1500m at the Atlanta Olympics, missing out on a medal by a tenth of a second. When the games were over Holmes spent many weeks with her injured leg in plaster. More bad luck followed. In 1997 Holmes became the UK record holder over 1500m and favorite to win the event at the world championships in Athens. But she suffered a ruptured Achilles tendon in her heat and finished almost 200m behind the rest of the field.

For the next five years Holmes battled with injury and illness. Although she managed to take the silver medal in the 800m in the 1998 Commonwealth Games and the bronze medal for the same distance at the Sydney Olympics in 2000, Holmes admitted that she had reached a low point and was struggling. In 2001, the same year she underwent stomach surgery, she could only manage sixth place in the 800m at the world championships and did not compete in the 1500m. She told Peter Sissons on the BBC's *Breakfast with Frost* talk show in 2002 that for the previous three years she had stuck to the 800m because injury had prevented her from doing the stamina training needed for the longer event. She has since said that she considered giving up competitive running after her success at the Manchester Commonwealth Games in 2002, where she took back the 800m title.

But 2002 proved to be a turning point for the then 32-year-old Holmes. That year she also won her tenth national title for 1500m and a European bronze medal in the 800m. She also switched coaches, making a fresh start with Margo Jennings after almost 18 years with Dave Arnold. Holmes began training in South Africa alongside close friend and world-class 800m runner Maria Mutola. In the build-up to the 2003 season Holmes was optimistic. That year she set personal bests over 600m, 800m (indoors), and 1500m (indoors), as well as taking second place in the 800m at the world championships in Paris and the world indoor silver medal at 1500m.

Fulfilled Olympic Dreams

As a child Holmes admired the outstanding British middle-distance runner of the 1980s, Sebastian Coe, whose win at the 1984 Olympics to retain his 1500m title inspired her as a child athlete. Although she dreamed of matching his success the years of injury and underperforming suggested it would not be possible. Even so Holmes trained hard throughout the winter of 2003 and found herself in the spring of 2004 fully fit and "in the best shape of my life." In the build-up to the Athens Olympics she won four 1500m races in Super Grand Prix meetings in Europe, the 1500m Grand Prix race at Eugene, Oregon, as well as the Golden League 1500m competition in Zurich.

Still uncertain of her ability to perform well in both 800m and 1500m races, Holmes decided to race in the Olympic 800m only two days before the event. As a former Olympic bronze medalist she was among the favorites for a medal placement, but her recent form in the 1500m had been better than at 800m and the line-up for the final was strong, including four of the top ten women over the distance in 2004 and the African record holder, Mutola. Seemingly unphased by the pressure Holmes ran a perfect race, taking the lead on the final bend and bringing the field home to a tight finish in 1-minute 56.38-seconds, a personal best.

With the 1500m competition only six days away Holmes began her preparation with the 800m gold medal dominating her thoughts. She told the *Guardian* newspaper that in the days after the 800m final she had looked at the medal every day and was an "emotional wreck" for the whole week leading up to the 1500m. Holmes again began the race from the back of the field, but matched the fast pace set of the Russian competitors, who included Tatyana Tomashova, the

world champion. She moved towards the front on the final lap and took the lead on the home straight to finish in 3-minutes 57.90-seconds, a British record. By winning Olympic gold medals in 800m and 1500m races Holmes became only the third woman in history to achieve the middle-distance double, the others being Tatyana Kazankina of the Soviet Union in 1976, and Svetlana Masterkova of Russia in 1996. She is the only British athlete to have won two gold medals at a single Olympics since Albert Hill in 1920.

Sources

Periodicals

The Guardian (London and Manchester, UK), August 27, 2004; August 30, 2004.
The Independent (London), August 30, 2004.
The Observer (London), August 29, 2004.
The Scotsman, September 2, 2004.

On-line

"Kelly Holmes Profile," *UK Athletics,* www.ukathletics.net/vsite/vcontent/page/custom/0,8510,4854-132151-133459-21084-77218-custom-item,00.html (September 15, 2004).
"Kelly Holmes, Athlete, and Steve Parry, Swimmer," *BBC Breakfast with Frost* (transcript of television interview by Peter Sissons), http://news.bbc.co.uk/1/hi/programmes/breakfast_with_frost/2142402.stm (September 15, 2004).
"Mother's Joy at 'Amazing' Kelly," *BBC News Online,* http://news.bbc.co.uk/1/hi/england/kent/3608878.stm (September 15, 2004).
"Holmes Keeps on Running," *BBC Sport World Edition,* http://news.bbc.co.uk/sport2/hi/olympics_2004/athletics/3609426.stm (September 15, 2004).
"The Golden Girl on a Publicity Whirl," *BBC News Online,* http://news.bbc.co.uk/1/hi/england/kent/3639640.stm (September 15, 2004).

—Chris Routledge

Cowan F. "Bubba" Hyde

1908-2003

Negro Leagues baseball star

The full and fascinating history of baseball's Negro Leagues remains to be written. While African-American baseball players gained attention from white audiences in the years before and just after the integration of Major League Baseball in 1947, and "Satchel" Paige and other charismatic players became household names, many other highly talented players emerge from history only in outline form. One of those players was outfielder Cowan F. "Bubba" Hyde, who entertained fans by racing horses around the bases and was an unusually consistent performer over his long career.

Hyde was born on April 10, 1908, in Pontotoc, Mississippi. His baseball talents showed up at an early age. When he was only 14, he had a tryout with the Negro Leagues' Memphis Red Sox. The team was apparently willing to sign him up, but either out of homesickness or due to parental pressure he left the Red Sox training camp and returned home. He returned for another short stint with the Red Sox in 1927 but once again departed and pursued his education. At Rust College in Holly Springs, Mississippi, and at Morris Brown College in Atlanta, his athletic skills were on display as he became a member of the baseball, football, and track teams.

Playing for various baseball teams in the early 1930s, including the Birmingham Black Barons (where he finally began his career in earnest in 1930) and the Indianapolis Athletics, Hyde made a strong impression on Cincinnati Tigers manager "Double Duty" Radcliffe while playing for that squad in 1937. A small player at

5-foot, 8-inches tall and 150 pounds, Hyde made up for his lack of size with his speed on the bases. Radcliffe brought Hyde with him to Memphis when he signed on to manage the Red Sox, and he gave Hyde standing permission to steal a base whenever could get a long lead. On the Negro American League-leading 1938 Red Sox, Hyde played left field. He also played other outfield positions and could move to second base as needed.

Hyde remained with the Red Sox until 1950, taking only the 1940 season off. He played for a team in Santa Rosa, Mexico, that year and then returned to the United States and played briefly for an independent Chicago team, the Palmer House All-Stars. He was also said by his daughter to have played for teams in Cuba and the Dominican Republic. In the years before multimillion-dollar salaries it was common for baseball players to supplement their incomes by playing in winter leagues in Latin America, and the incentive to do so for the poorly paid players of the Negro Leagues was doubly strong.

Hyde was a threat at home plate as well as on the bases. He consistently batted close to .300 for the Red Sox, with a Negro Leagues career best of .313 in 1942. Twice, in 1943 and 1946, he played for the West squad in the popular Negro Leagues East-West All-Star Game. Coming to bat three times, he notched two hits. In those same two years he played in exhibition games against white major-league teams and faced the top pitchers of the day. A right-hander, he often batted leadoff.

At a Glance . . .

Born on April 10, 1908, in Pontotoc, MS; died on November 20, 2003, in St. Louis, MO; married, wife's name Edith; one daughter, Almerth. *Education:* Attended Rust College, Holly Springs, MS, and Morris Brown College, Atlanta, GA.

Career: Memphis Red Sox, professional baseball player, 1927; Birmingham Black Barons, professional baseball player, 1930; Indianapolis Athletics and Cincinnati Tigers, professional baseball player, 1937; Memphis Red Sox, professional baseball player, 1938-50; played in Mexican League and for Palmer House All-Stars, 1940; Bridgeport (CT), Colonial League, professional baseball player, 1949; Chicago American Giants, professional baseball player, 1950-51; Canadian leagues, professional baseball player, 1951-54. General Cable Corporation, St. Louis, MO, employee, early 1960s-early 1980s.

Awards: Negro Leagues East-West All-Star Game, 1943, 1946; inducted into Milwaukee's County Stadium Negro Leagues Wall of Fame, 1997.

Whatever his skills as a hitter, it was his speed that really endeared him to fans. His daughter Almerth Owens-Long recalled to the *St. Louis Post-Dispatch* that Hyde was a "speed demon." He beat the horses he took on in his pregame base-running contests, which were an ongoing attraction. "But the horses couldn't round the bases," Owens-Long told the *Post-Dispatch.* "That's why he always outran them." He was also said to have taken on famed Olympic sprinter Jesse Owens in a similar contest, beating him for the same reason: Owens wasn't used to the sharp turns on the base paths. "With exceptional speed on the bases, this Memphis Red Sox outfielder could run as fast looking back as anyone in baseball," opined author James A. Riley.

After Jackie Robinson's epochal breaking of Major League Baseball's color barrier in 1947, Hyde was one of a number of players who tried to land spots in the majors themselves. He played for a Bridgeport, Connecticut, team in the Colonial League in the major-league farm system, hitting an impressive .327 even though he was over 40 years old. The following year he won a place at the training camp of the major-league Boston Braves. With major-league slugger Jimmy Foxx serving as Bridgeport's manager, Hyde seemed a strong candidate for elevation to the majors. Once again, however, he chose family over baseball. In a prime example of the hardships and discrimination early black major-leaguers faced, he was cut from the squad after leaving camp to accompany his wife Edith to the hospital for the birth of the couple's only child, Almerth.

Hyde left American baseball altogether after playing briefly for the Chicago American Giants, but he didn't close the book on his career. He went to Canada and played for various professional teams there, performing well even into the second half of his fifth decade. He played for the Elmwood Giants, Winnipeg Giants, and Brandon Greys teams in Canada's Mandak League, notching a batting average of .348 for Elmwood in 1951. That year, he also played for the Farnham team in the Canadian Provincial League. In 1954 he finally left the game, having first taken the field with a professional team 30 years earlier.

Settling in St. Louis, Missouri, Hyde worked for 20 years for the General Cable company, retiring in the early 1980s. He continued to play baseball at Negro League reunion games into his eighties, and he stayed active for 20 years as a Meals on Wheels volunteer until he turned 90. In later years he lived with his daughter Almerth, and his family finally talked him into taking a break from Meals on Wheels. In 1997, Hyde became one of the first group of players inducted into the Negro Leagues Wall of Fame at Milwaukee's County Stadium, and his uniform was displayed at the Negro Leagues Baseball Museum in Kansas City. Hyde died at age 95 on November 20, 2003, in St. Louis after a short illness.

Sources

Books

Riley, James A., *The Biographical Encyclopedia of the Negro Baseball Leagues,* Carroll & Graf, 1994.

Periodicals

Milwaukee Journal-Sentinel, November 25, 2003, p. B5.
St. Louis Post-Dispatch, November 24, 2003, p. B4.

On-line

"The Conscience of the Trade," *Mudville: The Voice of Baseball,* www.mudvillemagazine.com/archives/ 12_2003 (August 14, 2004).
"News and Notes," *Western Canada Baseball,* www.attheplate.com/wcbl/news3.html (August 14, 2004).

—James M. Manheim

Shoshana Johnson

1973—

Army specialist

Johnson, Shoshana, photograph. Mike Theiler/Getty Images.

U.S. Army Specialist Shoshana Johnson was captured by Iraqi forces during the first week of the 2003 U.S.-led war against Iraq, and became the first African-American female prisoner of war (P.O.W.) in U.S. history. Images of a frightened and injured Johnson were televised around the world shortly after her capture, and her family waited for three long weeks before she was rescued U.S. Marines. Though it was a tense time, her sister Nikki told CNN News reporters she had been hopeful her sister would return home safely. "She always had an angel following her around," Nikki Johnson told the cable-news organization. "She always manages to get out of stuff."

Johnson was born in Panama, the Central American nation, on January 18, 1973. Her family had West Indian roots, and her father was a U.S. military veteran. They later settled in El Paso, Texas, and Johnson served in her high school's Reserve Officer Training Corp (ROTC). She took classes at the University of Texas at El Paso, and enlisted in the Army in 1998 hoping to earn tuition money to enroll at a culinary-arts school.

Johnson, stationed at Fort Bliss in Texas, trained as an Army cook. Attached to the 507th Maintenance Company, which fixes the diesel tankers, generators, and Patriot missile batteries for infantry divisions, Johnson was dismayed to learn that she was being sent overseas once U.S. troops began to mobilize in preparation for the invasion of Iraq. By then, in early 2003, she was the single mother of a two-year-old daughter, Janelle, and was forced to leave her daughter in the care of her parents.

Johnson's 507th Maintenance Company unit was attached to the Third Infantry Division, which moved into Iraq during the week of March 20 after landing in nearby Kuwait. On March 23, Johnson was part of a convoy heading toward Baghdad on Highway 1, Iraq's main north-south artery. Her convoy made a wrong turn and was left alone and defenseless when Iraqi troops ambushed it near Nasiriya. The truck in which she was riding rolled over in the melee, and she and another specialist hid under it to return fire. "I got off one round and then my gun jammed," she recalled in an interview with *Essence* writer Veronica Byrd. "All of our weapons jammed because of the sand, so we had no way to return fire. Then I felt a burning sensation in my legs."

Eleven American soldiers were killed in the firefight before the ranking officer in Johnson's group, a sergeant, came out to surrender. Johnson had been shot in both feet, and the Iraqis ordered her and the others to come forward. "The Iraqi soldiers came and got me because I couldn't stand up," she said in the *Essence* interview. The Iraqi soldiers began beating the American soldiers with rifle butts, but when her helmet was knocked off and her cornrows became visible, they realized she was a woman and separated her from others. "Then they took me to what looked like an office," she told Byrd. "I was terrified. There was blood coming out of my boots."

Johnson's wounds were treated by an Iraqi doctor, and she was offered a painkiller. "More than once, a doctor said that they wanted to take good care of me to show that the Iraqi people had humanity," she told a writer for London's *Independent* newspaper, Andrew Gumbel. The captured Americans—who by now included two Apache helicopter pilots—were videotaped by Iraqi military officials, and the footage was sent to the media. Within hours, the images found their way onto the television in her parents' living room back in Texas. Later that day, Fort Bliss officials contacted them and confirmed reports that their daughter had become a prisoner of war.

Johnson was taken to Baghdad and held there until the city was captured by coalition forces two weeks later. While in custody, she underwent surgery on one ankle, after being required to write out her own waiver before submitting to anesthesia. She and the others were moved a total of seven times during their 22-day ordeal. Twice their cell walls shook because of bombs

dropped nearby. She was not sexually harassed or assaulted because of her gender, but did tell Byrd in the *Essence* interview that "in one prison the guards kept commenting that I should stay and marry an Iraqi man. At first I thought it was a joke, but after they kept saying it, I started to think they were going to keep me." She also recalled that one of her guards kept trying to hold her hand, which was noticed by an older guard, who came and slept outside her cell that night; she never saw the other guard again.

Johnson and her fellow captives were worried that they might be killed when prison officials fed them an unusually rich meal one evening. "On that Sunday morning I remember it was really quiet, so quiet I felt worried," she recalled in the *Essence* interview. By then she was in the city of Samarra, being guarded by ordinary Iraqi police officers who had even taken up a collection amongst themselves in order to buy the prisoners necessary food and medicine.

On April 12, Marines heading toward Tikrit learned that the American P.O.W.s were nearby, and stormed the facility the next day. Telling everyone to stand up if they were American, the Marines at first did not believe that the still-injured Johnson was an American, but her fellow captives vouched that she was one of them. The Marines instructed them to run for their vehicle when they gave the signal, and "I started crying," she told Byrd. "I was like, 'I can't run.' Another Marine said, 'Come here.' I went over and he half-carried and half-dragged me to the vehicle."

Johnson and the others were shuttled to safety, treated, and debriefed. They were then flown home and reunited with their families days later. No longer able to serve because of her injured feet, she retired from the Army with a pension in early 2004, not long after helping New York City Mayor Michael Bloomberg press the button that dropped the famous ball over Times Square at midnight on December 31.

Despite such honors, Johnson did not receive the level of publicity attached to another female American soldier who had been captured, eighteen-year-old Jessica Lynch. The West Virginian received a book deal and was even the subject of a made-for-television movie, and was granted higher disability payments than Johnson as a result of injuries suffered. Johnson appealed the military's decision and won a pension that amounted to 50 percent of her salary during the time she served. She dismissed any hints that she was a hero. "I'm a survivor, not a hero," she told Byrd in the *Essence* interview. "The heroes are the soldiers who paid the ultimate price and the Marines who risked their lives to rescue us. Who knows what they could have walked into? It could have been a trap. But just the thought of getting us out was enough. They took a chance, and because they did, I'm here."

Sources

Periodicals

Ebony, August 2003, p. 46.
Essence, March 2004, p. 166.
Independent (London, England), April 15, 2003, p. 5.
Knight Ridder/Tribune News Service, November 8, 2003.
New York Times, March 28, 2003, p. B1.
Time, April 7, 2003, p. 64.

On-line

"Ex-POW Planned on Cooking, Not Fighting," *CNN,* www.cnn.com/2003/US/04/13/sprj.irq.pow.johnson (August 10, 2004).

—Carol Brennan

Kem

196?—

R&B vocalist, songwriter

Kem, photograph. Quantrell Colbert/Getty Images.

Kem has carved a niche for himself in the music world. His jazz-influenced contemporary R&B vocal styles are claiming a loyal following in an African-American musical environment dominated by hip-hop sounds. When he signed to the venerable Motown music label and his debut release, *Kemistry,* climbed to the top reaches of industry urban-music sales charts, these events marked the beginning of a new chapter in Kem's life. His career accomplishments were personal milestones as well, for they came at the end of a series of trials that extended down to the depths of homelessness. With a five-album deal inked at Motown, Kem stood ready to make music that fit neatly into a set of retro trends that had appeared in African-American music, and at the same time was rooted in his own experiences.

Born in Nashville, Tennessee, Kem has refused to discuss his age, and his characteristic shaven-headed appearance makes it difficult for observers even to feel confident that a guess is reasonably accurate. But he told the *New York Amsterdam News* that "I grew up in the late '70s, early '80s, when most of the radio stations were Top 40." He said in 2002 that he had

been sober for 12 years, and the period of his life that he lost to drug and alcohol abuse took place during his late teens and early 20s. Kem was probably born, therefore, in the late 1960s. His birth name was Kim Owens; the "Kem" spelling was a mistake on an associate's part that the singer adopted because he thought it sounded distinctive and marketable.

Kem's family moved from Tennessee to the Detroit suburb of Southfield, Michigan, when he was young. When he was four, he began to explore the keyboard. "My grandparents had a piano in their house and my earliest memory of playing was on that piano," he told *Jet*. "There's something about a piano that turns me on." He made little headway at first. A babysitter taught him to play the harmonically ambitious "Color My World," by the pop group Chicago. "I played that song for about three years straight," Kem told Cleveland's *Scene Entertainment Weekly*. "But what that did was it gave me an idea of what chords were all about."

Also influenced by R&B giants of the day like Stevie Wonder and Marvin Gaye and by jazz-popsters Steely Dan and Grover Washington Jr., Kem became

At a Glance . . .

Born Kim Owens in Nashville, TN, 196?; *Pseudonym:* Kem; children: Troi (daughter). *Education:* Self-taught as musician. *Religion:* Nondenominational Christian.

Career: Ritz-Carlton hotel, Dearborn, MI, waiter, and various other nonmusical jobs, 1990-2001; full-time musician, 2001–; Motown Records, recording artist, 2003–.

Addresses: *Office*—Kemistry Records, P.O. Box 37156, Oak Park, MI 48237. *Web*—http://www.kemistryrecords.com.

fascinated by music in high school. He sang in the choir, kept up with releases by Michael Jackson, Prince, and jazz-pop phenomenon Al Jarreau, and gravitated toward musically talented classmates like keyboardist Brian O'Neal. The two spent their lunch hours in the school's band room. "Kem would come in and just watch me, and I started teaching him a couple of things," O'Neal recalled to *Ebony*. (Other than that, however, Kem was essentially self-taught.) The two dreamed of a musical career. "But after high school, he went in one direction and I went the other," O'Neal said.

Kem couldn't attribute his later problems to the surroundings in which he grew up; he remembered his childhood as a happy one, and he was raised, he told *Ebony,* in a "professional, middle-class family." Underneath, however, his feelings told a different story. "I left my parents' home when I was 19," he told the magazine. "And I left as a teenager who was lost, depressed, insecure, full of fear and trying to mask all of that with alcohol and drugs." His descent into homelessness was gradual; at first he limped along by staying with friends, and then, when he had to take to the streets, he stayed at first in shelters in Detroit's affluent suburbs and was relatively well taken care of.

Kem has refused to discuss his life on the streets in much detail, but it seems clear that his life went into a downward spiral. He ended up at a downtown Detroit shelter not far from the city's notorious Cass Corridor drug markets. "I was down in the corridor doing the shuffle," he told the *Detroit Free Press*. "My homelessness was a result of addiction." Finally things got even worse, and he took to sleeping outside, near a newspaper printing plant on the Detroit River. And that was when he bottomed out and, he says, turned to God.

"He was waiting on me," the singer told *Ebony*. "There was no flash of light or anything—I was just tired and I

didn't know how to fix it…. On that particular day, I realized that I was not living the life that I wanted to live. I'd always had these high hopes and expectations of what I wanted out of my life, and I was nowhere near achieving those." The first step in Kem's recovery was to seek help; he has chosen not to identify the program to which he turned, but he later became a member of the Renaissance Unity Church in the Detroit suburb of Warren, then led by pastor and nationally famous author and radio host Marianne Williamson.

After becoming sober around 1990, Kem put his life back together with a series of nonmusical jobs. For a time he worked as a waiter at the Ritz-Carlton Hotel in suburban Dearborn, Michigan. Estranged from his family during the period when he was homeless, he reconciled himself with them, and they supported him strongly when he returned to music once again. Looking back on his experiences, Kem never talked in terms of regret. "The journey is where it's at—getting here," he told the *Detroit News*. "All of the things that have happened to me in the past are definitely what brought success to the Kem CD."

The most important thing that happened to Kem during this period of recovery was that he began to get together once again with some of his musical friends. O'Neal performed with his band sometimes, although the keyboard sound heard in most of Kem's music is his own. Saxophonist David McMurray joined Kem in a band and became the group's musical director. Other members of Kem's lineup, which remained remarkably stable over a decade of performing, were guitarist Quentin Baxter, bassist Fred Robinson, and percussionists Andre Driscoll and Wild Bill Curry.

While most of the musical world was headed toward the exploitation of electronics, Kem moved in the opposite direction. The *Kemistry* album, almost alone among recent R&B charting releases, was the creation of live musicians. "That's the key to the magic of this record," McMurray told *Ebony*. "I think he has something really unique." The group began playing around 1993 and had its first major gig when it won an opening slot for singer MeShell NdegeOcello at the Royal Oak Music Theater outside Detroit.

From then on, Kem's rise to national prominence was mostly due to the hard work he put into the enterprise of self-promotion. Other opening slots, for War and Donald Byrd, followed, and the singer made some outside income by writing music for a McDonald's commercial and singing for weddings. He also sang with the Church of Today choir, based at Renaissance Unity Church. His band performed at Detroit's African World Festival and began to generate a buzz among frequenters of the city's active urban music scene. Along the way, he became the father of a daughter, Troi (as of 2003 he was engaged to be married, but kept the details private). In 1999, he recorded a live version of what became the *Kemistry* CD at a Detroit coffeehouse. A severe self-critic, he wasn't pleased with the results. "I just didn't like it, and I decided not to release it," he told the *Scene Entertainment Weekly.*

Detroit music fans had a different opinion of the music, though, and unofficial copies of the album circulated around the city. Kem passed an important turning point when he quit a nine-to-five job in 2001 in order to devote full time to his music. Aware of the demand for his music, he decided to record a studio version of *Kemistry.* He financed the project by running up debt on a credit card.

When *Kemistry* appeared in 2002 on Kem's own label, also called Kemistry, it was rare for a completely independent release to make much of an impact in urban music business. But Kem marketed his CD to beauty salons and black-oriented restaurants, persuading them to play the music on their sound systems and to sell the disc on consignment. "I gave lots of CDs away," he told the *Washington Informer.* Word of his talents continued to build, and version two of *Kemistry* sold an impressive 10,000 copies over a five-month period.

That got the attention of executives at the Motown label, who signed Kem to a five-album contract in 2003 and released *Kemistry* for the third time. National critics like *Ebony's* Lynn Norment praised Kem's "emotionally rich" music; his sound was often compared to Al Jarreau's, but his lyrics had a depth and a tendency to take unexpected turns even when they dealt with conventional romantic subjects. "With my stuff, you have to pay attention to the words," Kem explained to the *Michigan Chronicle.* "There is not a lot of kick behind it, not a whole lot of driving beat." The singer's four-octave range was another musical attraction. The album's leadoff single, "Love Calls," received heavy airplay on jazz and adult contemporary radio stations; Kem took to the road nationally; and the album cracked the top 20 of *Billboard's* Top Hip-Hop/R&B Albums chart.

A sign of Kem's rising profile was that he successfully recruited Marsha Ambrosius of the innovative hip-hop duo Floetry to participate in a remix of "Love Calls." The singer looked toward a more specifically spiritual project for his second release and often stressed that his own past life had played a role in the music he eventually made. "The rough spots in our lives give us character," he explained to *Jet.* "I don't regret the past…it's an integral part of who I am." Music fans were just happy to hear such a fresh take on old-school traditions. "What I'm most grateful for is that I didn't give up," Kem told the *Detroit News.* "Don't quit before your miracle happens."

Selected discography

Kemistry, Motown, 2003.

Sources

Periodicals

Atlanta Journal-Constitution, April 10, 2003, p. C2.
Chicago Defender, April 6, 2004, p. 15.
Detroit Free Press, April 19, 2002, p. D6; August 24, 2003, p. E1.
Detroit News, February 27, 2003, p. E1.
Ebony, May 2003, p. 32; October 2003.
Jet, September 1, 2003, p. 40.
Michigan Chronicle, March 13, 2002, p. D1.
Michigan Citizen, March 8, 2003, p. B1.
New York Amsterdam News, May 29, 2003, p. 20.
Scene Entertainment Weekly (Cleveland, OH), December 24, 2003.
Washington Informer, March 19, 2003, p. 20.
Washington Post, August 22, 2003, p. T7.

On-line

"Kem," *All Music Guide,* www.allmusic.com (August 4, 2004).

—James M. Manheim

Femi Kuti

1962—

Nigerian singer, songwriter, bandleader

Nigeria's Femi Kuti calls his band Positive Force, and that name illustrates some of the differences between Kuti and his famous father. Kuti is the son of Fela Anikulapo-Kuti, an icon of Nigerian music whose protest lyrics were a constant thorn in the side of the country's military government, and who often ended up in prison as a result of songs that seemed to portend rebellion among Nigeria's masses of impoverished young people. Femi Kuti carries forward his father's legacy in many respects, but his is a Nigerian music for a different country, one that is making steps toward democracy and trying to get a grip on endemic corruption. Protest is certainly present in his music, but it is measured rather than incendiary.

One of numerous children of Fela, who had at least 27 wives, Femi Kuti was born on June 16, 1962. Some sources place his birth in Britain; others in Lagos, Nigeria. His mother Remi was born in Britain and was of mixed African-American, Native American, English, and Nigerian background. Kuti soaked up his father's pathbreaking "Afrobeat" fusion of American funk with Yoruba rhythms, shaped during visits to the United States in the late 1960s. He took up the saxophone at age 16 and within a couple of years was playing in Fela's band, which featured an entourage of well over 20 musicians and dancers. During a Nigerian army raid on Fela's home, Kuti's mother died after falling from a window—a tragedy he has laid at the feet of Nigerian president Olusegun Obasanjo.

The first sign that Kuti might inherit his father's mantle came in 1984, when he stepped in to lead Fela's Egypt 80 band and run his Shrine club in Lagos after Fela ran afoul of the government. At a Hollywood Bowl concert the following year, after Fela was taken into custody at the Lagos airport on the way to the concert, Kuti presented a reasonable facsimile of his father's performing style. But two years later he formed his own band, Positive Force, and the son's music turned out to be different from the father's. (He also gave up cigarettes and marijuana, both of which Fela indulged in heavily.) His first album, *No Cause for Alarm,* featured his jazz-style saxophone playing and brought him a cadre of fans in France, where he remains popular.

Fela wanted to install his son as a club manager and heir apparent, but Kuti refused, precipitating a five-year period of silence between the two. They finally buried the hatchet after running into each other at a Lagos club in the mid-1990s, but some of Fela's band members never became reconciled to the son's independent career. In the meantime, Kuti recorded several albums for labels in Europe and looked for chances to emerge from his father's shadow. In 1994 he recorded an album, *Femi Kuti,* for the Motown label's short-lived Tabu world music imprint.

Without support from its moribund label, that album made little impact in the United States. With an eye toward expanding his influence in Nigeria, however, Kuti kept looking for opportunities to record. "An international career is my number one priority," he told London's *Independent* newspaper. "If I can make money in Europe I'll subsidize my African activities." Kuti toured Europe in 1996 and 1997, and in 1998 he

At a Glance . . .

Born on June 16, 1962, in Lagos, Nigeria; son of Nigerian superstar Fela Anikulapo-Kuti and his wife Remi; married Funke; children: one son, Omrinmade.

Career: Musician; joined father Fela's band Egypt 80 as a teen; formed band Positive Force, 1986.

Address: *Label*—c/o MCA Records, Universal Music Group, 2220 Colorado Avenue, Santa Monica , CA 90404.

formed a student-oriented political group called M.A. S.S.—Movement Against Second Slavery—that aimed to promote pan-African culture and fired a few shots across the bow of Nigeria's government. "I don't want power," Kuti told the *Independent*. "I don't care who's in power as long as he provides electricity, petrol, water. The President should be like a houseboy."

Kuti seemed to become more politically oriented after his father's death in 1997, from AIDS-related complications. "When you are born, you are in politics," he observed sardonically to the *Financial Times*. "Don't fool yourself—that's why the baby cries." Kuti's sister, Sola, with whom he shared both parents and who was one of the original members of Positive Force, also died that year, and it was in the late 1990s that he really became a familiar name on the international scene. His album *Shoki Shoki*, released in the United States on the MCA label, was his big international breakthrough.

On that album, Kuti avoided the half-hour-long (or longer) jams that his father often indulged in, focusing on catchy rhythms that might generate a piece seven or eight minutes long. He addressed social themes in the widely heard "Blackman Know Yourself," but also had fun with the raunchy "Beng Beng Beng." Kuti's songs attracted the attention of hip-hop and dance remix artists, including Lauryn Hill, as well as Ahmir Thompson of the Roots, who sampled them repeatedly. A host of dance-club remixes (collected on a CD called *Shoki Remixed*) turned Kuti's songs into true party anthems for a time. Despite these modernizing trends, Kuti rooted his music strongly in Fela's, which at the time was being widely marketed in posthumous reissues. "He is still growing into Fela's shoes, but he hasn't fudged an iota on his father's ferocious funk," noted the Minneapolis *Star Tribune*.

Kuti's attempt to modernize Afrobeat continued on his second MCA album, *Fight to Win*, released in late 2001; the album featured rappers Mos Def and Com-

mon, and showed the results of Kuti's effort to incorporate hip-hop into African music. The album also contained a composition, "97," in which Kuti reflected on the family tragedies of that year. Generally praised by critics, *Fight to Win* moved the All Music Guide to state that "Kuti has made his first great album." Kuti's ongoing success inspired the recording of a tribute album, *Red Hot + RIOT*.

In contrast to Fela and his phalanx of wives, Femi Kuti has been monogamously married to his wife, Funke, for many years. She is a member of Positive Force, and the couple has one son, Omrinmade, whose lack of places to go in Lagos worries his father. Kuti has begun to think big about Africa, and its situation. "I know Africa is full of abundant talent which has not developed to its fullest," he told *Interview*. "I would love to see great Africa rise again. But honestly speaking, what I see in Africa is that young people want to get out because they don't want to get involved in all the gangsterism or the corruption."

"I think that Europeans mistake Africa's anger for desperation," he continued. Sounding very much like his father, whatever changes he had made to his music, Kuti took to the road in Europe and the United States in 2004, appearing at the Playboy Jazz Festival in Los Angeles and at Guilford, England's Guilfest. "I look like him, dance like him, and even talk like him sometimes," Kuti said of Fela in a *Maclean's* interview. "I will never run away from the fact that I am his son."

Selected discography

No Cause for Alarm, 1987.
Femi Kuti, Tabu, 1994.
Shoki Shoki, MCA, 1999.
Fight to Win, MCA, 2001.

Sources

Books

Contemporary Musicians, Vol. 29, Gale, 2000.

Periodicals

Daily News (Los Angeles), January 21, 2000, p. L21; August 8, 2000, p. L5; June 22, 2004, p. U3.
Financial Times (London), October 5, 2002, p. 9.
Independent (London), May 7, 1999, p. 13; December 1, 2001, p. 74.
Interview, May 2001, p. 76; November 2001, p. 48.
Maclean's, May 1, 2000, p. 68.
Star Tribune (Minneapolis, MN), July 19, 2002, p. E5.

On-line

"Femi Kuti," *All Music Guide*, www.allmusic.com (August 9, 2004).

Femi Kuti, www.mcarecords.com/ArtistMain.asp?Ar-
tistId=174 (August 17, 2004).

—James M. Manheim

Bob Lanier

1948—

Professional basketball player, businessman

Bob Lanier—6-foot, 11-inches tall and filling size 22 shoes—entered the National Basketball Association (NBA) in 1970 as the number one draft pick of the Detroit Pistons. He played nine and one-half seasons for the Pistons and four and one-half seasons for the Milwaukee Bucks. During his 14 years in the NBA, Lanier amassed 19,248 points, 9,698 rebounds, and 1,100 blocks. He averaged over 20 points per game over his entire career, yet he retired in 1984 without ever winning an NBA title. After leaving the court, Lanier remained close to the game as a special assistant to the NBA commissioner, in charge of community services.

Too Big Too Fast

Robert Jerry Lanier Jr. was born on September 10, 1948, in Buffalo, New York, the son of Robert and Nannette Lanier. The family lived in one of Buffalo's poorest neighborhoods, and Lanier, who grew to 6-foot, 8-inches by the time he was 14 years old, had to wear men's clothes when he attended Bennett High School, making him feel awkward and out of place. He later told *The Buffalo News,* "I remember my first day [of high school]. To me it seemed like the biggest building in the world, and there were so many people. It gave me a feeling of inadequacy because the kids here had nice clothes. They wore khaki pants and penny loafers, and I didn't have all that stuff."

Because Lanier's coordination had not yet caught up to his height, he did not win a place on his grammar school basketball team and was told by the coach that his feet (size 11 at age 11) were too big for him to ever become a good athlete. As a high school sophomore he was cut from the basketball team by coach Nick Mogavero because he was too clumsy. Emotionally hurt by the rejection, Lanier joined a Boys' Club, where he worked out and practiced continually. The following year, with the encouragement of his biology teacher, Fred Schwepker, who had since become the basketball coach, Lanier tried out again. That year, as the center of the Bennett Tigers, Lanier averaged 21.5 points per game and was named to the All-City team. In his senior year, his average increased to 25 points per game and he earned All-Western New York State honors. Both years he led his team to city titles.

Becoming the team's star player helped Lanier overcome his feelings of alienation. His parents, who always stressed the need for getting an education, were also supportive of their son. Lanier was particularly close to his father, who encouraged him and helped him through his awkward years. Despite being courted by over one hundred schools for his basketball skills, Lanier, who was a poor student, was unable to secure a place at Canisius, his first choice for college, because of his grades. Instead, he attended St. Bonaventure University, located in the southwest corner of New York State, near Buffalo.

Became College All-Star

Because National Collegiate Athletic Association

Born on September 10, 1948, in Buffalo, NY; son of Robert and Nannette Lanier; married Shirley (divorced); married Rose; children: four from first marriage; four from second marriage. *Education:* St. Bonaventure University, BA in business administration, 1970.

Career: Detroit Pistons, professional basketball player, 1970-80; Milwaukee Bucks, professional basketball player, 1980-84; National Basketball Association, executive, 1989-93, 1996-2004; Golden State Warriors, assistant coach, 1993-94, interim head coach, 1995; Bob Lanier Enterprises, Milwaukee, WI, founder and president, 1996–.

Selected Awards: Eastern College Athletic Conference Player of the Year, 1970; NBA All-Rookie Team, 1971; NBA All-Star Team, 1972-75, 1977-79, 1982; NBA All-Star Game, Most Valuable Player 1974; Walter J. Kennedy Citizenship Award, 1978; Jackie Robinson Award, 1981; Oscar Robertson Leadership Award, 1984; NBA Hall of Fame, 1992; Schick Achievement Award, 1993; Horizon Award, 2000.

Addresses: *Office*—Bob Lanier Enterprises, 8316 N. Steven Road, Milwaukee, WI 53223-3355. *Office*—c/o Basketball Hall of Fame, 1150 W. Columbus Avenue, Springfield, MA 01101.

(NCAA) rules at the time did not allow freshmen participation in collegiate sports, Lanier did not join the Bonnies' team until his sophomore year. Now 6-foot, 11-inches tall and 265 pounds, Lanier led the team to a record 22-0 regular season record (23-2 overall), and the team ranked third in the national standings at the end of the season. With an average of 26.2 points and 15.6 rebounds per game, Lanier was named All-American Second Team. In his junior year, his performance improved to an average of 27.2 points and 15.5 rebounds per game. During his junior year Lanier was approached by the American Basketball Association's New Jersey Nets, who offered him $1.2 million to join the team. However, following his father's advice, Lanier chose to remain in school.

During his senior year Lanier averaged 29 points and 16 rebounds per game and was a unanimous pick for All-American. Once again setting a school record, the

Bonnies posted a 25-1 season (the one blemish was a 2-point loss to Villanova University) and earned a bid to the 1970 NCAA tournament. In the first two rounds of the tournament, the Bonnies breezed by Davidson College and North Carolina State. In the third round, St. Bonaventure laid claim to the Eastern Regional title by beating Villanova, 97-74. However, after scoring 18 points in the game, Lanier suffered a season-ending knee-ligament injury. Without his presence on the floor for the next game, the Bonnies' dream season came to an end when they were upset in the national semifinals. Lanier ended his college career as St. Bonaventure's all-time scoring leader (he now ranks third) with 2,067 points. He graduated in 1970 with a bachelor's degree in business administration.

In 1970, even though he was still rehabilitating his injured knee, Lanier was selected first in the NBA draft by the Detroit Pistons, who had posted losing seasons for 13 consecutive years and were in desperate need of a shot in the arm. In fact, the Pistons were so eager to secure Lanier that the NBA contract was presented to him while he was still in the hospital recuperating from knee surgery. He showed up to training camp still limping, in significant pain, and overweight from his long period of inactivity.

Starred for the Pistons

During his first year in the NBA, in which he played in all 82 games, Lanier posted outstanding numbers for a rookie, averaging 15.6 points and 8.1 rebounds per game. At the end of the season he was named to the NBA All-Rookie Team, and the Piston's overall record improved to 45-37. During his second season, with his knee finally healing and his mobility improving, Lanier's performance jumped to 25.7 points and 14.2 rebounds per game, which placed him eighth best in the NBA for scoring and ninth best in rebounding. In 1972 he was invited to his first NBA All-Star game. Over the course of his 14-year career, he was named an NBA All-Star eight times.

Lanier, nicknamed the Big Dobber, took up a lot of room under the basket, and he dominated the middle on defense. On the offensive end, he had an almost unstoppable left-handed hook shot and a range of up to 15 feet. He was also a good free-throw shooter, averaging better than 75 percent from the line over his career. Lanier was also known as a tough and physical player who played through pain, which he did all too often. During his career, Lanier had knee surgery five times, as well as a broken right hand, a bad toe, a sore back, a broken finger, and chronic shoulder problems.

Despite his best efforts, Lanier could not carry the weight of the entire team, and the 1972-73 season started off poorly. After 12 games, coach Bill Van Breda Kolff resigned, and four more coaches quickly filed in and out of Detroit. Lanier, who was often blamed for getting coaches fired, was slowly watching his chance at winning a national championship slip away. Of his nine full seasons at Detroit, the Pistons made the playoffs just four times and only advanced out of the first round series once; they never got past the second round. Injuries also continued to plague Lanier. Although he never missed more than two games in each of his first four seasons and only sat out six during the 1974-75 season, he missed 18 games in both the 1975-76 and the 1977-78 seasons and 19 games during the 1978-78 season.

Traded to Milwaukee

By the late 1970s Lanier was feeling the emotional burden of losing and was frustrated with the team's managerial instability—during his nine years in Detroit, he had played for eight different coaches. In 1979, in the midst of the franchise's worst season ever (16-66), Lanier decided he had had enough and asked out. The Pistons' obliged and, in February 1980, Lanier was traded to the Milwaukee Bucks for Kent Benson and a future first-round pick. During his time in Detroit, Lanier had amassed 15,488 points and 8,063 rebounds.

When Lanier arrived in Milwaukee, the Bucks were nursing a mediocre 29-27 record. But, during the final months of the regular season, Lanier helped the team go on a 20-6 run to end season 49-33. Lanier, now 31 years old and called "Coach" by his teammates in deference to his age and experience, was not expected to carry the team or play as many minutes. According to *Sports Illustrated,* which ran a story titled "Big Boost from Big Bob," Lanier said, "I don't have the emotional burden. Here I help on defense, set picks and pass the ball, things I do well anyway. It makes life easier. My playing time has gone down but the [wins] are up." In Milwaukee, Lanier hoped to finally chase down that elusive championship ring. Unfortunately, although the Bucks won the division title for five consecutive years and claimed the Eastern Conference championship twice, Lanier never won the NBA title.

Tragedy struck in October 1980 when Lanier's 59-year-old father was killed in a late-night hit-and-run accident. Lanier was paged by the police in La Guardia Airport, returning from a game, and asked to identify the body. "More so than any other time in my life I'm drained emotionally," Lanier told *Jet* after the accident. "I've never been so down." Three months later, Lanier's wife, Rose, filed for legal separation and moved out, taking the couple's four children with her. This was the second time in their 11-year marriage that the couple had split. Lanier was devastated. During the tumultuous 1980-81 season, Lanier played in 67 games, averaging 26 minutes and 14.5 points per game. Although he reconciled with his wife, the couple would later divorce.

Retired without Title

During the 1981-82 season Lanier played in 72 games and averaged 13.5 points per game. The following season he was once again hindered by injuries and only played in 39 games, averaging 10.7 points per game, the lowest of his NBA career. Returning to the court full time for the 1983-84 season, he appeared in 72 games, playing nearly 28 minutes and scoring 13.6 points per game. After the season ended, Lanier, whose knees could no longer hold up, announced his retirement. "Basketball is a game because it's fun and it's a job because I get paid," Lanier said, according to *The Washington Post.* "I don't need a championship to have made my career a successful one. I think the importance of it to me has been overplayed."

After his retirement, Lanier founded Lanier Enterprises, Inc., a company that specializes in advertising and promotional products. He also took on some sportscasting assignments. In the late 1980s Lanier helped the NBA launch its "Stay in School Program" and later its "Read to Achieve" and "Team-Up" programs. As a special assistant to the NBA commissioner, Lanier traveled around the country speaking with kids about the importance of staying in school and learning to read.

During the 1993-94 NBA season, Lanier accepted an invitation from his former coach Don Nelson, now the head coach of the Golden State Warriors, to join him on the bench as an assistant. Nelson was looking for help with his big men, and Lanier was pulled in to work as both coach and mentor to the younger players. After posting a record of 7-30 in the first half of the 1994-95, Nelson resigned under pressure. Lanier was tagged to take over the job as interim head coach, inheriting an injury-laden and demoralized team. Despite his best efforts, the Warriors finished out the season 12-25. Although he expressed interest in remaining as the team's coach, Rick Adelman was named to fill the position.

Lanier returned to his work as a special assistant to the NBA commissioner with responsibilities for the league community outreach programs as well as refereeing and basketball operations. In 2003 Lanier became a published children's author with the introduction of his series "L'il Dobber," co-authored with Heather Goodyear. Targeted for children ages six to nine, the four-book series includes the titles *It's All in a Name, Hey, L'il D: Take the Court, Stuck in the Middle,* and *Out of Bounds.* Lanier told *Inside Stuff Magazine,* "I've thought about doing a book series for a few years now. Using basketball as the carrot to [raise] kids' interests, I wanted to share some of life's lessons through some endearing characters." Lanier, who has received numerous awards for his outstanding community service over the years, lives in Scottsdale, Arizona, with his wife Rose and their four children.

Selected writings

(With Heather Goodyear) *It's All in a Name, Hey, L'il D: Take the Court, Stuck in the Middle,* and *Out of Bounds* (for children), Scholastic, 2003.

Sources

Periodicals

Associated Press, April 10, 1995; September 24, 1984; June 20, 1995.

Buffalo News, March 22, 2003, p. C1; March 24, 2004, p. B4.

Commercial Appeal (Memphis, TN), February 14, 1995.

Jet, March 6, 1995, p. 46.

Los Angeles Times, June 16, 2004, p. S2.

Milwaukee Journal Sentinel, September 29, 1998, p. S1.

New York Times, April 6, 1981, p. C1; May 20, 1995, p. S35.

Newsbytes, June 13, 2003.

Pittsburgh Post-Gazette, February 25, 1996, p. D9.

San Antonio Express-News, January 26, 2004, p. D1.

San Francisco Chronicle, February 13, 1995, p. B5; February 15, 1995, p. E1.

Sports Illustrated, February 27, 1995, p. 78-79.

Times-Picayune (New Orleans), June 16, 2004.

USA Today, February 4, 1997, C6.

Washington Post, May 14, 1983, p. D1.

On-line

"Bob Lanier," *HoopHall: Basketball Hall of Fame,* www.hoophall.com/halloffamers/Lanier.htm (July 12, 2004).

"Bob Lanier," *NBA,* www.nba.com/history/players/lanier_bio.html (July 12, 2004).

"Bob Lanier to Visit St. Bonaventure for Children's Book Signing," *Inside Bona's,* www.sbu.edu/insidebonas/July03/insidebonas_July_18.html (July 12, 2004).

"One-on-One with Bob Lanier," *76ers,* www.nba.com/sixers/community/rta_week_lanier.html (July 12, 2004).

—Kari Bethel

Carl Lumbly

1952—

Actor

In the role of Agent Dixon on the hit television program *Alias* in the early 2000s, Carl Lumbly conveyed a streak of edgy intensity lurking beneath the veneer of a traditional supporting actor's sidekick part. That intensity has run through much of Lumbly's acting work and has its roots in the dynamics of the actor's early life. Praised by critics, Lumbly built a successful acting career in spite of his reluctance to accept many of the roles that fell to African-American actors.

Lumbly, Carl, photograph. © Glenn Weiner/Auma/Corbis.

Lumbly was born to Jamaican immigrant parents in Minneapolis, Minnesota, on August 14, 1952. His family had recently come to chilly Minnesota after meeting a local radio host, Cedric Adams, while he was vacationing in Jamaica. Lumbly's father Carrol got a job as a welder but never felt at ease in the United States, and his mother mostly stayed at home. Lumbly's parents raised their children with an appreciation of the Jamaican culture. About his family's home Lumbly recalled to the Minneapolis *Star Tribune* that "Once you stepped in the door, you were in Jamaica."

Out of sight of his father, who brooked no disrespect, Lumbly would amuse his sister Amy (a future television news reporter) by imitating their father's finicky way of aligning his tableware. He showed an interest in theater while he was attending South High School in Minneapolis, but most of his free time was taken up by playing basketball and trombone—sometimes in the course of the same game. He would change clothes during the coach's halftime pep talk and come out onto the court with his trombone for the band's halftime show. "I like to work real hard," Lumbly told the *Star Tribune*.

Winning admission to Minnesota's competitive Macalester College, Lumbly majored in English and took roles in two student theater productions. Urged to pursue a professional career by his father, he thought about attending law or medical school, and he had no thoughts of trying to act professionally. After graduating, Lumbly accepted a public relations job at the 3M corporation and also did some freelance newspaper writing on the side. One evening in the mid-1970s, he visited an innovative new theater company called Brave New Workshop to observe its open auditions, hoping to write an article about them but not planning to audition himself.

Through a mixup that began when Lumbly stood in the wrong line of people, he ended up auditioning. Three

At a Glance . . .

Born on August 14, 1952, in Minneapolis, MN, to Jamaican immigrant parents; married Vonnetta McGee (an actor); children: Brandon. *Education:* Macalester College, BA, English, 1973.

Career: 3M Corporation, Minneapolis, public relations writer, mid-1970s; Associated Press, freelance writer, mid-1970s; Brave New Workshop theater company, Minneapolis, member, mid-1970s; actor, mid-1970s–

Addresses: *Office*—ABC Television, 500 S. Buena Vista St., Burbank, CA 91521

weeks later, the Workshop directors asked Lumbly to join the company. He did and soon found himself enjoying acting quite a bit. He appeared in several revues, signed on with several other theater companies, and even wrote a comic play of his own, *Badd High.* The high points of his experiences were some episodes of improvisational theater he performed at Brave New Workshop. "I lived with many, many strictures in my life, and adhered to lots of things that other people believed I should adhere to," Lumbly told the *Star Tribune.* In an improv skit, on the other hand, he found that anything goes. "Whenever I could, I would try to see just how strange and how weird and how far away from myself I could be." But when he veered into questionable humor, he worried about how his father would react if he saw him.

Despite his stage appearances, Lumbly didn not yet consider himself an actor. Partly to get away from Minnesota's cold winters, he moved with a girlfriend to San Francisco in 1977 and decided to try to make a living as an Associated Press writer. But he saw a classified ad in a newspaper seeking two black actors for parts in a pair of short plays by South African writer Athol Fugard. After an audition with director Robert Woodruff, Lumbly was hired for one of the parts, and future superstar Danny Glover got the other. That break led to other stage parts. Especially active in live theater during the 1980s, Lumbly finally won his ill father's approval of his new career after appearing in a 1983 Minneapolis production of the musical *The Gospel at Colonus.* He also appeared at such prestigious venues as the New York Shakespeare Festival, where he played the role of Oberon in Shakespeare's *A Midsummer Night's Dream* in 1988.

Soon after moving to California, Lumbly began to attract television and movie parts as well, beginning with a bit part in the film *Escape from Alcatraz* in 1979. What made him a familiar face to the public at large was his ongoing role as Sgt. Marcus Petrie in the hit television series *Cagney & Lacey,* which he joined beginning with the pilot episode in 1982. He also appeared in several films with specifically African-American themes; in the 1991 Public Broadcasting System film *Brother Future,* he played slave rebel Denmark Vesey.

That was the first of several roles in which Lumbly played figures from the slavery era; he would later appear in a film devoted to Nat Turner, and his first television film starring role came in *Nightjohn,* which featured him as a slave who teaches others to read. Lumbly generally declined roles that he felt relegated African-American actors to stereotypical urban action tales, and he has been a consistent voice speaking out in favor of increased opportunities for black performers. When he did take an action role, it was an unusual one: he starred in the 1994 Fox network series *M.A. N.T.I.S.* as the disabled Dr. Miles Hawkins, who takes on the powers of a giant insect. Featuring television's first black superhero, the series gained a cult following but lasted only one season.

Lumbly won an NAACP Image Award nomination for his performance in the 1997 television film *Buffalo Soldiers,* and he kept his profile high with appearances in the hit film *How Stella Got Her Groove Back* and with guest slots on the television series *The X-Files* and *The West Wing.* In 2001 he was cast opposite actress Jennifer Garner in the ABC network's over-the-top spy series *Alias;* Lumbly and Garner played espionage partners enmeshed in a giant web of deception that led them to keep secrets from their loved ones and from each other. *Alias* creator J.J. Abrams cast Lumbly in the role of Agent Marcus Dixon because he felt Lumbly would bring a sense of gravity to stories that otherwise risked running into campy territory.

Married to actress Vonnetta McGee, Lumbly has one son, Brandon. He continues to enjoy writing in his spare time, and he stays in shape as a marathon runner. In 2003 he starred in a made-for-TV remake of the classic film *Sounder,* and he looked to a future in which he challenged himself with a wider range of roles in theatrical feature films. He didn't rule out playing the evil characters he had long avoided, but, he told the *Star Tribune,* he had always followed an overriding set of principles. "A lot of what has guided me in the past is the history of black men in this industry and the history of black men in this country. There's also the personal history with my father."

Selected works

Films

Escape from Alcatraz, 1979.
Hardcore, 1979.
Lifepod (also known as *Life Pod*), 1980.

Caveman, 1981.
The Adventures of Buckaroo Banzai: Across the Eighth Dimension (also known as *Buckaroo Banzai*), 1984.
The Bedroom Window, 1987.
Judgment in Berlin (also known as *Escape to Freedom*), 1988.
Everybody's All-American (also known as *When I Fall in Love*), 1988.
To Sleep with Anger, 1990.
Pacific Heights, 1990.
South Central, 1992.
How Stella Got Her Groove Back, 1998.

Plays

Meetings, 1981.
Nevis Mountain Dew, 1981.
The Tempest, 1981.
The Gospel at Colonus, 1983.
Eyes of the American, 1986.
A Midsummer Night's Dream, 1988.
Miss Evers' Boys, 1989-90.

Television

Undercover with the KKK (also known as *The Freedom Riders* and *My Undercover Years with the KKK*; television movie), 1979.
Conspiracy: The Trial of the Chicago Eight (television movie), 1987.
Cagney and Lacey (series), 1982-88.
LA Law (series), 1989-90.
Brother Future (television movie), 1991.
Eyes of a Witness (also known as *Circumstantial Evidence*; television movie), 1991.
Back to the Streets of San Francisco (television movie), 1992.

Going to Extremes (series), 1992-93.
M.A.N.T.I.S. (series), 1994.
On Promised Land (also known as *My Precious T-Top*; television movie), 1994.
EZ Streets (series), 1996.
Nightjohn (television movie), 1996.
The Ditchdigger's Daughters (television movie), 1997.
Buffalo Soldiers (television movie), 1997.
Border Line (television movie), 1999.
Alias (series), 2001–.
Nat Turner: A Troublesome Property (television movie), 2003.
Sounder (television movie), 2003.

Sources

Books

Contemporary Theatre, Film and Television, volume 27, Gale, 2000.

Periodicals

Rocky Mountain News (Denver, CO), September 2, 1994, p. D36.
San Francisco Chronicle, February 16, 1997, p. 33.
Star Tribune (Minneapolis, MN), January 23, 1994, p. F1; January 18, 2003, p. E1.
Times Picayune (New Orleans, LA), September 2, 1994, p. E1.
Variety, March 17, 2003, p. 35.

On-line

"Alias: The TV Show," *ABC Television,* www.alias-tv.com/carl.html (July 30, 2004).

—James M. Manheim

Steve McNair

1973—

Professional football player

The starting quarterback for the National Football League's Tennessee Titans, Steve McNair has developed into one of the most effective quarterbacks in the league. Following a spectacular college career, McNair progressed smoothly as a pro player. By 2003, he had led the Titans to the Super Bowl, though not to victory, and shared the title of the league's Most Valuable Player. Throughout his career, McNair has adopted a dependable and workmanlike approach rather than going for the flashy, high-risk play. McNair has the power to rocket the ball 75 yards downfield with pinpoint accuracy and is also one of the league's best scramblers, both inside and outside of the pocket.

McNair's life is a classic American success story. He was born on February 14, 1973. His father, Selma McNair, left the family when Steve was young, leaving McNair and his four brothers to be raised by their single mother, Lucille, in a ramshackle house in rural Mount Olive, Mississippi. She toiled as a factory worker, and money was scarce. Despite material hardships, she instilled an unshakable set of values in her sons—including loyalty, fairness, an appreciation for education, and a strong work ethic. Fred, the oldest brother and star athlete, served as the family's father figure, and carefully instructed Steve in every aspect of sports. Quoted in *Sports Illustrated*, McNair said, "Fred has taught me absolutely everything I know. I can't thank him enough for giving me a map and then showing me how to take the short road when he's taken the longer one." In fact, Steve's nickname, "Air McNair," was borrowed from Fred, who was the original "Air" in the family.

Showed Early Signs of Greatness

In a family with deep athletic gifts, Steve McNair was especially blessed—and not only with extraordinary talent (as well as huge hands), but also the determination and discipline to cultivate it. He had multiple options for pursuing a professional sports career. He starred in three sports at Mount Olive High: baseball, as a shortstop and outfielder, all-state four years running; basketball, at point guard; and football, in which he played both offense and defense. As cornerback, McNair set a state record for single-season pass interceptions (15) and tied the career mark (30). In 1989, he quarterbacked Mount Olive to a small-school state title when he was a junior. A strapping 6' 2", 220-pounder who could run 40 yards in 4.6 seconds and hurl a baseball 90 mph, McNair had both the strength and speed to play a multitude of positions. McNair was strongly tempted when the Seattle Mariners baseball team picked him in the 14th round of the amateur draft, but with some guidance from Fred and Lucille he opted to pass up that opportunity, as well as several college basketball offers.

McNair's first pivotal decision in football concerned his choice of college. Many of the powerhouse schools courted McNair, including Louisiana State, Miami, Ohio State, Nebraska, and Mississippi State. But they all wanted him as a defensive back, whereas he was determined to be a quarterback. Again, Fred's counsel helped him set a course, this time to Alcorn State, in Lorman, Mississippi, where Fred had starred as a quarterback and where Steve was guaranteed a shot at the position.

Alcorn, a predominantly black school, was the country's first black land-grant institution, the first black state-supported school, and the first to provide the NFL with a black player—Jack Spinks, drafted in 1952 as a fullback by the Pittsburgh Steelers. It is a member of the Division I-AA Southwestern Athletic Conference (SWAC), which comprises other mostly black schools and has produced several football immortals, including all-time touchdown leader Jerry Rice (Mississippi Valley) and all-time rushing leader Walter Payton (Jackson State). It was virtually a foregone conclusion that attending a Division I-AA school, rather than an I-A, would seriously impair or even scuttle McNair's shot at a Heisman Trophy and potentially hurt his chances for the NFL. But the assurance of a quarterback role and the proximity to home were major pulls for him, and he decided to take the chance.

Glory Years at Alcorn State

McNair's college career became the stuff of legend, a true story of the all-conquering hero. As a mere freshman, McNair set nine records and was named Southwestern Athletic Conference player of the year. In his sophomore year, he led the nation in total offense, average 405.7 yards per game. McNair racked up numerous 500-plus-passing-yard games, and many times he added another 100 or so rushing.

After his junior year, McNair again faced a choice—should he shoot for an NFL contract or stay for his senior year of college? Once he found out his draft status was first- or second-round, the enticement was especially strong to try for the kind of deal that Tennessee quarterback Heath Shuler got when he left school early to sign with the Washington Redskins—$19.25 million over eight years. Steve wanted to take care of his mother and family financially and to get on with his professional career. But both Lucille and Fred urged him to finish his education—as well as strengthen his hand even further with one more outstanding college season.

McNair opted to remain in school, as he was quoted in *Jet*: "I am an Alcornite and will continue to be an Alcornite. I want my degree." During his senior year his game improved in several capacities. He learned how to hang in the pocket longer and find his receiver, while his rushing grew even more devastating. Among his other accomplishments that season, he finished with a phenomenal 44/17 touchdown/interception pass ratio.

Though McNair had a great year, his team fared poorly in post-season play. (Historically the SWAC champs had racked up an appalling 0-15 record in the I-AA playoffs.) In the first round of the playoffs, defending champion Youngstown (Ohio) State College destroyed Alcorn, 63-20. McNair showed great heart in playing with a badly-pulled hamstring. His rushing ability crippled, he still nailed 514 passing yards and three touchdowns. The game did not hurt his stature as a potential NFL draft pick, but it did not enhance his shot at clinching the coveted Heisman Trophy either. At season's end, McNair was third in voting for the prestigious award.

Signed with Oilers

On April 22, 1995, following a successful showing at the Senior Bowl and at the NFL scouting combine, McNair was chosen as the third pick in the first round of the draft by the Houston Oilers. Clearly, playing I-AA ball had not impeded McNair's standing. He became the highest-drafted black quarterback ever—a berth previously occupied by Andre Ware, who was chosen seventh in 1990 by the Detroit Lions. When the negotiations were finalized in August of 1995, McNair signed a contract for $28.4 million over seven years. At 22, he had become the Oilers' highest-paid player—not bad for the guy who had told *Jet*, "No matter what happens, I'm just Steve, the country boy from Mount Olive." Quarterbacks usually develop more gradually than other players. Not only is it the highest-profile position, with the most pressure, but it is also the most mentally challenging. NFL playbooks are vast, and reading the opposition's defense to make split-second play changes is incredibly complex. Plus, the pace of NFL play is far faster than in college ball and even the finest quarterback athletes can be intimidated by the speed of the action surrounding the pocket. As ESPN draft analyst Mel Kiper, discussing the development curve, said in *USA Today*, "With any quarterback, you really need to figure three years."

Oiler management made sure to cultivate McNair carefully; they did not want to rush him into play abruptly and expose him to damaging and unnecessary pressure. He was tutored intensively throughout the off-season by offensive coordinator Jerry Rhome, a premier quarterback teacher. Later, Les Steckel took on this role. During the 1995 and 1996 seasons, McNair's primary mission was to absorb knowledge and make the leap from the shotgun offense at Alcorn to the far more elaborate and turbo-charged conditions in the NFL.

Some of McNair's first games were rough initiations indeed, with the Arizona Cardinals blitzing him mercilessly in an exhibition game with as many as five pass rushers. But this merely fortified McNair's will; he knew this was part of his initiation. When starting quarterback Chris Chandler was injured late in McNair's first season, the rookie went into action. The results were impressive: in the December 11, 1995, game against the Detroit Lions, McNair entered after halftime with the Oilers down 17-7 and played out the game. He completed 16 of 27 passes for 203 yards, including a touchdown. In fact, McNair nearly pulled off a come-from-behind upset. There was little question in anyone's mind as to whether he could hack it as a pro. He started the next two games, helping the Oilers end the season with back-to-back victories over the New York Jets and the Buffalo Bills.

In the 1996 season McNair played in ten games (starting in four), and completed an impressive 88 of 103 pass attempts for 1197 yards and six touchdowns. The team went 8-8, missing the playoffs by one game. In his first six starts, McNair threw seven touchdown passes with only two interceptions. However, his leadership most impressed the coaches. In a *Sports Illustrated* piece Steckel said, "Even though he's the most humble athlete I've encountered in pro sports, he's also a leader who exudes extreme confidence." Head coach Jeff Fisher said in the same article, "If you were going to put together a list of all the things you can't coach—poise, ability to lead, competitiveness, responsibility—he has them all."

In February of 1997, the Oilers traded Chandler to the Atlanta Falcons, and McNair's career as a starter began in earnest. Meanwhile, the franchise relocated to Tennessee that same year. With big changes afoot, there was a lot more pressure on McNair.

Rose to NFL Elite

As the steady starter at quarterback, McNair steadily accrued impressive stats on third-down conversions and pass completions, touchdowns per starts, and rushing, among others. In the 1997 season, for example, his 674 yards rushing was the third-highest for a quarterback in NFL history. By the end of that season, McNair had garnered the second-best overall rating of any quarterback drafted in the previous six years (trailing only the Jacksonville Jaguars' Mark Brunell). According to Bob Sherwin of the *Knight-Ridder/Tribune News Service*, McNair is "a quarterback on the cusp of greatness," one who "is beginning to make his impact on the NFL." In the article, McNair said: "The last part of the [1997] season it finally clicked for me."

From that point on, McNair has steadily become one of the league's best quarterbacks. At the end of the 1998 season, the Titans—the Oilers' new name—had placed second in the AFC Central. In 1999 McNair led to the Titans to an AFC championship. When he took the field as the starting quarterback against the St. Louis Rams, he became just the second black quarterback to start in the Super Bowl. Though the Titans lost the game to the Rams, McNair's strong performance did not go unnoticed around the league, where McNair was considered a rising star. The Titans signed McNair to a six-year, $47 million contract extension in July of 2001.

McNair's rise to prominence has not come without a great deal of pain. During the 1999 season, McNair had midseason surgery on a ruptured disk in his lower back, then shocked football fans by returning to led his team through the playoffs. McNair's back pain had been so severe that season that he could not sit for more than 15 minutes at a time, yet he played like a champion in games. Coach Jeff Fisher told *Sports Illustrated for Kids* that during the 2001 season, "We literally had to help him off the plane when we landed because of his lower back and two or three other [injuries]. Twenty-four hours later, we're beating Oakland, with Steve running around making plays. That's how he is." McNair overcame great pain again in 2002, when turf toe, strained rib cartilage, and an injured thumb kept him from practicing throughout November and December, though he player in games. Michael Silver wrote in *Sports Illustrated* that "the mild-mannered Mississippian is becoming a mythical figure in a sport in which the athletes pride themselves on playing hurt," but McNair's wife Mechelle offered a softer image when she explained "he's a big baby at home…. He'll be limping, grimacing, complaining all week, saying there's no way he'll play, and then I'll see him on Sunday running around like nothing's wrong." Coach Jeff Fisher told *Football Digest,* "Steve is the toughest player I have ever coached."

In 2002, the Titans rebounded from a 1-4 start by winning 10 of their last 11 games and taking the AFC

Central championship. The *Football Digest* gave much of the credit for the turnaround to McNair, who inspired his teammates by overcoming a series of nagging injuries. Team owner Bud Adams told the magazine: "[McNair] doesn't know what pain is. He's a warrior." Ever humble, McNair explained: "We are professionals. We had to start playing like it. We had to look into ourselves and find a way to win. We couldn't allow things to keep going the way they started off." Their spectacular comeback season was ended when they lost 41-24 to the high-powered Oakland Raiders in the AFC Championship game. McNair came in third in league MVP voting, but was not named to the Pro Bowl.

McNair's shining reputation was somewhat tarnished in the summer of 2003 when he was arrested on drunken driving charges and also found to be in illegal possession of a loaded handgun. McNair quickly acknowledged his fault in the incident. According to *Jet*, McNair announced: "It's something you don't usually see out of me. But I put myself in a situation. I've got to get out of it, and I will bounce back from it."

During the 2003 season, McNair put the troubles of the summer behind him and embarked on the most successful year of his career. Starting in 14 games, McNair piled up 3,215 passing yards while completing 62.5 percent of his passes. With 24 touchdowns and just seven interceptions, he led the NFL in quarterback ratings with a rating of 100.4. With running back Eddie George playing a smaller role in the team's offense, McNair was now clearly the star. The Titans finished the regular season 12-4, but were eliminated from the playoffs in a game played in frigid, snowy conditions against the New England Patriots.

In January of 2004 McNair was named the league's co-MVP, along with Indianapolis Colts quarterback Peyton Manning. McNair was the first black quarterback ever to win the NFL's highest honor. "I would like to thank the guys who paved the way for myself and a lot of other guys," McNair told *Jet*, naming quarterbacks Warren Moon, Doug Williams, and Randall Cunningham. "Those guys paved the way for us as Black quarterbacks to come into the league and be successful." Later, McNair was named the league's

MVP by the Associated Press. By the end of the 2003 season, he was one of just five quarterbacks to have passed for 20,000 yards and rushed for 3,000 yards.

Reflecting on his successes in a 2003 interview with the *Sporting News*, McNair said: "This is all I've ever wanted to do, what I dreamed about in Mississippi, playing on Sundays in the NFL. I'm not surprised by what is happening to me now. I just want to enjoy it and have fun with it. The opportunity is here. I don't want to waste it." As 2004 season began, many Titans fans hoped that soon McNair would achieve the greatest NFL dream of all: a Super Bowl title.

Sources

Books

Stewart, Mark, *Steve McNair: Running and Gunning*, Millbrook Press, 2001.

Periodicals

Football Digest, April 2003, p. 52; February 2004, p. 48.
Jet, January 31, 1994, p. 50; September 26, 1994, p. 49; January 26, 2004, p. 46.
Knight-Ridder/Tribune News Service, November 27, 1998.
New York Times, September 28, 1994, p. B11; January 22, 1995, p. 2.
Sports Illustrated, August 30, 1993, p. 76; September 26, 1994, p. 40; December 5, 1994, p. 85; September 1, 1997, p. 188; November 17, 2003, p. 56; September 6, 2004.
Sports Illustrated for Kids, November 1, 2003, p. 58.
The Sporting News, August 22, 1994, p. S8; November 28, 1994, p. 6; August 12, 1996, p. 42; January 3, 2000, p. 16; November 24, 2003, p. 14.
USA Today, April 12, 1995.

On-line

"Steve McNair," *Tennessee Titans*, www.titansonline.com (September 15, 2004).

—Mark Baven and Tom Pendergast

S. Epatha Merkerson

1952—

Actor

S. Epatha Merkerson has made a name for herself playing Lt. Anita Van Buren on the long-running, Emmy award-winning police drama, *Law & Order*. For more than a decade, fans have tuned in to watch the show's ensemble cast portray gritty, often straight-from-the-headlines, New York crime stories. Merkerson is also an accomplished stage and screen actor, having performed on and off Broadway, in film, and on television. Her talents have earned her attention from the industry's most prestigious award granting organizations.

Merkerson, S. Epatha, photograph. © Michael Kim/Corbis.

S. Epatha Merkerson was born on November 28, 1952, in Saginaw, Michigan, and raised by her mother, a divorced postal employee, in Detroit, Michigan, along with four siblings. At the age of 13 Merkerson's family moved to an all-white neighborhood and experienced racism that she remembers well. During the 1960s, Detroit erupted in racial riots that made relations between blacks and whites living there uneasy. "Each day my brother Zephry and I would guess how many new For Sale signs had gone up," she told *People Weekly* magazine. In Detroit, Merkerson also had a scary run-in with the police. While driving with her brother in 1967, Merkerson had a police officer point his gun at the back of her head while his partner inspected her brother's identification. The police were looking for a suspect driving a similar car. Although she and her brother were released, Merkerson remembered the encounter to *People Weekly* as "terrifying."

Merkerson did well in school and continued her education at Wayne State University in Detroit. While earning a bachelor of fine arts degree from the university, Merkerson experienced racial discrimination. As "the only black person" in Wayne State's drama program at the time, "I was actually told not to audition for things," she told *People Weekly*.

Upon graduation in 1975, Merkerson left Detroit for Albany, New York, to pursue her acting career. She soon joined a children's theater company. At the same time she met Toussaint L. Jones Jr. whom she would date for many years. The couple married in March of 1994.

In 1986 with a little bit of luck and a lot of hard work Merkerson entertained millions of children and adults as Reba the Mail Lady on the popular *Pee-wee's*

At a Glance . . .

Born Sharon Epatha Merkerson on November 28, 1952, in Saginaw, MI; married Toussaint L. Jones, 1994. *Education:* Wayne State University, BA, fine arts, 1975.

Career: Actor, 1975–.

Awards: Obie Award, 1991, for *I'm not Stupid*; Helen Hayes Award, for Outstanding Lead Actress in a Resident Play, 1999, for *The Old Settler*.

Addresses: *Agent*—David Nesmith, PMK/HBH Public Relations, 650 5th Avenue, 33rd Floor, New York, NY 10019.

Playhouse television show. As a spin-off of *Pee-wee's Big Adventure,* actor Paul Reuben's first feature film combined old educational film segments, puppets, marionettes, and human characters with fun and games, and an irreverent take on societal conventions. Racial, social, and sexual conventions were challenged, always in good humor. On one show Pee-wee marries a bowl of cereal; on another, a white female character goes on a date with an African-American cowboy. The cast used a hilarious mix of camp, surprise, and silliness to win six Emmy Awards during its first season. The show developed a cult following and soon became part of popular culture, spawning a second movie and *Pee-wee's Playhouse Christmas Special* in 1988. Dolls, toys, and *Pee-wee's Playhouse* themed paraphernalia found a brisk market until the craze came to an end when Reubens was arrested for indecent behavior in August 1991.

Merkerson's role on *Pee-wee's Playhouse* caught the attention of Dick Wolf, the executive producer of *Law & Order.* In 1993 Dick Wolf, the show's executive producer, was urged to "add a woman to the regular cast or the show would be cancelled," Merkerson said during an interview with National Public Radio. But Wolf admitted to *People Weekly* that he "fell in love with her" for her role on *Pee-wee's Playhouse* and cast her on *Law & Order* without an audition. Merkerson had landed a part on what would become the longest-running crime series and the second longest-running drama series in the history of television. On *Law & Order,* Merkerson plays Lt. Anita Van Buren, a tough, no-nonsense type who can hold her own against the male-dominated police department. Van Buren is also the mother of a child killed because of a gunman's inability to read. A series regular, she dispenses wisdom and supervision to New York City detectives. The cast earned an Emmy in 1997 and holds the record for the

most consecutive Emmy nominations (11) for Outstanding Drama Series. *Law & Order* has spawned successful spin-offs—*Law & Order: Special Victims Unit* and *Law & Order: Criminal Intent.* A third show, *Law & Order: Trial by Jury,* premieres in 2005.

Despite her career success, Merkerson still finds she has to struggle at times to bring some rather obscure African-American realities to her roles. Merkerson told the *St. Louis Post-Dispatch* that "I came into this business with no illusions, especially about television. It's very stereotyped." Citing a particular *Law & Order* episode involving a black man passing for white unbeknownst to his white wife, Merkerson felt the child playing their offspring in reality wouldn't have been dark-skinned. She lobbied vigorously for a more fair-skinned child but for the episode but was overruled. "We try to do shows that are correct," she explained to the *St. Louis Post-Dispatch.* "Not politically correct, not artistically correct, but correct in reality. It's the minutiae, those little things that present themselves in our culture that I've spent my career fighting for."

In addition to her television work, Merkerson has performed in a long list of theater productions and films. For her work in theater she earned an Obie Award in 1991 for *I'm not Stupid* and a Helen Hayes Award in 1999 for her work in *The Old Settler.* The Pulitzer Prize-winning play *The Piano Lesson* earned her both a Tony and Drama Desk nomination for Best Actress. She also appeared in such films as *Prizzi's Honor, Postcards from the Edge, Jacob's Ladder, Terminator 2: Judgment Day, An Unexpected Life,* and *Radio.* Merkerson is scheduled to complete production on the movie *Lackawanna Blues* in 2004, co-starring Jimmy Smits and Rosie Perez.

But acting is not Merkerson's only activity. Having lost one of her close friends to lung cancer, Merkerson decided in 1994 to quit smoking herself. She told the *Los Angeles Daily News,* "I woke up one morning and it just felt like an elephant was standing on my chest." A year later she lost another friend to the disease. Merkerson dedicates time to lung cancer prevention, working with kids to spread awareness about the dangers of smoking. She told the *Los Angeles Daily News,* "One thing I've realized is celebrity can be used for real important things. People seem to listen a little more acutely to those who are in front of the camera. If you're going to hear it from me because I'm Lt. Van Buren, then that's really cool." She is an active participant with the Campaign for Tobacco-free Kids and organizations such as Cancercare have honored Merkerson for her work.

Selected works

Films

Prizzi's Honor, 1985.
Navy Seals, 1990.

Jacob's Ladder, 1990.
Terminator II, 1991.
Radio, 2003.
Jersey Girl, 2004.
Lackawanna Blues, 2004.

Plays

The Piano Lesson, 1990.
I'm Not Stupid, 1991.
The Old Settler, 1998.
F**king A, 2003.

Television

The Cosby Show, 1984.
Pee-wee's Playhouse, 1986.
Elysian Fields, 1989.
Equal Justice, 1990.
Here and Now, 1992.
Mann and Machine, 1992.
Law & Order, 1993—.
A Place for Annie, 1994.
A Mother's Prayer, 1995.
Breaking Through, 1996.

An Unexpected Life, 1998.
It's a Girl Thing, 2001.

Sources

Periodicals

Daily News (Los Angeles), November 12, 2001, p. L7.
Essence, September 2003, p. 122.
Hollywood Reporter, October 21, 2002, p. 11.
People Weekly, August 13, 2001, p. 93.
St. Louis Post-Dispatch, June 10, 1998, p. E8.

On-line

"S. Epatha Merkerson," NBC, www.nbc.com (July 23, 2004).
"Pee-Wee's Playhouse," Nostalgia Central, www.nostalgiacentral.com/tv/kids/pee.htm (July 24, 2004).
"Audio Interview with S. Epatha Merkerson," National Public Radio, www.npr.org/features/feature.php?wfId=1069210 (July 25, 2004).

—Sharon Melson Fletcher

Steve Mills

1960(?)—

Sports executive

Mills, Steve, photograph. © Mike Segar/Reuters/Corbis.

As president and chief operating officer of MSG (Madison Square Garden) Sports, Steve Mills is one of the most important executives in the world of professional sports. He oversees the business operations of three New York teams that play at Madison Square Garden: the New York Knickerbockers of the National Basketball Association (NBA), the New York Rangers of the National Hockey League (NHL), and the New York Liberty of the Women's National Basketball Association (WNBA). With a staff of 150 and responsibility for an estimated $700 million in assets, Mills supervised day-to-day operations, including finances, business strategies, and marketing for all three teams. Only the activities of players on the court (or ice) remained officially beyond his purview, but he exercised increasing influence over those as well.

A native of Roosevelt, New York, near New York City, Mills was born around 1960. His father was a teacher and basketball coach, his mother a social worker. He grew up a Knickerbockers fan and lived around the corner from future NBA legend Julius "Dr. J" Erving, who made a career in basketball seem like something worth striving for. At the Ivy League's Princeton University, from which Mills graduated with a sociology major and an economics minor, Mills was a three-year starter at the position of guard and helped lead Princeton to two Ivy League championships.

Played Professional Basketball in Ecuador

At six-feet, one-inch tall, Mills was small for a professional basketball player, but he still hoped for an NBA career. After he was passed over during the NBA draft, he took a job as manager of new business development at New York's Chemical Bank. The officer who recruited him was a former Brown University basketball player and was sympathetic to Mills's continuing dreams of making the pros, offering to defer Mills's start date until. after Mills played professional basketball in Ecuador for a year. But after that year, Mills called a halt to his basketball career. "I had committed to myself that if I wasn't good enough to play in the NBA, I wasn't going to be one of those guys who spend years and years bouncing around playing semi-professional basketball," Mills told Black Enterprise.

At a Glance . . .

Born in 1960(?) in Roosevelt, NY; father a teacher and basketball coach, mother a social worker; married; wife's name Beverly; two daughters, Kristen and Danielle. *Education:* Princeton University, B.A. in sociology.

Career: Ecuador, professional basketball, 1981-82; Chemical Bank, New York, manager of new business development, 1982-83; NBA Properties, account executive, 1983-86; NBA Properties, national programs manager, 1986; NBA special events department, 1987-93; NBA special events department, vice president, 1989; NBA commissioner's office, vice president for corporate development, 1993-95; NBA, vice president for basketball and player development, 1995-99; New York Knickerbockers, executive vice president for franchise operations, 1999-2001; Madison Square Garden sports team operations, president, 2001-03; Madison Square Garden Sports, president and CEO, 2003—.

Selected memberships: Board of Trustees, Basketball Hall of Fame; Board of Directors, USA Basketball; Board of Directors, Salvation Army of Greater New York.

Addresses: *Office*—Madison Square Garden, 2 Pennsylvania Plaza, New York, NY 10121.

hands-on training for an executive career ahead, as Mills explained to *Black Enterprise*: "I was able to develop a skill set that touched every aspect of the business." He also helped develop the "Dream Team" concept that united NBA stars Earvin "Magic" Johnson, Michael Jordan, Larry Bird, and Charles Barkley on the gold medal-winning United States 1992 Olympic basketball team.

Became Involved with Player Development, Community Relations

The next step for Mills was closer involvement with the game of basketball itself. After he spent two years (1993-95) as vice president of corporate development with the NBA Commissioner's office, he took on the newly created position of vice president for basketball and player development in 1995. Here he supervised the programs that moved high school and college players up the pipeline to the NBA and got a taste of the high-stakes world of player salaries and team finances. His most visible effort during the late 1990s, though, was his central role in the creation of the WNBA in 1997. By this time, Mills was the highest-ranking African American in the NBA organization.

In 1999, motivated by a desire to be involved with the fortunes of an individual team, Mills joined the New York Knickerbockers as executive vice president of franchise operations, with a 14th-floor office at Knicks headquarters and responsibility for the revenue side of the team's existence. "There are guys out there that I…came into the league with, and they played, and I'm doing this, and my NBA career's going to be a lot longer than theirs is," Mills reflected in conversation with the *New York Times*. He was promoted to the position of president, MSG Sports Team Operations, in June of 2001. Mills was officially involved with such tasks as business planning and the identification of new revenue streams, but he soon found that his new job put him in the day-to-day crucible of New York sports headlines.

Mills plunged into controversies such as the withdrawal of the Knickerbockers' playoff training camp from South Carolina in protest of that state's refusal to stop flying the Confederate battle flag at its statehouse, and he was among the Knicks executives who tried to deal with the difficulties caused by player Latrell Sprewell. He was instrumental in bringing former NBA star Isiah Thomas to New York to serve as Knicks president in 2003. Rumored to be a favorite of Cablevision CEO James Dolan, the executive with ultimate responsibility over Madison Square Garden and all its teams, Mills proved to be an expert at navigating the byzantine corporate structure that governed Madison Square Garden. Mills was credited with instituting fan-friendly policies and with a new emphasis on community relations.

Returning to Chemical Bank, Mills found his way back to basketball after a high school friend tipped him off in 1983 to a job as an account executive in an NBA office dealing with corporate sponsorships. Mills submitted a resume that same evening, and five weeks later was hired. Although he told *Princeton Alumni Weekly* that the job was "as low as you can start on the totem pole," it was an advantageous time to be joining the NBA, for the league was in the process of branching out to become an international marketing empire. Mills was promoted to national programs manager for the NBA's properties division in 1986, and then spent from 1987 to 1993 in the NBA's special events department, becoming its vice president in 1989.

There, Mills oversaw such events as the league's McDonald's Championship, which featured a game between the Milwaukee Bucks and a team from the former Soviet Union. Mills traveled the globe, working with venues, hotels, and broadcasters. It was all

For example, he expanded the Madison Square Garden Cheering for Children Foundation to provide after-school programs for over 30,000 New York City children. Mills was selected as one of *Savoy* magazine's 100 People of Influence and as one of *Sports Illustrated*'s 101 Most Influential Minorities in Sports. He participated in an African American Heritage Celebration organized by New York Senator Hillary Clinton, and among his community service posts were seats on the boards of directors of the Salvation Army of Greater New York, the Arthur Ashe Institute for Urban Health, and USA Basketball. Mills, his wife Beverly, and their two daughters made their home in South Orange, New Jersey.

Promoted to the position of president and CEO of MSG Sports at the end of 2003, Mills took on responsibility for all the sports-related activites of Madison Square Garden, which included collegiate as well as professional sports. In a sense, he was the person in charge of the total sports "product" offered at the famous arena. For all his business expertise and accomplishments, though, the onetime pro basketball aspirant remained focused on the game itself. Asked by *Black Enterprise* what his next goal might be, he answered, "For us to win some championships here in New York." Some observers, though, predicted that Mills would become basketball's first African-American commissioner.

Sources

Periodicals

Black Enterprise, October 2002; September 2003, p. 114.
New York Daily News, October 8, 2002, p. 56; December 23, 2003, p. 57.
New York Times, February 29, 2000, p. B2.
Princeton Alumni Weekly, February 21, 2001.
USA Weekend, February 17, 2001.

On-line

"Steve Mills," *The League: Black Ivy Alumni League,* www.theleagueonline.org/ASmills.php (September 16, 2004).
"Steve Mills," *MSG Sports,* www.thegarden.com/inandaroundgarden_SteveMills.html (September 12, 2004).

—James M. Manheim

Arthur Mitchell

1934—

Choreographer, dancer

Members of the Dance Theatre of Harlem call Arthur Mitchell the "Pied Piper of Dance." Mitchell, one of the first blacks to succeed in the field of classical ballet, founded the Dance Theatre of Harlem in 1969 in an effort to provide minority students with a chance to learn and perform classical ballet. He has been leading the troupe ever since and has presided over an extensive ballet school, worldwide tours, and performances of both classical and modern dance. *Boston Globe* contributor Christine Temin called Mitchell "a preacher of sorts," an artist whose "gospel is one of discipline, hard work, education, goals set and then met. His own goal, of course, was to show that blacks could dance classical ballet. He realized that aim with his Dance Theatre of Harlem, now famous for its energy, purity of style, dedicated dancers and diverse repertory."

Since its founding, Mitchell's Dance Theatre of Harlem has included a school educating hundreds of would-be dancers, as well as a group of professionals—graduates of the school—who perform. The school is located in Harlem and draws many of its pupils from that struggling neighborhood. Many are on scholarship, and all are encouraged to pursue a well-rounded education. Mitchell told the *Philadelphia Inquirer* that his goal is to use dance "to build better human beings." He added: "The young people today, particularly minority kids and inner-city kids, they need some kind of motivation as well as compassion. We live in a very technological society. Very few people are spending time to develop the soul."

Raised on Modern Dance

No one—least of all Arthur Mitchell—would have predicted that he would become a classical ballet star, an artist of the first rank in one of the nation's best companies. He was born and raised in Harlem, and his early interest in dancing and dramatics was encouraged by his school teachers. As a teenager he enrolled in New York's High School of the Performing Arts, a public institution made famous by the television show *Fame.* There he excelled in jazz and modern dance but was determined to try his luck with classical ballet.

He came to the demanding art form relatively late, and of course he was one of only a few black students in his classes. Instructors told him he had little chance of breaking into the all-white ranks of classical ballet, but he persisted. Mitchell told the *Philadelphia Inquirer* that he chose ballet because of "prejudice." He explained: "I wasn't getting work, and I thought I'd better get classical technique, because then I'd be so good I couldn't be turned down." He soon landed a scholarship with the School of American Ballet, where he became the student of renowned choreographer George Balanchine.

In 1955, Balanchine invited Mitchell to join the New York City Ballet. Mitchell told the directors of the company that he didn't want to work with them if a massive publicity campaign would be built around his being the first black to be so honored. "I didn't want any Jackie Robinson stuff about breaking the color

At a Glance . . .

Born on March 27, 1934, in New York City. *Education:* Attended New York High School of the Performing Arts; studied under choreographer George Balanchine at the School of American Ballet.

Career: New York City Ballet, principal dancer, 1955-69; National Ballet Company of Brazil, founder, 1966; Dance Theatre of Harlem, co-founder, with Karel Shook, and artistic director, 1969–.

Memberships: National Endowment for the Arts Council; President's Commission on White House Fellowships; Market Theatre Foundation, South Africa, honorary patron; New York State Council on the Arts; New York City Cultural Affairs Advisory Commission.

Awards: National Medal of Arts, 1987; Kennedy Center Honor for lifetime contribution to the performing arts, 1993; American Academy of Arts and Letters, Award for Distinguished Service to the Arts, 1994; MacArthur Foundation Fellowship, 1994; inducted into Cornelius Vanderbilt Whitney Dance Hall of Fame, 1999; Heinz Award, 2001; Dance/USA Honors, 2004.

Addresses: *Office*—Dance Theatre of Harlem, 466 W. 152nd St., New York, NY 10031. *Web*—www.dancetheatreofharlem.com.

barrier," he said in the *Philadelphia Inquirer.* "I wanted to be tested on the merits of my dancing. Balanchine…felt the same way. Of course I knew I was the only black person there, but there was no issue about it. No problem. Balanchine cast me in ballets like he cast everyone else." The imaginative Balanchine even created a duet called *Agon* specifically for Mitchell, a work *Philadelphia Inquirer* dance critic Nancy Goldner described as "Balanchine's profoundest exploration of partnering as both a physical exercise and a metaphor of the tensions in love relationships."

Became Pioneer in Ballet

As a principal dancer with the New York City Ballet, Mitchell traveled all over the world giving performances. He was the first black man to perform classical ballet in the Soviet Union, where ballet is considered a pinnacle art form. The dancer told the *Washington*

Post that his Soviet hosts "were mind-boggled at the sight of a black man dancing classical ballet." In fact, Mitchell began to find such special notice annoying. He knew that other black dancers could perform ballet as well as he could, if they were allowed the same opportunities—especially dance scholarships—that helped launch his career.

Mitchell was in a taxicab on his way to the airport in 1968 when he heard over the radio that Martin Luther King Jr. had been assassinated in Memphis. The news stunned Mitchell, and it proved a turning point in his career. He had planned to continue his work with the National Ballet Company of Brazil, which he had established two years earlier. Instead, he told the cab driver to turn around and head back into Harlem. Mitchell told the *San Jose Mercury News:* "After hearing of King's death, I came back to Harlem and set up a dance school in a garage. Nobody said I could do it. I started with 30 kids and two dancers, and inside of four months I had 400 kids."

Mitchell wanted to give black children another route out of the ghetto—one through the arts, especially dance. He also wanted to prove, once and for all, that classical ballet need not be the exclusive realm of whites. "What we started out to do, to prove, was that black children, given the same opportunity as white children, could be great dancers," he told the *Lexington Herald-Leader.* "We proved that in just a few years. Then we wanted to take that company of black dancers and showcase them in the city, the country, the world, to show people what black artists could do. We did that."

Formed Unique Dance Company

The energetic Mitchell had strong opinions about how he wanted his company to perform. He sought to preserve an American dance repertory, calling attention to the unique contributions this country has made to ballet. Over the years his repertory has included balletic versions of *A Streetcar Named Desire* and *John Henry,* the latter based on the American ballad pitting a man against a machine. He also drew widely on the works of Balanchine, his former mentor. Mitchell told the *Chicago Tribune:* "In the early days, I figured, 'What better way to grow but to dance Balanchine's repertory?'… But it's the eclecticism of the American dancer that is his and her strong point—their versatility…. I was criticized as being too eclectic, not knowing what kind of company I wanted. We did jazz and classical, for instance." Mitchell defended his actions by pointing out that his productions appeal to a broad base of people, rather than those who merely like classical ballet. "Notice we used the word dance and not ballet," he said in the *Philadelphia Inquirer.* "That other word tends to turn people off. Then, we chose theater, so audiences will know that we want to attract more than just the dance public. We're after the public."

Initial fears that the nation's dance enthusiasts would not support an all-black ballet troupe soon vanished, and Mitchell's Dance Theatre of Harlem forged a reputation for both innovative modern works and imaginative staging of old classics. "When the curtain goes up, the first thing the audience sees is that the dancers are black," he told the *Philadelphia Inquirer.* "If they don't see it, something is wrong. The real questions are, 'What are they doing? And, how well are they doing it?' Dance Theatre of Harlem is a major ballet company." In the *Philadelphia Daily News,* Mitchell explained that his decision to cater to mass tastes is actually one of the company's strengths. "Dance Theatre of Harlem is an example of American classicism," he said, "And by that I mean that we stress eclecticism and strong dramatic elements. There's a difference between being classic and being classical. When you are classical, you are an imitation of an original. But if you're a classic, you are unique. This notion I got from Balanchine."

The Dance Theatre of Harlem has toured in the United States and abroad. The company even mounted a full-length ballet for the Public Broadcasting System, an honor accorded only the finest of troupes. A high point came in 1987, when the group made a two-month visit to the Soviet Union for a series of performances. Not only was Mitchell invited to teach in Russia—the first American artist of any race to receive such a request—but his company met full houses and standing ovations everywhere it went. Mitchell told the *Chicago Tribune:* "In Leningrad, on the stage where the Kirov Ballet performs, they came onstage and gave us a champagne salute. It was like being a rock star. I think that brought the company as artists to another level, that feeling of acceptance by the best." Over the years the company has grown increasingly eclectic in its dance offerings, leading some to charge that it is watering down classical ballet. Yet Mitchell has remained a staunch defender of eclecticism and innovation, and the Dance Theatre has consistently won accolades for the variety and interest of its performances.

Struggled through Financial Crises

Beginning in about 1990, the Dance Theatre of Harlem faced the first in a series of recurring financial crises. The cancellation of several performance dates, the withdrawal of some corporate sponsors, and a continued shortfall in government funding for the arts led to a significant reduction in revenues. Mitchell was forced to lay off his dancers and most of his staff and cancel much of the 1990 season's roster. At the time Mitchell told the press that the move did not mean the end of the company; instead, it was a means to keep the operation from plunging into deep debt. Fortunately, new corporate sponsors appeared to help defray expenses, and the troupe was back in business by early 1991. Mitchell was far from relieved, however. "We have taken our first step back on land," he told the *Boston Globe.* "But if we take a wrong step, we'll be back in the sea."

Through the mid-1990s and into the 2000s, financial troubles became distressingly commonplace. In 1995 the company was forced to reduce its staff of dancers from 52 to 36, and in 1997 dancers walked out, charging that the company had become overly reliant on apprentices and non-union dancers. In 2004, the company was forced to slash its budget in half, to about $5 million, and to lay off the remaining paid employees. "Dance Theatre is in an unprecedented crisis,"' a dance executive close to the company told *Crain's New York Business.* "The obligations they've incurred and the financial mismanagement are so over the top that, unless there's a big infusion of cash, the place will probably close down in a month or two."' By the fall of 2004, however, the company remained in business. The Dance Theatre of Harlem's financial problems are not unique in an age when federal funding of the arts is dwindling and corporate sponsorship must be spread broadly across numerous charities and organizations. Mitchell has been able to sustain his dance company because of its fine reputation, his own personal charisma, and the laudable goals of the company and its satellite school. By the mid-2000s, however, many supporters of the company charged that Mitchell must relinquish control to professional managers if the company is to survive.

Whatever the future of the Dance Theatre of Harlem, there can be no doubt that Mitchell created one of the most important American dance companies in history. A true pioneer, Mitchell has always recognized the importance of the arts. "Put the arts first, give us the children first, and there won't be any AIDS or homelessness," he once told the *Boston Globe.* "The kids you see in the street get their hope from something chemical—and it doesn't last. Our society doesn't have enough real hope. That's what the arts give you." Mitchell sees the dawn of the twenty-first century as a precarious time for art, and hence for the health of American youth. Voicing his concerns in the *Boston Globe,* he expressed a fear that someday, "people [will] wake up and realize there is no art in their lives. And then it will be too late."

Sources

Periodicals

Arizona Republic, November 23, 1987.
Boston Globe, November 11, 1990.
Chicago Tribune, May 7, 1989.
Crain's New York Business, April 19, 2004.
Dance Magazine, July 1994; October 1996.
Jet, September 27, 1993; August 9, 1999.
Lexington Herald-Leader, June 25, 1989.
Nation, January 3, 2000.
Orlando Sentinel, March 11, 1990.
Philadelphia Daily News, November 17, 1987.

Philadelphia Inquirer, November 15, 1987; February
13, 1991; June 14, 1991; July 24, 1991.
San Jose Mercury News, February 14, 1988.
Washington Post, March 14, 1989; March 13, 1990.

On-line

Dance Theatre of Harlem, www.dancetheatreofhar-
lem.com (September 14, 2004).

—Mark Kram and Tom Pendergast

Cecil Murray

1929—

Religious leader

The Rev. Cecil (Chip) Murray is the religious leader every spiritually-conscious person would like to follow. A man of exceptional integrity, he heads a church whose congregants have included Dionne Warwick and Arsenio Hall, a church supported by an annual budget of tens of millions of dollars, which is nevertheless a church that takes loving care of the less fortunate in Los Angeles' inner-city black community. He is a tireless campaigner for jobs and training programs, never turns anyone in need away from his door, and somehow has also found the time to spearhead the construction of low-income housing projects, start drug rehabilitation programs, and organize funds for college scholarships. He is a truly focused man, whose life is his work, and whose work is his life.

Born on September 26, 1929, Chip Murray grew up in a middle-class black neighborhood in West Palm Beach, Florida, the second of three children. The family lost their mother when they were very young and were sent to stay with relatives for a short time. But their father remarried and brought them back to their home, where their stepmother gave them the loving support they needed to ease their way to adulthood.

Pledged Oath with Father

The principal of the school his son Chip attended, Edward Murray was commonly known as "Prof." He was a powerful influence upon his children, teaching them by personal example to practice what they preached. What Prof Murray preached was never to knuckle down to racism, a lesson that was painfully slammed home one night when he and his two sons confronted three white bigots who had been bullying indigent blacks on their way to collect government-issue food. Edward Murray tried to reason with the whites, but met only flying fists and curses. After the fight was over, he took some blood from one of his cuts and sealed a blood oath with each of his two sons, to make them swear to love and protect their fellow blacks.

"I guess my dad was about the most fearless person I knew," Reverend Murray told the *Los Angeles Times* in August, 1992: "I'm sure he must have felt the fear, so he must have gone on in spite of it." Go on Prof Murray did, but the pain and fear of that night were so overwhelming that he began to turn to alcohol in order to dull them. Insidiously the bottle began to claim him, until it finally broke up his second marriage. Alcohol-sodden, he died in 1952 at just 52 years of age, leaving behind nothing for his son Chip but the memory of the oath to protect black people from racism and to help them in any way possible.

For seven years, this promise lay fallow in Cecil Murray's mind. He had chosen to enter the Air Force after his 1951 graduation from Florida A&M University, and the demands of his first post as a jet radar intercept officer in the Air Force's Air Defense Command left him little time for public service of any kind. He was just as busy after he moved on to the post of navigator in the Air Transport Service, but the essence of his father's blood oath was brought forcibly back into

At a Glance . . .

Born on September 26, 1929, in Lakeland, FL; son of Edward W. and Minnie Lee Murray; married Bernadine Cousin, 1958; children: Drew David. *Education:* Florida A & M University, BA, 1951; School of Theology at Claremont, Doctor of Religion, 1964. *Military Service:* US Air Force, captain, Jet Raider interceptor and navigator; US Air Force Reserves, 1951-61.

Career: First African Methodist Episcopal Church, minister; religious posts in Los Angeles, Seattle, Kansas City, and Pomona, 1977–.

Memberships: African Methodist Episcopal Church, general board, 1972-92; National Council of Churches, general board, 1972-92; NAACP; SCLC; Urban League; United Nations Association of the USA; National Council on Aging, general board, 1988-93;.

Awards: Soldiers' Medal for Heroism, 1958; William Nelson Cromwell Award, 1977; Ralph Bunche Peace Prize, 1992; AME Church Daniel Alexander Payne Award, 1992; NAACP, Los Angeles Community Achievement Award, 1986; National Association of University Women, Outstanding Role Model, 1992.

Addresses: *Office*—Senior Minister, First AME Church, 2270 S Harvard Blvd, Los Angeles, California, 90018.

his memory when tragedy stalked into his life for the second time.

Found Calling

Catastrophe announced itself with an explosion in the nose tank of a jet in which he was flying, just as it was lifting up from a runway. Within moments, escaping jet fuel covered the plane in a seething mass of flames. Moving swiftly, Murray managed to hurl himself free. Then, when his own danger had passed, he saw to his horror that the pilot had not been as lucky. He had managed to climb out of the cockpit, but he had then slipped in the burning oil pouring along the wing, and his body was being consumed by the blaze. Murray ran to help, smothering the blaze as best he could. Nevertheless the flames burned 90 percent of the pilot's body, leaving injuries too great for him to overcome. The pilot died a few weeks later, leaving a legacy that

Murray treasured far more than the medal he won for his valor. According to the *Los Angeles Times*, "I love you," were his last words to his brave fellow crew-member—an accolade indeed from a white man born in South Carolina.

Fulfilling at least the "help your fellows" part of Murray's father's request, this incident proved to be a turning point. He continued to enjoy flying for a further three years, but his sights were no longer set on the Air Force as a long-term career. Recognizing that his true mission in life was to help his fellow blacks, and that the most powerful way of doing this was via the pulpit, he began to think of entering the ministry serving the First African Methodist Episcopal Church.

The First African Methodist Episcopal Church (FAME) was originally part of the Methodist Episcopal Church founded in 1784 in Philadelphia. Its own history as an institution began to crystallize shortly after the supposedly multiracial St George's Church built a gallery, to which black worshippers were banished. They resented being sidelined, but made no official protest until one Sunday in November 1787, when a group of white congregants tried to pull several of them away from the altar rail. The furious group of black worshippers was led from the church by a former slave named Richard Allen, who happened also to be a licensed Methodist preacher. Allen, a prosperous business man, immediately started an African-American-oriented church, and bought an abandoned blacksmith's shop in which to base it.

Studied Theology

Despite their separation by 150 years, there was no denying that FAME's origins and Prof. Murray's blood oath had sprung from the same struggle against racism. Chip Murray felt strongly that destiny was beckoning. Without further delay he entered the School of Theology at Claremont and found himself a part-time janitor's job in order to support himself while his wife added to this slender income by working as a clerk at the school.

In 1964 Murray graduated with a doctorate in religion. His first post was in Pomona, in a church too tiny even to boast plumbing. Next came a transfer to a larger church in Kansas City, after which Murray was transferred to Seattle, Washington, where he settled for a six-year stay that saw his congregation soar to reach 2,000 members.

In 1977 Reverend Murray was transferred again, this time to Los Angeles. On the surface this seemed an extremely challenging assignment, since it involved a debt-ridden church with only 300 elderly congregants, but it was not long before the Herculean task of giving the church an inviting, black-oriented identity was well under way. As a first step Murray added a liberal helping of gospel flavor to the music, which now featured drums, cymbals, and other percussion to give it a throbbing beat. Next, in order to attract young black men who could go out into the poverty-stricken inner-city community, he honored the church's founding father by starting the Richard Allen Men's Society. Today this association is involved in the nationwide fight against drugs, and is also active in mentoring fatherless children.

Struggled to Improve Life in Los Angeles

By 1990 a wide variety of activities to improve the lives of poor black Americans was making Reverend Cecil Murray's name a familiar one outside the world of the church. His style was forthright, his candid comments frequently discomforting. Unperturbed by the embarrassed sniggers of self-righteous congregants, he did not hesitate to hand out AIDS-awareness kits containing condoms whenever he found it necessary. With blistering scorn he criticized the "Just Say No, " slogan suggested by the Reagan White House as an antidote to drug use; he even took great care, in a *Los Angeles Times* article in March, 1990, to list some of the tragic social and economic consequences of such ineffectual White House equivocation.

In August 1990 *Los Angeles Times* readers felt the lash of Murray's uncompromising honesty again. His subject this time was the bitter relationship between black Californians and the 267,000-strong Korean community—a subject that was common knowledge. But the problem had seldom been treated to the media spotlight, and Murray now felt it was time to correct this deficiency. He chose to do so in an article called "Body Language Stokes the Anger," using as a painful example the contempt he found in Korean retailers in their day-to-day dealings with black customers.

As always, he did not content himself with a mere outline of the situation. Instead, he proposed a crisply-worded three-point plan for improving this obviously acrimonious relationship. First, he noted, it was vital that the two communities get together and talk, so they could understand each other's viewpoints. His next suggestion was that the Korean merchants hire some black workers, so that potential customers from the black community would be comfortable shopping in their stores. His third recommendation, the most daring one of all, proposed that the Koreans sponsor some scholarships for black youth and some workshops for budding black entrepreneurs. Murray's article was thoughtful and boldly forthright, but it did not bring a break in the cloud of bigotry. Sadly, it proved to be prophetic of further suffering to come.

Stepped into the Middle of the Racial Tensions

The storm broke in early 1991, when a high school student named Latasha Harlins was shot in the back of the head by a Korean storekeeper after an argument involving a carton of orange juice. This tragic, needless death was neither the first nor the last in the blood-spattered list that would claim the lives of 13 Korean storekeepers before another year had passed. But for inner-city Los Angeles blacks, the teenager's murder was a special symbol; the epitome of an unconcerned government, an ever-dwindling supply of jobs and a powerlessness that they were no longer prepared to endure. Latasha Harlins' death was the tinder of a long-smoldering black rage that would shortly burst forth across Los Angeles.

The detonator to the definitive explosion was set just after midnight on March 3, 1991, when four white police officers forced a speeding Hyundai to a stop on the Los Angeles freeway. They handcuffed and arrested two of the three black men traveling in the car, but found the driver, Rodney King, much more intimidating because of his hefty build and 6 feet 3-inch stature. So they hit King with two Taser darts, each carrying 50,000 volts of electricity, and followed up with 56 blows to his body. Then, as far as they were concerned, the literally long-arm-of-the-law had triumphed again.

At the time the case seemed a simple one. However, the following day it took a complicated turn after amateur photographer George Holliday produced a videotape he had made of King's brutal beating. Disciplinary Police Department action was taken against the police officers, but a horrified America demanded some public legal action. On March 3, 1992, this demand was met. After the proceedings were moved from seething Los Angeles to a county that was more friendly to the police, the televised trial of the four white officers began. It came to an end on April 29, 1992, with a verdict of "not guilty."

Inspired Peace during Riots

If the Los Angeles Police Department had imagined that their troubles were now over, they were destined for disappointment. About two hours after the verdict was announced, a liquor store in South Central Los Angeles called for police help in settling a disturbance. Four patrol cars arrived to find a swelling crowd of bystanders, who soon started throwing rocks and shouting at the police. It took just one hour for Los Angeles to start writhing in the grip of a full-blown race riot; within a day, television newscasts showed gut-wrenching footage of beatings, showers of broken glass, and laden looters staggering triumphantly through the charred wreckage of once-flourishing businesses.

On the first night of the disturbance, Rev. Murray and 5,000 of his 8,500 parishioners were praying together for peace. One-half a block away, a fire was burning, as he later said, "like Dante's Inferno," yet the firemen would not come to help unless they were guaranteed protection. Rev. Murray did not hesitate. For three hours, he and 100 other men stood between the rioters and the firemen, acting as a human shield.

An uncompromising realist, he had anticipated trouble on the very night the King verdict was announced. As reported by the *Los Angeles Times* of May 3, 1992, his message now to his flock must have come over loud and clear: "Under no circumstances will we pretend that the looting, the burning, and the arson are excusable. And in the same breath that we say that, we must say that this miscegenation of justice in the courtroom...was injurious to us all." (The entire country agreed with him. Such vociferous protests resulted from this verdict that the four policemen were retried in a Federal courtroom, and two of them were found guilty and punished for their brutal beating of Rodney King.)

The Federal trial, however, was still in the future. The immediate problem now was to stem the fury that was destroying Los Angeles. Meeting the crisis took about a week, plus 2,000 National Guardsmen, 1,000 federal officers, and 4,500 military troops mobilized by President George Bush. When the city lay in an uneasy calm again, there was time to count the unnecessary injuries, the wasted opportunities, and the ruined businesses. For everyone, the toll for the long-simmering lack of communication between the black and white citizens of Los Angeles was high–Police Department figures showed 52 dead, 20,000 jobs lost, and $735 million in property damage.

While a mere seven days saw the end of the violence, the entire country understood that years would pass before Los Angeles' deeply-rooted scars truly began to heal. For Reverend Murray, the message of difficult recuperation came as an ominous personal warning, delivered to him while the city was still in flames. It happened on the second night of the riot, just after television journalist Ted Koppel had finished taping his show at the First African Methodist Episcopal Church. Murray and a couple of companions were walking through the parking lot when several gang members suddenly stepped into their path. Menacing shouts of "You sellout!" followed Murray to his car, but he was unconcerned about the threat to his personal safety. His companions, however, viewed the incident quite differently.

Endured Threats to Build Strong Congregation

Their anxiety was quite justified, for this was not the first alarming episode Murray had experienced. For two years before the riots both he himself and the church had been the targets of a steady stream of hate mail, which had swelled to a river in mid-1991 after church members had launched a petition calling for the resignation of Los Angeles Police Chief Darryl Gates. Now the city's turmoil had brought out the true intention of these vicious attacks—to assassinate Rev. Murray and burn down the church, in order to start a full-blown race war between America's black and white citizens.

On June 20, 1993 Rev. Murray received a call from Special Agent Parsons of the FBI. Parsons warned him that his life was in danger and told him that there were hate groups bent on destroying his church. Parsons also asked him to keep their conversation private, since the FBI was currently wrapping up an investigation of a number of white supremacist groups and was expecting to make several arrests. As promised, the FBI pounced on July 15, arresting members of the White Aryan Resistence, the Fourth Reich, and a relatively new group of Nazi sympathizers called the Fourth Reich Skinheads, whose ranks included a Continental Airlines flight engineer named Christian Nadal and his wife Doris.

The Sunday following the arrests found the First African Methodist Episcopal Church buzzing with more than 2,000 congregants at each of its three morning services. Each group found its pastor calm, unshaken, and secure in his long-time philosophy of conciliation and universal redemption. In its issue of August 2, 1993, widely- read *People* magazine quoted from the sermon Rev. Murray gave on that fateful Sunday: "Soul force is greater than sword force. In this lovely city we have 146 different nations. We've got to learn how to love together. There's enough room for everybody." Amen.

A decade later, Murray has continued his mission to nurture fellowship among Americans in Los Angeles and beyond. His efforts increased membership in his congregation to nearly 18,000. One of the cornerstones of his ministry has been to encourage blacks to see themselves in a positive light. He told the *Christian Science Monitor* that "Black communities across America are bombarded from every angle with a model of black life that is full of violence, drugs, and mayhem. It's time for blacks to become more savvy about how destructive these models are, and how to quit contributing to the problem." For his part, Murray conducts seminars and workshops in local churches to help parents and educators create positive examples for black children. Under his direction FAME organizes employment programs, financial aid and counseling for the poor, and youth programs. The massive size of his church is part of Murray's plan. He told *Ebony* that "You must think big. If you think big, you will have big returns. But we must go beyond worship and praise. We must help the homeless, heal the sick, find jobs, make loans and worry about the environment. Then the megachurch will endure into the next century."

Sources

Books

Cohen, Jerry, and William S. Murphy, *Burn, Baby, Burn! The Los Angeles Race Riot, August 1965,* E.P. Dutton, 1966.

Gooding-Williams, Robert, ed., *Reading Urban Uprising,* Routledge, 1993. Melton, J. Gordon, ed., *Encyclopedia of American Religions,* volume I, McGrath, 1978.

Wall, Brenda, *The Rodney King Rebellion,* African-American Images, 1992.

Periodicals

Christian Science Monitor, October 23, 2000.
Chicago Tribune, February 16, 2003.
Ebony, December 2001.
Essence, November 1992, p. 56.
Humanist, November/December 1992, p. 11.
Los Angeles Sentinel, July 22, 1993.
Los Angeles Times, March 21, 1990; August 29, 1991; October 14, 1991, sec. B. p. 1; May 3, 1992, sec. M., p. 3; August 16, 1992, p. 12.
New York Times, September 13, 1992, Sec. 4, p. 7.
People, August 2, 1993, p. 82.
Time, July 26, 1993, p. 49.
U.S. News & World Report, May 18, 1993, p. 34.

On-line

"Celebrities Pack Heroes Gala at Paramount Lot," *Black AIDS Institute,* http://www.blackaids.org/kujisource/kuji0303/Heroes_gala.htm (August 18, 2004).
First African Methodist Episcopal (FAME) Church, www.famechurch.org (August 18, 2004).

—Gillian Wolf and Sara Pendergast

Tai Murray

1982—

Violinist

Violinist Tai Murray is a rising young star within the world of classical music, and only in her early 20s, she has already been rising for over a decade. Known for her beautiful, mature phrasing and graceful bow work, Murray has received critical acclaim from coast to coast. She has also drawn attention as one of the few African-American musicians involved in classical music.

Murray first asked to play the violin when she was just two years old. Finally, just before her fifth birthday, Murray received her first violin. She began to take lessons at the Sherwood Conservatory of Music in Chicago "because I wanted to," she told the *Salt Lake Tribune.* "I started asking at a younger age, but my mother thought I should wait until I was older. I've always been drawn to music." Although Murray's one sister has taken up the flute, none of her four brothers play an instrument.

Within a few years Murray was drawing attention for her exceptional ability. As a result, her family made a beginning commitment to her future in music by spending $1,600 for a new violin and bow when Murray was just seven years old. The investment paid off, and at the age of nine she made her debut with the Chicago Symphony Orchestra. When she was young, Murray practiced her instrument between three and four hours every day. At the beginning of her fifth-grade year of school, she began being homeschooled to allow more time for her to practice, which she stepped up to five hours a day. She also began to travel to performances on a more regular basis.

At the age of 16, Murray was invited to perform as soloist with the Utah Symphony. The symphony's conductor Joseph Silverstein had heard her perform in a master class in Chicago when she was just 14 years old and again at a chamber-music performance at the University of Indiana, and he was duly impressed. Following her performance, Jeff Manookian reported in his review for the *Salt Lake Tribune,* "[Murray's] elegant demeanor was the complete antithesis of the opulent music gushing from this rare talent. Every note from the 16-year-old Murray was marked with superhuman intonation amid abundant pyrotechnical display. Throw in her magical bowing technique (at times, bow changes were imperceptible), and what comes is an awe-inspiring execution." Edward Reichel, the reviewer for Salt Lake City's *Deseret News,* noted, "Despite her young age, Murray is an incredible violinist. She possesses the technical mastery of her instrument that is needed to dazzle her audience. She coaxes a fine, mellow tone out of her violin, and she has an enticing vibrato."

In 2001 Murray made her debut in San Antonio, Texas, as guest soloist with the San Antonio Symphony. In his review in the *San Antonio Express-News,* Mike Greenberg wrote, "Murray impressed immediately with her depth of tone, mature phrasing and steely sweetness.…In temperament, she was more like a chamber musician than the typical concert artist. Though she projected a big assertive sound, she also melded into the orchestral backdrop with uncommon grace."

Murray returned to the Chicago Symphony Orchestra to perform once again when she was 21 years old. Wynee Delacoma, who reviewed her performance for the *Chicago Sun-Times,* wrote, "Murray's supple, clean violin line was front and center.... In Berstein's rapt passages, she established an extraordinary psychological relationship with the audience. She was completely absorbed with her meandering melody line, at time sounding like she was improvising, at other times as if she were following some musical voice audible only to herself."

Murray studied music at the University of Indiana and graduated with honors from the school's Artist Diploma program. Following her tenure at the University of Indiana, she enrolled in a three-year program at New York's Julliard School of Music to study under Joel Smirnoff. After a performance with the Julliard Orchestra in 2002, Dennis Rooney wrote in *The Strad,* "Displaying sophisticated bowing and vibrato, her performance was at times deliberate but never stolid. It was enhanced by a warm tone that easily soared above the orchestra...." She graduated from Julliard in the spring of 2004.

By 2004 Murray stage appearances included the Chicago Youth Symphony Orchestra, the St. Ambrose Chamber Orchestra, and the Oakland-East Bay Symphony, as well as the symphonies in St. Louis, San Antonio, Greensboro, North Carolina, and Washington, D.C. Her performance with the Sacramento Philharmonic in 2002 was named the classical performance of the year by the *Sacramento Bee.* Her awards include top honors in the Indiana University Concerto

Competition, the Sphinx Competition, and the Julliard School Concerto Competition. She also earned a Certificate of Honor for musicianship by the Accademia Chigiana in Siena, Italy. In 2004 she was awarded a $15,000 career grant from the Lincoln Center's Avery Fisher Artist Program.

Although Murray's home base has moved from Chicago to New York, her family is still very involved with supporting her career, both emotionally and financially. For lessons, wardrobe, travel, rehearsing, Murray and her family have spent approximately $30,000 annually to maintain and promote her career. "Playing the violin is a very expensive endeavor, which is why you don't see many Black violinists," Murray's mother Ellen Murray told *Ebony.* "It takes the efforts of the whole family to help us in this endeavor. It takes a village to raise a Black violinist."

Another financial strain for Murray is acquiring an instrument. A high-quality instrument, such as an Italian-made Guarneri or Stradivarius, can cost from $150,000 to upwards of $1 million. Throughout her career, Murray, who doesn't own an instrument of this caliber, has used the standard practice of borrowing a violin from a music store when she is on tour. During her days at Julliard, she played a school-issued 1727 Guarneri del Gesu.

In the fall of 2004, 22-year-old Murray earned a spot in a two-year professional residency program at the Chamber Music Society of Lincoln Center. She also performs regularly with chamber ensembles in New York, Philadelphia, and Jacksonville, including the Ritz Chamber Players, the only black chamber orchestra in the country. Her third tour is planned for 2005, during which she will tour with Musicians from Marlboro, an extension of Vermont's Marlboro Music Festival.

Despite her intense practice and performance schedule, Murray finds time to enjoy life. She loves dance, both as an observer and a participant, including tango, salsa, ballet, swing, and modern. She also likes to read, knit, and spend time with her friends. In an interview with the Chamber Music Society of Lincoln Center, she described a typical day: "I like to get in two or three hours of practicing as soon as I get out of bed.... Late afternoon I might take a walk or read a book. I'm a bit of a night owl so after dinner...I like to practice into the wee hours of the morning." Her advice to young musicians: "Practice makes perfect, and quality over quantity."

Sources

Periodicals

Charleston Daily Mail (WV), May 20, 2004.
Chicago Sun-Times, April 3, 2004.
Ebony, January 2001, December 2003.

Deseret News (Salt Lake City, UT), November 22, 1998; November 28, 1998.
Florida Times-Union (Jacksonville), January 12, 2003.
News & Record (Greensboro, NC), May 8, 2004.
Salt Lake Tribune, November 22, 1998; November 30, 1998.
San Antonio Express-News, February 6, 2001.
St. Louis Post-Dispatch, October 19, 2003.
The Strad, August 2002; July 2003.

On-line

"Tai Murray," *Chamber Music Society of Lincoln Center,* www.chambermusicsociety.org/artists/art ist_detail.php?id=242 (August 11, 2004).
"Tai Murray: Graceful Fire," *FinalCall.com News,* www.finalcall.com (August 11, 2004).

—Kari Bethel

Samuel Milton Nabrit

1905-2003

Biologist, educator, university president

A celebrated marine biologist who specialized in studying the ability of fish to regrow their fins after injury or disease, Samuel Nabrit was the first black representative on the United States Atomic Energy Commission. In a long career, Nabrit found success on many fronts. He was the first alumnus of Morehouse College to receive a doctorate and the first black to be awarded a Ph.D. at Brown University. He served on various committees under three United States presidents and as president of Texas Southern University he steered the institution through many years of civil rights protests and change. Commenting late in life on the difficulties he experienced in advancing his own career, Nabrit is reported to have said that "no kite can rise unless it's going against the wind."

Born on February 21, 1905, in Macon, Georgia, Samuel Milton Nabrit was the son of James M. Nabrit, a Baptist minister and teacher, and Augusta G. West. He was one of eight children, all of whom received a college education; his brother James became president of Howard University. Nabrit attended schools in Macon and received his bachelor's degree in biology from Morehouse College in 1925. Nabrit was hired as an instructor in zoology at Morehouse in the same year and taught there until 1931; he was made professor of biology in 1928, the same year as he married Constance Crocker. At the same time he attended Brown University, where he was awarded an M.S. in 1928 and a Ph.D. in biology in 1932. He was the first African American to be awarded a Ph.D. at Brown and the first Morehouse graduate to receive a doctorate. He

later became Brown University's first black trustee, serving between 1967 and 1972.

Nabrit's doctoral research was conducted at the Marine Biological Laboratory in Woods Hole, Massachusetts, where he studied the ability of fish to regenerate their fins after injury. He continued his research after becoming chairman of the biology department at Atlanta University in 1932, and the scientific papers he published during this period remained influential in the field until well into the 1980s. He became dean of the graduate school of arts and sciences at Atlanta in 1947, where he stayed until 1955, when he became the second president of Texas Southern University. Besides being a committed researcher Nabrit was also a keen sportsman, playing baseball and football while he was at college, but excelling at the game of bridge, which he played regularly in competitions until the 1940s.

From his earliest days as a researcher Nabrit was committed to encouraging more black students to stay on at college and pursue advanced research. After moving to Texas, Nabrit was involved in the Upward Bound program, a scheme to encourage scholarship winners to stay in college beyond their first year. In his eleven years at Texas Southern University Nabrit attracted a great deal of outside funding and more than doubled the enrollment of black students. As university president he also supported students in their successful protests against segregation in public buildings in Houston, declaring that no student would be expelled for civil

At a Glance . . .

Born Samuel Milton Nabrit on February 21, 1905, in Macon, Georgia; died December 30, 2003; married Constance Crocker, August 8, 1927. *Education:* Morehouse College, BS, biology, 1925; Brown University, MS, 1928, PhD, 1932. *Religion:* Baptist.

Career: Morehouse College, Atlanta, GA, instructor in zoology, 1925-27; Morehouse College, professor of biology, 1928-31; Atlanta University, professor of biology, 1932-55; Atlanta University, dean of graduate school, 1947-55; University of Brussels, Belgium, research fellow, 1950; Texas Southern University, president, 1955-66; appointed member of United States Atomic Energy Commission, 1966-67; Southern Fellowship Fund, Atlanta, GA, executive director, 1967-81.

Memberships: American Society of Zoologists; Institute of Medicine of the National Academy of Sciences; National Association for Research in Science Teaching; National Institute of Science (president 1945); Societe d'honneur Francaise; Society for Developmental Biology; Phi Beta Kappa.

Awards: Brown University, William Rogers Award.

rights activities while he was president of the university. He also encouraged black students who had been expelled from other colleges to move to Texas Southern. At the same time he worked with the protesters to prevent violence and managed to persuade white local businessmen and politicians that he was doing all he could to control the protests. Nabrit was not afraid of confrontation, however, and was respected for his strong sense of integrity. He is reputed to have fired the coach of Texas Southern's acclaimed track team when he learned that students were being recruited for their sporting prowess alone. When he left Texas Southern to join the Atomic Energy Commission in 1966 he was involved in a dispute with the university's board of regents over the amount of influence they had on university policy.

Nabrit dedicated his life to public service, sitting on many committees and boards, including a period as president of the Association of Colleges and Secondary Schools and various government committees. From 1956 until 1962 Nabrit served on President Eisenhower's National Science Board and was then selected by President Kennedy to be the United States representative to Niger. In 1966 President Johnson asked him to serve on the Atomic Energy Commission and he became the first black to do so. In 1967 Nabrit became director of the Southern Fellowships Fund, an organization he founded to support and mentor black students studying for doctorates. He continued to work for the fund until his retirement in 1981. In 1985 Brown University established the Nabrit Fellowship to assist graduate students from minority groups and in 1999 Nabrit was once again was honored by Brown University with a portrait hanging in Sayles Hall, alongside portraits of the university's most distinguished faculty. Nabrit died of a heart attack following a bout of pneumonia on December 30, 2003, at the age of 98.

Selected writings

Periodicals

"The Role of the Fin Rays in Tailfins of Fishes Fundulus and Goldfish," *Biological Bulletin*, April 1929.
"Human Ecology in Georgia," *Science Education*, October 1944.
"The Negro in Science," *Negro History Bulletin*, January 1957.

Sources

Periodicals

Jet, January 26, 2004.
New York Times, January 6, 2004, p. B8

On-line

"Conversation with President Lyndon B. Johnson," *Scripps Library Presidential Recordings* (sound recording), millercenter.virginia.edu/scripps/diglibrary/prezrecordings/johnson/1966/06_1966.html (August 24, 2004).
"Always a Smile, Always in Control. Farewell: Samuel M. Nabrit '32 PhD," *Brown Alumni Magazine Online*, brownalumnimagazine.com/storydetail.cfm?ID=2321 (August 24, 2004).
"Samuel Nabrit," *Biography Resource Center*, www.galenet.com/servlet/BioRC (August 24, 2004).
"Samuel Nabrit, Scientist and Scholar," *University Faculty Voice*, www.facultyvoice.com/News/news2004/01-January/Obituary.html (August 24, 2004).

Other

Sammons, Vivian O., *Blacks in Science and Technology*, Beta Kappa Chi, text of citation, April 30, 1980.

—Chris Routledge

Christina Norman

1960(?)—

Television executive

Norman, Christina, photograph. Scott Gries/Getty Images.

Christina Norman was named president of the cable channel VH1 in early 2004, a career achievement that made her one of the highest-ranking African Americans in the television industry. For two years prior to that, Norman had been instrumental in helping revive ratings at VH1, which had been struggling to lure and keep new viewers with a mix of music videos and its music- and pop-culture-centered original fare. Norman enjoys a reputation for being able to lead the various creative teams at VH1 and before that, at MTV, where she had worked for much of the 1990s. Judy McGrath, MTV Networks Music Group president, summed up Norman's talents in a *Crain's New York Business* profile. "When kids are kicking the backseat in the car, you need someone who can drive," McGrath told journalist Elizabeth MacBride.

Born in the early 1960s, Norman grew up in the New York City boroughs of the Bronx and Queens, and earned a degree in film production from Boston University. She began her career in the advertising business as a specialist in the tabletop shot, which is the static image of the product in a commercial. Many television-commercial professionals dread having to undertake the task, considered the least creative part of the thirty- or sixty-second ad. "I still remember my last spot," Norman told *Advertising Age* writer Richard Linnett. "It was for Tylenol Allergy Sinus. It was all night shooting because the pill was the wrong color and we were using a motion control camera, which takes forever to set up."

Norman was hired at MTV Networks in 1991 as a production manager for its own unique in-house promotional spots. Her first big break came in the lead-up to the premiere of the *Beavis and Butt-Head* series. One of her supervisors was trying to recruit staff for the animated series, which quickly became one of the top-rated shows on the cable channel and a pop-culture phenomenon. The boss came through the office asking if anyone knew about animation, and Norman volunteered—though she had no experience in the field. She assumed she would just learn on the job, she recalled in the interview with *Crain's New York Business*. "I can figure anything out," she told MacBride.

During the 1990s, Norman put together the campaigns for MTV shows or promotional features like *The*

Osbournes and the *10 Spot*. She rose to the post of senior vice president for marketing, advertising, and on-air promotion, and gained the attention of executives at Viacom, which owns MTV, as an executive able to both inspire and lead creative professionals. In April of 2002, she moved over to sister network VH1 as an executive vice president and general manager. McGrath had brought Norman on board to help revive its fortunes. At the time, VH1 was logging poor ratings in prime-time hours, though the network had experienced surges of new viewers thanks to original programming such as *Pop-Up Video* and *Behind the Music* just a few years before. Norman recognized the need to find a new batch of programs to lure an audience. "A hit can change anything," she told *Daily Variety*'s Melissa Grego. "I think the game is just to have more at bats for VH1. We've got to keep feeding that pipeline with more ideas, more fresh series, and episodes of things people like."

Norman set the creative teams to work and also oversaw a new identity campaign for VH1. In less than a year, the channel launched several new hit series under her watch, beginning with *I Love the '80s*, a look back at music and trends for one year in the decade. It was such a success that it spawned spin-offs about the 1970s and the 1990s. *Bands Reunited* also proved a popular show, as did a barb-filled look back at the week's celeb- and entertainment-business events

called *Best Week Ever.* There were just a few foul balls in that series of at-bats that Norman spoke of: *Rock Behind Bars,* a series showcasing bands formed by prison inmates, was one. It prompted objections from victims' families in some cases. There was also a contract for a Liza Minnelli-David Gest reality-television show that was inked just before rumors that the marriage was disintegrating reached the tabloids.

The other shows were a success, however, and VH1's prime-time viewers in a key age demographic jumped from 243,000 to 339,000. Norman's efforts were further rewarded when Viacom executives named her VH1's president in January 2004. The promotion made her one of the top African-American women among the ranks of entertainment executives. She had previously landed on lists such as *Ebony* magazine "Top 10 African-Americans in Television" and the *Hollywood Reporter*'s "Top 100 Women in Entertainment." Though she recognized the significance of her achievement, she also noted that Viacom and other companies were working to ensure that a new era was underway. "There have been times when certain viewpoints were not being represented but now they're being heard," she said in an interview with *Multichannel News* writer Diana Marszalek. "We are doing diverse programming. That's good for business, good for viewers and good for our branding."

Norman's office is in the Viacom headquarters on Times Square in the heart of midtown Manhattan. She lives in the city with her husband and two daughters, and is active in a New York City program called PENCIL (Public Education Needs Civic Involvement in Learning). Designed to bring together the city's public-school system and the private sector, its most popular feature—in which Norman has participated—is "Principal for a Day," in which executives take over a school for a day. But VH1 and its fortunes remain her primary focus. "When I first took this job, friends would say, 'I love VH1 but I'm not watching it anymore,'" she told *Brandweek* writer Becky Ebenkamp. "Now, they're calling up and saying, 'Oh, I loved that show!'"

Sources

Periodicals

Advertising Age, September 23, 2003, p. S26.
Brandweek, March 22, 2004, p. 26.
Broadcasting and Cable, April 22, 2002, p. 10.
Crain's New York Business, January 27, 2003, p. 24.
Daily Variety, April 19, 2002, p. 1.
Ebony, October 2002, p. 86.
Hollywood Reporter, December 2, 2003.
Multichannel News, March 24, 2003, p. 8A.

—Carol Brennan

Charles Ogletree, Jr.

1952—

Lawyer

Charles Ogletree, Jr., is considered one of the most tenacious and successful trial lawyers in the United States. The Harvard University professor is a passionate advocate of a defendant's right to a fair trial within the American justice system—a Constitutional right one might find it difficult to receive if a member of a minority group. For several years Ogletree worked in Washington, D.C.'s public defender's office, a difficult area of law which generally attracts only the most ideologically dedicated and stamina-imbued law school graduates. Those experiences were carried over to the Ivy League halls of Harvard Law School, where Ogletree has single-handedly made significant inroads into how students at the country's most prestigious legal training ground view both the African-American community and the criminal justice system.

Ogletree was born on December 31, 1952, to Charles Sr. and Willie Mae Ogletree, the first of their five children. He grew up in a rural northern California community called Merced, which had a small African-American population that lived south of its railroad tracks. His maternal grandparents, known as Big Daddy and Big Mama, were an important influence on the young Ogletree. With his grandfather he would fish for hours, and from Big Mama he learned how to cook and thus, learning self-sufficiency. Both grandparents he would later credit as having a profound influence on his demeanor and tactics as a trial lawyer. The marriage of Ogletree's parents, however, was plagued by periodic violence, and they eventually divorced, although they remained on good terms. A bright child who spent free hours in the public library and brought home good grades from school, his first brushes with the law—especially watching his father being taken away in cuffs after incidents of domestic violence at the Ogletree house—instilled in him a deep distrust of and feelings of powerlessness toward the law enforcement community.

The Ogletree family was part of the migrant worker community around Merced, and when Charles, Jr., became old enough he also began working in the fields, picking figs and other fruit. From this he learned a certain inner competitiveness—every day he would strive to pick more than he had the day before. As an adult, Ogletree compared his humble upbringing with that of his own children, raised in relatively affluent African-American middle-class surroundings: "In the normal course of their lives they meet professors, lawyers, doctors," he recalled for Sara Lawrence in *Lightfoot in I've Known Rivers: Lives of Loss and Liberation*. "Before I got to college I had never met any of these kinds of people." Another incident that occurred in his teens severely impacted Ogletree's views on law, order, and justice, especially for members of the African-American community. In high school he was part of a tight-knit group of young African-American males that were determined to stay out of trouble. All earned good grades, were involved in athletics, and respected Eugene Allen, considered the brightest of the clique. After Allen had a run-in with Merced's high school football coach—and incurred the wrath of the town's white community by dating the daughter of a white judge—Allen was accused of setting fire to the coach's residence. He was convicted and

At a Glance . . .

Born on December 31, 1952, in Merced, CA; son of Charles Sr. and Willie Mae (Reed) Ogletree; married Pamela Barnes, 1975; children: Charles J. III, Rashida Jamila. *Education:* Stanford University, BA, political science (with distinction), 1974; Stanford University, MA, political science, 1975; Harvard Law School, JD, 1978.

Career: District of Columbia Public Defender Service, Washington, DC, staff attorney, 1978-82, director of staff and training, 1982-83; American University, Washington, adjunct professor, 1982-84, deputy director, 1984-85; Antioch Law School, Washington, adjunct professor, 1983-84; Jessamy, Fort & Ogletree (law firm), Washington, partner, 1985-89, Jessamy, Fort & Botts, of counsel, 1989–; Harvard Law School, Cambridge, MA, visiting professor, 1985-89, director, introduction to trial advocacy workshop, 1986, assistant professor, 1989-93; director, Criminal Justice Institute, 1990–; professor, 1993; director of clinical programs, 1996; Jesse Climenko Professor of Law, 1998; associate dean for the clinical programs, 2002; vice dean for the clinical programs, 2003; director, Charles Hamilton Houston Institute for Race and Justice, 2004.

Selected Memberships: National Legal Aid and Defender Association (defender committee member); Southern Prisoners Defense Committee (chair, board of directors); Society of American Law Teachers (board member); National Mentor Program (member, advisory committee); Stanford University Board of Trustees; University of the District of Columbia Board of Trustees.

Selected Awards: Award of Merit, Public Defender Service Association, 1990; Personal Achievement Award, National Association for the Advancement of Colored People and the Black Network, 1990; Nelson Mandela Service Award, National Black Law Students Association, 1991; National Bar Association, Presidential Award for The Renaissance Man of the Legal Profession, 1996; Washington Bar Association, Charles Hamilton Houston Medallion of Merit, 2001.

Addresses: *Office*—Harvard Law School, Hauser Hall, Room 516, 1575 Massachusetts Ave., Cambridge, MA 02138.

sent to a youth camp, where he was involved in a race riot and charged with the death of a white inmate. Sent to San Quentin for the crime, he was co-charged with killing a prison guard, although the decision was overturned and Allen was removed from Death Row. The sad story of one of his closest friends made Ogletree painfully aware of how difficult it was for young African-American males to receive fair treatment once inside the criminal justice system.

Ogletree himself stayed out of trouble. In 1970, after high school, Ogletree enrolled in Stanford University outside San Francisco. His dormitory marked the first time he had ever had his own room. At college, Ogletree became dismayed by the elitism of the institution. Fortunately, he was also quite near the epicenter of the Black Power movement that had coalesced around San Francisco, the city of Oakland, and the University of California at Berkeley at that point in history. Ogletree became a campus radical, organizing an Afrocentric (though still integrated) dormitory, where he met his future wife, Pamela Barnes. He edited a campus Black Panther newspaper called *The Real News* and traveled to Africa and Cuba as part of student activist groups.

Ogletree's first intensive experience in the courtroom sparked his intent to pursue trial law as a career. He attended nearly every day of the trial of Black Power activist and Communist Angela Davis. Some of parts of the Davis trial were tedious, Ogletree recalled in *I've Known Rivers*, but "the process and strategies were fascinating. I sat there wondering how they were going to tie all this together." After graduating with a bachelor's degree in political science from Stanford in 1974, Ogletree stayed on a year to earn a master's degree. At the urging of his soon-to-be wife, he applied to Harvard Law School; the newlyweds moved to the Boston area upon his acceptance and enrollment in the fall of 1975. From the start, Ogletree recalled, he felt unease in the markedly different, monied East Coast enclave. Furthermore, the city was then in the middle of a vicious battle over busing that pitted its ethnic-American communities against the African-American populace. Academia itself was also especially tedious, and at one point he nearly quit the prestigious School of Law. "At Harvard the pressure was on, participation was mandatory, there was always a lot of competition and tension in the air," Ogletree recalled in *I've Known Rivers*. He survived by closely allying himself with other African-American students and continued his political activism, even becoming national president of the Black Law Students Association.

After receiving a juris doctor degree from Harvard in 1978, Ogletree was hired by the District of Columbia's Public Defender's Service, which provided free legal counsel to those accused of a crime who were unable to afford an attorney guaranteed them by the U.S. Constitution. With wife Pamela and son Charles III (a family made complete with the arrival of daughter Rashida in 1979), Ogletree moved to the nation's capital, also home to some of the most blighted and crime-ridden urban pockets in the country. He had originally thought that perhaps he had not gained very much from his experiences at Harvard, but later asserted that everything he learned came back in surprising ways as he began to argue cases before the bench—and win. Soon Ogletree had gained a reputation as a formidable courtroom presence, although it took him a while to understand that himself. Initially, he would attribute most victories to luck, but then, as he told Lawrence-Lightfoot in *I've Known Rivers*, "it was only after I kept on winning and began to gain a strong reputation among my peers...that I began to admit to myself that I had a special talent for this work."

Ogletree became known for a cool, collected courtroom demeanor, which he has said was inherited from his grandfather and their fishing expeditions together, during which the elder man would sit impassively for long stretches of time. Ogletree himself took up fishing in his thirties as a means of relaxation from his hectic schedule that not only included his grueling hours in the Public Defender's Service—where he was named director of staff training in 1982—but his teaching position at American University and later Antioch Law School, rounded out by his involvements in numerous professional organizations. After a time Ogletree left the Public Defender's Service, and between 1985 and 1989 Ogletree was a partner in the Washington law firm of Jessamy, Fort, & Ogletree while concurrently serving as a visiting professor at Harvard Law School.

In 1986 Ogletree became director of Harvard's introduction to trial advocacy workshops, a program he founded to inject a more clinical, hands-on approach into a curriculum known to be a bit too focused on the theory of law. Through the intensive workshops, students—even if they are not planning a career in trial law—will walk away with a sense that the law can be "an instrument for social and political change...a tool to empower the dispossessed and disenfranchised... and a means to make the privileged more respectful of differences," as Ogletree explained in *I've Known Rivers*. He also founded and became director of the School's Criminal Justice Institute in 1990, a broad program heavily involved with the poorer communities in Boston, and began a Saturday School so African-American students could learn from other professionals of their own heritage. The conferences are often sold out and well integrated.

Ogletree also gained prominence in 1991 when he was asked by the National Association for the Advancement of Colored People to write up an investigation into the legal career of a former Equal Employment Opportunity Commission chief and African-American judge Clarence Thomas, a staunch Republican. The group thought they should cast their support of the presidential nominee for the Supreme Court on the basis of race, even though Thomas's legal rulings and writings consistently seemed to work against the civil rights principles upon which the NAACP had been founded. Ogletree drafted a 30-page report on Thomas that was instrumental in the NAACP's vote of no confidence for the nominee. He later became further embroiled in the battle against Thomas when charges of sexual harassment were leveled against the judge by a law professor and former EEOC subordinate named Anita Hill; Ogletree served as her attorney during the contentious Senate confirmation hearings in the fall of 1991.

The following year, Ogletree's career at Harvard—whose decision-makers had named him assistant professor in 1989—became the subject of controversy when a paper he had submitted to the school's *Law Review Journal* was called into question by some of the publication's staff. However, the prestigious university's dearth of tenured African-American professors as well as vicious rivalry between political camps among the student body seemed to be behind much of the flap. The *Wall Street Journal* as well as the *New Republic* covered the incident, but Ogletree was granted tenure and the *Law Review* editor censured. The fractious atmosphere that has replaced the elitism of Ogletree's student days at the school make him question his own reasons for staying on. "Am I doing right by my people working here at the university?" he wondered in *I've Known Rivers*. "This remains an open question."

Ogletree remained with Harvard, however. He became the Jesse Climenko professor of law in 1998, the vice dean for Clinical Programs at Harvard in 2003, and in 2004 he was appointed director of the Charles Hamilton Houston Institute for Race and Justice. His work in the legal profession and advocacy for racial justice brought him a great deal of media attention. He became a sought-after expert, appearing as a guest commentator on the *McNeil-Lehrer News Hour*, *Nightline*, and *This Week With David Brinkley*. He also served as the co-chair of the Reparations Coordinating Committee, a group pursuing a lawsuit to win reparations for descendants of African slaves. The group of distinguished lawyers and other experts on the committee sought to reconcile the past wrongs brought by slavery. His legal work was recognized, and the *National Law Journal* named him one of the "100 Most Influential Lawyers in America" in 2002.

In addition to legal issues, Ogletree committed himself to other causes. Determined to improve the educational opportunities for minority and needy students, Ogletree established a college scholarship fund for students in Merced, California. He is also a founding member of the Benjamin Bannekrer Charter School in Cambridge, Massachusetts, which provides after-school programs to minority children.

Selected writings

Books

Beyond the Rodney King Story: An Investigation of Police Conduct in Minority Communities, Northeastern University Press, 1995.

All Deliberate Speed: Reflections on the First Half-Century of Brown v. Board of Education, W.W. Norton and Company, 2004.

Sources

Books

Lawrence-Lightfoot, Sara. *I've Known Rivers: Lives of Loss and Liberation,* Addison-Wesley, 1994.

Periodicals

Bay State Banner, April 28, 1994, p. 17.
Boston Globe, September 9, 2004.
Jet, June 28, 1993, p. 10.
New Republic, June 7, 1993, p. 11.
Wall Street Journal, December 4, 1992.

—Carol Brennan and Sara Pendergast

John Pinderhughes

1946—

Photographer

New York-based photographer John Pinderhughes has combined careers in advertising and fine art photography. His commercial work includes advertising campaigns for major corporations while his fine art has developed quite separately. Pinderhughes is known for expansive landscapes and pictures that explore the relationship between people and their environment, traditions, and points of view. Although he describes himself as "primarily self-taught," his photographs display a deep understanding of light, shape, and form. His work has been exhibited at many galleries, including New York City's Museum of Modern Art and The Studio Museum in Harlem, and has appeared in several books, including Barbara Millstein's *Committed to the Image: Contemporary Black Photographers* (2001). He has published several books of his own, including cookbooks and children's books.

John Pinderhughes was born on January 28, 1946, in Washington, D.C. He was raised in Alabama and New Jersey, where he attended Montclair High School before going on to Howard University to major in marketing. Though he attended from 1964 to 1968, Pinderhughes did not complete his degree, dropping out in his senior year to take up photography. He later attended the WNET Film and Television Training School in 1971 and 1972.

Pinderhughes was introduced to photography while on Operation Crossroads Africa between his sophomore and junior years at college. He worked mostly in Ethiopia, where he helped to build a school, but spent time taking photographs of the landscape and people with a camera borrowed from another member of the group. Pinderhughes recalls being smitten by photography almost at once, but the trip was formative in other ways too. Unlike the other volunteers Pinderhughes refused to eat Western food, opting instead to eat in local bars and making lots of friends; his interest in food and his heritage resurfaced with the publication of his 1990 cookbook *Family of the Spirit*, in which he recorded recipes handed down from his grandmothers and other loved ones.

Returning to the United States, Pinderhughes photographed anti-war and civil rights protests at Howard University and began taking portraits to earn some money, learning how to use the camera as he went along. In 1969 he contributed photographs to a book, *Centennial Plus One: A Photographic and Narrative Account of the Black Student Revolution, Howard University, 1964-1968*. By the early 1970s he was gaining experience working in graphics departments at publisher McGraw Hill and Cowles Communications, publisher of *Venture Magazine*. It was while working for Cowles Communications doing "paste-ups and mechanicals"—setting up magazine pages for printing—that art director Tom Huestis encouraged him to help out with photographic jobs. He also became friendly with the "lab guy" at *Look Magazine* and spent time there learning the technical aspects of the craft from professional photographers who saw him as "just a black kid" and therefore no threat.

Unlike most photographers who focus on one particular type of photography, Pinderhughes enjoys two careers running alongside one another. On the one hand he is a highly successful, award-winning commercial photographer, one who has worked on advertising campaigns for big clients such as McDonald's, Miller beer, Equitable Life Insurance, and the United States Army. And on the other he is a fine art photographer whose thoughtful, cool, carefully crafted images have been exhibited continuously since the early 1970s. Such achievements in fields that few photographers manage to combine is highly unusual, but in fact the way he works—he told *Contemporary Black Biography (CBB)* that he likes to be working on two or three things at the same time—might actually be the key to his success.

Pinderhughes told Patsy Southgate in 1997 that he specializes in "warm and fuzzy" in his commercial advertising work, but as with his art images he plans each shot meticulously. For example he explained to *CBB* that when photographing landscapes he keeps maps of the areas he is interested in photographing, keeping a diary of the way light changes at different times and going back repeatedly to exactly the same spot to capture the image he wants. And light is the key to his fine art work. Pinderhughes described his fascination with "the way light falls on line and delineates line," explaining that the photographer's job is to "make [light] reveal itself." He is also interested in making the viewer work to understand or interpret his images; despite the careful planning and deliberate attempts to achieve a given effect, he would prefer his audience to figure it out for themselves.

Fascinated by people and their relationship to the past, culture, and the natural world, Pinderhughes has been called a "people photographer." One of his most successful exhibitions, at the Museum of Modern Art in 1991, consisted of a series of portraits of old people. A passionate cook, he has also explored these relationships in the two cookbooks he published in 1990 and 2003, using recipes handed down by his grandmothers and other family members and friends. He has also collaborated on children's books and is involved with the Nature Conservancy, an organization that favors a non-confrontational approach to environmental issues. Pinderhughes's work with the Nature Conservancy combines his love of the sea with a passion for conserving the natural world for his children and their children. He told *CBB* that he had come to realize that in terms of conservation we hold the future in our own hands: "If you don't think about [nature conservancy] other people will make the wrong decisions." This intensity seems to run through his work too. When asked what he most enjoyed about photography he likened his relationship with the camera to love: "When you are in love with a woman how do you say why you love her?"

Selected works

Solo Exhibitions

Dry Bones & Burnt Offerings, Bronx Museum of the Arts, New York City, 1990.
One Photographer's View, AT&T, Holmdel, NJ, 1993.
A Celebration of Nature, Holland & Holland, New York City, 1999.
John Pinderhughes: Soliloquies, Sherry Washington Gallery, Detroit, MI, 2000.
Majestic Vista: The Landscape of Eastern Long Island, June Kelly Gallery, New York City, 2000.

Group Exhibitions

The Pleasures and Terrors of Domestic Comfort, Museum of Modern Art; New York City, 1991.

Jazz Plus / Kamoinge, UFA Gallery, New York City, 1999.
Reflections In Black: A History of African American Photographers 1840 to Present, Arts & Industries Gallery, Smithsonian Institution, Washington, D.C., 2000.
Committed To The Image: A Half Century Of Black Photographers In America, Brooklyn Museum Of Art, Brooklyn, New York City, 2001.

Books

(With Vanessa Howard) *A Screaming Whisper*, Holt, Rinehart and Winston, 1972.
Family of the Spirit: Recipes and Remembrances from African American Kitchens, Simon & Schuster, 1990.
Hurt No Living Thing, McClanahan Book Company, 1999.
The Golden Rule .. .And Other Words to Live By, McClanahan Book Company, 1999.
(With Harriette Cole) *Coming Together: Celebrations for African American Families*, Jump At The Sun / Hyperion, 2003.

Periodicals

(With John Carafoli) "Thanksgiving …With All the Fixings," *New Choices Magazine* November 1991.

Sources

Books

Millstein, Barbara, *Committed to the Image: Contemporary Black Photographers*, W.W. Norton & Co., 2001.

Periodicals

East Hampton Star (East Hampton, NY), October 9, 1997.

Other

Additional material for this profile was obtained through an interview with John Pinderhughes on September 14, 2004, and from documents kindly supplied by him.

—Chris Routledge

Gene Anthony Ray

1962-2003

Actor, dancer

Gene Anthony Ray shot to fame in the early 1980s when he took on his first—and only important—role of his acting career. As Leroy Johnson in both the movie and television versions of *Fame,* Ray used his street-honed disco moves, good looks, and tough-guy personality to win over a generation of teenagers. A talented dancer, Ray's problems with drugs and alcohol prohibited him from achieving a successful comeback after *Fame*'s popularity faded.

Street Dancer

Ray was born on May 24, 1962, in New York, New York. He grew up with his mother, Jean Ray, and a younger brother on West 153rd Street in Harlem, surrounded by an extended family of aunts and uncles. Although Ray denied that he was very much like Leroy Johnson, the tough, street-kid *Fame* character that made him famous, similarities abound. Like Leroy, Ray grew up on the streets, in the rough, urban center of New York during the 1960s and 1970s. Also like Leroy, he was not trained as a dancer, but rather honed his skills dancing at neighborhood block parties. According to the London *Times,* Ray later recalled, "All the blocks had parties, not just ours. And I'd go to them and scoop all the prizes." He once claimed the award as the best male disco dancer at New York's Roseland Ballroom.

After showcasing his talent in a dance class at Julia Richmond High School, Ray was accepted into Manhattan's School of Performing Arts, the same school in

which *Fame* was based. He did not last long, however, and was expelled for disruptive behavior after a year. He later told *Seventeen,* "I got kicked out. I had beefs with the teachers and settled them the way Leroy would, by cursing the teachers out." According to Ray, as a dancer he had to carry some attitude around with him. He told *The Express,* "Because I danced, I couldn't afford to be a wimp. I mean, wherever I went to school I had to come back to that area and survive in the streets."

On the day of the auditions for the movie *Fame,* Ray skipped school to attend. One of 2,800 teenagers trying out for a part, 17-year-old Ray knocked the producers off their feet. According to *The Daily Telegraph,* the film's choreographer Louis Falco said of Ray's audition: "Gene uncovered something inside me that I hadn't witnessed before. He was just incredible. I felt like I was in the same shoes as the person who had maybe seen Fred Astaire for the first time." His brash attitude, stunning good looks, and flashy disco moves earned him the role of Leroy Johnson.

"Fame" Brought Fame

Fame hit theaters in 1980 and received widespread attention, especially from the teenage audience. Critical reviews were mixed. "*Fame* is the spur to some authentic exhilaration," noted John Coleman of the *New Statesman,* but he continued, "It is also sadly glib in its determination not to miss a contemporary trick." Despite his misgivings, Coleman did comment that

Leroy was "splendidly done" by Ray. In *The New Republic* review, Stanley Kauffman sang the movie's praises: "You keep *Star Wars* and all the sequels, with their special-effect, lab-coddled cosmic powers, and I'll take the *real* comic power of these kids."

The film follows the lives of students and several of the teachers of the School of Performing Arts, and the plot is driven along by the hard-rocking disco music and dance routines intermixed with the dialogue. The film won Academy Awards for best musical score and best song. In the film Ray's character, Leroy, is a streetwise kid who, like Ray, earned his place in the elite school by sheer, raw talent. Also like Ray, what Leroy had in dance moves, he lacked in social skills. He was rough, tough, and untouchable, in a way that made teenage girls swoon. His character, who helped make Lycra pants and leg warmers a hit trend during the early 1980s, was so popular that it was one of the few that was reused in the television series *Fame,* which ABC began airing in 1982.

Just twenty years old when the television series began to air, Ray's personal fame was at its peak. He hired two secretaries to answer the some 17 thousand fan letters he received daily. He also began to show up to work wearing a platinum diamond-studded medallion and made little secret of his love of partying. Although the television series was positively reviewed in the United States, it failed to gain an audience and was dropped by ABC. However, *Fame* had developed a strong following of 11 million regular viewers in the United Kingdom and was, consequently, picked up by MGM Television, which distributed it in syndication from 1983 to 1987. In 1982 Ray toured Britain with other *Fame* cast members. The show *The Kids from Fame* played to adoring teenage audiences. The following year, a television special based on the tour was aired in the United States.

Troubles Took Over

By 1983 Ray's life was beginning to spiral out of control. In June, the $400,000 house he had purchased in a white neighborhood of Rockland County, New York, was intentionally set afire. Ray, who was only using the house on weekends, had planned to move into the house permanently after his younger brother finished high school in the Bronx. The two-story home was set ablaze in four separate locations on the outside of the house, reportedly aided by gasoline. No one was ever convicted, although it was rumored that the fire may have been racially motivated.

The following summer, in 1984, Ray's mother was arrested in a drug raid along with 14 others, including his grandmother, three aunts, and three uncles. Ray's mother, 46-year-old Jean Ray, was charged with dealing heroin and cocaine. His grandmother, 66-year-old Viola (Lilly) Ward, was carrying six ounces of cocaine and a loaded .38-caliber pistol when she was taken into custody. In March 1984, after a two-week trial, Ray's mother was convicted. According to police, she sold heroin and cocaine to undercover officers in several buys in 1983 that took place in Harlem bars. In April 1984 she was sentenced to at least 15 years, with parole eligibility in 1999.

Although Ray, who remained very loyal to his mother, was never implicated in the drug dealings, he was under tremendous stress. After failing to show up for *Fame* rehearsals 100 times and self-admittedly using drugs between shoots, he was fired from the show in 1984. Ray's use of drugs and alcohol continued unabated. His personal and professional life in shambles, he sat idle for five months, during which time he gained nearly thirty pounds. Eventually Ray began to work out, slimming down again to his normal 28-inch waist size. He spent the remainder of his life attempting to reclaim his place in the spotlight but was never successful.

He briefly revived his dance career with his performance in the Weather Girls' musical video of "It's Raining Men," and he received positive reviews for his performance as Billie in the British stage production of *Carrie* in 1988. However, he failed both in his attempt to set up a European dance tour and then to open a *Fame*-style dance school in Milan, where he shared a flat with a porn actress. In 1992, with his use of alcohol out of control, Ray stole a bottle of wine from a Milan supermarket and used it to attack two men who were taunting him. He was arrested, although the charges were later dropped. Having squandered his wealth to feed his drug habit, Ray was unemployed, and rumors spread that he was sleeping on park benches in Milan. In 1995 a rumor also circulated that Ray had died of AIDS.

Once again Ray made an attempt to regain control of his life. In 1995 he had a cameo role in *Out of Sync*, a film co-produced by *Fame* co-star Debbie Allen. The following year he appeared briefly in the movie *Eddie*, starring Whoopi Goldberg. In 1996 Ray was diagnosed HIV-positive. The high toxicity of the drugs he was then required to take made him weak, although he did appear in Dr. Pepper and Diet Coke advertisements during the late 1990s. His mother, now released from prison, helped care for him. When Ray was interviewed by the British Broadcasting Association in the early 2000s, as part of a *Fame* reunion special, he appeared thin and weak. He suffered a stroke in June 2003, and died on November 14, 2003 in Manhattan. Ray, who brushed aside questions of his sexuality, never married.

Selected works

Films

Fame, 1980.
Out-of-Sync, 1995.
Eddie, 1996.

Television

Fame, 1982-87.

Sources

Periodicals

Daily Telegraph (London), November 20, 2003.
Express (London), November 21, 2003, p. 66.
Independent (London), November 20, 2003.
Jet, June 13, 1983, p. 59; July 11, 1983, p. 18; March 19, 1984, p. 61; April 23, 1984, p. 39; April 11, 1994, p. 53; December 8, 2003.
National Post (Ontario), November 21, 2004, p. S7.
New Republic, June 7, 1980, pp. 22-24.
New Statesman, July 25, 1980, pp. 26-27.
New York Times, November 19, 2003, p. C14.
Scottish Daily Record, September 28, 2002, p. 34.
Seventeen, December 1982, pp. 126ff.
Times (London), November 26, 2003.

—Kari Bethel

Jimmy Rodriguez

1963(?)—

Restaurateur

Jimmy Rodriguez's story has all the elements of a fairy tale. In this story, a high school dropout helps his Puerto Rican father sell seafood from a pushcart alongside a highway. Slick cars whoosh past, ferrying baseball stars to nearby Yankee stadium, or across the river to Manhattan penthouses. The boy, possessed of a kinetic personality that any politician would envy, parlays the pushcart into a storefront, then upgrades that to a restaurant. A decade later he oversees a chain of four restaurants, each bearing his name: Jimmy. He is the one

Rodriguez, Jimmy, photograph. Thos Robinson/Getty Images

whirring down the highway in a Jaguar convertible; his friends are the baseball stars, his girlfriend a famous actress. And his restaurants, featuring fresh seafood like he once sold on the street, pull down over $10 million a year. By 2004, however, the ending of this fairy tale was clouded by the sale or closure of each of his restaurants. Would they reopen, returning Jimmy to fame? Or had something gone disastrously wrong?

Started Selling Seafood on the Street

Born Jaime Rodriguez Jr. in 1963 to Puerto

Rican immigrants, Rodriguez—known as "Jimmy"—grew up above a grocery store in the Bronx. It was a tight-knit community and Rodriguez blossomed in it, developing his trademark mile-wide smile and unflappable charm. A close friend later described Rodriguez to *Crain's New York Business,* saying "Jimmy walks into a room, and he'll say hello to 100 people before he leaves." Rodriguez was particularly impressed by his grandfather Francisco Rodriguez. "He taught me the value of a job, and that patience and kindness can make or break a person," Rodriguez told *Crain's New York Business.*

While in high school, Rodriguez joined his father selling seafood from the trunk of their car parked near the Major Deegan Expressway. Soon they added a seafood chowder Rodriguez's father whipped up from leftovers. The duo eventually set up a stand on a shady corner and added other Puerto Rican seafood dishes. Next they opened a 50-seat storefront named Marisco del Caribe—Spanish for Caribbean seafood. By this time Rodriguez had dropped out of high school to help run the business full-time.

complex included a nightclub that featured live Latin music, from local bands to living legends like Tito Puente. The combination, headed up by Rodriguez's non-stop charm, proved a winner. It served $5 million in meals its first year and soon had 125 people on its payroll.

Rodriguez didn't just score a lucky hit with the café. He worked behind the scenes to acquire the secret ingredient that would guarantee the restaurant's success: celebrities. His uncle, Ellie Rodriguez, was a player's agent for Major League Baseball. He made sure that players who visited nearby Yankee Stadium stopped off at his nephew's restaurant. Soon, Jimmy's became a New York Yankees hangout. Ruben Sierra, a Yankees outfielder, invested $450,000 in the restaurant. Shortstop Derek Jeter held parties in the restaurant. The entire team donated signed jerseys to decorate the restaurant's walls.

With the sports stars in tow, other celebrities followed. Bill Cosby, Jennifer Lopez, President Bill Clinton, legendary Cuban singer Celia Cruz, rap star Fat Joe, and a host of Big Apple movers-and-shakers dined at Jimmy's. The celebrity presence guaranteed press coverage and a steady stream of clientele. One prominent client, however, brought Jimmy's not only notoriety, but controversy. During Fidel Castro's 1995 visit to New York, Rodriguez hosted a dinner for the Cuban dictator. Though 300 guests jammed the dinner to hear Castro speak, Cuban groups protested vocally in person and in the press.

Over the next five years, Jimmy's Bronx Café continued to attract celebrities and money. Rodriguez became a man-about-town. He sponsored over 100 Little League teams and supported Bronx-based charities from food shelters to senior citizen housing. He also implemented a series of Bronx business mixers that regularly drew enthusiastic crowds of up to 500 small business leaders. "They don't have to sit around and listen to speeches," Rodriguez told *The Bronx Beat,* explaining the event's appeal. "Deals can be cut here. Someone can work a floor and meet three to four hundred people, all in one night."

Moved His Magic to Manhattan

In 2000 Rodriguez helped spark the Harlem Renaissance when he opened Jimmy's Uptown in Harlem. "The inner city is underdeveloped, and whoever gets there first is gonna cash in," Rodriguez told W. Rodriguez's piece of the action was a 17,000 square-foot restaurant he bought for $900,000. He sunk in another half million in renovations. Even before construction was finished, Rodriguez proved his celebrity pull when Woody Allen hosted an opening party for his film *Sweet and Lowdown* in the half-finished restaurant.

At a Glance . . .

Born Jaime Rodriguez Jr. in 1963(?), in Bronx, NY.

Career: Restaurateur. Marisco del Caribe, Bronx, NY, owner/manager, late 1980s-1993; Jimmy's Bronx Café, Bronx, NY, owner/manager, 1993-2003; Jimmy's Uptown in Harlem, New York, NY, owner, 2000-04; Jimmy's Downtown, New York, NY, owner, 2002-04; Jimmy's City Island, Bronx, NY, owner, 2003-04.

Memberships: Hispanic Federation of New York City; Bronx Chamber of Commerce; South Bronx Board of Trade.

Awards: House of Representatives, New York, The Bronx, Tribute to Jaime 'Jimmy' Rodriguez, 1997; *Crain's New York Business,* 100 Top Minority Business Leaders, 2003.

Addresses: *Office*—c/o Jimmy's Downtown, 400 E. 57th St., New York, NY, 10022.

The restaurant industry proved the perfect environment for Rodriguez's infectious personality. He thrived on the hustle and bustle, the constant hand-shaking. He later told the *New York Times,* "I love being the host." By the 1990s, Rodriguez decided to expand. He found an abandoned car dealership located on the same expressway where he and his father had once hawked seafood. With a clean credit rating and a successful restaurant, he turned to local banks for the $2.5 million asking price. "I figured we'd just be arguing over the interest rate," Rodriguez told *Crain's New York Business.* But he was wrong: every bank turned him down. Desperate, he even considered approaching a local loan shark. Fortunately Mother Nature stepped in. A snowstorm caused severe damage to the dealership, and the seller lopped the price in half. A friend of Rodriguez's agreed to lend him the money and, in 1993, Jimmy's Bronx Café opened.

Launched First Jimmy's Restaurant

Perched on a hillside, Jimmy's Bronx Café included a 300-seat dining room with wrap-around windows looking out to Manhattan. An outdoor deck sat another 400 guests. The food drew directly from the menu at Marisco del Caribe. "This is food from the Latin Caribbean—Cuba, the Dominican Republic, PuertoRico," Rodriguez told *The Kansas City Star.* The

Rodriguez cemented his role in Manhattan nightlife in 2002 when he opened Jimmy's Downtown, an oasis of posh urban design. A 100-foot long bar lit by candles and boasting 10 flat-screen TVs led to a white oval dining room punctuated by a giant red pillar. The food was again Caribbean but with modern touches—yucca crusted scallops, duck empanadas, black bass in grapefruit mustard salsa. The crowd was again celebrity-studded, though decidedly more white than Latino or African-American. Paying heed to the quirks of the Manhattan elite, Rodriguez even had a doggie bar installed to provide pampered pets with bottled water and tasty treats.

Rodriguez soon became famous city-wide for barbecues thrown on the terrace of the sleek penthouse he had rented in upscale Sutton Place. Ambassadors, rap stars, socialites, and regular folk rubbed shoulders and munched on spicy ribs and chicken. "I like to introduce people who wouldn't normally meet each other," Rodriguez told *The New York Times*. "There are so many diverse cultures in New York and they need to mix more or else life gets really boring." Rodriguez began popping up in the society columns and he appeared in a celebrity fashion show. He also nabbed a role playing himself in the 2002 film *Death of a Dynasty*. Meanwhile, he began a relationship with Michael Michelle, former actress on the hit show *ER*.

In 2003 Rodriguez opened his fourth restaurant, Jimmy's City Island, in a nautical area of the Bronx. Like his other places, Jimmy's City Island was slickly designed and featured fresh seafood and Latin-themed dishes. Rodriguez's empire now had nearly 300 employees and raked in sales of $10 million per year. Rodriguez was named one of *Crain's New York Business's* top minority business leaders on a list that included musician Wynton Marsalis, American Express CEO Ken Chenault, and lawyer Johnnie Cochran.

Hit Hard Times

Rodriguez's fortunes took a downward spiral at the end of 2003. After being rejected for a renovation loan, Rodriguez decided to sell Jimmy's Bronx Café. He shut the doors New Year's Eve 2003. Patrons were disappointed. "It was a place that everybody identified as very much our own," Bronx politician Jose Serrano told *The New York Times*. Within the next six months, Rodriguez sold Jimmy's City Island and Jimmy's Uptown in Harlem. In July of 2004, patrons found Jimmy's Downtown shuttered with a sign announcing renovations. After avoiding the press for several days, Rodriguez finally gave an interview to *The New York Times*. "I love being around people, but the day-to-day operations of working with 300 employees—I don't love the day-to-day." He said his future plans were to reopen Jimmy's Downtown and then open another restaurant either in Miami or Europe. Patrons already hooked on his signature mix of Caribbean seafood and Latin sounds are eagerly waiting, forks poised, dancing shoes polished. By mid-2004, it was unclear how long they would have to wait.

Sources

Periodicals

The Bronx Beat, April 3, 1995.
Crain's New York Business, March 30, 1998; December 3, 2001; July 22, 2002; June 30, 2003.
Daily News Record, May 22, 2000.
The Kansas City Star, July 29, 2002.
The New York Times, July 28, 2002; January 3, 2004; July 3, 2004.
Newsday, August 23, 1995.
W, February 1, 2000.

—Candace LaBalle

Janna Scantlebury

1984(?)—

Ceremonial guard

England's Janna Scantlebury became the first black woman to serve in an elite mounted regiment attached to the royal household. As a member of the King's Troop of the Royal Horse Artillery, Scantlebury participates in the lavish, colorful pageants such as the Trooping of the Colours every June in honor of Queen Elizabeth II's birthday. The London-born nineteen-year-old made headlines in 2003 when she became one of the historic ceremonial guards, who have guarded the royal family since the 1600s.

Scantlebury grew up in the neighborhood of Bow, part of the Tower Hamlets borough in East London. Tower Hamlets, named because of its proximity to the famed Tower of London, is a part of the city known to have been continually inhabited since the Bronze Age (c. 2500-600 B.C.E.). Her mother, Jennifer, was a local official at the borough office, and her father, Sherwin, came from Barbados. Sherwin Scantlebury had served in the British Army as well, and had been a member of the Queen's Royal Irish Hussars until 1976.

Scantlebury was the second of four children in her family, and was an outstanding athlete during her youth. She took karate and represented Tower Hamlets in a citywide track and field competition for the shot-put and discus-throwing events. Her older brother, Kenton, joined the school Cadets, Britain's version of the Reserve Officers' Training Corps, and she followed him into it. When she finished school at the age of 16, she was unsure of her career direction. She worked in an office, which she found dull, but had liked her Cadets' training, and so decided to enlist in the British

Army. "I wasn't sure what else I wanted to do," she told Wayne Veysey of London's *Evening Standard*. "I thought that if I didn't like it I could always leave."

Scantlebury's first experience with a horse came when she mounted one at the Army Foundation College in Harrogate during her basic-training stint. She was wary of the animal, but liked it anyway. As she told the *Evening Standard*'s Elizabeth Hopkirk, "I just sat on them while they held them. I was even too scared to get them out of the stables. But then I just thought 'if you don't try you don't know, so I am going to do it.'"

In May of 2002, Scantlebury began training for the King's Troop, one of the ceremonial regiments in London. The tradition of a mounted regiment to guard the king or queen dated back to 1660, during a time when intrigues and plots landed some regents or heirs to the throne in prison or even in the grave. The King's Troop dated back to 1947, when the father of Queen Elizabeth II, King George VI, revived the idea of using a mounted guard for ceremonies of state. It retains the "King" name in his honor.

Scantlebury officially joined the King's Troop in August of 2003 as one of its ten gunners, becoming the first black woman in British history to serve in a ceremonial mounted regiment. Her regiment was based in stables and barracks located in St. John's Wood, an affluent and leafy area of northwest London. She was given her own "mount," or horse, named Hackney. Many of the horses in the prestigious regiment are bred in Ireland, and arrive as five-year-olds for training. Scantlebury

At a Glance . . .

Born 1984(?), in London, England; daughter of Sherwin and Jennifer (a municipal official) Scantlebury. *Education:* Attended the Army Foundation College, Harrogate. *Military Service:* British Army, c. 2000–.

Career: Enlisted in British Army, c. 2000; became member of the King's Troop, Royal Horse Artillery, Household Guards, August 2003.

Addresses: *Office*—The King's Troop, Royal Horse Artillery, Ordnance Hill, St. John's Wood, London NW8 6PT, United Kingdom.

and her colleagues then train them to pull a heavy artillery gun and the two-wheeled cart, called a limber, on which it sits, which together weigh one and one-half tons. By tradition, the horses must pull them at a full gallop in parade events.

Some of those parades are magnificent spectacles of pomp and British pageantry held on official holidays or anniversaries. The King's Troop cannons of Scantlebury's regiment are fired for official salutes to the queen—21 rounds by custom—on days that include the Queen's birthday in April, her official birthday in June, the anniversary of her coronation, the state opening of Parliament, and when a royal birth is announced. The Queen's June birthday event is known as the Trooping of the Colours, and dates back to the 1700s. Its name comes from a tradition in which regiments are supposed to show their flags, or "colors," annually so that other regiments will recognize them in battle. Their official uniform consists of an ornate jacket with a plumed busby-style hat. The busby has a red flap that traditionally was to be filled with sand, to protect against enemy sabers. Scantlebury carries no gun, but does carry a special saber.

On occasion, Scantlebury and others in the King's Troop are posted at Buckingham Palace, the official residence of Queen Elizabeth, as ceremonial guards. Though the regiment traditionally recruits its members from the countryside, where many youth grow up riding horses, such experience is not a necessary requirement to be admitted. Scantlebury is one of just a few who come from London proper, however. She still lives at home with her parents in Bow, and commutes to the St. John's Wood barracks in time for morning reveille. Her day includes exercising Hackney and the other horses. She hopes to become a show jumper for the Army, as many in her regiment are encouraged to do, and she is certainly no longer wary of horses. "Hackney threw me off three times at first but I kept getting back on," she told Veysey. "Now I feel comfortable on most horses, apart from the really big ones."

Scantlebury's mother was proud of her achievement, but not surprised. "She's always been very strongwilled and if she sets her sights on something, she's determined to succeed," Jennifer Scantlebury told *Daily Mail* journalist Sam Greenhill. "I'm so proud of her, not because she's the first black woman to do it but because she's my daughter."

Sources

Periodicals

Daily Mail (London), August 27, 2003, p. 7.
Daily Post (Liverpool), July 23, 2004, p. 5.
Daily Telegraph (London), June 16, 2001.
Evening Standard (London), August 26, 2003, p. 9; August 27, 2003, p. 7.

On-line

The Royal Artillery Kings Troop, www.army.mod.uk/kingstprha (August 2, 2004).

—Carol Brennan

Ras Shorty I

1941-2000

Musician

Ras Shorty I, photograph. AP/Wide World Photos.

One of the few musicians of modern times who could claim to have almost single-handedly created a long-lasting musical genre, Ras Shorty I, formerly known as Lord Shorty, was one of the most creative figures to emerge from the Caribbean island of Trinidad. With hits such as "Indrani" and his 1974 album *Endless Vibrations,* Shorty created a new variant of Trinidadian calypso music; known as soca, it was still vital and flourishing at the time of Shorty's death almost 30 years later. Shorty's own musical career was durable as well; he changed directions several times without losing any of his popularity in Trinidad.

Shorty was born Garfield Blackman in the southern Trinidadian community of Lengua on October 6, 1941. The area in which he grew up was heavily populated by the descendants of indentured servants Trinidad's British colonizers had brought from India, and he heard their music along with the lilting but satirical local calypso sounds that gained international popularity after they were adopted by American performers like the Andrews Sisters and Harry Belafonte. Beginning his life as a performer at age seven, Blackman took the name Lord Shorty early in his career.

Most calypsonians took nicknames and Blackman's served humorously to point up the imposing presence of his six-foot-four-inch frame.

Gaining musical experience as a teenager by working out musical arrangements for Trinidad's spectacular steel pan bands, Shorty began to record in the early 1960s. After several modestly successful releases like "Long Mango" (1962), he had a hit with "Cloak and Dagger" in 1963. Fired from a carpentry job in 1967, he decided to make music a full-time career. The way to fame and fortune in Trinidadian music was in the island's annual calypso competitions, and in 1970 Shorty took top honors at a regional contest, losing only in the national finals in the capital of Port of Spain. In these early years he was influenced by the classic calypsonian Lord Kitchener

His calypso career on the rise, Shorty was what Trinidadians called a "saga boy," living what he described (according to the *Guardian*) as an "orgy of the flesh" and becoming regarded as a sex symbol. Some called him "the Love Man." He used drugs, alcohol, and women, fathering 14 children or more but eventually marrying a woman named Claudette. In the early

1970s, Shorty worked with calypso musicians from the island of Dominica, wrote and produced songs for other artists, recorded a song in Creole French, and cast about for a way to counter the growing popularity of Jamaica's reggae music throughout the Caribbean region. "I felt [calypso] needed something brand new to hit everybody like a thunderbolt," Shorty was quoted as saying in *The Times* of London.

Shorty began to draw on the music of Trinidad's Indian minority, using such Indian instruments as the dholak, tabla, and dhantal in such songs as "Indrani." After combating obscenity charges that arose in the wake of his racy "Lesson in Love" single (Trinidad's prime minister Eric Williams came to his aid), Shorty released the song "Soul Calypso Music" in 1973. That song was widely assumed to have given the new genre of soca its name by contributing the first two letters of each of the two genres it mentioned, but Shorty himself explained the term's etymology differently, pointing to the Indian elements of the style. In his version, the syllable "so" came from "calypso" and "ca" from the Indian percussion rhythms he introduced to the music. The word was variously spelled as "solka" or "sokah" on early releases.

It was Shorty's 1974 album *Endless Vibrations* that put soca on the international music map. Other calypso singers, including the biggest star of them all, the Mighty Sparrow, jumped on the soca bandwagon, and Shorty continued to deliver innovative recordings like "Om Shanti," a song based on a Hindu chant that was even covered in India itself and became a hit there. A charismatic figure who dressed in designer shoes and suits and sported a long cigarette holder, Shorty turned to calypso's traditional function of political satire when he jabbed at Trinidad and Tobago's prime minister in "The PM Sex Probe" and in "Money Ent No Problem" (from the *Soca Explosion* album of 1979), which sliced up one of leader's speeches and re-formed it into comment on Trinidad's decaying infrastructure.

By the late 1970s, however, Shorty was tiring of his hedonistic life, and his disillusionment with the fast life grew when his fellow musician and friend Maestro was killed in an auto crash. He converted to the Rastafarian faith, traded in his fancy clothes for togas and sandals, grew dreadlocks, and moved with his wife and children to the forested Trinidadian region of Piparo. In 1980 he was christened Ras Shorty I.

Unlike other musicians who have turned to an existence filled with spirituality, Ras Shorty's new life did not portend any decline in his popularity. He criticized the sexual orientation of soca music as enthusiastically as he had previously participated in it, pointing especially to Lord Kitchener's hit "Sugar Bum Bum" as an example of soca's moral decline. Younger musicians criticized Ras Shorty's polemical songs like "Latrine Singers" in turn, but Ras Shorty continued to connect with ordinary Trinidadians. He formed a band called the Home Circle (later the Love Circle) which featured 13 of his children, and he proclaimed the birth of another new style. This new music he called jamoo, an abbreviation of the words "jah music."

Ras Shorty's new style, as heard on his 1984 release *Jamoo: The Gospel of Soca,* featured elements of reggae music and of African-American gospel. He continued to come up with new ideas, once again incorporating Indian instruments into his music and influencing a younger group of musicians that forged the so-called "chutney soca" style at the century's end. Many of his songs addressed social issues, and his 1997 hit "Watch Out My Children" was a major antidrug anthem that gained international airplay and was said to have been translated into ten languages. The song warned against "a fella called Lucifer with a bag of white powder; he don't want to powder your face but bring shame and disgrace to the human race."

In April of 2000, as he was preparing for the release of his CDs *Jamoo Victory* and *Children of the Jamoo Journey,* Ras Shorty broke a bone in his hand. Friends worried when the break did not heal, and he was diagnosed with bone cancer. "I am not worried because whether in death or life Jesus Christ will be glorified," he was quoted as saying in *The Times.* He declined chemotherapy and put himself in the hands of a Haitian-born herbalist, but after his condition worsened and he was hospitalized at Trinidad's Langmore Foundation and Southern Specialist Centre, he issued an appeal for financial assistance. A concert and radio telethon raised $27,000, and a government fund gave him a monetary advance on a possible future cultural prize, but the money came too late to help. Ras Shorty I died on July 12, 2000, in Port of Spain.

Selected discography

"Long Mango" (single), 1962.
"Cloak and Dagger" (single), 1963.
Endless Vibrations, 1974.
Sweet Music, 1976.

Sokah, Soul of Calypso, 1977.
Soca Explosion, 1979.
Jamoo: The Gospel of Soca, 1984.
"Watch Out My Children" (single), 1997.
Jamoo Victory, 2000.
Children of the Jamoo Journey, 2000.
Gone, Gone, Gone (collection), 2002.

Sources

Books

Sweeney, Philip, *The Virgin Directory of World Music,* Henry Holt, 1991.

Periodicals

Guardian (London, England), July 15, 2000, p. 22.
Independent (London, England), July 17, 2000, p. 6.
New York Times, July 16, 2000, p. 30.
Times (London, England), July 24, 2000, p. 19.
Trinidad Guardian, July 13, 2000, p. 1.

On-line

"Lord Shorty," *All Music Guide,* www.allmusic.com (August 10, 2004).
"Soca," *CaribPlanet,* http://caribplanet.homestead.com/101_Soca-ns4.html (August 10, 2004).

—James M. Manheim

Fred Shuttlesworth

1922—

Minister, civil rights leader

The Rev. Martin Luther King and his associates, who waged the battle for civil rights on a national scale, are remembered today as the movement's leaders. Less well known, even though a statue of him stands in front of the Birmingham, Alabama, Civil Rights Institute, is the Rev. Fred Shuttlesworth. But it was the Rev. Shuttlesworth who battled Birmingham's notorious police chief, Eugene "Bull" Connor, year in and year out, surviving bombings and numerous instances of violence from official or non-uniformed thugs. "Shuttlesworth is one of those persons who was on fire, and the most important thing to know about him is that he has no equal in terms of courage and putting his life in the line of fire to challenge segregation," his biographer Andrew Manis told the *Atlanta Journal-Constitution*.

Shuttlesworth was born Freddie Lee Robinson on March 18, 1922, in Mt. Meigs, in Alabama's Montgomery County. He grew up in Oxmoor, a segregated community near Birmingham, and received a new last name after his mother married coal miner William Nathan Shuttlesworth. The family raised money on the side by sharecropping and by making moonshine liquor, which got Shuttlesworth sentenced to two years' probation in 1940. Shuttlesworth's mother worked as a white family's maid, and Shuttlesworth himself held various jobs including cement plant worker. After marrying the former Ruby Lanette Keeler in 1942, Shuttlesworth worked as a civilian truck driver at a U.S. Army air base in Mobile during World War II.

Invited to Give Sermons

Though raised in the African Methodist Episcopal (A.M.E.) church, Shuttlesworth began attending a Baptist church in 1943. Within a few months the church's preacher was inviting him to give guest sermons, and Shuttlesworth was attending Cedar Grove Academy Bible College in Prichard, Alabama, outside Mobile. After leaving Mobile with his growing family of two daughters and one son, Shuttlesworth enrolled at Selma University. He earned a bachelor's degree there, a master's in education at Alabama State College, and an advanced divinity degree at Birmingham Baptist College. In 1948 Shuttlesworth began his preaching career in a series of small Alabama churches. After the birth of one more daughter in 1949, he became the pastor at Selma's First Baptist Church.

Returning to Birmingham late in 1952, Shuttlesworth became pastor of Bethel Baptist Church the following spring. On May 17, 1954, he noticed newspaper headlines announcing the U.S. Supreme Court's *Brown vs. Board of Education* decision outlawing school segregation. It was, he told the Cleveland *Plain Dealer,* the second biggest day of his life; the first was when he became a Christian. "I felt like I was a man, like I had rights." His first foray into social activism came in July of 1955, when he petitioned Birmingham's city council to hire black police officers. Rosa Parks' epochal bus ride in Montgomery was still several months away.

Shuttlesworth's petition was ignored, but over the next decade he was in constant motion, challenging the city's white power structure on every front. In 1956 he founded the Alabama Christian Movement for Human Rights, one of whose first actions was to demand the desegregation of Birmingham's city buses in the wake of the successful Montgomery bus boycott that followed Parks' ride. The following year, he helped organize the better-known Southern Christian Leadership Conference (SCLC). Shuttlesworth preached a 1956 Christmas sermon in which he said (as quoted in the *Plain Dealer*), "If it takes being killed to get integration, I'll do just that thing. For God is with me all the way." That night, Ku Klux Klan members threw dynamite sticks into the basement of Shuttlesworth's house, a parsonage attached to Bethel Baptist. Even the mattress on which he slept was destroyed, but he was unhurt. "The bomb had my name on it, but God erased it," he told the crowd that gathered.

Outfoxed Segregationist Police Commissioner

In September of 1957, Shuttlesworth was beaten with bicycle chains and baseball bats as he tried to enroll two of his daughters at an all-white elementary school. That November his nemesis, "Bull" Connor, a high school dropout and former baseball announcer, was elected public safety commissioner and soon suggested that Shuttlesworth himself had engineered the Christmas Day bombing. Asked to take a polygraph test, Shuttlesworth agreed to do so if Connor would do the same, but Connor refused. Bethel Baptist was bombed again on June 29, 1958. As the Birmingham Transit Company dragged its feet on bus integration, Shuttlesworth called on blacks to ignore the company's policies and was jailed for five days.

Having for some time urged the Rev. Martin Luther King to adopt more confrontational tactics (and not always finding support among Birmingham's black middle class), Shuttlesworth got a boost in 1960 when African-American college students in North Carolina began a series of sit-ins at segregated department stores. By March of that year, Shuttlesworth had been arrested after organizing a parallel effort by Birmingham students. In early 1961 a CBS television documentary, *Who Speaks for Birmingham?*, called Shuttlesworth (according to Manis) "the man most feared by southern racists and the voice of the new militancy among Birmingham Negroes."

In the summer of 1961 Shuttlesworth accepted the pastorate of Revelation Baptist Church in Cincinnati, Ohio, a larger congregation than the one at Bethel. But he kept in close touch with events in Birmingham and continued to play a decisive role in the civil rights struggle there, flying in after Bethel was bombed for a third time on December 14, 1962, as children rehearsed a Christmas pageant. In the spring of 1963, Shuttlesworth, working with King and the SCLC, launched Project C (which stood for "confrontation") with a series of department store sit-ins by students from Miles College. Demonstrations grew after King's arrest on Good Friday and the publication of his "Letter from the Birmingham Jail," and they were paced by repressive police tactics.

Injured by Fire House

During a May 6 demonstration, Shuttlesworth was hit by a fire hose, thrown against the wall of the Sixteenth Street Baptist Church—five months before it too was bombed, killing four young girls—and hospitalized with a rib injury. Shuttlesworth and King disagreed over whether to call off the demonstrations after white merchants offered partial concessions, with King ultimately carrying the day. Segregation was already in retreat when the U.S. Congress passed the 1964 Civil Rights Act and the Voting Rights Act of 1965—the two cornerstones of modern equal-rights laws.

Shuttlesworth continued to live and preach in Cincinnati, sometimes tangling with city officials and local institutions over hiring practices. His Revelation Baptist congregation split in two at one point, with some claiming that he had misused church funds; others, however, followed him and created a new congregation, Greater New Light Baptist Church. In 1967 Shuttlesworth tried to calm violent demonstrations in Cincinnati over the ongoing issue of police brutality. National consciousness of his courageous struggles faded after King's assassination in 1968.

Returning to Birmingham in 1988 at the invitation of Mayor Richard Arrington to help lobby for a new civil rights museum, Shuttlesworth saw a statue of himself erected in front of the building when it opened in 1992. He also served on the institution's board of directors. But he wasn't ready for retirement of any kind, even as he approached 80 years of age in the early 2000s. After the Rev. Martin Luther King III, son of the slain civil rights leader, stepped down as head of a fractured SCLC, Shuttlesworth served a term as interim president in 2003 and 2004. Outraged over widely publicized voting irregularities in Florida during the 2000 U.S. presidential election, he vowed to take to the streets to prevent a repeat.

"Laptops won't do it," Shuttlesworth told the *Plain Dealer,* ridiculing the high-tech methods of his younger successors. "We will have demonstrations down there. I want to create an external interest in the right to vote all over again." Looking back on his brushes with death at the height of the civil rights struggle, Shuttlesworth was philosophical. "It helps to have a little divine insanity," he told the *Tampa Tribune.* "That's when

you're willing to suffer and die for something. Christ did it for us, so I don't think it's asking too much to do it for him."

Sources

Books

Garrow, David J., ed., *Birmingham, Alabama, 1956-1963: The Black Struggle for Civil Rights,* Carlson, 1989.

Hampton, Henry, *Voices of Freedom: An Oral History of the Civil Rights Movement from the 1950s Through the 1980s,* Bantam, 1980.

Manis, Andrew M., *A Fire You Can't Put Out: The Civil Rights Life of Birmingham's Reverend Fred Shuttlesworth,* University of Alabama Press, 1999.

White, Marjorie L., comp., *A Walk to Freedom: The Reverend Fred Shuttlesworth and the Alabama Christian Movement for Human Rights, 1956-1964.* Birmingham Historical Society, 1998.

Periodicals

Atlanta Journal-Constitution, August 28, 1993, p. A2; May 23, 2002, p. A12; December 25, 2003, p. D1; July 26, 2004, p. A6.

Plain Dealer (Cleveland, OH), April 11, 2004, p. 9.

Tampa Tribune, September 7, 1999, p. Nation/World-1.

—James M. Manheim

Walter Sisulu

1912-2003

Political activist

Walter Sisulu was one of South Africa's most important leaders in its decades-long struggle to end apartheid. A key figure in the African National Congress (ANC) of the 1940s, it was he who brought future South African president Nelson Mandela into the organization. Both Sisulu and Mandela were later imprisoned for 25 years by the South African government for their political activities. Sisulu was released from jail in 1989, at the age of 77, and continued to play a vital role in shaping South Africa's emergence as a free, democratic nation until his death in 2003.

Grew Up in Tribal Area

Sisulu was born on May 18, 1912, in a village called Qutubeni in the Transkei reserve. His mother was a Xhosa, one of the major tribes of South Africa, while his father was a local magistrate and of European background. The relationship between his parents, who never married, also produced a younger sister, Rosabella, but neither she nor Sisulu knew their father's name until much later in life. Such unions between blacks and whites were generally taboo at the time, though not technically illegal, as they would later be declared.

Sisulu was raised by his uncle, a respected Xhosa chief and village council leader, whose leadership style was likely a tremendous influence on him. He attended a local village school and then a mission school run by the Anglican church. His family had a bit of land to farm and a small herd of cattle, and Sisulu looked after both as a boy. When his uncle died, Sisulu dropped out of school to find a job, for it fell to him to support his family. In 1928, the year he turned 16, he boarded a train for the first time in his life and went to look for work in Johannesburg, South Africa's main city, some 600 miles from his home.

For many years Sisulu worked menial jobs, the only kind available to blacks without a university education. He delivered milk by horse-drawn cart, working twelve hours a day, seven days a week for the monthly salary of one pound. Early on, he realized the importance of speaking English fluently if he was to survive in the European-dominated cities. He remained close to his Xhosa roots, however, traveling back to Qutubeni for his tribal initiation ceremony and later writing articles about Xhosa history for a black journal.

Settled in Johannesburg permanently by the mid-1930s, Sisulu brought his mother and sister to live with him, and together they bought a small red brick home in a district called Orlando West. It later became part of Soweto, the acronym given to the southwest townships of Johannesburg, where blacks had been allowed to settle. Sisulu worked in a factory and a bakery, and also in South Africa's famous gold mines, before taking night-school courses to become a real-estate agent. His office helped blacks buy and sell property in Johannesburg, though such freedoms later ended.

At a Glance . . .

Born Walter Max Ulyate Sisulu on May 18, 1912, in Qutubeni, Engcobo district, Transkei, South Africa; son of Victor Dickinson (a magistrate) and Alice Manse Sisulu (a laundress and domestic worker); died May 5, 2003, in Orlando West, South Africa; married Nontsikelelo Albertina Totiwe, 1944; eight children. *Education:* Took night school courses in Johannesburg, South Africa to become a real estate agent. *Politics:* African National Congress.

Career: Worked as a dairy deliveryperson in Johannesburg, South Africa, c. 1928, and as live-in household help in East London, South Africa; also worked in a factory, a gold mine, and a bakery before opening a real estate office in Johannesburg; African National Congress, various roles, including treasurer of the Youth League, c. 1944, Secretary-General, 1949-55; African National Congress, special advisor to President Nelson Mandela.

Worked to Reorganize ANC

Sisulu formally joined the African National Congress (ANC) in 1940. The political party had been founded the year he was born, in 1912, as the South African Native National Congress, in part to protest the 1913 Land Act that forced blacks into designated homelands that were for the most part unsuitable for farming. The Land Act forced them to earn a living by working on white-owned farms, or in factories or mines, and bred the seeds of a deep discontent in the country.

The ANC was a weak organization at the time Sisulu joined. Its strongest actions were to present formal petitions to the white government. Sisulu came to believe that the organization needed new blood and a new direction. He found someone who shared his ideas when a young student came into his downtown Johannesburg office one day seeking a job recommendation. Nelson Mandela, eight years younger than Sisulu, had just been fired from a mining job. He hoped to find work for a lawyer in the city, and eventually to become a lawyer himself. Like Sisulu, Mandela was a Xhosa from Transkei, but he came from an elite royal bloodline. Sisulu later said that he recognized Mandela's leadership potential that day, and convinced him to join the ANC.

The two became good friends, with Sisulu lending Mandela tuition money to finish his degree. They then joined with another black activist, Oliver Tambo, to create the ANC Youth League in 1944. Their goal was to reenergize the ANC with an influx of young, politically articulate new members. In 1948, however, the racist Nationalist Party (NP) won South Africa's general elections. Drawn from South Africans of Dutch descent, the NP had come to power with a political platform that declared the superiority of the white race over all others. Once in power, the NP began putting into place stringent laws that enshrined *apartheid,* or racial "apartness" in the Afrikaans language, across the land.

Fought Dreaded "Pass Laws"

There were three classifications for people under apartheid: white, black, and colored or mixed-race. Under this system, which touched every part of daily life, everything was segregated based on these racial categories. In stores, whites were served first. If an ambulance was needed, the caller was required to give the race of the victim first, and lying about it was punishable by law. Hospitals and schools for blacks were dreadfully inadequate. Since Sisulu's father was white, he could have formally registered as a colored under the new law, thus protecting himself from the worst treatment. But Sisulu believed he had been raised entirely in black culture and refused to reject it.

One of the most hated parts of apartheid were the "Pass Laws." These required any black who lived outside of the tribal homelands to carry an identification document if they wanted to work in an area like Johannesburg, which was the only place there were jobs. The passes were difficult to get, and a man who obtained one would not be able to bring his wife or children to live with him. A police officer could stop any black and ask to see his pass; not carrying it made a person subject to immediate deportation back to one of the homelands.

The horrific situation energized the ANC, which elected Sisulu as Secretary General at its 1949 conference. He called for a series of strikes and boycotts to protest apartheid laws, and in 1952 devised a sweeping plan of civil disobedience. He called on blacks to openly disobey the government, with the aim of overcrowding the jails. Some 8,000 were arrested, including Sisulu several times, but South African authorities simply found new and more dreadful places to house detainees. ANC membership skyrocketed during the early 1950s, as the party became the dominant force resisting apartheid.

Went into Hiding

In December of 1956, Sisulu and other senior ANC leaders were arrested under the Suppression of Communism Act. Their four-year-long treason trial attracted international attention and ended in acquittal. But the turning point in South African history came in March of 1960, when police opened fire on a demonstration of 20,000 blacks and killed 69; many of the dead were shot in the back. The South African government officially outlawed the ANC after what became known as the Sharpeville Massacre.

In response, Sisulu and the ANC leaders created an adjunct group, Umkhonto We Sizwe (Spear of the Nation). This was the ANC's secret militant wing and carried out acts of sabotage. Sisulu served as its political advisor. He remained under constant watch by authorities, followed wherever he went and his home subject to surprise raids. Fortunately he had wed a staunch ally in the struggle, Albertina Totiwe, a former nurse, with whom he had eight children. She was also subject to "banning," a law that restricted a person from a social gathering of two or more people.

Sisulu decided that he could better serve the movement by going underground, as Mandela had done. Sisulu disappeared for four months, but in July of 1963 police raided the secret ANC hideout in a farmhouse outside of Johannesburg. Sisulu and the others were arrested with incriminating documents. His trial—which included Mandela and several other ANC leaders—also gained international notoriety, and Sisulu delivered memorable, reasoned answers that likely helped save him and the others from the death penalty. The government prosecutors, for example, claimed that the ANC was misrepresenting black Africans, that the majority of them were happy with the situation. "Why doesn't the government put the matter to the test by having elections in which everyone could vote?," Sisulu asked in response, according to the Africa News Service.

Spent Years in Jail

In the end, Sisulu and the others were sentenced to life imprisonment. They were housed on Robben Island, one of the world's most notorious prisons. Opened in 1961 to house black political prisoners, Robben Island was considered impossible to escape, for escape would have required swimming or rafting three miles through shark-infested Atlantic Ocean waters with deadly currents. Sisulu spent the years from 1964 to 1982 in this prison, with just two visitors allowed per year. His cell measured just seven feet square, and was lit all night. There was no bed, just a straw mat, and for a number of years he and the others, including Mandela, did hard labor by crushing gravel with hammers or quarrying lime. Their conditions improved late in their term, thanks to hunger strikes and international pressure, and they were allowed to read newspapers for the first time in 1980.

Both Sisulu and Mandela were moved to Pollsmoor Prison in Cape Town in 1982. Meanwhile, Sisulu's children carried on the fight. His son Zwelakhe, a

newspaper editor, was arrested in 1986, and his daughter Lindiwe was also detained and tortured. International pressure, including harsh sanctions against the South African economy, finally helped end apartheid in what was one of the most surprisingly bloodless handovers of power in world history. Sisulu was released on October 15, 1989, by recently elected South African president F.W. de Klerk, and the government did not even impose restrictions on the jubilant celebrations that took place in Soweto when he came home that evening. Mandela was released four months later, after 28 years in prison.

By the time he was released much had changed in South African politics. Sisulu and other members of the ANC leadership helped usher in the era in which apartheid was dismantled and Mandela was elected president in historic 1994 elections, the first in South African history in which blacks were allowed to vote. Even during his 25 years in prison, Sisulu had believed change was possible in his lifetime, and knew that education and an end to propaganda were the keys to a freer society. "In my cell I was alone but guarded all the time by a [white] warder," he told *Time* writer Scott MacLeod not long after his release. "He would make comments and become very hostile when he saw certain things about the A.N.C. on TV. I then took a chance to talk to him, to educate him. In the end, he understood."

Sisulu declined a position in the government, but continued to play an important role as an advisor to Mandela. Unlike other ANC leaders who moved into new homes once apartheid no longer restricted their residency, Sisulu and Albertina stayed in the same Orlando West home where he had lived in the 1930s. He died on May 5, 2003, at the age of 90. Thousands mourned him, and a state funeral was held at which Mandela eulogized him. "From the moment when we first met, he has been my friend, my brother, my keeper, my comrade," South Africa's first black president said of the man who had introduced him into the ANC. "The spear of the nation has fallen. Let us pick up the spear to build a country after the example that Walter Sisulu has set for us."

Selected writings

(With George M. Houser and Herbert Shore) *I Will Go Singing: Walter Sisulu Speaks of His Life and the Struggle for Freedom in South Africa,* Robben Island Museum, 2001.

Sources

Books

Sisulu, Elinor, *Walter and Albertina Sisulu: In Our Lifetime,* David Philip Publishers, 2002.

Periodicals

Africa News Service, May 13, 2003; May 16, 2003; May 18, 2003.

Daily Telegraph (London), May 7, 2003.

Economist, October 21, 1989, p. 41; May 10, 2003.

Guardian (London), May 7, 2003, p. 25.

Independent (London), May 7, 2003, p. 16.

New York Times, April 27, 1977, p. 3; December 15, 1986, p. A23; October 19, 1989, p. A6; May 6, 2003, p. C17.

Time, October 30, 1989, p. 66, p. 70.

On-line

South African History, www.sahistory.org.za/pages/chronology/main-chronology-1940s.html (August 12, 2004).

"Walter Max Ulyate Sisulu," *African National Congress,* www.anc.org.za/ancdocs/history/people/sisulu_wmu.html (August 16, 2004).

—Carol Brennan

Natalie Manns Taylor

1959—

Corporate executive

Natalie Taylor grew up surrounded by adults who believed that hard work would lead to success and who demonstrated that belief in the way they lived their lives. Taught to aim high and expect a lot of herself, she has set and achieved one goal after another throughout her career. Beginning with paying for her college education by working several part-time jobs as a teenager, Taylor worked her way up the corporate ladder rung by rung to attain a top position in a large grocery chain. Even then, she continued to reach for new goals. Supported by her family and her deep religious belief, Natalie Taylor left an executive position in a major corporation to fulfill her lifelong dream of starting her own company.

Taylor was born Natalie Manns in the summer of 1959 in Columbus, Ohio. Within a year, her mother, Betty Manns Casey, took her new baby daughter to live with her parents, James and Hattie Manns, in the small southwestern Virginia town of Radford. James Manns had worked for the Virginia and Tennessee Railroad, once a central part of the Radford economy. Later, both he and his wife Hattie worked in the housekeeping division of St. Albans Hospital. Betty Casey worked at the Radford Army ammunition plant for more than thirty years, changing often between early morning and late evening shifts. Living in an extended family with her parents enabled her to care for her young daughter even while working long hours with an unpredictable schedule.

Cherished by her mother and her grandparents, young Natalie flourished in Radford. She not only attended

school, but was also active in many community activities. She joined a softball team, Girl Scouts, and 4-H, an agriculture-oriented club for youth growing up in rural areas. She was also active in her church, singing in the choir and first attending, then teaching, Sunday school. By the age of 16, she also had her first part-time job, working at a McDonalds restaurant.

Education was highly valued in the Manns household. Taylor's grandparents believed that a college education was the way to a better life, and they expected their granddaughter to continue her education past high school. James and Hattie Manns had worked hard to send their children to college during a time when it was very difficult for many African Americans to pursue higher education. Before the civil rights movement of the 1960s, many traditionally white colleges and universities did not allow blacks to attend, or admitted very few. This led African-American educators to establish a network of 105 colleges and universities specifically for black students, though they did not exclude students of other races. These colleges are now commonly referred to as "historically black colleges."

By the time Natalie Manns was ready to choose a college in 1978, however, she had more choices than her mother's generation had had. She did not choose an historically black college, but chose Radford University, partially because of its excellent academic programs and partially because it was close to home and her supportive family. She paid for her education by continuing to work at part-time jobs, sometimes holding two or three jobs while attending classes full time.

It was during her college years that she began her career with Food Lion, a large chain of supermarkets with stores throughout the Southern and Mid-Atlantic states. She took a job as a cashier, balancing that with her college classes and another job at a bank. This experience managing several jobs and tasks at the same time would be helpful when she rose to a high management position in the company.

After her college graduation, Taylor moved to Ohio for a short time. However, she missed the support of her family and community in Radford and soon moved back to Virginia. She went to work again as a cashier for Food Lion again and was soon promoted to the customer service department at the Roanoke, Virginia,

store. Anxious to keep advancing her career, she entered Food Lion's management training program. In less than two years, she earned promotions to assistant manager and then to store manager.

In 1985, as she was training for her management positions, Natalie Manns had married Timothy Taylor. The young couple was separated almost immediately when Natalie had to leave for Tennessee for the twelve-week training program. By the late 1980s, the Taylors had relocated to North Carolina, where Timothy had taken a job. Natalie applied to work at the corporate headquarters of Food Lion in Salisbury, North Carolina. Though she often had to commute more than an hour to work, she continued to rise within the company, working in various positions in employee training and community relations. By 1995 she had become Director of Diversity Planning; in 1997 she became Vice President in charge of Diversity.

Diversity means variety and difference. The word is often used in the fields of business or education to mean the inclusion of a variety of people from different racial, ethnic, or economic backgrounds. One part of Taylor's job as Director of Diversity Planning and Vice President of Diversity was to make sure the company hired and promoted employees from many different groups and that those employees and managers learned to understand and appreciate their differences. Another part of the Diversity process involved the role of Food Lion in the community. For example, Taylor worked hard to develop Food Lion's relationship with the Central Intercollegiate Athletic Association (CIAA), a college athletic organization of historically black colleges. Under Taylor's leadership, Food Lion not only sponsored several CIAA tournaments, but the company also offered a management trainee program where graduates of historically black colleges could learn about the grocery business. Because of Taylor's work, these young graduates had the chance to enter the business on a management level, rather than working their way up from cashier as she had done.

Taylor's work in the field of diversity helped Food Lion win several community awards, including the National Association for the Advancement of Colored People Fair Share Award in 1995 and 1997, the North Carolina NAACP Corporate Supporter Award in 1996, and the Corporation of the Year Award in 1999.

In 2004, after 21 years with Food Lion, Taylor decided to leave the company and pursue her own dream. Ever since her marriage, she had wanted to start her own business, and her hard work and success within the Food Lion corporation had convinced her that she could be successful on her own. With the support of her husband and son Ryan, she started Capture Communications Resource Group, a video production and executive coaching company. In athletics, a coach is the person in charge of training and encouraging the team. Many corporations employ executive coaches to teach their high-level employees to meet the challenges of their jobs. Having risen step by step through the levels of a corporate system, Natalie Taylor felt that she had learned many skills that would make her an excellent executive coach to help others negotiate the complex world of business.

Sources

Periodicals

Black EOE Journal, Summer 1996, p. 14.
Crisis, August 1995, p. 12.

On-line

"Historically Black Colleges and Universities," *Department of the Interior,* www.doi.gov/hrm/black.html (September 24, 2004).

Other

Information for this profile was obtained through an interview with Natalie Taylor on September 20, 2004.

—Tina Gianoulis

Marsha Thomason

1976—

Actor

Thomason, Marsha, photograph. Vince Bucci/Getty Images.

Actress Marsha Thomason began her career in British television, and moved quickly into starring roles opposite such Hollywood heavyweights as Eddie Murphy and James Caan. In 2003 she began appearing in the NBC series *Las Vegas,* which starred her opposite Caan's Las Vegas casino-surveillance chief in what quickly became one of the breakout shows of the fall season. "When I started in the series I knew nothing about gambling," she told John Millar of Glasgow's *Daily Record.* "I did not even know how to shuffle a deck of cards. Now I can do some neat tricks."

Thomason was born in Manchester, England, on January 19, 1976. That same year, *Bugsy Malone,* a lighthearted Hollywood film about mobsters, was released. The musical by Alan Parker featured a roster of child stars, including a young Jodie Foster, portraying well-known 1930s underworld figures. Thomason has said she was fascinated by it. "I think my inspiration to become an actress is down to the film Bugsy Malone," she told Sally Morgan, a writer for the London newspaper the *Mirror.* "After I saw it, I used to invent plays and create a makeshift theatre, with sheets as curtains, in my bedroom. I bribed my little sister Kristy to appear

in my productions, then made our parents watch."

At the age of twelve, Thomason's at-home stagings had gained her enough experience to win a place with the Oldham Theatre Workshop, a renowned children's ensemble in Lancashire. She appeared in a number of its plays and musicals, and took her first professional job at the age of 14 on a Saturday-morning children's show called *The 8:15 from Manchester.* Her breakout role came in 1993, when she was cast in a British Broadcasting Corporation (BBC) television film, *Safe,* about a community of homeless people in London. A year later, she won a small role as a nurse in her first feature film, *Priest.*

After Thomason finished at the North Manchester High School For Girls, she went on to Manchester Metropolitan University, and earned her undergraduate degree in English there. She worked during her college years, winning an especially plum role opposite Helen Mirren in the critically acclaimed crime series, *Prime Suspect.* In 1997, she was cast in a regular role on a BBC comedy-crime drama, *Pie in the Sky.* It starred Richard Griffiths, who later went on to play Uncle Vernon in the *Harry Potter* films, as a top police detective whose boss refuses to let him retire to run his restaurant.

By 1998, Thomason had moved to London and was cast as Sharon "Shazza" Pearce in *Playing the Field,* a hit BBC series about a women's soccer team. As one of the Castlefield Blues, Thomason's Shazza was a loose cannon, prone to substance abuse. "It's a very physical part," she told Morgan in the *Mirror* interview. "In one scene I headbutt a player from a rival team and call her a fat cow." Thomason worked overtime during these years, having taken a part on another British television series, *Where the Heart Is.*

Thomason's first attempt to tackle an American accent in her work came when she played a prostitute in a West End theater production of *Breath Boom* at the Royal Court Theatre. That experience came in handy when she was cast alongside Martin Lawrence in the hit 2001 comedy film *Black Knight.* Lawrence played a hapless medieval theme-park employee who time-travels back into the past. Thomason was cast as Victoria, a chambermaid in the royal court with some unusually modern ideas.

Thomason made two more British films, *Long Time Dead,* a 2002 horror tale that also featured Lukas Haas and Alec Newman, and *Pure,* another work released that year in which she once again played a prostitute. This time, she was a heroin addict as well. Hollywood offered her a more sedate role as Eddie Murphy's on-screen wife in *The Haunted Mansion,* a horror tale from 2003. The story was based on one of the venerable attractions at the Disney theme parks, much as the "Pirates of the Caribbean" ride had been turned into a successful big-screen story earlier that year. Thomason played the wife of Murphy's workaholic real-estate agent, and is trapped in the eerie manor with her husband and children when the ghost who haunts it believes she is a long-lost lover. Though it was

her second big-budget Hollywood feature, she was still nervous, she told Millar in the *Daily Record* interview. "The first day was bizarre. I felt a bit intimidated because I was doing my American accent," she recalled, and "was terrified that they would think I was rubbish and sack me."

By the time *The Haunted Mansion* was released—to generally dismal reviews—Thomason had already made her American network series debut in *Las Vegas.* The NBC drama starred a top-notch ensemble cast that included the veteran actor Caan as a former Central Intelligence Agency operative who serves as head of security at a casino. Thomason sported a glamorous wardrobe for her role as Nessa Holt, the pit boss who keeps an eye on the tables and their gamblers on the casino floor while intrigues roil behind the scenes. The series was filmed at the Mandalay Bay casino, and Thomason told one journalist that the hardest part of the job was the standard "whoosh" shot in each episode, when the camera sweeps through the casino floor. "Every single person has to freeze and hold for a while, for a minute, and then, action," she told the *Washington Times*'s Christian Toto, and said that she and her castmates dreaded being the one who made a mistake and forced another take.

Thomason also appeared in *My Baby's Daddy,* released in early 2004, and *The Nickel Children,* a film about a child prostitution ring. She remains in awe of the differences between British and American television and film sets. "Here, there are so many more people involved in the shows," she told Toto. "Even the sound stages and sets dwarf their British counterparts."

Selected works

Films

Priest, 1994.
Black Knight, 2001.
Long Time Dead, 2002.
Pure, 2002.
The Haunted Mansion, 2003.
My Baby's Daddy, 2003.
The Nickel Children, 2004.

Plays

Breath Boom, 2000.

Television

The 8:15 from Manchester, 1990.
Safe, 1993.
Playing the Field, 1998.
Where the Heart Is, 1998.
Las Vegas, 2003.

Sources

Periodicals

Daily Record (Glasgow, Scotland), February 13, 2004.
Entertainment Weekly, December 5, 2003, p. 25.
Essence, December 2003, p. 146.
Huddersfield Daily Examiner (Huddersfield, England), July 10, 2004, p. 33.
Jet, December 10, 2001, p. 57.
Mirror (London), April 18, 1998, p. 20.
People, October 20, 2003, p. 41; December 8, 2003, p. 34.
People (London), February 6, 2000, p. 28.
Washington Times, November 10, 2003, p. B6.

—Carol Brennan

Conrad Tillard

1964—

Religious leader

The Rev. Conrad Tillard is both a charismatic religious leader and a man on a quest. As one of the central figures in the New York City branch of the Nation of Islam, in the 1990s he took the name Conrad Muhammad. He later broke with the leaders of the Nation of Islam and returned to his birth name and his Christian roots. Along the way, he plunged into the controversies that swirled around hip-hop music and its sometimes violent messages, became one of the early proponents of using hip-hop to organize young people politically, studied at the Harvard Divinity School, and tried to break into politics himself, flirting with the Republican Party in the process. Throughout his varied career, Tillard demonstrated a distinctive intelligence and curiosity even in the midst of activist controversies.

Conrad Tillard was born on September 15, 1964, in St. Louis, Missouri. From an early age he realized that the date of his birth fell exactly a year after the deaths of four young girls in the white terrorist bombing of the Sixteenth Street Baptist Church in Birmingham, Alabama, and he was marked as a child by the horror of that event. Tillard's father was a jazz musician who divorced his mother Jackie and remained only sporadically involved in his son's life—and not at all after Tillard became involved with the Nation of Islam. Tillard's family later moved to Washington, D.C., and he was skilled enough academically to win admission to competitive Middlebury College in Vermont.

Worked on Jackson Campaign

Tillard lasted only a semester at that geographically isolated school. "My skin is dark brown, and Middlebury is a very white campus, and I found that I was uncomfortable with my darkness," he told *Esquire*. "I would go for a long time without looking in the mirror, and when I finally did look, I thought, 'Oh, man, that does not look right.'" Tillard transferred to the equally rigorous University of Pennsylvania in Philadelphia, and there he flourished. Fellow students remembered his leadership skills, and in 1984 he signed on to work for the Rev. Jesse Jackson's presidential campaign.

After encountering the Nation of Islam at a summer rally in Washington, D.C., that same year, Tillard joined the sect and changed his name first to Conrad X and then to Conrad Muhammad. He was disillusioned by the failure of Jackson's campaign and entranced by the rhetoric of the controversial New York Nation of Islam minister Khalid Muhammad. It wasn't long before the intelligent, well-educated young convert came to the attention of Nation of Islam leader Louis Farrakhan. In 1988, the year Conrad Muhammad won admission to the prestigious Georgetown Law School, Farrakhan asked him to embark on a career in the ministry instead. Muhammad, newly married to a fellow Penn student and future doctor, agreed.

Muhammad rose quickly in the Nation of Islam hierarchy, and by 1991 he had become minister of the Nation's Mosque No. 7 in New York's Harlem neighborhood. His ascent was so rapid that some began to tout him as an eventual successor to Farrakhan, especially since the mosque had launched the careers of both Minister Farrakhan and Malcolm X himself. In his

At a Glance . . .

Born Conrad Tillard on September 15, 1964, in St. Louis, MO; married Michele, 1988 (divorced); children: Amir, Najmah Muhammad, Conrad Muhammad II. *Education:* Attended Middlebury College, Middlebury, VT; University of Pennsylvania, bachelor's degree; attended Harvard Divinity School, Cambridge, MA. *Religion:* Baptist; formerly Nation of Islam.

Career: Jesse Jackson for President campaign, campaign worker, 1984; became Nation of Islam minister, 1988; Nation of Islam Mosque No. 7, New York, minister, 1991-97; radio station WBLS, talk show host; Eliot Church of Roxbury, MA, interim pastor, 2004–.

Memberships: Movement for CHHANGE (Conscious Hip-Hop Activism Necessary for Global Empowerment), founder.

Addresses: *Office*—Eliot Church of Roxbury, 56 Dale Street, Roxbury, MA 02119.

first years as minister, Muhammad revitalized Mosque No. 7, started a school there, and increased the contributions the congregation made to the Nation of Islam's central headquarters in Chicago. He ran into controversy when he called a Brooklyn state legislator a "snotty-nosed Jewish politician" during a radio interview that centered on a disputed housing project policing contract that had been withdrawn from a Nation-affiliated security force. In general, though, his rhetoric was milder than that of the confrontational Khalid Muhammad.

Organized "Day of Atonement" after Shakur Killing

Part of Conrad Muhammad's success came from his ability to expand the Nation's reach beyond the walls of the mosque and into the culture of young African-American New Yorkers. He plunged into the feuds that surrounded hip-hop music, organizing what he called (as quoted in the *New York Post*) a "day of atonement" after the 1996 murder of rapper Tupac Shakur. Muhammad was often critical of hip-hop's violent themes, even after he left the Nation, and he entered into something of a feud of his own when hip-hop

mogul Russell Simmons urged New Yorkers not to attend a 2001 meeting Muhammad organized to discuss ways of toning down hip-hop's incendiary qualities.

This clash, of course, raised Muhammad's profile still higher. Despite their religious differences, Muhammad closely studied the headline-grabbing ways of New York's activist Rev. Al Sharpton, who became a presidential candidate in 2004. At the same time, Muhammad cultivated his intellectually curious side, enrolling in the master's program at Harvard University's Divinity School.

In February of 1997, Muhammad's world came crashing down: he was summoned to Mosque No. 7 and stripped of his ministry, according to an order delivered by one of Farrakhan's lieutenants. Allegations of financial improprieties were raised against the notably frugal Muhammad, but the Nation's tendency toward internecine feuding may also have played a role. "I am a minister without a ministry," Muhammad told *Esquire* after his removal. "I have learned some hard lessons. I am out of the only job I was ever prepared for…. I am broke—bankrupt, in fact. My wife has informed me that we cannot eat press clippings. My marriage is in trouble. I cannot afford my Harvard tuition."

Hosted Talk Show

Muhammad's marriage soon ended in divorce, but he remained close to his wife and three children. Though his position in the Nation of Islam was gone, he retained a strong following in Harlem. For a time he explored the possibility of converting to orthodox Islam, as Malcolm X had done at the end of his life. He hosted a talk show on radio station WBLS, founded a group called the Movement for CHHANGE (Conscious Hip-Hop Activism Necessary for Global Empowerment), and began to bill himself as the hip-hop minister. In 2000, Muhammad suggested the formation of a slate of political candidates drawn from the hip-hop community.

All the while, Muhammad was spiritually restless. He spent time in Brooklyn and then in Baltimore, Maryland, where he attended an African Methodist Episcopal (A.M.E.) church. In 2002 he announced his intention to challenge Harlem's entrenched Democratic congressional representative, Charles Rangel. Offering a platform based on strong adherence to traditional morality, Muhammad proclaimed his support for President George W. Bush's conduct of the war in Iraq and hoped to run as a Republican. Although he garnered support from the conservative *New York Post*, Muhammad was rebuffed by Republicans leery of his past controversial statements and his personal Democratic voter registration. He then attempted to gather signatures to challenge Rangel in the 2002 Democratic primary, but that effort failed.

Finally, he began to question whether he was really drawn to the tenets of Islam or simply to the Nation's message of black empowerment. By 2003 Muhammad had returned to the name Conrad Tillard and converted back to Christianity. Something of a mentor was the Rev. Calvin O. Butts III, the pastor of Harlem's famed Abyssinian Baptist Church. Tillard began giving sermons at Christian churches in Harlem and considered the idea of becoming a pastor. Tillard refused to criticize his former Nation of Islam associates, and he found that Harlem audiences were sympathetic to his spiritual searches. "I have departed from the notion of judging people exclusively by their race.... I have grown and seen a lot," Tillard told the *New York Times.* "A number of my views have changed." Though just entering middle age, Tillard is a charismatic leader and thinker whose most influential days might well lie ahead of him. Perhaps the first step in the next stage of his career came when he was named interim pastor of the Eliot Church of Roxbury, Massachusetts, in 2004.

Sources

Periodicals

Entertainment Weekly, June 16, 2000, p. 87.
Esquire, November 1998, p. 118.
New York Post, May 8, 2001, p. 55; June 3, 2002, p. 27.
New York Times, March 5, 1994, sec. 1, p. 8; September 22, 1996, sec. 1, p. 42; August 5, 2002, p. B4; August 17, 2002, p. B4; June 16, 2003, p. B1.
Star-Ledger (Newark, NJ), September 23, 1996, p. 3.
Times-Picayune (New Orleans, LA), July 4, 2003, Metro section, p. 1.

On-line

Heimlich, Adam, "A Great Race in Harlem: Will 'Hiphop Minister' Conrad Muhammad Go from N.O.I. to G.O.P?," *New York Press,* www.nypress. com/15/29/news&columns/feature.cfm (August 2, 2004).

—James M. Manheim

Askia Touré

1938—

Poet, editor, activist

Askia Muhammad Abu Bakr el Touré is one of the founding members of the black arts movement of the 1960s and 1970s. As a poet, editor, and activist, Touré helped define a new generation of black consciousness that sought to affirm through the arts the community's African heritage as a means to create an uplifting and triumphal identity for the modern black experience. Touré is the author of several books of poetry and has been published in numerous anthologies.

Early Life

Touré was born as Rolland Snellings on October 13, 1938, in Raleigh, North Carolina, to Clifford R. and Nancy (Bullock) Snellings. He spent his early childhood, along with his younger brother, in La Grange, Georgia, where he lived with his paternal grandmother until the age of six. At that time he moved with his family to Dayton, Ohio. Although he spent the remainder of his childhood in Ohio, he made frequent trips back to North Carolina and Georgia to visit relatives, and the South had a profound influence on his early poetic images.

Touré wrote his first poem in the seventh grade, but after his teacher insisted that he could not have been the actual author of the work, he was duly dissuaded from further writing at the time. He attended public school and graduated from Dayton's Roosevelt High School in 1956. By that time Touré had begun singing in nightclubs, imitating the doo-wop style of popular 1950s groups such as the Ravens and the Platters. Although he considered heading straight into the music business, after graduating Touré decided instead to join the Air Force, serving from 1956 to 1959.

Upon his discharge from military service, Touré headed to New York, and from 1960 to 1962 he studied visual arts at the Art Students League of New York. In 1963 Touré, working with illustrator Tom Feeling and artist Elombe Brath, helped produce a brief, privately published illustrated history of Samory Touré, who resisted French colonialism in Guinea in the 1800s and was the grandfather of Sékou Touré, former president of Guinea who successfully led his country's struggle for independence from the French in the 1950s. This publication marked the beginning of his life-long interest in the history of Africa.

Developed Poetic Voice

In 1962 Touré began providing illustrations to *Umbra* magazine, whose staff included several prominent poets, authors, and activists. Here, in this company he began to focus on his poetry and to develop his own poetic style. Turning first to W.E.B. De Bois for inspiration, Touré's influences eventually came from a broad range of writers, including Irish poet William Butler Yeats, Chilean poet Pablo Neruda, and Harlem Renaissance writer Langston Hughes, among others. Ultimately, Touré found his poetic home in the rhythm, phrasing, and tonality of black music, with particular homage paid to the jazz saxophone of John Coltrane.

At a Glance . . .

Born Rolland Snellings on October 13, 1938, in Raleigh, NC; changed name to Askia Muhammad Abu Bakr el Touré, 1970; son of Clifford R. and Nancy (Bullock) Snellings; married Dona Humphrey, 1966 (divorced); married Helen Morton Hobbs (Muslim name, Halima), 1970 (divorced); married Agila; children: (first marriage) Tariq Abdullah bin Touré; (second marriage) Jamil Abdus-Salam bin Touré. *Education:* Attended Art Students League of New York, 1960-62. *Military service:* U.S. Air Force, 1956-59. *Religion:* Muslim.

Career: Staff member, *Umbra* magazine, 1962-63; member of the editorial board, *Black America,* 1963-65; cofounder, *Afro World* newspaper, 1965; staff member, *Liberator Magazine,* 1965-66; associate editor, *Black Dialogue*; editor-in-chief, *Journal of Black Poetry* (now *Kitabu Cha Juai*); poet, essayist, artist, editor, activist, and lecturer in African history, black studies, and creative writing.

Awards: Modern Poetry Association award, 1952; Columbia University Creative Writing grant, 1969; American Book Award for Literature, for *From the Pyramids to the Projects,* 1989; Gwendolyn Brooks Lifetime Achievement Award, 1996; Stephen Henderson Poetry Award, African-American Literature and Culture Society, for *Dawnsong,* 2000.

Addresses: *Office*—89 Ruthven Street, Boston, MA 02121; *Web site*—www.askiatoure.com.

During the early 1960s Touré solidified his growing role as a leader of the emerging black arts movement by working with several new black arts publications. From 1963 to 1965 he served on the editorial board of *Black America,* the literary arm of the black nationalist Revolutionary Action Movement (RAM). For the following two years he was on the staff of *Liberator Magazine,* and then he served as an associate editor on the staff of *Black Dialogue,* which had begun publication in the spring of 1965. Eventually the *Journal of Black Poetry* (now *Kitabu Cha Juai*) emerged from *Black Dialogue,* Touré was named editor-in-chief. Through all these forums, Touré sought to redefine black identity and strengthen the movement against racial injustice and oppression.

Touré was deeply affected by the assassination of Malcolm X on February 21, 1965. In response he joined with influential scholar Larry Neal to found the newspaper *Afro World,* which went to press just one week after Malcolm X's death. That spring Touré, again partnering with Neal, took the black arts movement to the streets of Harlem by organizing the Harlem Uptown Youth Conference. They invited artists from the Black Arts Repertoire Theatre School to perform music, poetry, and plays in the blocked-off streets of Harlem. Among the many Harlem-based artists, Touré performed some of his own poetry in this massive block party. This event spawned the creation of Harlem's Black Arts School.

Found Political and Religious Identity

As Touré's poetic voice matured, so did his political life. In 1965 he helped author the Student National Coordinating Committee's Black Power position paper that, among other things, called for the creation of black-led political groups across the United States. Touré married Dona Humphrey in June of 1966, and the following year rejoined *Black Dialogue* as an associate editor. He shook the black nationalist movement by printing a caustic letter denouncing LeRoi Jones (also known as Amiri Baraka), a prominent leader in the movement. Touré challenged Baraka for what he saw as Baraka's antiwhite bias and a failure to provide positive images of the African-American culture.

Shortly thereafter Touré moved to San Francisco and became active in RAM. He also taught African history at San Francisco State University, which eventually established the country's first Africana Studies program to be housed at a major university. During this period Touré came under the influence of the Nation of Islam and converted to the faith in 1970, changing his name from Rolland Snellings to Askia Muhammad Abu Bakr el Touré. In the midst of this tumultuous period of his life, Touré's marriage suffered severe strain, and Touré and Humphrey divorced shortly after the birth of their son, Tariq Abdullah bin Touré.

Returning to New York, Touré immersed himself in the theology and spirituality of Nation of Islam. In 1970 he married Helen Morton Hobbs, a writer and editor, who went by the Muslim name Halima. In the same year Touré published his first collection of poetry, *JuJu: Magic Songs for a Black Nation,* which included three poems and an essay by Touré. Playwright Ben Caldwell contributed a poem and penned the introduction. Imitating the cadence of black music, Touré's epic poem links the modern black experience with *juju,* the West African word for magic, which he, in turn, equates with black music. Touré suggests that when all else is stripped away—dress, customs, language, religion—the modern black experience can still be linked to an African past through music.

A "Griot"

During the early 1970s Touré worked with the John Oliver Killens Writers Workshop at Columbia University and taught courses at the Community College of New York. In 1972 he published *Songhai!,* his second volume of poetry, for which Killens wrote the introduction. Once again Touré undertook a cosmic and epic view that not only sought a return to African roots but also a fulfillment of the modern black experience that results in a triumphal future. His tone is hopeful, uplifting, and revolutionary. Touré's poetry earned him the title of a *griot,* a storyteller who keeps alive the memories of the people, serving also as a means to approach the future.

By the mid-1970s, shortly after the birth of his son, Jamil Abdus-Salam bin Touré, Touré's second marriage dissolved. His relationship with his mosque had also grown very strained, eventually leading him to break from the community. In 1974 he moved to Philadelphia, where he began teaching courses at the Community College of Philadelphia.

Touré continued to write, lecture, and teach throughout the next three decades. In 1984 he helped organize the Nile Valley Conference at Morehouse College, which sought to reestablish the Nile Valley as the source of Western civilization, and in 1986 he co-founded an Atlanta chapter of the Association for the Study of Classical African Civilizations. In 1990 he published his third major work, *From the Pyramids to the Projects: Poems of Genocide and Resistance,* which won the American Book Award for Literature.

"Dawnsong" and Beyond

In 1998 Touré caused a stir by writing a poem in defense of exiled Black Panther activist Assata Shakur, who had been living in Cuba since escaping from prison in 1979, where she was serving a life sentence for the murder of a state trooper in a highly publicized and contested case with racial overtones. Reprinted on AfroCubaWeb.com, the poem is a strong statement: "Hands off Assata, Republican witch! This Sista you won't kill or turn into Oprah, hanging out with Uncle Sam. She is ours; this Oya Woman, this Liberations Fighter, this Warrior-queen, this child of Harriet Tubman is ours—the Black Nation's Champion."

Dawnsong: The Epic Memory of Askia Touré, published in 2000, was awarded the Stephen Henderson Poetry award from the African-American Literature and Culture Society. Formulated on the Egyptian and Nubian civilizations along the Nile River, *Dawnsong* carries the reader through a history that predates slavery by thousands of years from the development of early human history to the triumphant creation of a highly cultured society. Once again using highly imagistic images, Touré's epic poetry depends on the cadence and tonality of jazz to develop a free-flowing verse, uplifting African history and culture and transposing it onto the modern black experience. "I'm part of what's been called the Afro-centric movement," he told Riverdeep.net. "But I prefer to call it African restoration because I try to restore and resurrect the ancient archetypes of the African people."

Touré, who is the artist in residence at Boston's Ogunamaile Gallery, continues to be active in the literary and political world. In 2003 he was working on making his play "Double Dutch: A Gather of Women" into an independent film. He was also collaborating with Boston composers to create a libretto from his epic poem "From the Pyramids to the Projects, From the Projects to the Stars." The Official Askia Touré Web site (www.askiatoure.com) became fully operational in August of 2004, with plans, according to Touré, to develop into a forum for interviews, dialogues, discussions, and political, cultural, spiritual, and historical analyses. Touré also continues to be a sought-after speaker.

Selected writings

Earth: For Mrs. Mary Bethune and the African and Afro-American Women, Broadside Press, 1968.
(With Ben Caldwell) *JuJu: Magic Songs for the Black Nation,* Third World Press, 1970.
Songhai!, Songhai Press, 1972.
From the Pyramids to the Projects: Poems of Genocide and Resistance!, African World Press, 1990.
Dawnsong! The Epic Memory of Askia Touré, Third World Press, 2000.

Sources

Books

Dictionary of Literary Biography. Volume 41: Afro-American Poets Since 1955, Gale Group, 1985.
Propaganda and Aesthetics: The Politics of African American Magazines in the Twentieth Century, University of Massachusetts Press, 1991.

Periodicals

African American Review, Summer 2002.
Black Issues Book Review, September 2000.

On-line

"Askia Touré," *AfroCubaWeb,* www.afrocubaweb.com/askiatoure.htm (September 13, 2004).
"Askia M. Touré: Poet, Activist, Africana Studies Pioneer," *The Official Web Site of Askia Toure,* www.askiatoure.com (September 13, 2004).

Contemporary Authors Online, www.galegroup.gale net.com (September 13, 2004).

"Reviving the Memory of a People," *Riverdeep.net,* http://www.riverdeep.net/current/2000/10/1005 00_askia.jhtml (September 21, 2004).

—Kari Bethel

Gene Upshaw

1945—

Football player, union executive

As a guard for pro football's Oakland Raiders, Gene Upshaw established a reputation as one of the most dominating players on the field. As the longtime executive director of the NFL Players' Association, he is widely regarded as one of the most powerful players on the sidelines. Upshaw helped the Raiders win two Super Bowls during his playing career, and became the standard by which all offensive linemen of the period were measured. During his long tenure at the helm of the Players' Association, Upshaw led the bargaining that led to free agency, big increases in profits from product licensing, and the best benefit package in professional sports.

Grew Into Football

Eugene Upshaw, Jr., was born on August 15, 1945, in Robstown, Texas. His father, Eugene Sr., worked for the local oil company, while his mother, Cora, was a domestic laborer. Upshaw was the oldest of three brothers. One of his brothers, Marvin, also went on to enjoy a successful NFL football career. As a child, Upshaw and his brothers attended a four-room schoolhouse. They earned extra money picking cotton, for which they were paid $1.25 for every 100 pounds of cotton they picked.

The only time the Upshaw brothers were allowed to avoid cotton-picking duties was when they were playing baseball. Needless to say, they spent as much time on the diamond as they could. Gene became a standout pitcher, and Marvin served as his catcher. The brothers carried their little league team to within one game of the Little League World Series in 1958. Gene went on to star for his high school baseball team. At only 5' 10" and 185 pounds, however, he had neither the size nor the aggressive nature to make much of a splash on the football field. He did play one year of varsity football, but it was brother Marvin who excelled at that sport. Eugene Sr.—a former semi-pro baseball player himself—warned Gene that if he signed a bonus to pitch in the minors instead of going to college, he would be kicked out of the house. Upon graduating from Robstown High School, Gene obediently enrolled at nearby Texas A&I.

Although he did not especially care for the contact and violence of football, Upshaw decided to try out for the football team at Texas A&I, in the hope of translating his natural athletic ability into a scholarship. The plan worked. The minute coach Gil Steinke saw the powerfully-built Upshaw, he said, according to the *Hartford Courant*, "Get a uniform on him." Three days later, Upshaw had his scholarship. By this time, Upshaw had begun to grow, and he continued to grow throughout college, reaching an imposing 6' 5" and 265 pounds by his senior year.

Playing center and tackle, Upshaw had a stellar career at Texas A&I. He was named First Team All-Lone Star Conference and received honorable mention Little All-America from the Associated Press in his senior year. Pro scouts projected that Upshaw would be selected in the third round of the 1967 National Football League (NFL)-American Football League

At a Glance . . .

Born Eugene Upshaw, Jr., on August 15, 1945, in Robstown, TX; son of Eugene (an oil company employee) and Cora (a domestic worker; maiden name, Riley) Upshaw; married Jimmye Hill, December 30, 1967 (divorced); married Teresa Buich, 1986; children: (first marriage) Eugene III; (second marriage) Justin, Daniel. *Education:* Texas A&I University, Kingsville, BS, 1968; additional study at California State University, 1969, and Golden Gate University Law School, 1982. *Politics:* Democrat. *Religion:* Baptist.

Career: Oakland (later Los Angeles) Raiders, professional football player, 1967-82; Gene Upshaw and Associates (management consulting firm), partner, 1970-78; NFL Players' Association, Raiders player representative, 1970-76, member of executive committee, 1976–, president, 1980-82, executive director, 1983–.

Awards: American Football Conference (AFC) Lineman of the Year, 1973, 1974, and 1977; National Football League (NFL) Lineman of the Year, 1977; named to NFL Pro Bowl six times; Byron "Whizzer" White Humanitarian Award, 1980; inducted into Pro Football Hall of Fame, 1987; elected to All-Time NFL team, 1994.

Addresses: *Office*—NFL Players Association, 2021 L Street NW, Suite 600, Washington, DC 20036.

(AFL) draft. He performed so well at the Senior Bowl, the Coaches All-American Bowl, and the College All-Star game, however, that he quickly came to be considered one of the top linemen available. The Oakland Raiders of the AFL selected Upshaw in the first round, making him the 17th player chosen overall in the entire draft.

All-Pro Guard

As a rookie for the Raiders, Upshaw was switched to the guard position. His combination of speed, strength, and mobility quickly made him the prototype for the next generation of NFL guards. Upshaw's impact on the field was immediate, as the Raiders made it into the playoffs in each of his first three seasons with the team, and 11 times overall during his career, which lasted from 1967 until 1982. Three times during that span,

the Raiders won the AFL (later the American Football Conference (AFC) championship, and in two of those seasons, 1977 and 1981, they won the Super Bowl. Upshaw was the only pro football player to play in the Super Bowl in the 1960s, 1970s, and 1980s.

In addition to his talents as a player, Upshaw's natural leadership skills quickly became apparent. He was a team leader on and off the field. For ten years, Upshaw was a Raider team captain. In 1970 he became the Raiders' representative to the players' union, the NFL Players' Association (NFLPA). Around the time he was becoming active in football union issues, Upshaw began to take an interest in general politics as well. He joined the Democratic Party Central Committee of Alameda County, California, in 1970, and later served on the Alameda County Planning Commission, the California Board of Governors for Community Colleges, and the Governor's Council on Wellness and Physical Fitness. He was also actively involved with numerous charitable organizations.

Meanwhile, Upshaw was showered with awards for his performance on the field. He played in the Pro Bowl six times. In 1977 he was named NFL Lineman of the Year, and he earned AFC Lineman of the Year honors in 1973 and 1974. In 1976, after six years as the Raiders' players' representative, Upshaw was elected to the NFLPA Executive Committee. He was named union president, under executive director Ed Garvey, in 1980. As president of the NFLPA, Upshaw was cast in the role of the heavy, taking serious flack from both sides during the NFL players' 57-day strike in 1982. As the point person in communicating the union's stance to team owners, the public, and the players' association's own members, Upshaw was criticized for being too inflexible and militant. When Garvey resigned as head of the union the following year, Upshaw—who, as a freshly-retired player, had more credibility among players than Garvey ever did—was perceived as the best candidate to succeed him.

Meanwhile, Upshaw continued to receive recognition for his community service contributions. In 1980 he received the prestigious Byron "Whizzer" White Humanitarian Award for outstanding contribution to "team, community, and country." Two years later he was presented with the A. Phillip Randolph Award for significant accomplishments as one of the outstanding black leaders in America. Among the groups he worked with were the Muscular Dystrophy Association and the National Committee on Drug Prevention.

Led NFL Players Union

The NFLPA that Upshaw took over in 1983 was an organization in disarray. Still reeling from the devastating effects of the 1982 strike, the union was broke, lacked the confidence of its own members, and had a terrible public image. Upshaw quickly took measures to address each of these problems. Although still taking a tough stance in negotiations, he worked to develop a positive relationship with Jack Donlan, chief negotiator for the team owners, and a man whom Upshaw's predecessor Garvey had clashed with frequently. Despite these efforts, Upshaw was perceived as being "militant," a term that he complained was racially charged. According to Upshaw, a white person who takes a strong position is "viewed as 'taking a strong position.' But if you're black and you take a strong position, you're viewed as militant," he told the *Washington Post*. Upshaw's credentials as a labor leader received a boost in 1985, when he was elected to the executive council of the AFL-CIO, one of the most powerful national labor unions.

In 1987 Upshaw was inducted into the Pro Football Hall of Fame. His biggest challenges as a union man remained ahead of him, however. When pro football's collective bargaining agreement expired in the fall of 1987, Upshaw called for a player strike to protest the owners' inflexible bargaining position on the issue of free agency, a contract provision that gives players the right to sell their labor to any team. The strike failed miserably. The owners hired strikebreakers to play for them and convinced the television stations to broadcast the games. Players began to cross the picket line in droves, and in mid-October they voted to end the strike. To add insult to injury, the owners locked the players out for an additional week.

Undaunted, Upshaw came up with a new strategy. He decertified the players' union, which essentially made all players free agents from a legal standpoint. The move caught the owners off-guard, and led to another five years of legal maneuvering and negotiations, including at least twenty lawsuits filed against the league by Upshaw on the players' behalf. The end result was the 1993 signing of a new seven-year contract that gave players some free-agency rights and gave the owners a salary cap. Although some players and owners were not pleased with the deal, it represented a compromise that both sides could live with. More importantly, football was no longer the only major sport without some form of player free agency. The *New York Times* called free agency Upshaw's "crowning jewel" in a collection of football treasures. In reality, the deal Upshaw helped forge was a double-edged sword for some. While it led to spectacular new contracts for many up-and-coming stars, a lot of aging veterans found themselves cast aside, or were forced to play for dramatically reduced salaries.

In the years since 1993, Upshaw, the NFLPA, and NFL team owners have worked together to decrease the adversarial nature of labor talks and to ensure that pro football is profitable for all involved. The result of the labor-management cooperation was the signing, in 2002, of a third-straight extension of the collective bargaining agreement, good through the year 2007. The 2002 agreement gave players full free agency and ensured that 65 to 70 percent of NFL revenues would be dedicated to player salaries and benefits. In exchange, team owners won salary cap provisions that allow them to keep their total payroll under control. Upshaw attributes the long period of peaceful labor relations in pro football to the shared interests of players and owners. He told *Business Week* in 2003: "We both understand that it's in everyone's best interest to have a league that is well run. We don't want to blow a good thing."

In addition to his work with the union, in 1994 Upshaw helped launch an organization, called National Football League Players, Inc. (or simply Players Inc.), that aimed to maximize the players' profits from licensing and marketing activities. Players Inc. became the first players association devoted to "taking the helmets off" players and marketing them as personalities as well as professional athletes. With Upshaw as its Chairman of the Board, Players Inc. has moved far beyond typical licensing activities, becoming involved in the creation, ownership and marketing of special events, promotions, publishing, and recording and broadcasting projects. Players Inc. produced its first nationally syndicated television special, the "NFL Players Rookie Premiere," in 1997; by 2000, the program was reaching over 40 million homes annually. Other activities have included the promotion of special appearances by players, scheduling of golf events, production of radio shows, and negotiation of corporate sponsorships. By 2001, Players Inc. had licensed over 100 companies for retail products, including trading cards and collectibles, video games and sports apparel.

Upshaw is widely acclaimed for his role in ensuring the stability and success of professional football in the 1990s and early 2000s. In fact, *The Sporting News* has regularly placed him on its list of the 100 most powerful people in sports. In 1997 Upshaw signed a new salary contract with the NFLPA and Players Inc. worth $11.2 million over seven years, making him the highest paid union boss in all of professional team sports. In 2003, Players Association representatives elected Upshaw to his seventh consecutive term as executive director. Upshaw promised that his seventh term would be his last, announcing in 2003 that he would retire from his position at the end of his contract in 2007.

Sources

Periodicals

Business Week, January 27, 2003, p. 91.
Ebony, December 1983, p. 76.
Football Digest, March 2003, p. 48.
Jet, November 25, 1985, p. 38; October 19, 1987, p. 49; October 20, 1997, p. 51.
New York, September 26, 1994, pp. 24-28.
New York Times, August 11, 1996, p. S3.
PR Newswire, March 19, 2003.
Sports Illustrated, September 14, 1987, pp. 64-74.

On-line

"Gene Upshaw," *Pro Football Hall of Fame,* www.
  profootballhof.com/hof/member.jsp?player_id=220
  (August 18, 2004).
National Football League Players Association, www.
  nflpa.org (August 18, 2004).
NFL Players, www.nflplayers.com (August 18, 2004).

—Robert R. Jacobson And Tom Pendergast

Iyanla Vanzant

1953—

Counselor, lawyer, writer, lecturer

Iyanla (pronounced EE-yan-lah) Vanzant has overcome overwhelming personal difficulties to become a lawyer, minister, talk show host, best-selling author, and national advocate for literacy. Through her self-named "dark valley experiences," those that like real valleys are necessarily traversed on the path from one mountain or peak to the next, Vanzant has emerged at a far different place from where she started and with a far more positive perspective on life than most anyone could imagine. *Emerge* magazine has hailed her as "one of the four most dynamic African-American speakers in the country." In 1992 Thomas Bradley, then Mayor of Los Angeles, called her "an inspiration to all women, particularly young African-American women growing through hardships in the inner city."

Using her powerful speaking and writing abilities, Iyanla Vanzant has been on a mission to educate women, especially those of color, to create a better life for themselves and their communities, by discovering the kingdom of God within. This best-selling author and spiritual-life counselor was ordained a "Yoruba Priestess" in 1983 (in New York). The Yoruba religion (from Nigeria) blends and adapts ancient African spirituality with contemporary African American culture. For Vanzant and her ancestors, African spirituality has been essential, since around 4000 B.C., to healing and transforming the mind, body, and soul. More recently, in September of 1997, she was a gospel minister with Dr. Barbara King, at Hillside Chapel and Truth Center, in Atlanta.

Iyanla Vanzant had a troubled childhood. After her mother died when she was two or three years old,

Vanzant was raised by her grandmother. Rather than a haven of safety, Vanzant found her new home exposed her to physical and sexual abuse. She received good grades, even though she was not encouraged to do so. On a self-professed search for love and security, she found herself pregnant by age 16, and had three children by 21. She was married when she was 18 and nine years later, when she finally left her abusive husband, Vanzant said in an article written for *Essence*, "I accumulated several black eyes, three fractured ribs, a broken jaw, a displaced uterus, and something far worse: the death of my personhood. In a fit of depression, I attempted suicide."

After being released from the hospital psychiatric ward, Vanzant, with her three children in tow, went on welfare. She was on welfare for eight years before, struck by the unfulfilled purpose in her life, she applied to Medgar Evers College, despite protests from family members, and began attending classes. Three-and-a-half years later she left welfare forever after graduating summa cum laude with a bachelor's degree in public administration and being offered a job that, as she said in *Essence*, "paid more than my former caseworker made!"

Three years after graduation, she attained a law degree from the City University of New York. Despite more than 20 years of practical study in the fields of spirituality and empowerment, however, Vanzant chose not to go into academics. Rather than intellectual analyses, she offered very apt spiritual guidance. In all her books and talks, Vanzant has offered ancient, but still contemporary wisdom and common sense,

At a Glance . . .

Born Rhonda Harris on September 13, 1953, in Brooklyn, New York; changed name to Iyanla, 1983; daughter of Horace Harris (a numbers runner for illegal gamblers) and Sarah Jefferson (a maid on a railroad car); married (fourth marriage) Adeyemi Bandele, 1996; children: Damon, Gemmia, Nisa. *Education:* Medgar Evers College, BA, public administration, summa cum laude, 1983; City University of New York, JD, 1988; University of Santa Monica, MA, spiritual psychology, 2001.

Career: Public defender, Philadelphia, 1988-92; ordained Yoruba priestess, 1983; founder and president of Inner Visions Spiritual Life Maintenance Center and Bookstore, Silver Springs, Maryland, 1988–; author, 1992–; ordained a gospel minister, 1997, talk show host, ABC, 2001.

Awards: International Congress of Black Women, Oni Award, 1991; National Association for Equal Opportunity in Education, Alumni of the Year, 1994; Blackboard Book of the Year, 1994 , 1995, 1996; NAACP Image Award for Outstanding Literary Work, Non-Fiction, for *Yesterday I Cried,* 1999; City University of New York, Medgar Evers College, Honorary Doctor of Humane Letters, 1999; Theological Seminary, Atlanta, Georgia, Honorary Doctor of Divinity, 2000.

Addresses: *Office*—PO Box 3231, Silver Spring, Maryland 20910.

leading her readers in and out of the "dark experiences."

Vanzant has experienced the healing journey from despair to self-reliance that she so fervently wants others to take. From her troubled past, she has emerged a winner, committed to an eclectic message of divine power and self-determination. This popular motivational speaker and prolific author has taken her audience by the hand and led them down the path of self-discovery, self-help, self-empowerment, and self-love. Vanzant stressed that all this social and self-improvement was made possible, however, only by "tapping the power within."

In confronting discrimination, racism, rejection, and alienation, Vanzant took an approach that, for a feminist, was very non-traditional—less political and more spiritual. She asserted in a telephone interview, "Spiritual consciousness does not make your problems go away; it does, however, help you view them from a different vantage point.... Your political reality is determined by your personal reality.... Racism and sexism in and of themselves are not what limit black women in America. It is our perception of them." Vanzant's *Faith in the Valley*, the companion book to her best-selling *Acts of Faith*, has inspired thousands of black women to seriously consider how their own behavior might have been causing certain avoidable problems. Her own journey served as an inspiring model for others.

According to Vanzant in *Faith in the Valley*, Black women, like many others, have found it "difficult to accept that life is more than hopping from one mountaintop experience to another.... Somehow we forget there is a valley between every mountain.... Eventually we [must] do the work it takes to get out of those dark experiences called valleys." Vanzant the counselor reminds her readers that "valleys are purposeful," that the highs and the lows, the light and the dark, have all balanced out and each experience was necessary to appreciate the other.

As she said in *Faith in the Valley*, "If we think of life as a twenty-four hour day, we know to expect twelve hours of light and twelve hours of darkness." Arriving at this realization would point the way up and out of a valley. The way out always involves a choice: spiritual growth, faith, and strength, or in Vanzant's words, "the stuff our grandmothers were made of." Women are to choose faith in God instead of the things that provide illusory comfort.

The author's pain and triumph, coming through her deepest spiritual valley, was most poignantly told in her memoirs *Interiors: A Black Woman's Healing in Progress*. While *Interiors* told of one woman's trip to insanity and her journey back, this survivor's suffering and recovery were told in a way that they became the story of all women. It was important, she said, for women to have discovered who they were so they would have made their decisions accordingly.

However, Iyanla has said that who she was has had nothing to do with her having been raped by her uncle at age nine. Nor did Iyanla see herself as having been crushed by the nine years spent in an abusive marriage before she found the strength to leave it. She has said that being a welfare recipient did not make her the person she has become. Nor did Iyanla define herself by a successful career as a public defender, spiritual counselor, best-selling author, or doting grandmother.

So just who is Iyanla Vanzant? In a phone interview with Dietrich Gruen she said, "I used to be just another Black woman, but today I am a child of God! This means I am unique, but I am not special. I am an ordinary person who is dedicated to doing very special things." And it would seem that others would agree with her. On the back cover of *Faith in the Valley*, fellow author and soul mate Julia Boyd commended her sister in the faith, whose message "comes right from the heart and goes straight to the soul....Thank you, sister Iyanla, for your gifts (of) wisdom, courage, and faith sprinkled with lots of blessings and love. Iyanla truly loves and cares about us sisters and it shows."

The small Harlem-based publishing house, Writers & Readers, took a first-time author and "put her on the map," when they published *Tapping the Power Within* (1992), at a time when few inspirational works were marketed specifically to African Americans. Vanzant went on to establish herself as a best-selling author, with more than 400,000 in sales of *Acts of Faith* (1993) and 100,000 of *The Value in the Valley* (1995). Vanzant's later books have been lined up with mainstream publishers, with a promise of more in 1998.

Widely regarded as America's leading authority on spirituality and empowerment for Black women, Iyanla Vanzant went on to offer her insights into the history and souls of Black men in *The Spirit of a Man : A Vision of Transformation for Black Men and the Women Who Love Them* (Harper San Francisco, 1996). This book provided a blend of ancient African spirituality, practical self-help advice, and contemporary faith. This effective blend has stimulated self-knowledge and courage for Black men in the struggles, crises, and victories they experienced in confronting the powerful social, political, and economic forces at work against them.

The best-selling author who has empowered countless Black women has also reached out to women of all races, all who have yearned for love. Her book *In the Meantime: Finding Yourself in the Love You Want* talked about love, sex, and marriage in the 1990s. About what it takes for men and women surviving the current gender wars in a successful marriage, Vanzant has this to say, "When your life is working, it is not a dramatic production. We have to break our addiction to drama and crisis. And we have to stop competing." Vanzant has touched men and women at all levels, and has tried to teach them to pursue their lives with success and faith.

Three years in a row this celebrated author has won the coveted "Blackboard Book of the Year"–for *Acts of Faith* (1993), *The Value in the Valley* (1995), and *Faith in the Valley* (1996). Vanzant was honored "Alumni of the Year" in 1994 by the National Association for Equal Opportunity in Education, an organization made up of the presidents and administrators of the 117 predominantly Black colleges in America. As one of the nation's "unsung heroes," she was given the "Oni" award by the International Congress of Black Women. In 1997 she founded and became president of Inner Visions Spiritual Life Maintenance Center. The next year she served as a national spokesperson for the Literacy Volunteers of America.

Vanzant continued to reach out to as many people as possible. In the late 1990s and early 2000s, she was a regular guest speaker on *The Oprah Winfrey Show*. In 2001 she hosted her own talk show for ABC. When the network canceled the show after one season, Vanzant continued her spiritual counseling undeterred. Working through her Inner Visions organization, Vanzant lectures, records inspirational and motivational compact discs, and writes books. Her books have sold billions of copies. In 2004 she joined the reality show *Starting Over* on ABC as a counselor. On the show Vanzant worked with six women who agreed to live together in a house while participating in life-changing counseling sessions. For all her work, Vanzant's appeal and power continued to spread. *Ebony* magazine recognized Vanzant as one of the 100 Most Influential African-Americans, *Vibe* magazine called her one of "100 Leaders of the New Millennium," and *Newsweek* featured her as one of the "Women of the New Century."

Selected writings

Tapping the Power Within: A Path to Self-Empowerment for Black Women, Writers & Readers, 1992.
Acts of Faith: Daily Meditations for People of Color, Simon & Schuster, 1993.
Interiors: A Black Woman's Healing in Progress, Writers & Readers, 1995.
The Value in The Valley: A Black Woman's Guide Through Life's Dilemmas, Simon & Schuster, 1995.
Faith in the Valley: Lessons for Women on the Journey Toward Peace, Simon & Schuster, 1996.
The Spirit of a Man: A Vision of Transformation for Black Men and the Women Who Love Them, Harper San Francisco, 1996.
The Big Book of Faith, Simon & Schuster, 1997.
In the Meantime: Finding Yourself and the Love That You Want, Simon & Schuster, 1998.
One Day My Soul Just Opened Up: 40 Days and 40 Nights Toward Spiritual Strength and Personal Growth, Fireside Books, 1998.
Yesterday I Cried: Celebrating the Lessons of Living and Loving, Simon & Schuster, 1998.
Every Day I Pray: Prayers for Awakening to the Grace of Inner Communion, Simon & Schuster, 2001.
Living Through the Meantime: Learning to Break the Patterns of the Past and Begin the Healing Process, Simon & Schuster, 2001.

Sources

Books

Murphy, Joseph M. *Working the Spirit*. Beacon Press, 1994.

Periodicals

Essence, October, 1989, p. 80; July, 1996 p. 104; March, 1997, p. 62; July, 1997, p. 65; August 2001, p. 112.
Philadelphia Tribune, January 9, 1998, p. C1.
Publishers Weekly, January 29, 1996, p. 16; March 18, 1996, p. 14.
Jet, September 22, 1997, p. 14.

Other

Dateline, NBC, November 22, 1998.
Inner Visions, www.innervisionsworldwide.com (September 15, 2004).

—Dietrich Gruen, Catherine V. Donaldson,
and Sara Pendergast

Gladys Gary Vaughn

1942(?)—

Organization leader

A recognized expert in family and social science, Gladys Gary Vaughn has forged a 30-year career in helping people improve the quality of their lives. "I've always believed in social justice. It is a deeply held belief of mine," she told *Contemporary Black Biography* (*CBB*). To that end, she has spoken before Congress and on the talk show *Geraldo*. She has published scholarly papers, appeared at international seminars, and been quoted in *The New York Times*. More importantly, her expertise has guided policies and programs that have positively affected thousands throughout the world.

Juggled Full Schedule as Child

Born Gladys Gary in the early 1940s in Ocala, Florida, Vaughn was the middle of five children of Homer and Ollie Colden Gary. Her mother was an elementary school teacher while her father ran the family's large farm. The combination led to a very disciplined household. "In our family we were expected to do well in the sense that my mother and father were determined to see all of us through high school and college," Vaughn told *CBB*. "So they provided a home environment that encouraged that." She continued, "In addition to school we were sent to music lessons (I took piano), and were expected to participate in school and church activities. I was very active in 4H [and] New Homemakers of America (NHA). I was also in student govern-

ment, played basketball, participated in the yearly school play, and was a cheerleader."

If that wasn't enough to keep the young Vaughn busy, there was always farm work. "We had to feed the animals and help during planting and harvesting season," Vaughn told *CBB*. On the weekends there was church. "We belonged to the African Methodist Church and our parents expected us to not only go to church but to go to Sunday school and all church-related activities," Vaughn explained. Though it may seem a heavy schedule for a child, Vaughn explained that her parent's expectations were typical of the time. "I grew up in the segregated years and it was the pattern of your life," Vaughn told *CBB*. "Everybody knew everybody and the parents formed a community to protect the children. We were kept active as much to keep us safe as to help us to do well in life."

Following high school Vaughn attended Florida A&M University and earned a degree in home economics in 1964. She returned to Florida where she worked for two years as a high school teacher before receiving a scholarship to Iowa State University in 1966. "[The scholarship] was part of a program from the Johnson Administration to improve secondary school education," Vaughn explained to *CBB*. "It was designed to increase the educational background of people who would become principals and administrators in secondary schools. There were 20 scholarship recipients at Iowa State, 18 were white males, one was a white female, and there was me." Vaughn earned a master's degree in home economics education from the school in 1968.

Began Career in Home Economics

In 1969 Vaughn and husband Dr. Joseph B. Vaughn, Jr., moved to North Carolina. "He was doing graduate school [at North Carolina Central University] and I took a job in the Home Economics department," Vaughn told *CBB*. In 1972 the university gave Vaughn a sabbatical from her teaching duties to pursue a doctorate. At the University of Maryland Vaughn earned a Ph.D. in home economics and educational administration in only two years. "North Carolina had given me a two year leave of absence to get my doctorate, so I got it done in that time and then returned to work at North Carolina again," Vaughn explained to *CBB*.

While at the University of Maryland, Vaughn had worked part-time at the American Home Economics Association (now the American Association of Family and Consumer Science AAFCS) in Washington, D.C., and in 1976 the organization offered her a full-time job. She and her husband moved to Washington, D.C., where he set up a medical practice, and as Vaughn explained to *CBB*, she "stayed with [AAFCS] for more than 20 years." AAFCS is dedicated to improving individual and family life by providing educational programs and influencing public policy. During Vaughn's two decades with the group she contributed extensively to this mission, holding positions in fundraising, research, program development, international planning, and grant writing.

After retiring from the AAFCS in 1995, Vaughn focused her efforts on the Odyssey Group, a family and consumer science consultancy she founded in 1994. The firm provided curriculum creation, grant writing, proposal development, and leadership training. Vaughn also offered seminars on professional, societal, and family life topics. Some of Odyssey's more prominent projects included *Families First: Nutrition Education and Wellness System*, a nutritional education program for food stamp recipients; *Teen Leadership Connection*, a youth development program sponsored by Texas's Prairie View A&M University; and the *Team Nutrition Community Action Kit*, a nutrition education program for the Cooperative State Research, Education, and Extension Service (CREES), a division of the US Department of Agriculture (USDA). "All three of the programs won awards," Vaughn proudly noted to *CBB*.

Launched Second Career with USDA

In 1998 Vaughn joined CREES full-time as the National Program Leader for Human Sciences Research for the Families, 4-H and Nutrition Unit. In that role she acted as a liaison with civic, corporate, academic, and government groups, to provide advice and assistance on all types of human sciences programs. In addition she co-founded the successful Food and Nutrition Summer Institute, an annual seminar that encourages educators to introduce innovative nutrition and physical education programs into their schools. However one of Vaughn's proudest achievements at the USDA was the founding of a mentoring program within the department. The USDA, like most government agencies, ranks employees by grade. As you move up from position to position your grade also increases. "Often there is miscommunication between the grades, and between races," Vaughn told *CBB*. "Also those at the lower grades don't often recognize the opportunities they can have as they move up." To combat this Vaughn developed a program that allows employees in lower grades to be mentored by those in higher grades. "It created the opportunity to create a community of excellence," Vaughn told *CBB*. The USDA agreed and in 2004 the program was awarded its highest prize, the Secretary's Honor Award.

In May of 2004 Vaughn left CREES to become the director of outreach for the USDA. Each agency within the department has an outreach office and Vaughn's job was to coordinate the efforts of all of them. "The office is set up to ensure that citizens have access to all of the programs and services of the department. It is particularly aimed at un- and underserved clients," Vaughn told *CBB*.

Throughout her career with both the AAFCS and the USDA, Vaughn has built a reputation as one of the country's foremost authorities on family and consumer sciences, particularly related to the African-American and Hispanic communities. She authored dozens of papers and programs on topics as diverse as leadership, latchkey kids, developing nations, family planning, and legislative processes. She was a principal architect behind several ground-breaking social programs dealing with issues such as teenage pregnancy, childhood self-esteem, and physical activity. She has also been active in several initiatives in Africa and the Caribbean, from rural health care to agriculture and nutrition. Her skill in grant writing and fundraising has resulted in over $12 million in funding for many of these programs. These experiences have made her a sought-after public speaker and landed her on the advisory committees of several prominent universities. It has also earned her a slew of awards including the 2000 Distinguished Service Award from AAFCS, the highest honor in the field of family and consumer science.

Dedicated to Community Service

The discipline that carried Vaughn through a childhood of scheduled activity carried through in her career. In addition to her heavy work load, Vaughn has been very active in community service. She has served on the boards of many groups including the Black Patriots Foundation, Black Women's Agenda, and the National Consumer's League. She also co-founded the National Coalition for Black Development in Home Economics in 1980. Since childhood Vaughn has also remained very active in the African Methodist Church. However Vaughn's most active community service has been with The Links, Inc., an international service organization of women of African ancestry. Vaughn became involved in the group in 1982 when she became the founding president of the Potomac, Virginia, chapter. In 1986 she moved up to the national level when she was appointed to the group's executive council.

In 20 years with The Links, Vaughn has played a key role in initiatives from drug and alcohol prevention for minority youth in Washington, D.C., to national organ donor programs. She helped design and/or secure funding for several important national programs including *Links To Success: Children Achieving Excellence*, an early education program for underachieving minority children and *High Expectations!*, an adolescent pregnancy prevention project. Her activity propelled Vaughn to the group's vice presidency in 1998. In 2002 she became its president.

As national president of the 10,000-plus member group, Vaughn maintained a calendar full of meetings, consultations, and speaking appointments. Add that to what she told *CBB* was her "more than a full-time job" at the USDA and her resultant schedule was near bursting. It didn't phase Vaughn though. Drawing on a determination inherited from her parents, as well as her own commitment to social change, Vaughn told *CBB*, "I believe in doing your best no matter what your job is. And I believe deeply in a fair day's pay for a fair day's work. And I believe in being disciplined in your work."

Sources

On-line

"Soror Gladys Gary Vaughn, Ph.D.," Delta Sigma Theta, www.geocities.com/taunotabledeltas/ (August 22, 2004).

Other

Additional information for this profile was obtained through an interview with Gladys Gary Vaughn on September 19, 2004, and biographical materials from The Links, Inc.

—Candace LaBalle

Perry E. Wallace, Jr.

1948—

College basketball player; law professor

As the first African-American player in college basketball's Southeastern Conference (SEC), Perry Wallace pioneered the way for black players to excel in this sport. Yet his years on the Vanderbilt University varsity team were marked by racist incidents and by a sense of isolation on campus. Despite daunting obstacles, however, Wallace became one of the school's most celebrated athletes as well as a distinguished alumnus with a career in legal education.

Excelled in School Sports

Born in Nashville, Tennessee, in 1948 to Perry E. and Hattie Haynes Wallace, Perry Junior was the youngest of six children. He grew up in Nashville and attended racially segregated public schools. "It was segregation with an attitude," he commented to *Black Athlete Sports Network* writer Michael Hudson. "People had an attitude about where you were and what you were—and what they could do to you." Wallace showed early academic and athletic promise. At Pearl Senior High School, where he earned the nickname "king of the boards," he played center on the varsity basketball team. At six-feet, five-inches tall, he became famous for his powerful slam dunks. In 1965-66, the first year in which African-American students were allowed to participate in local, regional, and state championships, Pearl's team swept away the competition to become the first African-American team to win the Tennessee Secondary School Boys' State Basketball Tournament.

Wallace averaged 19 rebounds and 12 points per game, earning the distinction of high school All-American. Valedictorian of his graduating class with a straight-A average, he was recruited by more than 80 colleges and universities. "He was the best player in the region with major college aspirations, and he was smart," observed Roy Neel in *The Vanderbilt Hustler*. Faced with a wealth of college options, Wallace weighed his choices carefully. "When I was looking at schools," he commented in *The Vanderbilt Hustler*, "I was interested in a good education and playing major college basketball. But when you're black and growing up in the South, there are just not many opportunities."

Wallace expected to attend either a historically black college or a school in the North. "But then Vanderbilt came into the picture," he recalled. One of the country's top 20 universities, Vanderbilt, located in Wallace's hometown of Nashville, had been segregated for most of its history and did not accept its first black student until 1953. "I knew that it was going to take a lot of extra effort and resilience [to enroll there]," he remembered. "It was all a big unknown." Despite his doubts, Wallace chose Vanderbilt, mostly on the basis of its excellent engineering program.

Broke the SEC Color Barrier

Wallace entered Vanderbilt on an athletic scholarship in 1966. During his first year, he played on Vanderbilt's freshman squad because NCAA regulations prohibited freshmen from playing on the varsity team. Another black player, Godfrey Dillard, had come to Vanderbilt that year from Detroit and played with Wallace on the freshman squad. Dillard was later injured and did not go on to play on the varsity team. Though Vanderbilt fans accepted the black players, at away games Wallace and Dillard faced racist taunts and jeers from hostile crowds. "You could really hear the catcalls and threats and racial epithets," Wallace told *USA Today* reporter Jack Carey. "It was clearly racist stuff. They'd cheer when we made a mistake and yell 'Which one's Amos and which one's Andy?' It was literally chilling. There were times my hands were absolutely cold. That was a real baptism."

Wallace and Dillard supported each other as much as they could, but remained silent about the threats they received. "This was a horror," Wallace later told Hudson. "To even let it out and speak the words created the danger that you might actually realize what you had been through." Despite these intensely hostile conditions, Wallace finished his freshman season with an impressive average of 17 points and 20 rebounds per game.

When he joined the varsity squad the following year, becoming Vanderbilt's first African-American varsity

athlete and the first African American to play basketball in the SEC, Wallace confronted a different game than he was prepared for: the NCAA had decided that year to ban the slam-dunk in college play. Some coaches and players saw this decision as an attempt to stop "black basketball," as played by such stars as UCLA's Lew Alcindor (now Kareem Abdul-Jabbar), from dominating the sport. In any case, the new rule forced Wallace to learn a whole new style of play. According to Roy Skinner, who was head basketball coach at Vanderbilt from 1961 to 1976, the ban on slam-dunks presented Wallace with a significant handicap. "They took away his game," Skinner recalled in *The Vanderbilt Hustler.* "He couldn't shoot worth a damn.... He basically had to start all over. He had to learn to play basketball, but he worked hard at it."

Indeed, by the end of his Vanderbilt career, Wallace had proved himself one of the school's greatest athletes. During his three varsity seasons, he improved his free-throw percentage from 50 percent in his sophomore year to 77 percent in his senior year, and raised his point average from 9.7 per game to 17.7 per game. In his senior year, he averaged 13.5 rebounds per game and scored 461 points for a career total of 1,010 points, making him one of 33 members of Vanderbilt's 1,000 Points Club. More than 30 years after graduating, Wallace remained the school's second-leading rebounder with a total of 894 career boards, as well as its 35th-best scorer.

Endured Racist Assaults

Success, however, did not come easily. When Wallace joined the varsity squad and began participating in SEC games, the virulence of the racist attacks against him increased. According to *The Tennessee Encyclopedia of History and Culture,* "He experienced racism at its worst, particularly at SEC schools in Alabama and Mississippi. Cheerleaders led a volley of invective racist cheers. There were threats of beatings, castration, and lynching. He endured physical abuse on the court that referees refused to acknowledge as fouls. Wallace was harangued, taunted, and threatened throughout his SEC career." As the only black athlete on the court at away games, according to Hudson, Wallace felt like a "marked man."

In his first game at the University of Mississippi, in the Tad Smith Coliseum, Wallace was punched in the eye and badly injured while jumping up for a rebound. The crowd cheered after the attack. "It was an ugly incident," he recalled in *The Vanderbilt Hustler.* Determined not to allow such behavior to defeat him, he came back to the game in the second half to score 14 points and make 11 rebounds. "Struggling to stay inbounds between whites who wanted him to fail and African Americans who expected him to be a 'superstar,'" wrote a contributor to *The Tennessee Encyclopedia of History and Culture,* "Wallace became the quintessential 'organization man.'" He refused to retaliate for violence against him on the court, knowing that a fight would only confirm negative stereotypes against black athletes. Instead, he played with renewed passion and skill to defeat his adversaries. As Hudson put it, Wallace "kept his mouth shut, played hard, sacrificed for Vanderbilt—and for black America." In his senior year, Wallace was chosen captain of the Vanderbilt varsity squad and was second-team All-SEC. He also received the SEC Sportsmanship Trophy, determined by league player vote, in 1970.

Wallace was popular off the court as well. In fact, according to Brad Golder in *The Vanderbilt Hustler,* one of his professors described him as an "honorary white guy" on campus, and the senior class voted him "Bachelor of Ugliness," an award given to the most popular man in the graduating class. At the same time, however, Wallace felt extremely isolated. After his final game in 1970, according to Golder, he decided to go public about the pressures he had endured and, in an interview with a Nashville newspaper, said that "I don't have any faith at all that people who say 'Hi' to me are addressing me as a human being.'" Many Vanderbilt alumni resented this comment, and some went so far as to accuse Wallace of disloyalty to the university. As Hudson put it, "People wanted to paint his years at Vanderbilt as an uncomplicated success story [but] although it was against his nature to make waves, he believed it was time to set the record straight."

In 2002, Wallace told Golder in *The Vanderbilt Hustler* that he doubted that he would choose to do it all over again. "I've realized too well how much it took," he commented. "I understand now the physical, psychological and emotional problems it caused." Lonely and threatened as Wallace felt during that period, however, he played a crucial role in desegregating college basketball. In 1970, the first season after Wallace graduated, the universities of Alabama, Florida, Georgia, and Kentucky created desegregated varsity teams; within the next decade, black athletes were routinely dominating SEC teams.

Forged Successful Legal Career

After earning a bachelor's degree in electrical engineering and engineering mathematics from Vanderbilt, Wallace played briefly in the minor league but chose not to pursue a professional basketball career. He took a job with the National Urban League, where he worked for future U.S. Secretary of Commerce Ron Brown, and then attended Columbia University's School of Law, where he was awarded the Charles Evans Hughes Fellowship. He earned his J.D. in 1975. He worked in the U.S. Justice Department and taught at the University of Baltimore before joining the faculty at Washington College of Law at American University in Washington, D.C.

Specializing in environmental law and in corporate law and finance, Wallace is active in several organizations, including the National Advisory Council for Environmental Policy and Technology, the U.S. Environmental Protection Agency, and the National Panel of Arbitrators. He also continues to give interviews about his experience as a pioneer in the desegregation in college sports. He and his wife, a Howard University professor, have one daughter.

Though he retired from sports shortly after his college career, Wallace remains one of Vanderbilt University's most acclaimed athletes. In 1996 he was named one of five Silver Anniversary All-American team members by the National Association of Basketball Coaches. In 2003 he was inducted into the Tennessee Sports Hall of Fame, and in 2004 he represented Vanderbilt as an "SEC Living Legend" honoree at the SEC Basketball Tournament in Atlanta. Also that year, Vanderbilt retired his basketball jersey, making him only the third athlete in the school's history to receive this honor. "Perry Wallace is a Vanderbilt hero," said Chancellor Gordon Gee in a speech at the ceremony, quoted in *The Vanderbilt Commodores.* "It took great courage for him to come here, and he represented the university with great dignity and skill during a turbulent time. Perry's accomplishments—in the classroom, on the basketball court and throughout his life—are an inspiration to us all."

Sources

Books

Douchant, Mike, *Encyclopedia of College Basketball,* Gale, 1995, p. 134.

Periodicals

Jet, March 15, 2004, p. 50.
USA Today, February 20, 2004.
Vanderbilt Hustler, February 26, 2002.

On-line

"Breaking Barriers: The Story of Perry Wallace, the SEC's First Black Athlete," *Vanderbilt Commodores,* www.commodores.com/news (August 18, 2004).
"College Basketball: Trailblazer Grows from Experience," *Black Athlete Sports Network,* www.blackathlete.com (September 9, 2004).
"Faculty Profile: Perry Wallace, Jr.," *Washington College of Law,* www.wcl.american.edu/faculty/wallace (August 19, 2004).
"Perry E. Wallace, Jr.," *Tennessee Encyclopedia of History and Culture,* http://tennesseeencyclopedia. net (August 19, 2004).

—E. Shostak

Mark Whitaker

1957—

Journalist

Whitaker, Mark, photograph. AP/Wide World Photos.

Near the end of 1998, *Newsweek* announced it had named veteran staff journalist Mark Theis Whitaker to the post of editor. Whitaker, who had worked for the magazine in various capacities, became the first African American editor of a major news weekly in the United States. As Carl Swanson remarked about Whitaker in the *New York Observer*, "His quiet, seemingly inevitable rise through the thicket of Ivy-educated overachievers at *Newsweek* says much more about his ability to play quiet clubhouse diplomacy than anything else."

Whitaker was born on September 7, 1957, in Lower Merion, Pennsylvania, and grew up in Norton, Massachusetts. He graduated summa cum laude from Harvard College in 1979. His college roommate, Jonathan Alter (who would also become a senior editor at *Newsweek*) noted in the *New York Observer* that Whitaker "was the smartest person in our circle. A rare combination of powerfully intelligent and powerfully disciplined." While attending Harvard, Whitaker played tennis, served on the editorial board of the famed *Harvard Crimson*, and was elected Phi Beta Kappa. In 1977, he began his career at *Newsweek* as a reporting intern at the magazine's San Francisco bureau. His

boss at the time, *Newsweek*'s Washington bureau chief Mel Elfin, told the *New York Observer* that Whitaker was "relatively quiet, relatively funny and awfully good."

Upon graduating from Harvard in 1979, Whitaker won a Marshall Scholarship to study at Oxford University's Balliol College. He then returned to *Newsweek* and worked as a stringer for the Boston, Washington, and Paris bureaus. In 1981, he joined *Newsweek*'s full-time New York City staff. Six years later, Whitaker was named as *Newsweek*'s business editor, taking over the position only a few days before the stock market crash of 1987. "I got lucky," Whitaker told Swanson in the *New York Observer*. "We'd decided to put the jitters on the cover the week before. They were on the stands that Monday"–a day widely known as Black Monday, when the Dow Jones average slid to its greatest one-day drop since 1914.

As *Newsweek*'s business editor, Whitaker led readers through the complex stories of insider trading scandals and the savings and loan crisis of the late 1980s. In 1991, he was named assistant managing editor and, in this capacity, was able to expand the magazine's coverage of technology issues. *Newsweek* added a

At a Glance . . .

Born on September 7, 1957, in Lower Merion, Pennsylvannia; married Alexis Gelber (a journalist), 1985; children: Rachel Eva, Matthew Edward. *Education:* Harvard College, BA, 1979; attended Balliol College, Oxford University, Marshall Scholar, 1979-81; Wheaton College, LLD.

Career: *Newsweek,* San Francisco bureau, intern, 1977; *Newsweek,* stringer from Boston, Washington, and Paris; *Newsweek,* New York City, full-time journalist, 1981; *Newsweek,* business editor, 1987-91; *Newsweek,* assistant managing editor, 1991-96; *Newsweek,* managing editor and deputy to editor, 1996-97; *Newsweek,* interim editor, 1997-98, and editor, 1998–.

Memberships: National Association of Black Journalists; American Society of Magazine Editors, president, 2004–; Council on Foreign Relations; Century Association; Phi Beta Kappa.

Addresses: *Office*—Newsweek, 251 W. 57th St., New York, NY 10019-1894.

"Cyberscope" page, introduced a special monthly "Focus on Technology" section, and issued an annual special edition called *Computers and the Family.* As assistant managing editor, Whitaker also oversaw several special-issue editions of *Newsweek,* including issues devoted to the Olympic Games and the first Clinton inauguration. He also wrote essays on the issue of race and was widely praised for his article in *Newsweek* entitled "Whites v. Blacks." It was published immediately after O.J. Simpson's 1995 acquittal on charges that he murdered his wife and another man.

In 1996, Whitaker was named managing editor at *Newsweek* and served as deputy to the magazine's editor, Maynard Parker. Parker was known for his lively style and was credited with reviving *Newsweek* during the early 1980s. Whitaker's duties as managing editor included producing special issues, such as the retrospective of the 1996 presidential election. In August of 1997, the *Newsweek* staff had already put the magazine "to bed" for the week when news broke that Princess Diana had been killed in a Paris car crash. Whitaker returned to *Newsweek*'s offices, called in the staff, and put together a special report on her death. When Parker was diagnosed with leukemia in 1997, Whitaker became interim editor. During this time, he oversaw the magazine's coverage of the Bill Clinton-Monica Lewinsky affair as it unfolded.

After Maynard Parker's death from leukemia, Whitaker was named editor of *Newsweek* on November 10, 1998. He became the first African American to hold such an influential job at a weekly news magazine. "At a news weekly magazine–where the job of editor includes signing off on every story, cover headline, chart, photograph and 'pull quote'–the influence of the editor is felt to the core of the publication," explained Alex Kuczynski of the *New York Times.*

Whitaker, noted Kuczynski in the *New York Times,* "is regarded by his staff as a strong, even-keeled intellectual presence, less seismic in his deadline fervor than Mr. Parker." Whitaker immediately declared his intention to attract a younger demographic of readers to *Newsweek.* "I think we do an extremely good job covering the Baby Boom generation, and we will continue to do so as we get older," he remarked in the *New York Times.* "But I want this to be a must-read for younger readers as well."

Following his promotion to editor, Whitaker downplayed the issue of race. "I'm proud and I'm honored to be in this position," he told Kuczynski in the *New York Times,* "but my goal is to be the very best editor of *Newsweek* that I can be, not just the best black editor." He did concede, however, in an interview with Howard Kurtz of the *Washington Post,* that he was "very interested in the racial question here in America, not just between blacks and whites but Hispanics and Asians and the changing demographics of the country. Perhaps I have a little more sensitivity to that issue than other people might have." But Whitaker added in *Black Enterprise* that his appointment to the top position at *Newsweek* is a sign of improvements. "My experience says it's possible. If you go to work at a publication like *Newsweek,* put in the time, rise through the ranks and do a good job, it's possible to rise to the top. You no longer have to think what's the point of putting in those years because in the end you're going to knock your head against a ceiling."

Since his appointment, Whitaker has concentrated on increasing advertising dollars and paid subscriptions. While Whitaker felt he had inherited a "pretty good magazine," as he told *Black Enterprise,* he did institute some changes. Keeping the magazine's dedication to sound reporting techniques, Whitaker revamped coverage of several topics, including religion, science, and social issues, and added expanded coverage of technology. Under his editorship, *Newsweek* won the industry's most prestigious award, the National Magazine Award for general excellence, twice: in 2002 for coverage of the September 11th terrorist attacks and in 2004 for coverage of the war in Iraq.

Whitaker is married to Alexis Gelber, the managing editor of *Newsweek International,* with whom he has two children. They live in New York City, where despite his stature as one of the most influential editorial executives in the nation, Whitaker is largely unrecognized. "Editing a magazine is like conducting an orchestra," he told Kurtz in the *Washington Post*. "It's about getting the right sound. It's not about how flamboyant you are and what your personality is."

Sources

Periodicals

Black Enterprise, April 1999, p. 20.
Boston Globe, November 11, 1998, pp. F1, 4.
Jet, November 30, 1998, p. 31.
Los Angeles Times, November 11, 1998, p. A16.
Media Industry Newsletter, November 16, 1998, p. 1.
Mediaweek, November 16, 1998, p. 40.
New York Observer, November 16, 1998.
New York Times, November 11, 1998, p. A14.
Wall Street Journal, November 11, 1998, p. B14.
Washington Post, November 11, 1998, pp. D1, 9.

On-line

"Newsweek," *MSNBC,* www.msnbc.com (August 18, 2004).

Other

Additional information for this profile was provided by *Newsweek* magazine publicity materials.

—Carol Brennan and Sara Pendergast

Ray Wilkins

1951—

Corporate executive

Wilkins, Ray, photograph. AP/Wide World Photos.

Ray Wilkins's career blossomed at SBC Communications, Inc., as the company expanded over the years. Serving as group president for marketing and sales for the telecommunications giant in 2004, this Texas native began his career with the company when it was still Southwestern Bell, the local telephone company. Though his job certainly required him to keep up with changing communications technology in order to serve the voice and data needs of millions of business and residential customers across 13 states, Wilkins remained committed to making SBC a first-rate service provider. "I'm not a technology junkie," he told *San Antonio Express-News* Sanford Nowlin. "I'm a customer junkie. If you're going to succeed you have to start with the customer and work backwards."

Rayford Wilkins was born on August 9, 1951, in Waco, Texas. He pursued a college education by studying business administration at the University of Texas. Before earning his degree in 1974, he worked a series of retail jobs to help defray his college-tuition costs. Just after graduating, he was hired by Southwestern Bell into its manager trainee program in Houston, at a time when the company was the only local telephone service provider. These local utilities, usually known by their states' names, were part of the AT&T (American Telegraph and Telephone) corporate family, but a lengthy legal challenge forced the companies to split into separate, independently owned regional "Baby Bells" in 1984. Southwestern Bell became one of these, and Wilkins rose through the ranks at its Houston, Dallas, and San Antonio offices. He held a management position in customer service and another with the marketing department, and also worked in the comptroller's office as well. In 1987, he completed the Management Program for Executives at the University of Pittsburgh.

Wilkins was posted to Southwestern Bell company offices in St. Louis, Missouri, in the early 1990s, and was named a regional president in the summer of 1996 for Kansas City. In that position, he oversaw telecommunications sales and service for western Missouri and all of Kansas, and was the top-ranking local executive for the company. The 1996 Telecommunications Act gave Southwestern Bell and the other Baby Bells permission to become national phone-service providers, and Southwestern Bell began moving into larger territory. In 1998 it became SBC Communications when it acquired Ameritech and Pacific Bell, two other Baby Bells. By then Wilkins was serving as president of the company's Business Communications Services in San Antonio, which handled accounts for some three million non-residential customers.

In 1999, Wilkins was made president and CEO of Southwestern Bell, the remaining local phone-service provider, and a year later moved to California to take over as president and chief executive officer of SBC Pacific Bell/SBC Nevada Bell. He became the first locally-based president in charge of operations, marketing, customer service, and network services since the takeover. From its headquarters in San Ramon, California, SBC PacBell served as the leading phone company for California, but was suffering from several customer-service related issues. The company's new high-speed Internet connection service, the Digital Subscriber Line, or DSL, was an offering that was plagued with problems in the first year of its launch. It

was a potentially grievous public-relations disaster in the high-tech nexus that stretched from San Francisco to Silicon Valley, and new and waiting customers were irate. Wilkins moved quickly to find and fix the problems, and managed to slice the wait-time for DSL installation from 26 days to six. Determined to improve customer service, he visited the call centers often to boost morale. There were other issues as well: at the time, Californians were logging record numbers of complaints with the FCC over SBC/PacBell service, and the company was also heavily fined for using misleading marketing strategies.

In the next few years, Wilkins helped SBC/PacBell weather a recession and the sinking of the dotcom boom by cutting expenses and hiring new employees only when absolutely necessary. Resorting to such belt-tightening measures would help avoid layoffs, he told *Black Enterprise* writer Alan Hughes. It was crucial to "recognize the signs, and take action," Wilkins explained, as opposed to the company finding itself, "in a situation where they have to do something drastic and dramatic. And that hurts people."

Wilkins's excellent track record brought him another promotion, this one in May of 2002 to group president for sales and marketing at SBC. This meant that he and his wife, Lorena, would return to San Antonio, where they had lived for several years. His task was to reinvigorate marketing strategies and lure new customers in each of the thirteen states where SBC operates. Wilkins's wife is also a longtime SBC executive, and his stepson is also with the company in Houston.

In his spare time, Wilkins likes to golf and is a collector of sports memorabilia, but he has also been active in a number of local and civic groups in each of the cities that he has called home over the years. These include the Carver Academy in San Antonio, for which he has served on the board of directors, and the San Francisco YMCA. Vintage Foster, a publisher who had worked with Wilkins on a San Francisco-area scholarship program, told the *San Antonio Express-News*'s Nowlin that he was impressed with Wilkins's generosity and help when Foster was setting up the East Bay Leadership Foundation. "Ray gave me a $50,000 check for the foundation," Foster told Nowlin. "And the next words out of his mouth were, 'Who else do you need me to call?' He's not the kind of guy who just writes a check and moves on. He helped take (the foundation) from concept to fruition. There's very little ego involved with Ray. With him, something's either a good idea or it isn't."

Sources

Periodicals

Black Enterprise, March 2002, p. 30.
St. Louis Business Journal, March 10, 1997, p. 3.

San Antonio Express-News, July 27, 2002, p. 1D.
San Francisco Business Times, December 29, 2000,
  p. 27; September 15, 2000, p. 10; September 22,
  2000, p. 8.
San Francisco Chronicle, January 7, 2001, p. B1.

On-line

"Rayford Wilkins, Jr.," *SBC–Investor Relations*, www.
  sbc.com/gen/investor-relations?pid=5687
  (September 8, 2004).

—Carol Brennan

Pharrell Williams

1973—

Music producer

Pharrell Williams scored hit after hit beginning in 2002 thanks to his producing talents for an array of top musical acts. As one half of the Neptunes, Williams writes and puts a unique stamp on singles for Usher, Nelly, Justin Timberlake, and many others. He and his co-Neptune, high-school pal Chad Hugo, also put out music of their own under the "N.E.R.D." name. The music-industry powerhouse-duo are anything but geeks, however, with *Esquire* writer Neil Strauss declaring their music "the sparkling, clean chrome kitchen of hip-hop futurism. Nearly every song carries the Neptunes' brand-name sound: a syncopated bouncing beat, seductive keyboard chord progressions, and an unforgettable yet oddball hook." For his part, Williams claimed to be sometimes overwhelmed by his success. "There's no better feeling than walking into a club and hearing your song," he told *Newsweek* writer Lorraine Ali. "You'd think we'd get used to it, but I don't think I ever will. It still gives me the chills."

Born in 1973, Williams grew up in Virginia Beach, Virginia, one of three boys born to Carolyn, a teacher, and Pharoah, who worked as a housepainter and handyman. Williams remembers that there was no homegrown musical legacy in Virginia Beach to serve as any sort of future inspiration for him, but his aunt did introduce him to a world of influences. Together, he told *CosmoGirl* writer Lauren Brown, they would "sit in front of the stereo and just play records. She was a singer-songwriter type of person—like, she loved Stevie Wonder—and I got all that from her."

Scored Chart Success as Teen

Williams met Chad Hugo while both were playing in the school jazz band in seventh grade. They soon began making music on their own, with Williams on drums and Hugo playing the saxophone. Both went on to an art and music-focused high school in Virginia Beach, and Williams joined his first outfit around 1990, a rap act called Surrounded by Idiots. One of the other members was a local D.J. named Tim Mosely, who would later rename himself Timbaland and attain chart fame as well.

Around this same time, Williams and Hugo put together an act for their high school talent show, a noted local event that lured famed producer Teddy Riley, whose "New Jack Swing" style began to dominate the R&B charts in the late 1980s. Impressed, Riley signed Williams and Hugo to a production deal, and they began using the "Neptunes" name professionally. Their first hit came when both were still in high school. Wreckx-n-Effect's "Rump Shaker" helped propel the album to No. 6 on the R&B/Hip-Hop charts in 1992. But Williams recalled he had a tough time juggling school and the music business at times. "I'd work in the studio after school and wouldn't tell [my parents] about it," he told *Teen People*'s Mitsuka Ida. "My curfew was midnight, and I used to get into trouble for coming in late."

After spending a few more years under the tutelage of Riley, Williams and Hugo broke out on their own. Their

At a Glance . . .

Born on April 5, 1973, in Virginia Beach, Virginia; son of Pharoah (a housepainter) and Carolyn (a teacher) Williams.

Career: Musician and music producer, late 1980s–; N.E.R.D. musical group, co-founder and member, early 2000–; Star Trak record label, co-founder, 2003–.

Awards: National Academy of Recording Arts and Sciences, Grammy Award, for best producer (with Hugo), 2004.

Addresses: *Agent*—United Talent Agency, 9560 Wilshire Blvd., Ste. 500, Beverly Hills, CA 90212.

first Top Ten hit came in September of 1998 with "Lookin' at Me" from Mase and Puff Daddy, which reached No. 1 on *Billboard*'s Hot Rap Singles chart. It also cemented their reputation as up-and-comers in the production business, and they went on to achieve a string of notable successes, including Britney Spears' "I'm A Slave 4 U" in 2001. Rap and R&B acts such as Ludacris and Usher liked they way they mixed in unusual samples and sounds into the tracks. The duo's musical influences ranged from Afrika Bambaataa and Stevie Wonder to Tears for Fears and Stereolab.

Garnered Critical Accolades

"The result is a bold, dynamic, futurist-sounding brand of pop music," wrote *Daily Telegraph* journalist Craig McLean of Williams' and Hugo's studio talents, "part cutting-edge technology, part old-school soul and funk." *New York Times* music writer Jon Pareles had similar accolades. "They use the freeze-dried, uninflected tones of the digital era: the snap of drum samples, the blips and tweets of video games and cell-phone rings.... Although Neptunes' tracks revel in the mechanization of looped and programmed riffs pumped out by computerized sequencers, they often add an element that sounds winningly askew: the drooping, detuned notes in 'I'm a Slave for U' or a drum-machine accent that lands just behind the beat."

Eager to move forward, Williams and Hugo formed N.E.R.D., an acronym for "No One Ever Really Dies," with another friend from their magnet high school, Sheldon "Shay" Haley. The group released its first LP, *In Search of ...*, in 2001. It was a terrific mix of their production talents and songwriting skills, which *Newsweek*'s Ali termed "a frenetic concoction—mostly inspiring and occasionally off the rails. Though the lyrics

can sometimes be annoyingly immature...the music is terse, crisp and magnetic." The record's release was actually delayed for a few months because Williams and Hugo had done some work in the studio with Californian ska-pop band No Doubt, and realized they wanted to add live musicians to their own record.

In Search of... landed on several "best-of" lists for 2001 from music critics, and Williams went on to garner a slew of hit records for other artists over the next two years. These included Nelly's "Hot in Herre" and "Girlfriend" from N'Sync, which featured Nelly as well. Despite their string of successes, Williams and his Neptunes producing partner were bypassed for the 2002 Grammy Awards thanks to an oversight: neither the label nor Williams and Hugo entered their work for consideration in the nominations balloting.

Still, four of their singles were nominated for Grammy Awards, and Williams and Hugo went on to have another outstanding year in 2003. Songs they produced for Jay-Z, Justin Timberlake, and Snoop Dogg landed in the Top Ten, and they were singled out for particular praise for lending a certain depth to the more hardcore side of rap and R&B. "Taking somebody from A to B is cool," Williams told *Time*'s Josh Tyrangiel about his philosophy, "but when we produce, we want to take people from A to D, to challenge their artistic natures, their image, everything."

Aided by All-Star Line-Up

The first "Neptunes" album, a compilation titled *The Neptunes Present...Clones,* debuted at No. 1 in August of 2003 in the United States and sold 250,000 copies in its first week. Williams sang on the single "Frontin'," which also featured Jay-Z, and an array of rap stars joined in to help out on other tracks, including Busta Rhymes, Nelly, Snoop Dogg, and Ludacris. Proving they could work in a range of musical styles, in 2003 Williams and Hugo even did a remix of the 1968 Rolling Stones classic, "Sympathy for the Devil," for the band's *40 Licks* compilation. "We never want to be those people who specialize in a certain style," Williams told *Newsweek*'s Ali, "because once that dies, so do you."

At the 2004 Grammy Awards ceremony, Williams and Hugo walked away with the best producer award and Williams even took the stage that night in an all-star lineup that included country crooner Vince Gill, Dave Matthews, and Sting, to perform the Beatles track, "I Saw Her Standing There." Later in 2004 N.E.R.D. released their second LP, *Fly or Die,* with help from a Minneapolis rock band they used on the first album, Spymob. The songs sampled an array of 1970s progressive-rock tunes, from Steely Dan to Queen.

Williams's sudden fame led to a slew of other ventures. In early 2003, he and Hugo formed their own label,

Star Trak, which was part of the Arista family, and Williams inked a deal for a clothing line with Reebok called Billionaire's Boys Club, and a line of footwear called Ice Cream. "Because ice and cream are two things that run the world," he told *Guardian* journalist Paul Lester when asked about the name. "The jewellery—the ice—the diamonds; and the cream is the cash." He also penned the "Lovin' It" jingle for McDonald's, and signed a deal with a top talent agency for future film work. He remains grounded in Virginia Beach, however, where the Neptunes studio is located. "I have no complaints, man," he told Lester in the *Guardian* interview about his new status as pop star, producer to the stars, and teen heartthrob. "Tired, but no complaints. I could be somewhere else, doing something I really don't want to do…. I'd like to think I'd have become some sort of art teacher at least, or art professor at most, studying for my Ph.D. But life doesn't always end up that way."

Selected discography

In Search of…, Virgin, 2001.
The Neptunes Present…Clones, Star Trak/Arista, 2003.
Fly or Die, Virgin, 2004.

Sources

Periodicals

CosmoGirl, March 2004, p. 166.
Daily News Record, October 20, 2003, p. 21.
Daily Telegraph (London, England), June 5, 2002.
Daily Variety, April 8, 2004, p. 4.
Esquire, December 2002, p. 148.
Guardian (London, England), February 20, 2004, p. 4.
Interview, August 2003, p. 120.
Newsweek, March 18, 2002, p. 65; December 29, 2003, p. 105; March 29, 2004, p. 76.
New York Times, March 10, 2002, p. 1; January 14, 2003, p. E3; April 4, 2004, p. AR31.
People, October 13, 2003, p. 111; June 28, 2004, p. 115.
Teen People, February 1, 2004, p. 48.
Time, August 25, 2003, p. 64.
WWD, March 25, 2004, p. 20S.

—Carol Brennan

Cumulative Nationality Index

Volume numbers appear in **bold**

Wallace, Perry E. **47**
Wallace, Phyllis A. **9**
Wallace, Sippie **1**
Waller, Fats **29**
Ward, Douglas Turner **42**
Ward, Lloyd **21, 46**
Ware, Andre **37**
Ware, Carl H. **30**
Warfield, Marsha **2**
Warner, Malcolm-Jamal **22, 36**
Warren, Michael **27**
Warwick, Dionne **18**
Washington, Alonzo **29**
Washington, Booker T. **4**
Washington, Denzel **1, 16**
Washington, Dinah **22**
Washington, Fredi **10**
Washington, Grover, Jr. **17, 44**
Washington, Harold **6**
Washington, James, Jr. **38**
Washington, Kerry **46**
Washington, Laura S. **18**
Washington, MaliVai **8**
Washington, Patrice Clarke **12**
Washington, Regynald G. **44**
Washington, Val **12**
Washington, Walter **45**
Wasow, Omar **15**
Waters, Benny **26**
Waters, Ethel **7**
Waters, Maxine **3**
Waters, Muddy **34**
Watkins, Donald **35**
Watkins, Levi, Jr. **9**
Watkins, Perry **12**
Watkins, Shirley R. **17**
Watkins, Tionne "T-Boz" **34**
Watkins, Walter C. **24**
Watson, Bob **25**
Watson, Diane **41**
Watson, Johnny "Guitar" **18**
Watt, Melvin **26**
Wattleton, Faye **9**
Watts, J. C., Jr. **14, 38**
Watts, Rolonda **9**
Wayans, Damon **8, 41**
Wayans, Keenen Ivory **18**
Wayans, Marlon **29**
Wayans, Shawn **29**
Weathers, Carl **10**
Weaver, Afaa Michael **37**
Weaver, Robert C. **8, 46**
Webb, Veronica **10**
Webb, Wellington **3**
Webber, Chris **15, 30**
Webster, Katie **29**
Wedgeworth, Robert W. **42**
Weems, Renita J. **44**
Wells, James Lesesne **10**
Wells, Mary **28**
Wells-Barnett, Ida B. **8**
Welsing, Frances Cress **5**
Wesley, Dorothy Porter **19**
Wesley, Valerie Wilson **18**
West, Cornel **5, 33**
West, Dorothy **12**
West, Togo D., Jr. **16**
Westbrook, Peter **20**
Whack, Rita Coburn **36**
Whalum, Kirk **37**
Wharton, Clifton R., Jr. **7**
Wharton, Clifton Reginald, Sr. **36**
Wheat, Alan **14**
Whitaker, Forest **2**
Whitaker, Mark **21, 47**

Whitaker, Pernell **10**
White, Barry **13, 41**
White, Bill **1**
White, Charles **39**
White, Dondi **34**
White, Jesse **22**
White, John H. **27**
White, Linda M. **45**
White, Lois Jean **20**
White, Maurice **29**
White, Michael R. **5**
White, Reggie **6**
White, Walter F. **4**
Whitfield, Fred **23**
Whitfield, Lynn **18**
Whitfield, Van **34**
Wideman, John Edgar **5**
Wilder, L. Douglas **3**
Wiley, Ralph **8**
Wilkens, J. Ernest, Jr. **43**
Wilkens, Lenny **11**
Wilkins, Ray **47**
Wilkins, Roger **2**
Wilkins, Roy **4**
Williams, Anthony **21**
Williams, Armstrong **29**
Williams, Bert **18**
Williams, Billy Dee **8**
Williams, Clarence **33**
Williams, Clarence, III **26**
Williams, Daniel Hale **2**
Williams, Deniece **36**
Williams, Doug **22**
Williams, Eddie N. **44**
Aaliyah **30**
Williams, Evelyn **10**
Williams, Fannie Barrier **27**
Williams, George Washington **18**
Williams, Gregory **11**
Williams, Hosea Lorenzo **15, 31**
Williams, Joe **5, 25**
Williams, John A. **27**
Williams, Maggie **7**
Williams, Mary Lou **15**
Williams, Montel **4**
Williams, Natalie **31**
Williams, O. S. **13**
Williams, Patricia J. **11**
Williams, Paul R. **9**
Williams, Pharrell **47**
Williams, Robert F. **11**
Williams, Samm-Art **21**
Williams, Saul **31**
Williams, Serena **20, 41**
Williams, Sherley Anne **25**
Williams, Stanley "Tookie" **29**
Williams, Terrie M. **35**
Williams, Vanessa **32**
Williams, Vanessa L. **4, 17**
Williams, Venus **17, 34**
Williams, Walter E. **4**
Williams, William T. **11**
Williams, Willie L. **4**
Williamson, Mykelti **22**
Willingham, Tyrone **43**
Wilson, August **7, 33**
Wilson, Cassandra **16**
Wilson, Charlie **31**
Wilson, Debra **38**
Wilson, Ellis **39**
Wilson, Flip **21**
Wilson, Jimmy **45**
Wilson, Mary **28**
Wilson, Nancy **10**
Wilson, Natalie **38**

Wilson, Phill **9**
Wilson, Sunnie **7**
Wilson, William Julius **20**
Winans, Angie **36**
Winans, BeBe **14**
Winans, CeCe **14, 43**
Winans, Debbie **36**
Winans, Marvin L. **17**
Winans, Vickie **24**
Winfield, Dave **5**
Winfield, Paul **2, 45**
Winfrey, Oprah **2, 15**
Winkfield, Jimmy **42**
Witherspoon, John **38**
Witt, Edwin T. **26**
Wolfe, George C. **6, 43**
Wonder, Stevie **11**
Woodard, Alfre **9**
Woodruff, Hale **9**
Woods, Granville T. **5**
Woods, Sylvia **34**
Woods, Tiger **14, 31**
Woodson, Carter G. **2**
Woodson, Robert L. **10**
Worrill, Conrad **12**
Wright, Bruce McMarion **3**
Wright, Charles H. **35**
Wright, Deborah C. **25**
Wright, Jeremiah A., Jr. **45**
Wright, Lewin **43**
Wright, Louis Tompkins **4**
Wright, Richard **5**
Wynn, Albert R. **25**
X, Malcolm **1**
X, Marvin **45**
Yancy, Dorothy Cowser **42**
Yarbrough, Camille **40**
Yoba, Malik **11**
York, Vincent **40**
Young, Andrew **3**
Young, Coleman **1, 20**
Young, Jean Childs **14**
Young, Lester **37**
Young, Roger Arliner **29**
Young, Whitney M., Jr. **4**
Youngblood, Johnny Ray **8**
Youngblood, Shay **32**
Zollar, Alfred **40**
Zollar, Jawole Willa Jo **28**

Angolan
Bonga, Kuenda **13**
dos Santos, José Eduardo **43**
Neto, António Agostinho **43**
Savimbi, Jonas **2, 34**

Antiguan
Williams, Denise **40**

Australian
Freeman, Cathy **29**

Austrian
Kodjoe, Boris **34**

Bahamian
Ingraham, Hubert A. **19**

Barbadian
Arthur, Owen **33**
Brathwaite, Kamau **36**
Clarke, Austin C. **32**
Flash, Grandmaster **33**
Foster, Cecil **32**

Cumulative Occupation Index

Volume numbers appear in **bold**

Art and design

Adjaye, David **38**
Allen, Tina **22**
Alston, Charles **33**
Andrews, Benny **22**
Andrews, Bert **13**
Armstrong, Robb **15**
Bailey, Radcliffe **19**
Bailey, Xenobia **11**
Barboza, Anthony **10**
Barnes, Ernie **16**
Barthe, Richmond **15**
Basquiat, Jean-Michel **5**
Bearden, Romare **2**
Beasley, Phoebe **34**
Biggers, John **20**, **33**
Blacknurn, Robert **28**
Brandon, Barbara **3**
Brown, Donald **19**
Burke, Selma **16**
Burroughs, Margaret Taylor **9**
Camp, Kimberly **19**
Campbell, E. Simms **13**
Campbell, Mary Schmidt **43**
Catlett, Elizabeth **2**
Chase-Riboud, Barbara **20**, **46**
Cortor, Eldzier **42**
Cowans, Adger W. **20**
Crite, Alan Rohan **29**
De Veaux, Alexis **44**
DeCarava, Roy **42**
Delaney, Beauford **19**
Delaney, Joseph **30**
Delsarte, Louis **34**
Donaldson, Jeff **46**
Douglas, Aaron **7**
Driskell, David C. **7**
Edwards, Melvin **22**
El Wilson, Barbara **35**
Ewing, Patrick A.**17**
Feelings, Tom **11**, **47**
Freeman, Leonard **27**
Fuller, Meta Vaux Warrick **27**
Gantt, Harvey **1**
Gilliam, Sam **16**
Golden, Thelma **10**
Goodnight, Paul **32**
Guyton, Tyree **9**
Harkless, Necia Desiree **19**
Harrington, Oliver W. **9**
Hathaway, Isaac Scott **33**
Hayden, Palmer **13**

Hayes, Cecil N. **46**
Hope, John **8**
Hudson, Cheryl **15**
Hudson, Wade **15**
Hunt, Richard **6**
Hunter, Clementine **45**
Hutson, Jean Blackwell **16**
Jackson, Earl **31**
Jackson, Vera **40**
John, Daymond **23**
Johnson, Jeh Vincent **44**
Johnson, William Henry **3**
Jones, Lois Mailou **13**
Kitt, Sandra **23**
Lawrence, Jacob **4**, **28**
Lee, Annie Francis **22**
Lee-Smith, Hughie **5**, **22**
Lewis, Edmonia **10**
Lewis, Norman **39**
Lewis, Samella **25**
Loving, Alvin **35**
Manley, Edna **26**
Mayhew, Richard **39**
McGee, Charles **10**
McGruder, Aaron **28**
Mitchell, Corinne **8**
Moody, Ronald **30**
Morrison, Keith **13**
Motley, Archibald Jr. **30**
Moutoussamy-Ashe, Jeanne **7**
Mutu, Wangechi **44**
N'Namdi, George R. **17**
Nugent, Richard Bruce **39**
Olden, Georg(e) **44**
Ouattara **43**
Perkins, Marion **38**
Pierre, Andre **17**
Pinderhughes, John **47**
Pinkney, Jerry **15**
Pippin, Horace **9**
Porter, James A. **10**
Prophet, Nancy Elizabeth **42**
Puryear, Martin **42**
Ringgold, Faith **4**
Ruley, Ellis **38**
Saar, Alison **16**
Saint James, Synthia **12**
Sallee, Charles **38**
Sanders, Joseph R., Jr. **11**
Savage, Augusta **12**
Sebree, Charles **40**
Serrano, Andres **3**

Shabazz, Attallah **6**
Simpson, Lorna **4**, **36**
Sims, Lowery Stokes **27**
Sklarek, Norma Merrick **25**
Sleet, Moneta, Jr. **5**
Smith, Marvin **46**
Smith, Morgan **46**
Tanksley, Ann **37**
Tanner, Henry Ossawa **1**
Thomas, Alma **14**
Thrash, Dox **35**
Tolliver, William **9**
VanDerZee, James **6**
Wainwright, Joscelyn **46**
Walker, A'lelia **14**
Walker, Kara **16**
Washington, Alonzo **29**
Washington, James, Jr. **38**
Wells, James Lesesne **10**
White, Charles **39**
White, Dondi **34**
White, John H. **27**
Williams, Billy Dee **8**
Williams, O. S. **13**
Williams, Paul R. **9**
Williams, William T. **11**
Wilson, Ellis **39**
Woodruff, Hale **9**

Business

Abbot, Robert Sengstacke **27**
Abdul-Jabbar, Kareem **8**
Adams, Eula L. **39**
Adkins, Rod **41**
Ailey, Alvin **8**
Al-Amin, Jamil Abdullah **6**
Alexander, Archie Alphonso **14**
Allen, Byron **24**
Ames, Wilmer **27**
Amos, Wally **9**
Auguste, Donna **29**
Avant, Clarence **19**
Beal, Bernard B. **46**
Beamon, Bob **30**
Baker, Dusty **8**, **43**
Baker, Ella **5**
Baker, Gwendolyn Calvert **9**
Baker, Maxine **28**
Banks, Jeffrey **17**
Banks, William **11**
Barden, Don H. **9**, **20**
Barrett, Andrew C. **12**

Marable, Manning **10**
Markham, E.A. **37**
Marsalis, Wynton **16**
Marshall, Paule **7**
Masekela, Barbara **18**
Mason, Ronald **27**
Massey, Walter E. **5, 45**
Massie, Samuel P., Jr. **29**
Mayhew, Richard **39**
Maynard, Robert C. **7**
Maynor, Dorothy **19**
Mayo, Whitman **32**
Mays, Benjamin E. **7**
McCarty, Osceola **16**
McKay, Nellie Yvonne **17**
McMillan, Terry **4, 17**
McMurray, Georgia L. **36**
McWhorter, John **35**
Meek, Carrie **6**
Memmi, Albert **37**
Meredith, James H. **11**
Millender-McDonald, Juanita **21**
Mitchell, Corinne **8**
Mitchell, Sharon **36**
Mofolo, Thomas Mokopu **37**
Mollel, Tololwa **38**
Mongella, Gertrude **11**
Mooney, Paul **37**
Moore, Harry T. **29**
Moore, Melba **21**
Morrison, Keith **13**
Morrison, Toni **15**
Moses, Robert Parris **11**
Mphalele, Es'kia (Ezekiel) **40**
Mullen, Harryette **34**
Murray, Pauli **38**
Nabrit, Samuel Milton **47**
N'Namdi, George R. **17**
Naylor, Gloria **10, 42**
Neal, Larry **38**
N'Namdi, George R. **17**
Norman, Maidie **20**
Norton, Eleanor Holmes **7**
Ogletree, Charles, Jr. **12, 47**
Onwueme, Tess Osonye **23**
Onwurah, Ngozi **38**
Owens, Major **6**
Page, Alan **7**
Paige, Rod **29**
Painter, Nell Irvin **24**
Palmer, Everard **37**
Parker, Kellis E. **30**
Parks, Suzan-Lori **34**
Patterson, Frederick Douglass **12**
Patterson, Orlando **4**
Payton, Benjamin F. **23**
Peters, Margaret and Matilda **43**
Pickett, Cecil **39**
Pinckney, Bill **42**
Player, Willa B. **43**
Porter, James A. **11**
Poussaint, Alvin F. **5**
Price, Florence **37**
Price, Glenda **22**
Primus, Pearl **6**
Prophet, Nancy Elizabeth **42**
Puryear, Martin **42**
Quarles, Benjamin Arthur **18**
Rahman, Aishah **37**
Ramphele, Mamphela **29**
Reagon, Bernice Johnson **7**
Reddick, Lawrence Dunbar **20**
Redding, J. Saunders **26**
Redmond, Eugene **23**
Reid, Irvin D. **20**

Ringgold, Faith **4**
Robinson, Sharon **22**
Robinson, Spottswood **22**
Rogers, Joel Augustus **30**
Rollins, Charlemae Hill **27**
Russell-McCloud, Patricia **17**
Salih, Al-Tayyib **37**
Sallee, Charles Louis, Jr. **38**
Satcher, David **7**
Schomburg, Arthur Alfonso **9**
Senior, Olive **37**
Shabazz, Betty **7, 26**
Shange, Ntozake **8**
Shipp, E. R. **15**
Shirley, George **33**
Simmons, Ruth J. **13, 38**
Sinkford, Jeanne C. **13**
Sisulu, Sheila Violet Makate **24**
Sizemore, Barbara A. **26**
Smith, Anna Deavere **6**
Smith, Barbara **28**
Smith, Jessie Carney **35**
Smith, John L. **22**
Smith, Mary Carter **26**
Smith, Tubby **18**
Sowande, Fela **39**
Soyinka, Wole **4**
Spikes, Dolores **18**
Stanford, John **20**
Steele, Claude Mason **13**
Steele, Shelby **13**
Stephens, Charlotte Andrews **14**
Stewart, Maria W. Miller **19**
Stone, Chuck **9**
Sudarkasa, Niara **4**
Sullivan, Louis **8**
Swygert, H. Patrick **22**
Tanksley, Ann **37**
Tatum, Beverly Daniel **42**
Taylor, Helen (Lavon Hollingshed) **30**
Taylor, Susie King **13**
Terrell, Mary Church **9**
Thomas, Alma **14**
Thurman, Howard **3**
Tillis, Frederick **40**
Tolson, Melvin **37**
Tribble, Israel, Jr. **8**
Tucker, Rosina **14**
Turnbull, Walter **13**
Tutu, Desmond **6**
Tutuola, Amos **30**
Tyson, Andre **40**
Tyson, Asha **39**
Tyson, Neil de Grasse **15**
Usry, James L. **23**
van Sertima, Ivan **25**
Wade-Gayles, Gloria Jean **41**
Walcott, Derek **5**
Walker, George **37**
Wallace, Michele Faith **13**
Wallace, Perry E. **47**
Wallace, Phyllis A. **9**
Washington, Booker T. **4**
Watkins, Shirley R. **17**
Wattleton, Faye **9**
Weaver, Afaa Michael **37**
Wedgeworth, Robert W. **42**
Wells, James Lesesne **10**
Wells-Barnett, Ida B. **8**
Welsing, Frances Cress **5**
Wesley, Dorothy Porter **19**
West, Cornel **5, 33**
Wharton, Clifton R., Jr. **7**
White, Charles **39**
White, Lois Jean **20**

Wilkens, J. Ernest, Jr. **43**
Wilkins, Roger **2**
Williams, Fannie Barrier **27**
Williams, Gregory **11**
Williams, Patricia J. **11**
Williams, Sherley Anne **25**
Williams, Walter E. **4**
Wilson, William Julius **22**
Woodruff, Hale **9**
Woodson, Carter G. **2**
Worrill, Conrad **12**
Yancy, Dorothy Cowser **42**
Young, Jean Childs **14**

Fashion
Bailey, Xenobia **11**
Banks, Jeffrey **17**
Banks, Tyra **11**
Barboza, Anthony **10**
Beals, Jennifer **12**
Beckford, Tyson **11**
Berry, Halle **4, 19**
Boateng, Ozwald **35**
Bridges, Sheila **36**
Brown, Joyce F. **25**
Burrows, Stephen **31**
Campbell, Naomi **1, 31**
Dash, Damon **31**
Davidson, Jaye **5**
Henderson, Gordon **5**
Hendy, Francis **47**
Iman **4, 33**
Jay-Z **27**
John, Daymond **23**
Johnson, Beverly **2**
Jones, Carl **7**
Kodjoe, Boris **34**
Kani, Karl **10**
Kelly, Patrick **3**
Lars, Byron **32**
Malone, Maurice **32**
Michele, Michael **31**
Onwurah, Ngozi **38**
Powell, Maxine **8**
Rhymes, Busta **31**
Robinson, Patrick **19**
Rochon, Lela **16**
Rowell, Victoria **13**
Sims, Naomi **29**
Smaltz, Audrey **12**
Smith, B(arbara) **11**
Smith, Willi **8**
Steele, Lawrence **28**
Taylor, Karin **34**
Walker, T. J. **7**
Webb, Veronica **10**
Wek, Alek **18**

Film
Aaliyah **30**
Akomfrah, John **37**
Alexander, Khandi **43**
Allen, Debbie **13, 42**
Amos, John **8**
Anderson, Eddie "Rochester" **30**
Awoonor, Kofi **37**
Babatunde, Obba **35**
Baker, Josephine **3**
Banks, Tyra **11**
Barclay, Paris **37**
Bassett, Angela **6, 23**
Beach, Michael **26**
Beals, Jennifer **12**
Belafonte, Harry **4**
Bellamy, Bill **12**

Sinbad **1, 16**
Singleton, John **2, 30**
Sisqo **30**
Smith, Anjela Lauren **44**
Smith, Anna Deavere **6, 44**
Smith, Roger Guenveur **12**
Smith, Will **8, 18**
Snipes, Wesley **3, 24**
St. Jacques, Raymond **8**
St. John, Kristoff **25**
Sullivan, Maxine **37**
Tate, Larenz **15**
Taylor, Meshach **4**
Taylor, Regina **9, 46**
Thigpen, Lynne **17, 41**
Thomas, Sean Patrick **35**
Thurman, Wallace **16**
Tillman, George, Jr. **20**
Torry, Guy **31**
Toussaint, Lorraine **32**
Townsend, Robert **4, 23**
Tucker, Chris **13, 23**
Turner, Tina **6, 27**
Tyler, Aisha N. **36**
Tyrese **27**
Tyson, Cicely **7**
Uggams, Leslie **23**
Underwood, Blair **7, 27**
Union, Gabrielle **31**
Usher **23**
Van Peebles, Mario **2**
Van Peebles, Melvin **7**
Vance, Courtney B. **15**
Vereen, Ben **4**
Walker, Eamonn **37**
Ward, Douglas Turner **42**
Warfield, Marsha **2**
Warner, Malcolm-Jamal **22, 36**
Warren, Michael **27**
Warwick, Dionne **18**
Washington, Denzel **1, 16**
Washington, Fredi **10**
Washington, Kerry **46**
Waters, Ethel **7**
Wayans, Damon **8, 41**
Wayans, Keenen Ivory **18**
Wayans, Marlon **29**
Wayans, Shawn **29**
Weathers, Carl **10**
Webb, Veronica **10**
Whitaker, Forest **2**
Whitfield, Lynn **18**
Williams, Billy Dee **8**
Williams, Clarence, III **26**
Williams, Samm-Art **21**
Williams, Saul **31**
Williams, Vanessa **32**
Williams, Vanessa L. **4, 17**
Williamson, Mykelti **22**
Wilson, Debra **38**
Winfield, Paul **2, 45**
Winfrey, Oprah **2, 15**
Witherspoon, John **38**
Woodard, Alfre **9**
Yoba, Malik **11**

Government and politics--international
Abacha, Sani **11**
Abbott, Diane **9**
Achebe, Chinua **6**
Ali Mahdi Mohamed **5**
Amadi, Elechi **40**
Amin, Idi **42**
Amos, Valerie **41**
Annan, Kofi Atta **15**

Aristide, Jean-Bertrand **6, 45**
Arthur, Owen **33**
Awoonor, Kofi **37**
Azikiwe, Nnamdi **13**
Babangida, Ibrahim **4**
Baker, Gwendolyn Calvert **9**
Banda, Hastings Kamuzu **6**
Bedie, Henri Konan **21**
Berry, Mary Frances **7**
Biko, Steven **4**
Bishop, Maurice **39**
Biya, Paul **28**
Bizimungu, Pasteur **19**
Bongo, Omar **1**
Boye, Madior **30**
Bunche, Ralph J. **5**
Buthelezi, Mangosuthu Gatsha **9**
Charlemagne, Manno **11**
Charles, Mary Eugenia **10**
Chissano, Joaquim **7**
Christophe, Henri **9**
Conté, Lansana **7**
Curling, Alvin **34**
da Silva, Benedita **5**
Dadié, Bernard **34**
Davis, Ruth **37**
Déby, Idriss **30**
Diop, Cheikh Anta **4**
Diouf, Abdou **3**
dos Santos, José Eduardo **43**
Ekwensi, Cyprian **37**
Eyadéma, Gnassingbé **7**
Fela **1, 42**
Gbagbo, Laurent **43**
Gordon, Pamela **17**
Habré, Hissène **6**
Habyarimana, Juvenal **8**
Haile Selassie **7**
Haley, George Williford Boyce **21**
Hani, Chris **6**
Houphouët-Boigny, Félix **4**
Ifill, Gwen **28**
Ingraham, Hubert A. **19**
Isaac, Julius **34**
Jagan, Cheddi **16**
Jammeh, Yahya **23**
Jawara, Sir Dawda Kairaba **11**
Ka Dinizulu, Mcwayizeni **29**
Kabbah, Ahmad Tejan **23**
Kabila, Joseph **30**
Kabila, Laurent **20**
Kabunda, Kenneth **2**
Kenyatta, Jomo **5**
Kerekou, Ahmed (Mathieu) **1**
King, Oona **27**
Liberia-Peters, Maria Philomena **12**
Lumumba, Patrice **33**
Luthuli, Albert **13**
Maathai, Wangari **43**
Mabuza, Lindiwe **18**
Machel, Samora Moises **8**
Mamadou, Tandja **33**
Mandela, Nelson **1, 14**
Mandela, Winnie **2, 35**
Masekela, Barbara **18**
Masire, Quett **5**
Mbeki, Thabo Mvuyelwa **14**
Mbuende, Kaire **12**
Meles Zenawi **3**
Mkapa, Benjamin **16**
Mobutu Sese Seko **1**
Mogae, Festus Gontebanye **19**
Moi, Daniel **1, 35**
Mongella, Gertrude **11**
Mugabe, Robert Gabriel **10**

Muluzi, Bakili **14**
Museveni, Yoweri **4**
Mutebi, Ronald **25**
Mwinyi, Ali Hassan **1**
Ndadaye, Melchior **7**
Neto, António Agostinho **43**
Ngubane, Ben **33**
Nkomo, Joshua **4**
Nkrumah, Kwame **3**
Ntaryamira, Cyprien **8**
Nujoma, Samuel **10**
Nyanda, Siphiwe **21**
Nyerere, Julius **5**
Nzo, Alfred **15**
Obasanjo, Olusegun **5, 22**
Obasanjo, Stella **32**
Okara, Gabriel **37**
Oyono, Ferdinand **38**
Pascal-Trouillot, Ertha **3**
Patterson, P. J. **6, 20**
Pereira, Aristides **30**
Perkins, Edward **5**
Perry, Ruth **15**
Pitt, David Thomas **10**
Pitta, Celso **17**
Poitier, Sidney **36**
Ramaphosa, Cyril **3**
Rawlings, Jerry **9**
Rawlings, Nana Konadu Agyeman **13**
Rice, Condoleezza **3, 28**
Robinson, Randall **7, 46**
Sampson, Edith S. **4**
Sankara, Thomas **17**
Savimbi, Jonas **2, 34**
Sawyer, Amos **2**
Senghor, Léopold Sédar **12**
Sisulu, Walter **47**
Smith, Jennifer **21**
Soglo, Nicephore **15**
Soyinka, Wole **4**
Taylor, Charles **20**
Taylor, John (David Beckett) **16**
Touré, Sekou **6**
Toure, Amadou Toumani **18**
Tsvangirai, Morgan **26**
Tutu, Desmond (Mpilo) **6, 44**
Vieira, Joao **14**
Wharton, Clifton Reginald, Sr. **36**
Wharton, Clifton R., Jr. **7**
Zuma, Jacob G. **33**
Zuma, Nkosazana Dlamini **34**

Government and politics--U.S.
Adams, Floyd, Jr. **12**
Alexander, Archie Alphonso **14**
Alexander, Clifford **26**
Ali, Muhammad **2, 16**
Allen, Ethel D. **13**
Archer, Dennis **7, 36**
Arrington, Richard **24**
Avant, Clarence **19**
Baker, Thurbert **22**
Ballance, Frank W. **41**
Barden, Don H. **9, 20**
Barrett, Andrew C. **12**
Barrett, Jacqueline **28**
Barry, Marion S(hepilov, Jr.) **7, 44**
Bell, Michael **40**
Belton, Sharon Sayles **9, 16**
Berry, Mary Frances **7**
Berry, Theodore M. **31**
Bethune, Mary McLeod **4**
Blackwell, Unita **17**
Bond, Julian **2, 35**
Bosley, Freeman, Jr. **7**

Tubbs Jones, Stephanie **24**
Tucker, C. DeLores **12**
Turner, Henry McNeal **5**
Usry, James L. **23**
Vaughn, Gladys Gary **47**
Von Lipsey, Roderick K. **11**
Wallace, Phyllis A. **9**
Washington, Harold **6**
Washington, Val **12**
Washington, Walter **45**
Waters, Maxine **3**
Watkins, Shirley R. **17**
Watson, Diane **41**
Watt, Melvin **26**
Watts, J. C., Jr. **14, 38**
Weaver, Robert C. **8, 46**
Webb, Wellington **3**
Wharton, Clifton Reginald, Sr. **36**
Wharton, Clifton R., Jr. **7**
Wheat, Alan **14**
White, Jesse **22**
White, Michael R. **5**
Wilder, L. Douglas **3**
Wilkins, Roger **2**
Williams, Anthony **21**
Williams, Eddie N. **44**
Williams, George Washington **18**
Williams, Hosea Lorenzo **15, 31**
Williams, Maggie **7**
Wilson, Sunnie **7**
Wynn, Albert **25**
Young, Andrew **3**

Law

Alexander, Clifford **26**
Alexander, Joyce London **18**
Alexander, Sadie Tanner Mossell **22**
Allen, Samuel W. **38**
Archer, Dennis **7, 36**
Arnwine, Barbara **28**
Bailey, Clyde **45**
Banks, William **11**
Barrett, Andrew C. **12**
Barrett, Jacqueline **28**
Baugh, David **23**
Bell, Derrick **6**
Berry, Mary Frances **7**
Berry, Theodore M. **31**
Bishop Jr., Sanford D. **24**
Bolin, Jane **22**
Bolton, Terrell D. **25**
Bosley, Freeman, Jr. **7**
Boykin, Keith **14**
Bradley, Thomas **2**
Braun, Carol Moseley **4, 42**
Brooke, Edward **8**
Brown, Cora **33**
Brown, Homer S. **47**
Brown, Janice Rogers **43**
Brown, Joe **29**
Brown, Lee Patrick **1, 24**
Brown, Ron **5**
Brown, Willie L., Jr. **7**
Bryant, Wayne R. **6**
Burke, Yvonne Braithwaite **42**
Burris, Roland W. **25**
Butler, Paul D. **17**
Bynoe, Peter C.B. **40**
Campbell, Bill **9**
Carter, Stephen L. **4**
Chambers, Julius **3**
Cleaver, Kathleen Neal **29**
Clendenon, Donn **26**
Cochran, Johnnie L., Jr. **11, 39**
Colter, Cyrus J. **36**

Conyers, John, Jr. **4, 45**
Crockett, George, Jr. **10**
Darden, Christopher **13**
Davis, Artur **41**
Days, Drew S., III **10**
DeFrantz, Anita **37**
Diggs-Taylor, Anna **20**
Dillard, Godfrey J. **45**
Dinkins, David **4**
Dixon, Sharon Pratt **1**
Edelman, Marian Wright **5, 42**
Edley, Christopher **2**
Ellington, E. David **11**
Ephriam, Mablean **29**
Espy, Mike **6**
Farmer-Paellmann, Deadria **43**
Fields, Cleo **13**
Frazier-Lyde, Jacqui **31**
Freeman, Charles **19**
Gary, Willie E. **12**
Gibson, Johnnie Mae **23**
Glover, Nathaniel, Jr. **12**
Gomez-Preston, Cheryl **9**
Graham, Lawrence Otis **12**
Gray, Fred **37**
Gray, Willie **46**
Grimké, Archibald H. **9**
Guinier, Lani **7, 30**
Haley, George Williford Boyce **21**
Hall, Elliott S. **24**
Harris, Patricia Roberts **2**
Harvard, Beverly **11**
Hassell, Leroy Rountree, Sr. **41**
Hastie, William H. **8**
Hastings, Alcee L. **16**
Hatchett, Glenda **32**
Hawkins, Steven **14**
Haywood, Margaret A. **24**
Higginbotham, A. Leon, Jr. **13, 25**
Hill, Anita **5**
Hillard, Terry **25**
Hills, Oliver W. **24**
Holder, Eric H., Jr. **9**
Holton, Hugh, Jr. **39**
Hooks, Benjamin L. **2**
Houston, Charles Hamilton **4**
Hubbard, Arnette Rhinehart **38**
Hunter, Billy **22**
Hurtt, Harold **46**
Isaac, Julius **34**
Jackson Lee, Sheila **20**
Jackson, Maynard **2, 41**
Johnson, James Weldon **5**
Johnson, Norma L. Holloway **17**
Jones, Elaine R. **7, 45**
Jones, Star **10, 27**
Jordan, Vernon E. **3, 35**
Kearse, Amalya Lyle **12**
Keith, Damon J. **16**
Kennard, William Earl **18**
Kennedy, Florynce **12, 33**
Kennedy, Randall **40**
King, Bernice **4**
Kirk, Ron **11**
Lafontant, Jewel Stradford **3**
Lewis, Delano **7**
Lewis, Reginald F. **6**
Majette, Denise **41**
Mallett, Conrad, Jr. **16**
Mandela, Nelson **1, 14**
Marsh, Henry, III **32**
Marshall, Thurgood **1, 44**
Mathis, Greg **26**
McDonald, Gabrielle Kirk **20**
McDougall, Gay J. **11, 43**

McKinnon, Isaiah **9**
McKissick, Floyd B. **3**
McPhail, Sharon **2**
Meek, Kendrick **41**
Meeks, Gregory **25**
Moose, Charles **40**
Morial, Ernest "Dutch" **26**
Motley, Constance Baker **10**
Muhammad, Ava **31**
Murray, Pauli **38**
Napoleon, Benny N. **23**
Noble, Ronald **46**
Norton, Eleanor Holmes **7**
Nunn, Annetta **43**
O'Leary, Hazel **6**
Ogletree, Jr., Charles **12, 47**
Ogunlesi, Adebayo O. **37**
Oliver, Jerry **37**
Page, Alan **7**
Paker, Kellis E. **30**
Parks, Bernard C. **17**
Parsons, James **14**
Parsons, Richard Dean **11, 33**
Pascal-Trouillot, Ertha **3**
Patrick, Deval **12**
Payne, Ulice **42**
Perry, Lowell **30**
Philip, Marlene Nourbese **32**
Powell, Michael **32**
Ramsey, Charles H. **21**
Redding, Louis L. **26**
Richie, Leroy C. **18**
Robinson, Malcolm S. **44**
Robinson, Randall **7, 46**
Russell-McCloud, Patricia **17**
Sampson, Edith S. **4**
Schmoke, Kurt **1**
Sears-Collins, Leah J. **5**
Solomon, Jimmie Lee **38**
Steele, Michael **38**
Stokes, Carl B. **10**
Stokes, Louis **3**
Stout, Juanita Kidd **24**
Sutton, Percy E. **42**
Taylor, John (David Beckett) **16**
Thomas, Clarence **2, 39**
Thomas, Franklin A. **5**
Thompson, Larry D. **39**
Tubbs Jones, Stephanie **24**
Vanzant, Iyanla **17, 47**
Wagner, Annice **22**
Wainwright, Joscelyn **46**
Wallace, Perry E. **47**
Washington, Harold **6**
Watkins, Donald **35**
Watt, Melvin **26**
Wharton, Clifton Reginald, Sr. **36**
Wilder, L. Douglas **3**
Wilkins, Roger **2**
Williams, Evelyn **10**
Williams, Gregory **11**
Williams, Patricia J. **11**
Williams, Willie L. **4**
Wilson, Jimmy **45**
Wright, Bruce McMarion **3**
Wynn, Albert **25**

Military

Abacha, Sani **11**
Adams Early, Charity **13, 34**
Adams-Ender, Clara **40**
Alexander, Margaret Walker **22**
Amin, Idi **42**
Babangida, Ibrahim **4**
Black, Barry C. **47**

Bolden, Charles F., Jr. **7**
Brashear, Carl **29**
Brown, Erroll M. **23**
Brown, Jesse **6, 41**
Brown, Jesse Leroy **31**
Brown, Willa **40**
Bullard, Eugene **12**
Cadoria, Sherian Grace **14**
Chissano, Joaquim **7**
Christophe, Henri **9**
Clemmons, Reginal G. **41**
Conté, Lansana **7**
Davis, Benjamin O., Jr. **2, 43**
Davis, Benjamin O., Sr. **4**
Europe, James Reese **10**
Eyadéma, Gnassingbé **7**
Fields, Evelyn J. **27**
Flipper, Henry O. **3**
Gravely, Samuel L., Jr. **5**
Gregory, Frederick D. **8**
Habré, Hissène **6**
Habyarimana, Juvenal **8**
Harris, Marcelite Jordan **16**
Howard, Michelle **28**
Jackson, Fred James **25**
James, Daniel, Jr. **16**
Johnson, Hazel **22**
Johnson, Shoshana **47**
Kerekou, Ahmed (Mathieu) **1**
Lawrence, Robert H., Jr. **16**
Lyles, Lester **31**
Miller, Dorie **29**
Nyanda, Siphiwe **21**
Obasanjo, Olusegun **5, 22**
Petersen, Frank E. **31**
Powell, Colin **1, 28**
Pratt, Geronimo **18**
Rawlings, Jerry **9**
Reason, J. Paul **19**
Scantlebury, Janna **47**
Stanford, John **20**
Staupers, Mabel K. **7**
Stokes, Louis **3**
Touré, Amadou Toumani **18**
Vieira, Joao **14**
Von Lipsey, Roderick K. **11**
Watkins, Perry **12**
West, Togo, D., Jr. **16**
Wilson, Jimmy **45**
Wright, Lewin **43**

Music
Aaliyah **30**
Ace, Johnny **36**
Adams, Johnny **39**
Adams, Leslie **39**
Adams, Oleta **18**
Adams, Yolanda **17**
Adderley, Julian "Cannonball" **30**
Adderley, Nat **29**
Ade, King Sunny **41**
Albright, Gerald **23**
Alert, Kool DJ **33**
Anderson, Marian **2, 33**
Armatrading, Joan **32**
Armstrong, Louis **2**
Armstrong, Vanessa Bell **24**
Arroyo, Marina **30**
Ashanti **37**
Ashford, Nickolas **21**
Austin, Lovie **40**
Austin, Patti **24**
Avant, Clarence **19**
Ayers, Roy **16**
Badu, Erykah **22**

Bailey, Buster **38**
Bailey, DeFord **33**
Baiocchi, Regina Harris **41**
Baker, Anita **21**
Baker, Josephine **3**
Baker, LaVern **26**
Ballard, Hank **41**
Bambaataa, Afrika **34**
Barker, Danny **32**
Barnes, Roosevelt "Booba" **33**
Basie, Count **23**
Bassey, Shirley **25**
Baylor, Helen **36**
Bebey, Francis **45**
Bechet, Sidney **18**
Beenie Man **32**
Belafonte, Harry **4**
Belle, Regina **1**
Benét, Eric **28**
Benjamin, Andre **45**
Berry, Chuck **29**
Beverly, Frankie **25**
Blake, Eubie **29**
Blakey, Art **37**
Blanchard, Terence **43**
Bland, Bobby "Blue" **36**
Blige, Mary J. **20, 34**
Blondy, Alpha **30**
Blow, Kurtis **31**
Bolden, Buddy **39**
Bonds, Margaret **39**
Bonga, Kuenda **13**
(Lil') Bow Wow **35**
Brandy **14, 34**
Braxton, Toni **15**
Bridgewater, Dee Dee **32**
Brooks, Avery **9**
Brooks, Hadda **40**
Brown, Charles **23**
Brown, Foxy **25**
Brown, Uzee **42**
Bumbry, Grace **5**
Burke, Solomon **31**
Burns, Eddie **44**
Busby, Jheryl **3**
Butler, Jerry **26**
Butler, Jonathan **28**
Caesar, Shirley **19**
Calloway, Cab **1**
Campbell Martin, Tisha **8, 42**
Cannon, Nick **47**
Carey, Mariah **32**
Carroll, Diahann **9**
Cartíer, Xam Wilson **41**
Carter, Benny **46**
Carter, Betty **19**
Carter, Nell **39**
Carter, Regina **23**
Carter, Warrick L. **27**
Chapman, Tracy **26**
Charlemagne, Manno **11**
Charles, Ray **16**
Cheatham, Doc **17**
Checker, Chubby **28**
Chenault, John **40**
Christie, Angella **36**
Chuck D **9**
Clarke, Kenny **27**
Clark-Sheard, Karen **22**
Clemons, Clarence **41**
Cleveland, James **19**
Cliff, Jimmy **28**
Clinton, George **9**
Cole, Nat King **17**
Cole, Natalie Maria **17**

Coleman, Ornette **39**
Collins, Albert **12**
Collins, Bootsy **31**
Coltrane, John **19**
Combs, Sean "Puffy" **17, 43**
Common **31**
Cook, Charles "Doc" **44**
Cook, Will Marion **40**
Cooke, Sam **17**
Cortez, Jayne **43**
Count Basie **23**
Cox, Deborah **28**
Cox, Ida **42**
Craig, Carl **31**
Crawford, Randy **19**
Cray, Robert **30**
Creagh, Milton **27**
Crocker, Frankie **29**
Crothers, Scatman **19**
Crouch, Andraé **27**
Crouch, Stanley **11**
Crowder, Henry **16**
D'Angelo **27**
Dash, Damon **31**
Dash, Darien **29**
David, Craig **31**
Davis, Anthony **11**
Davis, Gary **41**
Davis, Guy **36**
Davis, Miles **4**
Davis, Sammy, Jr. **18**
Dawson, William Levi **39**
de Passe, Suzanne **25**
Dennard, Brazeal **37**
Dickenson, Vic **38**
Diddley, Bo **39**
Dixon, Willie **4**
DJ Jazzy Jeff **32**
DMX **28**
Dobbs, Mattiwilda **34**
Donegan, Dorothy **19**
Dorsey, Thomas **15**
Downing, Will **19**
Dr. Dre **10**
Dre, Dr. **14, 30**
Duke, George **21**
Dumas, Henry **41**
Dunner, Leslie B. **45**
Dupri, Jermaine **13, 46**
Dupri, Jermaine **13**
Eckstine, Billy **28**
Edmonds, Kenneth "Babyface" **10, 31**
Edmonds, Tracey **16**
Edwards, Esther Gordy **43**
Eldridge, Roy **37**
Ellington, Duke **5**
Elliott, Missy "Misdemeanor" **31**
Estes, Simon **28**
Estes, Sleepy John **33**
Eubanks, Kevin **15**
Europe, James Reese **10**
Evans, Faith **22**
Eve **29**
Evora, Cesaria **12**
Falana, Lola **42**
Farmer, Art **38**
Fats Domino **20**
Fela **1, 42**
Ferrell, Rachelle **29**
Ferrer, Ibrahim **41**
50 Cent **46**
Fitzgerald, Ella **8, 18**
Flack, Roberta **19**
Flash, Grandmaster **33**
Foster, George "Pops" **40**

King, Martin Luther, Jr. **1**
Kobia, Rev. Dr. Samuel **43**
Lester, Julius **9**
Lewis-Thornton, Rae **32**
Lincoln, C. Eric **38**
Little Richard **15**
Long, Eddie L. **29**
Lowery, Joseph **2**
Lyons, Henry **12**
Majors, Jeff **41**
Marino, Eugene Antonio **30**
Mays, Benjamin E. **7**
McClurkin, Donnie **25**
McKenzie, Vashti M. **29**
Muhammad, Ava **31**
Muhammad, Elijah **4**
Muhammad, Khallid Abdul **10, 31**
Muhammed, W. Deen **27**
Murray, Cecil **12, 47**
Patterson, Gilbert Earl **41**
Pierre, Andre **17**
Powell, Adam Clayton, Jr. **3**
Price, Frederick K.C. **21**
Reems, Ernestine Cleveland **27**
Reese, Della **6, 20**
Riley, Helen Caldwell Day **13**
Rugambwa, Laurean **20**
Shabazz, Betty **7, 26**
Sharpton, Al **21**
Shaw, William J. **30**
Shuttlesworth, Fred **47**
Somé, Malidoma Patrice **10**
Stallings, George A., Jr. **6**
Steinberg, Martha Jean "The Queen" **28**
Sullivan, Leon H. **3, 30**
Tillard, Conrad **47**
Thurman, Howard **3**
Turner, Henry McNeal **5**
Tutu, Desmond (Mpilo) **6, 44**
Vanzant, Iyanla **17, 47**
Waddles, Charleszetta (Mother) **10**
Walker, Hezekiah **34**
Waters, Ethel **7**
Weems, Renita J. **44**
West, Cornel **5, 33**
White, Reggie **6**
Williams, Hosea Lorenzo **15, 31**
Wilson, Natalie **38**
Winans, BeBe **14**
Winans, CeCe **14, 43**
Winans, Marvin L. **17**
Wright, Jeremiah A., Jr. **45**
X, Malcolm **1**
Youngblood, Johnny Ray **8**

Science and technology
Adkins, Rod **41**
Adkins, Rutherford H. **21**
Alexander, Archie Alphonso **14**
Allen, Ethel D. **13**
Anderson, Charles Edward **37**
Anderson, Michael P. **40**
Anderson, Norman B. **45**
Auguste, Donna **29**
Auguste, Rose-Anne **13**
Bacon-Bercey, June **38**
Banda, Hastings Kamuzu **6**
Bath, Patricia E. **37**
Benjamin, Regina **20**
Benson, Angela **34**
Black, Keith Lanier **18**
Bluford, Guy **2, 35**
Bluitt, Juliann S. **14**
Bolden, Charles F., Jr. **7**
Brown, Willa **40**

Brown, Vivian **27**
Bullard, Eugene **12**
Callender, Clive O. **3**
Canady, Alexa **28**
Cargill, Victoria A. **43**
Carroll, L. Natalie **44**
Carruthers, George R. **40**
Carson, Benjamin **1, 35**
Carter, Joye Maureen **41**
Carver, George Washington **4**
CasSelle, Malcolm **11**
Chatard, Peter **44**
Chinn, May Edward **26**
Christian, Spencer **15**
Cobb, W. Montague **39**
Cobbs, Price M. **9**
Cole, Rebecca **38**
Coleman, Bessie **9**
Comer, James P. **6**
Cooper, Edward S. **6**
Daly, Marie Maynard **37**
Davis, Allison **12**
Dean, Mark **35**
Delany, Bessie **12**
Delany, Martin R. **27**
Dickens, Helen Octavia **14**
Diop, Cheikh Anta **4**
Drew, Charles Richard **7**
Dunham, Katherine **4**
Elders, Joycelyn **6**
Ellington, E. David **11**
Ellis, Clarence A. **38**
Emeagwali, Dale **31**
Emeagwali, Philip **30**
Ericsson-Jackson, Aprille **28**
Fields, Evelyn J. **27**
Fisher, Rudolph **17**
Flipper, Henry O. **3**
Foster, Henry W., Jr. **26**
Freeman, Harold P. **23**
Fulani, Lenora **11**
Fuller, A. Oveta **43**
Fuller, Arthur **27**
Fuller, Solomon Carter, Jr. **15**
Gates, Sylvester James, Jr. **15**
Gayle, Helene D. **3, 46**
Gibson, Kenneth Allen **6**
Gibson, William F. **6**
Gourdine, Meredith **33**
Granville, Evelyn Boyd **36**
Gray, Ida **41**
Gregory, Frederick D. **8**
Griffin, Bessie Blout **43**
Hall, Lloyd A. **8**
Hannah, Marc **10**
Harris, Mary Styles **31**
Henderson, Cornelius Langston **26**
Henson, Matthew **2**
Hinton, William Augustus **8**
Imes, Elmer Samuel **39**
Irving, Larry, Jr. **12**
Jackson, Shirley Ann **12**
Jawara, Sir Dawda Kairaba **11**
Jemison, Mae C. **1, 35**
Jenifer, Franklyn G. **2**
Johnson, Eddie Bernice **8**
Johnson, Lonnie G. **32**
Jones, Randy **35**
Julian, Percy Lavon **6**
Just, Ernest Everett **6**
Knowling, Robert E., Jr. **38**
Kountz, Samuel L. **10**
Latimer, Lewis H. **4**
Lawless, Theodore K. **8**
Lawrence, Robert H., Jr. **16**

Leevy, Carrol M. **42**
Leffall, LaSalle, Jr. **3**
Lewis, Delano **7**
Logan, Onnie Lee **14**
Lyttle, Hulda Margaret **14**
Madison, Romell **45**
Manley, Audrey Forbes **16**
Massey, Walter E. **5, 45**
Massie, Samuel P., Jr. **29**
Maxey, Randall **46**
Mays, William G. **34**
Mboup, Souleymane **10**
McCoy, Elijah **8**
McNair, Ronald **3**
Millines Dziko, Trish **28**
Morgan, Garrett **1**
Murray, Pauli **38**
Nabrit, Samuel Milton **47**
Neto, António Agostinho **43**
O'Leary, Hazel **6**
Person, Waverly **9**
Peters, Lenrie **43**
Pickett, Cecil **39**
Pierre, Percy Anthony **46**
Pitt, David Thomas **10**
Poussaint, Alvin F. **5**
Prothrow-Stith, Deborah **10**
Quarterman, Lloyd Albert **4**
Riley, Helen Caldwell Day **13**
Robeson, Eslanda Goode **13**
Robinson, Rachel **16**
Roker, Al **12**
Samara, Noah **15**
Satcher, David **7**
Shabazz, Betty **7, 26**
Shavers, Cheryl **31**
Sigur, Wanda **44**
Sinkford, Jeanne C. **13**
Staples, Brent **8**
Staupers, Mabel K. **7**
Stewart, Ella **39**
Sullivan, Louis **8**
Terrell, Dorothy A. **24**
Thomas, Vivien **9**
Tyson, Neil de Grasse **15**
Wambugu, Florence **42**
Washington, Patrice Clarke **12**
Watkins, Levi, Jr. **9**
Welsing, Frances Cress **5**
Wilkens, J. Ernest, Jr. **43**
Williams, Daniel Hale **2**
Williams, O. S. **13**
Witt, Edwin T. **26**
Woods, Granville T. **5**
Wright, Louis Tompkins **4**
Young, Roger Arliner **29**

Social issues
Aaron, Hank **5**
Abbot, Robert Sengstacke **27**
Abbott, Diane **9**
Abdul-Jabbar, Kareem **8**
Abernathy, Ralph David **1**
Abu-Jamal, Mumia **15**
Achebe, Chinua **6**
Adams, Sheila J. **25**
Agyeman, Jaramogi Abebe **10**
Ake, Claude **30**
Al-Amin, Jamil Abdullah **6**
Alexander, Clifford **26**
Alexander, Sadie Tanner Mossell **22**
Ali, Muhammad, **2, 16**
Allen, Ethel D. **13**
Andrews, Benny **22**
Angelou, Maya **1, 15**

Morgan, Joe Leonard **9**
Morris, Garrett **31**
Morris, Greg **28**
Morton, Joe **18**
Mos Def **30**
Moses, Gilbert **12**
Moss, Carlton **17**
Murphy, Eddie **4, 20**
Muse, Clarence Edouard **21**
Nash, Johnny **40**
Neal, Elise **29**
Nichols, Nichelle **11**
Nissel, Angela **42**
Norman, Christina **47**
Norman, Maidie **20**
Odetta **37**
Onwurah, Ngozi **38**
Payne, Allen **13**
Peete, Holly Robinson **20**
Perkins, Tony **24**
Perry, Lowell **30**
Perry, Tyler **40**
Phifer, Mekhi **25**
Pinkett Smith, Jada **10, 41**
Pinkston, W. Randall **24**
Price, Frederick K.C. **21**
Price, Hugh B. **9**
Quarles, Norma **25**
Queen Latifah **1, 16**
Ralph, Sheryl Lee **18**
Randle, Theresa **16**
Rashad, Ahmad **18**
Rashad, Phylicia **21**
Raven, **44**
Ray, Gene Anthony **47**
Reese, Della **6, 20**
Reuben, Gloria **15**
Ribeiro, Alfonso **17**
Richards, Beah **30**
Richardson, Donna **39**
Roberts, Deborah **35**
Roberts, Robin **16**
Robinson, Max **3**
Robinson, Shaun **36**
Rochon, Lela **16**
Rock, Chris **3, 22**
Rodgers, Johnathan **6**
Roker, Al **12**
Rolle, Esther **13, 21**
Rollins, Howard E., Jr. **16**
Ross, Diana **1, 30**
Ross, Tracee Ellis **35**
Roundtree, Richard **27**
Rowan, Carl T. **1, 30**
Rowell, Victoria **13**
Rudolph, Maya **46**
Rupaul **17**
Russell, Bill **8**
Schultz, Michael A. **6**
Scott, Stuart **34**
Shaw, Bernard **2, 28**
Simpson, Carole **6, 30**
Simpson, O. J. **15**
Sinbad **1, 16**
Smiley, Tavis **20**
Smith, Anjela Lauren **44**
Smith, B(arbara) **11**
Smith, Roger Guenveur **12**
Smith, Will **8, 18**
St. Jacques, Raymond **8**
St. John, Kristoff **25**
Stewart, Alison **13**
Stokes, Carl B. **10**
Stone, Chuck **9**
Swann, Lynn **28**

Tate, Larenz **15**
Taylor, Karin **34**
Taylor, Meshach **4**
Taylor, Regina **9, 46**
Thigpen, Lynne **17, 41**
Thomas-Graham, Pamela **29**
Thomason, Marsha **47**
Torry, Guy **31**
Toussaint, Lorraine **32**
Townsend, Robert **4, 23**
Tucker, Chris **13, 23**
Tyler, Aisha N. **36**
Tyrese **27**
Tyson, Cicely **7**
Uggams, Leslie **23**
Underwood, Blair **7, 27**
Union, Gabrielle **31**
Usher **23**
Van Peebles, Mario **2**
Van Peebles, Melvin **7**
Vereen, Ben **4**
Walker, Eamonn **37**
Ware, Andre **37**
Warfield, Marsha **2**
Warner, Malcolm-Jamal **22, 36**
Warren, Michael **27**
Warwick, Dionne **18**
Washington, Denzel **1, 16**
Wattleton, Faye **9**
Watts, Rolonda **9**
Wayans, Damon **8, 41**
Wayans, Keenen Ivory **18**
Wayans, Marlon **29**
Wayans, Shawn **29**
Weathers, Carl **10**
Whack, Rita Coburn **36**
Whitfield, Lynn **1, 18**
Wilkins, Roger **2**
Williams, Armstrong **29**
Williams, Billy Dee **8**
Williams, Clarence, III **26**
Williams, Juan **35**
Williams, Montel **4**
Williams, Samm-Art **21**
Williams, Vanessa **32**
Williams, Vanessa L. **4, 17**
Williamson, Mykelti **22**
Wilson, Debra **38**
Wilson, Flip **21**
Winfield, Paul **2, 45**
Winfrey, Oprah **2, 15**
Witherspoon, John **38**
Yoba, Malik **11**

Theater
Adams, Osceola Macarthy **31**
Ailey, Alvin **8**
Alexander, Khandi **43**
Allen, Debbie **13, 42**
Amos, John **8**
Andrews, Bert **13**
Angelou, Maya **1, 15**
Arkadie, Kevin **17**
Armstrong, Vanessa Bell **24**
Babatunde, Obba **35**
Baraka, Amiri **1, 38**
Barrett, Lindsay **43**
Bassett, Angela **6, 23**
Beach, Michael **26**
Beaton, Norman **14**
Belafonte, Harry **4**
Borders, James **9**
Branch, William Blackwell **39**
Brooks, Avery **9**
Caldwell, Benjamin **46**

Calloway, Cab **14**
Cameron, Earl **44**
Campbell, Naomi **1**
Campbell, Tisha **8**
Carroll, Diahann **9**
Carroll, Vinnette **29**
Carter, Nell **39**
Cash, Rosalind **28**
Cheadle, Don **19**
Chenault, John **40**
Childress, Alice **15**
Clarke, Hope **14**
Cleage, Pearl **17**
Cook, Will Marion **40**
Corthron, Kia **43**
Curtis-Hall, Vondie **17**
Dadié, Bernard **34**
David, Keith **27**
Davis, Ossie **5**
Davis, Sammy, Jr. **18**
Davis, Viola **34**
Dee, Ruby **8**
Devine, Loretta **24**
Diggs, Taye **25**
Dodson, Owen Vincent **38**
Dourdan, Gary **37**
Duke, Bill **3**
Dunham, Katherine **4**
Dutton, Charles S. **4, 22**
Elder, Lonne, III **38**
Emmanuel, Alphonsia **38**
Esposito, Giancarlo **9**
Europe, James Reese **10**
Falana, Lola **42**
Fishburne, Larry **4, 22**
Franklin, J.E. **44**
Freeman, Al, Jr. **11**
Freeman, Morgan **2, 20**
Freeman, Yvette **27**
Fuller, Charles **8**
Glover, Danny **1, 24**
Glover, Savion **14**
Goldberg, Whoopi **4, 33**
Gordone, Charles **15**
Gossett, Louis, Jr. **7**
Graves, Denyce **19**
Greaves, William **38**
Grier, Pam **9, 31**
Guillaume, Robert **3**
Gunn, Moses **10**
Guy, Jasmine **2**
Hansberry, Lorraine **6**
Harris, Robin **7**
Hayes, Teddy **40**
Hemsley, Sherman **19**
Hill, Dulé **29**
Hill, Errol **40**
Hines, Gregory **1, 42**
Holder, Laurence **34**
Holland, Endesha Ida Mae **3**
Horne, Lena **5**
Hyman, Earle **25**
Hyman, Phyllis **19**
Ingram, Rex **5**
Jackson, Millie **25**
Jackson, Samuel L. **8, 19**
Jamison, Judith **7**
Jean-Baptiste, Marianne **17, 46**
Jones, James Earl **3**
Jones, Sarah **39**
Joyner, Matilda Sissieretta **15**
King, Woodie, Jr. **27**
King, Yolanda **6**
Kitt, Eartha **16**
Kotto, Yaphet **7**

Comer, James P. **6**
Cone, James H. **3**
Cook, Suzan D. Johnson **22**
Cooke, Marvel **31**
Coombs, Orde M. **44**
Cooper, Andrew W. **36**
Cooper, Anna Julia **20**
Cooper, J. California **12**
Cortez, Jayne **43**
Cosby, Bill **7, 26**
Cosby, Camille **14**
Cose, Ellis **5**
Cotter, Joseph Seamon, Sr. **40**
Couto, Mia **45**
Creagh, Milton **27**
Crouch, Stanley **11**
Cullen, Countee **8**
Cuney, William Waring **44**
Cunningham, Evelyn **23**
Curry, George E. **23**
Curtis, Christopher Paul **26**
Curtis-Hall, Vondie **17**
Dadié, Bernard **34**
Damas, Léon-Gontran **46**
Dandridge, Raymond Garfield **45**
Danticat, Edwidge **15**
Dash, Leon **47**
Davis, Allison **12**
Davis, Angela **5**
Davis, Frank Marshall **47**
Davis, George **36**
Davis, Miles **4**
Davis, Nolan **45**
Davis, Ossie **5**
Dawkins, Wayne **20**
de Passe, Suzanne **25**
De Veaux, Alexis **44**
Delany, Martin R. **27**
Delany, Samuel R., Jr. **9**
DeLoach, Nora **30**
Dickey, Eric Jerome **21**
Diesel, Vin **29**
Diop, Cheikh Anta **4**
Dodson, Howard, Jr. **7**
Dodson, Owen Vincent **38**
Dove, Rita **6**
Draper, Sharon Mills **16, 43**
Driskell, David C. **7**
Driver, David E. **11**
Drummond, William J. **40**
Du Bois, David Graham **45**
Du Bois, W. E. B. **3**
DuBois, Shirley Graham **21**
Due, Tananarive **30**
Dumas, Henry **41**
Dunbar, Paul Laurence **8**
Dunbar-Nelson, Alice Ruth Moore **44**
Dunham, Katherine **4**
Dunnigan, Alice Allison **41**
Dyson, Michael Eric **11, 40**
Early, Gerald **15**
Edmonds, Terry **17**
Ekwensi, Cyprian **37**
Elder, Lonne, III **38**
Elliot, Lorris **37**
Ellison, Ralph **7**
Elmore, Ronn **21**
Emanuel, James A. **46**
Emecheta, Buchi **30**
Estes, Rufus **29**
Evans, Mari **26**
Fair, Ronald L. **47**
Fanon, Frantz **44**
Farah, Nuruddin **27**
Farrakhan, Louis **15**

Fauset, Jessie **7**
Feelings, Muriel **44**
Feelings, Tom **11, 47**
Fields, Julia **45**
Figueroa, John J. **40**
Files, Lolita **35**
Fisher, Antwone **40**
Fisher, Rudolph **17**
Fletcher, Bill, Jr. **41**
Forbes, Calvin **46**
Ford, Clyde W. **40**
Ford, Nick Aaron **44**
Forman, James **7**
Forrest, Leon **44**
Fortune, T. Thomas **6**
Foster, Cecil **32**
Foster, Jylla Moore **45**
Franklin, John Hope **5**
Franklin, Robert M. **13**
Frazier, E. Franklin **10**
French, Albert **18**
Fuller, Charles **8**
Fuller, Hoyt **44**
Gaines, Ernest J. **7**
Gates, Henry Louis, Jr. **3, 38**
Gayle, Addison, Jr. **41**
Gaynor, Gloria **36**
George, Nelson **12**
Gibson, Althea **8, 43**
Gibson, Donald Bernard **40**
Giddings, Paula **11**
Giovanni, Nikki **9, 39**
Goines, Donald **19**
Golden, Marita **19**
Gomez, Jewelle **30**
Graham, Lawrence Otis **12**
Grant, Gwendolyn Goldsby **28**
Greaves, William **38**
Greenfield, Eloise **9**
Greenwood, Monique **38**
Griffith, Mark Winston **8**
Grimké, Archibald H. **9**
Guinier, Lani **7, 30**
Guy, Rosa **5**
Guy-Sheftall, Beverly **13**
Haley, Alex **4**
Hamblin, Ken **10**
Hamilton, Virginia **10**
Hansberry, Lorraine **6**
Hare, Nathan **44**
Harkless, Necia Desiree **19**
Harper, Frances Ellen Watkins **11**
Harper, Michael S. **34**
Harrington, Oliver W. **9**
Harris, Claire **34**
Harris, Eddy L. **18**
Harris, Jay **19**
Harris, Leslie **6**
Harris, Monica **18**
Harrison, Alvin **28**
Harrison, Calvin **28**
Haskins, James **36**
Hayden, Robert **12**
Hayes, Teddy **40**
Haywood, Gar Anthony **43**
Head, Bessie **28**
Heard, Nathan C. **45**
Hearne, John Edgar Caulwell **45**
Hemphill, Essex **10**
Henderson, Stephen E. **45**
Henries, A. Doris Banks **44**
Henriques, Julian **37**
Henry, Lenny **9**
Henson, Matthew **2**
Hercules, Frank **44**

Hill, Donna **32**
Hill, Errol **40**
Hill, Leslie Pinckney **44**
Hilliard, David **7**
Hoagland, Everett H. **45**
Hobson, Julius W. **44**
Holland, Endesha Ida Mae **3**
Holt, Nora **38**
Holton, Hugh, Jr. **39**
Hooks, Bell **5**
Horne, Frank **44**
Hrabowski, Freeman A. III **22**
Hudson, Cheryl **15**
Hudson, Wade **15**
Hughes, Langston **4**
Hull, Akasha Gloria **45**
Hunter-Gault, Charlayne **6, 31**
Hurston, Zora Neale **3**
Iceberg Slim **11**
Ifill, Gwen **28**
Jackson, Fred James **25**
Jackson, George **14**
Jackson, Sheneska **18**
Jarret, Vernon D. **42**
Jasper, Kenji **39**
Jenkins, Beverly **14**
Joachim, Paulin **34**
Joe, Yolanda **21**
Johnson, Charles **1**
Johnson, Charles S. **12**
Johnson, Dwayne "The Rock" **29**
Johnson, Georgia Douglas **41**
Johnson, James Weldon **5**
Johnson, John H. **3**
Johnson, Linton Kwesi **37**
Johnson, Mat **31**
Johnson, R. M. **36**
Jolley, Willie **28**
Jones, Edward P. **43**
Jones, Gayl **37**
Jones, Orlando **30**
Jones, Sarah **39**
Jordan, June **7, 35**
Josey, E. J. **10**
July, William **27**
Just, Ernest Everett **3**
Kamau, Kwadwo Agymah **28**
Karenga, Maulana **10**
Kay, Jackie **37**
Kayira, Legson **40**
Kennedy, Adrienne **11**
Kennedy, Florynce **12, 33**
Kennedy, Randall **40**
Khanga, Yelena **6**
Kimbro, Dennis **10**
Kincaid, Jamaica **4**
King, Coretta Scott **3**
King, Preston **28**
King, Woodie, Jr. **27**
King, Yolanda **6**
Kitt, Sandra **23**
Knight, Etheridge **37**
Kobia, Rev. Dr. Samuel **43**
Komunyakaa, Yusef **9**
Kotto, Yaphet **7**
Kunjufu, Jawanza **3**
Lacy, Sam **30, 46**
Ladner, Joyce A. **42**
Laferriere, Dany **33**
LaGuma, Alex **30**
Lamming, George **35**
Lampley, Oni Faida **43**
Larsen, Nella **10**
Lawrence, Martin **6, 27**
Lawrence-Lightfoot, Sara **10**

Cumulative Subject Index

Volume numbers appear in **bold**

AIDS Prevention Team
Wilson, Phill **9**

AIDS research
Mboup, Souleymane **10**

AIM
See Adventures in Movement

Akwaaba Mansion Bed & Breakfast
Greenwood, Monique **38**

ALA
See American Library Association

Alabama state government
Davis, Artur **41**
Gray, Fred **37**

Alamerica Bank
Watkins, Donald **35**

Alcoholics Anonymous (AA)
Hilliard, David **7**
Lucas, John **7**

All Afrikan People's Revolutionary Party
Carmichael, Stokely **5, 26**
Moses, Robert Parris **11**

Alliance for Children
McMurray, Georgia L. **36**

Alliance Theatre
Leon, Kenny **10**

Allied Arts Academy
Bonds, Margaret **39**

Alligator Records
Harris, Corey **39**

Alpha Kappa Alpha Sorority
White, Linda M. **45**

Alpha & Omega Ministry
White, Reggie **6**

Alvin Ailey American Dance Theater
Ailey, Alvin **8**
Clarke, Hope **14**
Dove, Ulysses **5**
Faison, George **16**
Jamison, Judith **7**
Primus, Pearl **6**
Rhoden, Dwight **40**
Richardson, Desmond **39**
Tyson, Andre **40**

Alvin Ailey Repertory Ensemble
Ailey, Alvin **8**
Miller, Bebe **3**

Amadou Diallo Foundation
Diallo, Amadou **27**

AMAS Repertory Theater
LeNoire, Rosetta **37**

Ambassadors
Braun, Carol Moseley **4, 42**
Cook, Mercer **40**

Dymally, Mervyn **42**
Watson, Diane **41**

AME
See African Methodist Episcopal Church

AMEN
See Active Ministers Engaged in Nurturance

American Academy of Arts and Sciences
Loury, Glenn **36**

American Art Award
Simpson, Lorna **4, 36**

American Association for the Advancement of Science (AAAS)
Cobb, W. Montague **39**
Massey, Walter E. **5, 45**
Pickett, Cecil **39**

American Association of University Women
Granville, Evelyn Boyd **36**

American Ballet Theatre
Dove, Ulysses **5**
Richardson, Desmond **39**

American Bar Association
Archer, Dennis **7, 36**
Thompson, Larry D. **39**

American Basketball Association (ABA)
Chamberlain, Wilt **18, 47**
Erving, Julius **18, 47**

American Beach
Betsch, MaVynee **28**

American Book Award
Baraka, Amiri **1, 38**
Bates, Daisy **13**
Bradley, David Henry, Jr. **39**
Clark, Septima **7**
Gates, Henry Louis, Jr. **3, 38**
Lorde, Audre **6**
Loury, Glenn **36**
Marshall, Paule **7**
Sanchez, Sonia **17**
Walker, Alice **1, 43**

American Broadcasting Company (ABC)
Christian, Spencer **15**
Goode, Mal **13**
Jackson, Michael **19**
Jones, Star **10, 27**
Joyner, Tom **19**
Mickebury, Penny **28**
Roberts, Robin **16**
Robinson, Max **3**
Simpson, Carole **6, 30**
Winfrey, Oprah **2, 15**

American Postal Worker's Union
Burrus, William Henry "Bill" **45**

American Cancer Society
Ashe, Arthur **1, 18**
Leffall, LaSalle, Jr. **3**
Riperton, Minnie **32**

American Choral Directors Association
Adams, Leslie **39**

American Civil Liberties Union (ACLU)
Baugh, David **23**
Murphy, Laura M. **43**
Murray, Pauli **38**
Norton, Eleanor Holmes **7**

American Composers Alliance
Tillis, Frederick **40**

American Communist Party
Patterson, Louise **25**

American Community Housing Associates, Inc.
Lane, Vincent **5**

American Counseling Association
Mitchell, Sharon **36**

American Dance Guild
Hall, Arthur **39**

American Economic Association
Loury Glenn **36**

American Enterprise Institute
Woodson, Robert L. **10**

American Express Company
Adams, Eula L. **39**
Chenault, Kenneth I. **4, 36**

American Express Consumer Card Group, USA
Chenault, Kenneth I. **4, 36**

American Federation of Labor and Congress of Industrial Organizations (AFL-CIO)
Fletcher, Bill, Jr. **41**
Randolph, A. Philip **3**

American Federation of Television and Radio Artists
Falana, Lola **42**
Fields, Kim **36**
Lewis, Emmanuel **36**
Daniels, Lee Louis **36**

American Guild of Organists
Adams, Leslie **39**

American Heart Association (AHA)
Cooper, Edward S. **6**
Richardson, Donna **39**

American Idol
Jackson, Randy **40**

American Institute for the Prevention of Blindness
Bath, Patricia E. **37**

American Library Association (ALA)
Franklin, Hardy R. **9**
Hayden, Carla D. **47**
Josey, E. J. **10**
McFadden, Bernice L. **39**
Rollins, Charlamae Hill **27**

Atco-EastWest
Rhone, Sylvia **2**

ATD Publishing
Tyson, Asha **39**

Athletic administration
Goss, Tom **23**
Littlpage, Craig **35**

Atlanta Association of Black Journalists
Pressley, Condace L. **41**

Atlanta Baptist College
See Morehouse College

Atlanta Beat
Scurry, Briana **27**

Atlanta Board of Education
Mays, Benjamin E. **7**

Atlanta Braves baseball team
Aaron, Hank **5**
Baker, Dusty **8, 43**
Justice, David **18**
McGriff, Fred **24**
Sanders, Deion **4, 31**

Atlanta Chamber of Commerce
Hill, Jessie, Jr. **13**

Atlanta City Council
Campbell, Bill **9**
Williams, Hosea Lorenzo **15, 31**

Atlanta city government
Campbell, Bill **9**
Franklin, Shirley **34**
Jackson, Maynard **2, 41**
Williams, Hosea Lorenzo **15, 31**
Young, Andrew **3**

Atlanta Falcons football team
Anderson, Jamal **22**
Buchanan, Ray **32**
Sanders, Deion **4, 31**
Vick, Michael **39**

Atlanta Hawks basketball team
Silas, Paul **24**
Wilkens, Lenny **11**

Atlanta Life Insurance Company
Hill, Jessie, Jr. **13**

Atlanta Negro Voters League
Hill, Jessie, Jr. **13**

Atlanta Police Department
Brown, Lee Patrick **1, 24**
Harvard, Beverly **11**

Atlantic City city government
Usry, James L. **23**

Atlantic Records
Franklin, Aretha **11, 44**
Lil' Kim **28**
Rhone, Sylvia **2**

Atlanta World
Scott, C. A. **29**

ATP
See Association of Tennis Professionals

Audelco awards
Holder, Laurence **34**
Rodgers, Rod **36**

Aurelian Honor Society Award
Lewis, William M., Jr. **40**

Authors Guild
Davis, George **36**
Gayle, Addison, Jr. **41**
Schuyler, George Samuel **40**

Authors League of America
Abrahams, Peter **39**
Cotter, Joseph Seamon, Sr. **40**
Davis, George **36**
Gayle, Addison, Jr. **41**

Aviation
Brown, Jesse Leroy **31**
Brown, Willa **40**
Bullard, Eugene **12**
Coleman, Bessie **9**
McLeod, Gus **27**
Petersen, Frank E. **31**

AVP
See Association of Volleyball Professionals

"Back to Africa" movement
Turner, Henry McNeal **5**

Bad Boy Entertainment
Combs, Sean "Puffy" **17, 43**
Harrell, Andre **9, 30**
Notorious B.I.G. **20**

Ballet
Ailey, Alvin **8**
Allen, Debbie **13, 42**
Collins, Janet **33**
Dove, Ulysses **5**
Faison, George **16**
Johnson, Virginia **9**
Mitchell, Arthur **2, 47**
Nichols, Nichelle **11**
Parks, Gordon **1, 35**
Rhoden, Dwight **40**
Richardson, Desmond **39**
Tyson, Andre **40**

Balm in Gilead, The
Seele, Pernessa **46**

Baltimore city government
Schmoke, Kurt **1**

Baltimore Black Sox baseball team
Day, Leon **39**

Baltimore Colts football team
Barnes, Ernie **16**

Baltimore Elite Giants baseball team
Campanella, Roy **25**
Day, Leon **39**

Kimbro, Henry A. **25**

Baltimore Orioles baseball team
Baylor, Don **6**
Blair, Paul **36**
Carter, Joe **30**
Jackson, Reggie **15**
Robinson, Frank **9**

Banking
Boyd, T. B., III **6**
Bradley, Jennette B. **40**
Bridgforth, Glinda **36**
Brimmer, Andrew F. **2**
Bryant, John **26**
Chapman, Nathan A. Jr. **21**
Chappell, Emma **18**
Ferguson, Roger W. **25**
Funderburg, I. Owen **38**
Griffith, Mark Winston **8**
Lawless, Theodore K. **8**
Louis, Errol T. **8**
Morgan, Rose **11**
Parsons, Richard Dean **11**
Utendahl, John **23**
Walker, Maggie Lena **17**
Watkins, Walter C. **24**
Wright, Deborah C. **25**

Baptist World Alliance Assembly
Mays, Benjamin E. **7**

Baptist
Austin, Rev. Junius C. **44**
Davis, Gary **41**
Gomes, Peter J. **15**
Jones, E. Edward, Sr. **45**
Long, Eddie L. **29**
Meek, Carrie **6**
Meek, Kendrick **41**

Barnett-Ader Gallery
Thomas, Alma **14**

Baseball
Aaron, Hank **5**
Anderson, Elmer **25**
Ashford, Emmett **22**
Baines, Harold **32**
Baker, Dusty **8, 43**
Banks, Ernie **33**
Barnhill, David **30**
Baylor, Don **6**
Bell, James "Cool Papa" **36**
Belle, Albert **10**
Blair, Paul **36**
Bonds, Barry **6, 34**
Bonds, Bobby **43**
Brock, Lou **18**
Brown, Willard **36**
Campanella, Roy **25**
Carew, Rod **20**
Carter, Joe **30**
Charleston, Oscar **39**
Clendenon, Donn **26**
Coleman, Leonard S., Jr. **12**
Cottrell, Comer **11**
Dandridge, Ray **36**
Davis, Piper **19**
Doby, Lawrence Eugene **16**
Day, Leon **39**
Edwards, Harry **2**
Fielder, Cecil **2**
Flood, Curt **10**

Chicago Cubs baseball team
Baker, Dusty **8, 43**
Banks, Ernie **33**
Bonds, Bobby **43**
Carter, Joe **30**
Sosa, Sammy **21, 44**

Chicago Defender
Abbott, Robert Sengstacke **27**
Holt, Nora **38**
Payne, Ethel L. **28**

Chicago Defender Charities
Joyner, Marjorie Stewart **26**

Chicago Eight
Seale, Bobby **3**

Chicago American Giants baseball team
Bell, James "Cool Papa" **36**

Chicago Housing Authority (CHA)
Lane, Vincent **5**

Chicago Library Board
Williams, Fannie Barrier **27**

Chicago Negro Chamber of Commerce
Fuller, S. B. **13**

Chicago Police Department
Hillard, Terry **25**
Holton, Hugh, Jr. **39**

Chicago Reporter
Washington, Laura S. **18**

Chicago Tribune
Page, Clarence **4**

Chicago White Sox baseball team
Baines, Harold **32**
Bonds, Bobby **43**
Doby, Lawrence Eugene Sr. **16, 41**
Thomas, Frank **12**

Chicago Women's Club
Williams, Fannie Barrier **27**

Child abuse prevention
Waters, Maxine **3**

Child Care Trust
Obasanjo, Stella **32**

Child psychiatry
Comer, James P. **6**

Child psychology
Hale, Lorraine **8**

Child Welfare Administration
Little, Robert L. **2**

Children's Defense Fund (CDF)
Edelman, Marian Wright **5, 42**
Williams, Maggie **7**

Children's literature
Berry, James **41**
Bryan, Ashley F. **41**
De Veaux, Alexis **44**

Feelings, Muriel **44**
Mollel, Tololwa **38**
Okara, Gabriel **37**
Palmer, Everard **37**
Yarbrough, Camille **40**

Chiropractics
Ford, Clyde W. **40**

Chisholm-Mingo Group, Inc.
Chisholm, Samuel J. **32**
Mingo, Frank **32**

Choreography
Ailey, Alvin **8**
Alexander, Khandi **43**
Allen, Debbie **13, 42**
Atkins, Cholly **40**
Babatunde, Obba **35**
Beatty, Talley **35**
Brooks, Avery **9**
Byrd, Donald **10**
Campbell-Martin, Tisha **8, 42**
Collins, Janet **33**
Davis, Chuck **33**
de Passe, Suzanne **25**
Dove, Ulysses **5**
Dunham, Katherine **4**
Ellington, Mercedes **34**
Fagan, Garth **18**
Faison, George **16**
Glover, Savion **14**
Hall, Arthur **39**
Henson, Darrin **33**
Jamison, Judith **7**
Johnson, Virginia **9**
Jones, Bill T. **1**
King, Alonzo **38**
Miller, Bebe **3**
Mitchell, Arthur **2, 47**
Nicholas, Fayard **20**
Nicholas, Harold **20**
Primus, Pearl **6**
Rhoden, Dwight **40**
Richardson, Desmond **39**
Robinson, Cleo Parker **38**
Robinson, Fatima **34**
Rodgers, Rod **36**
Tyson, Andre **40**
Zollar, Jawole **28**

Christian Financial Ministries, Inc.
Ross, Charles **27**

Christian Science Monitor
Khanga, Yelena **6**

Chrysler Corporation
Colbert, Virgis William **17**
Farmer, Forest **1**
Richie, Leroy C. **18**

Church for the Fellowship of All Peoples
Thurman, Howard **3**

Church of God in Christ
Franklin, Robert M. **13**
Hayes, James C. **10**
Patterson, Gilbert Earl **41**

CIAA
See Central Intercollegiate Athletic Association

Cincinnati city government
Berry, Theodore M. **31**

Cincinnati Reds baseball team
Blair, Paul **36**
Larkin, Barry **24**
Morgan, Joe Leonard **9**
Reese, Pokey **28**
Robinson, Frank **9**
Sanders, Deion **4, 31**

Cinematography
Dickerson, Ernest **6, 17**

Citadel Press
Achebe, Chinua **6**

Citigroup
Gaines, Brenda **41**
Jones, Thomas W. **41**

Citizens Federal Savings and Loan Association
Gaston, Arthur G. **4**

Citizens for Affirmative Action's Preservation
Dillard, Godfrey J. **45**

City government--U.S.
Archer, Dennis **7, 36**
Barden, Don H. **9, 20**
Barry, Marion S. **7, 44**
Berry, Theodore M. **31**
Bosley, Freeman, Jr. **7**
Bradley, Thomas **2, 20**
Brown, Lee P. **1, 24**
Burris, Chuck **21**
Caesar, Shirley **19**
Campbell, Bill **9**
Clayton, Constance **1**
Cleaver, Emanuel **4, 45**
Craig-Jones, Ellen Walker **44**
Dinkins, David **4**
Dixon, Sharon Pratt **1**
Evers, Myrlie **8**
Fauntroy, Walter E. **11**
Fields, C. Virginia **25**
Ford, Jack **39**
Gibson, Kenneth Allen **6**
Goode, W. Wilson **4**
Harmon, Clarence **26**
Hayes, James C. **10**
Jackson, Maynard **2, 41**
James, Sharpe **23**
Jarvis, Charlene Drew **21**
Johnson, Eddie Bernice **8**
Johnson, Harvey Jr. **24**
Kirk, Ron **11**
Mallett, Conrad, Jr. **16**
McPhail, Sharon **2**
Metcalfe, Ralph **26**
Millender-McDonald, Juanita **21**
Morial, Ernest "Dutch" **26**
Morial, Marc **20**
Powell, Adam Clayton, Jr. **3**
Powell, Debra A. **23**
Rice, Norm **8**
Sayles Belton, Sharon **9, 16**
Schmoke, Kurt **1**
Stokes, Carl B. **10**
Street, John F. **24**
Usry, James L. **23**
Washington, Harold **6**

Harlem Artist Guild
Nugent, Richard Bruce **39**
Wilson, Ellis **39**

Harlem Cultural Council
Nugent, Richard Bruce **39**

Harlem Junior Tennis League
Blake, James **43**

Harlem Globetrotters
Chamberlain, Wilt **18, 47**
Haynes, Marques **22**
Jackson, Mannie **14**

Harlem Renaissance
Alexander, Margaret Walker **22**
Christian, Barbara T. **44**
Cullen, Countee **8**
Cuney, William Waring **44**
Dandridge, Raymond Garfield **45**
Davis, Arthur P. **41**
Delaney, Beauford **19**
Ellington, Duke **5**
Fauset, Jessie **7**
Fisher, Rudolph **17**
Frazier, E. Franklin **10**
Horne, Frank **44**
Hughes, Langston **4**
Hurston, Zora Neale **3**
Imes, Elmer Samuel **39**
Johnson, Georgia Douglas **41**
Johnson, James Weldon **5**
Johnson, William Henry **3**
Larsen, Nella **10**
Locke, Alain **10**
McKay, Claude **6**
Mills, Florence **22**
Nugent, Richard Bruce **39**
Petry, Ann **19**
Thurman, Wallace **16**
Toomer, Jean **6**
VanDerZee, James **6**
West, Dorothy **12**
Wilson, Ellis **39**

Harlem Writers Guild
Guy, Rosa **5**
Wesley, Valerie Wilson **18**

Harlem Youth Opportunities Unlimited (HARYOU)
Clark, Kenneth B. **5**

Harvard University
Epps, Archie C., III **45**

Hallmark Channel
Corbi, Lana **42**

Hampton University
Harvey, William R. **42**

Harmolodics Records
Coleman, Ornette **39**

Harmonica
Bailey, DeFord **33**
Barnes, Roosevelt "Booba" **33**
Burns, Eddie **44**
Howlin' Wolf **9**
Neal, Raful **44**
Ross, Isaiah "Doc" **40**

Harness racing
Minor, DeWayne **32**

Harp
Majors, Jeff **41**

Harriet Tubman Home for Aged and Indigent Colored People
Tubman, Harriet **9**

Harrisburg Giants baseball team
Charleston, Oscar **39**

Harvard Law School
Bell, Derrick **6**
Ogletree, Charles, Jr. **12, 47**

Harvard University
Loury, Glenn **36**

HARYOU
See Harlem Youth Opportunities Unlimited

Hazelitt Award for Excellence in Arts
Bradley, David Henry, Jr. **39**

Head Start
Edelman, Marian Wright **5, 42**
Taylor, Helen (Lavon Hollingshed) **30**

Health care reform
Brown, Jesse **6, 41**
Carroll, L. Natalie **44**
Cooper, Edward S. **6**
Davis, Angela **5**
Gibson, Kenneth A. **6**
Norman, Pat **10**
Potter, Myrtle **40**
Satcher, David **7**
Williams, Daniel Hale **2**

Heart disease
Cooper, Edward S. **6**

Heidelberg Project
Guyton, Tyree **9**

Heisman Trophy
Ware, Andre **37**

The Heritage Network
Mercado-Valdes, Frank **43**

HEW
See U.S. Department of Health, Education, and Welfare

HHS
See U.S. Department of Health and Human Services

Hip-hop music
Ashanti **37**
Benjamin, Andre **45**
Patton, Antwan **45**
Smith, Danyel **40**
Williams, Pharrell **47**

Historians
Ballard, Allen Butler, Jr. **40**
Berry, Mary Frances **7**

Blassingame, John Wesley **40**
Blockson, Charles L. **42**
Bogle, Donald **34**
Chase-Riboud, Barbara **20, 46**
Cooper, Anna Julia **20**
Diop, Cheikh Anta **4**
Dodson, Howard, Jr. **7**
Du Bois, W. E. B. **3**
Franklin, John Hope **5**
Gates, Henry Louis, Jr. **3, 38**
Giddings, Paula **11**
Logan, Rayford W. **40**
Hansberry, William Leo **11**
Harkless, Necia Desiree **19**
Hine, Darlene Clark **24**
Marable, Manning **10**
Painter, Nell Irvin **24**
Patterson, Orlando **4**
Quarles, Benjamin Arthur **18**
Reagon, Bernice Johnson **7**
Reddick, Lawrence Dunbar **20**
Rogers, Joel Augustus **30**
Schomburg, Arthur Alfonso **9**
van Sertima, Ivan **25**
Williams, George Washington **18**
Woodson, Carter G. **2**

Hockey
Brashear, Donald **39**
Brathwaite, Fred **35**
Brown, James **22**
Carnegie, Herbert **25**
Doig, Jason **45**
Fuhr, Grant **1**
Grand-Pierre, Jean-Luc **46**
Grier, Mike **43**
Iginla, Jarome **35**
Mayers, Jamal **39**
McBride, Bryant **18**
McKegney, Tony **3**
O'Ree, Willie **5**

Homestead Grays baseball team
Charleston, Oscar **39**
Day, Leon **39**

Homosexuality
Carter, Mandy **11**
Clarke, Cheryl **32**
Delany, Samuel R., Jr. **9**
Gomes, Peter J. **15**
Harris, E. Lynn **12, 33**
Hemphill, Essex **10**
Julien, Isaac **3**
Lorde, Audre **6**
Norman, Pat **10**
Nugent, Richard Bruce **39**
Parker, Pat **19**
Riggs, Marlon **5, 44**
Rupaul **17**
Wilson, Phill **9**

Honeywell Corporation
Jackson, Mannie **14**

Horse racing
St. Julien, Marlon **29**
Winkfield, Jimmy **42**

House music
Knuckles, Frankie **42**

House of Representatives
See U.S. House of Representatives

Thomas, Derrick **25**

Kansas City government
Cleaver, Emanuel **4**, **45**

Kansas City Monarchs baseball team
Bell, James "Cool Papa" **36**
Brown, Willard **36**

KANU
See Kenya African National Union

Kappa Alpha Psi
Hamilton, Samuel C. **47**

Karl Kani Infinity
Kani, Karl **10**

KAU
See Kenya African Union

KCA
See Kikuyu Central Association

Kentucky Derby
Winkfield, Jimmy **42**

Kentucky state government
Kidd, Mae Street **39**

Kentucky Negro Educational Association
Cotter, Joseph Seamon, Sr. **40**

Kenya African National Union (KANU)
Kenyatta, Jomo **5**
Moi, Daniel arap **1**, **35**

Kenya African Union (KAU)
Kenyatta, Jomo **5**

Kenya National Council of Churches (NCCK)
Kobia, Rev. Dr. Samuel **43**

Keyan government
Maathai, Wangari **43**

Kikuyu Central Association (KCA)
Kenyatta, Jomo **5**

King Center
See Martin Luther King Jr. Center for Nonviolent Social Change

King Oliver's Creole Band
Armstrong, (Daniel) Louis **2**
Hardin Armstrong, Lil **39**
Oliver, Joe "King" **42**

King's Troop of the Royal Horse Artillery
Scantlebury, Janna **47**

King Sunny Ade Foundation
Ade, King Sunny **41**

Kitchen Table: Women of Color Press
Smith, Barbara **28**

Koko Taylor's Celebrity
Taylor, Koko **40**

Kraft General Foods
Fudge, Ann **11**
Sneed, Paula A. **18**

Kwanzaa
Karenga, Maulana **10**

Kwazulu Territorial Authority
Buthelezi, Mangosuthu Gatsha **9**

Labour Party
Amos, Valerie **41**

Ladies Professional Golfers' Association (LPGA)
Gibson, Althea **8**, **43**
Powell, Renee **34**

LaFace Records
Benjamin, Andre **45**
Edmonds, Kenneth "Babyface" **10**, **31**
Patton, Antwan **45**
Reid, Antonio "L.A." **28**
OutKast **35**

Lamb of God Ministry
Falana, Lola **42**

Langston (OK) city government
Tolson, Melvin B. **37**

LAPD
See Los Angeles Police Department

Latin American folk music
Nascimento, Milton **2**

Latin baseball leagues
Kaiser, Cecil **42**

Law enforcement
Alexander, Joyce London **18**
Barrett, Jacquelyn **28**
Bolton, Terrell D. **25**
Bradley, Thomas **2**, **20**
Brown, Lee P. **1**, **24**
Freeman, Charles **19**
Gibson, Johnnie Mae **23**
Glover, Nathaniel, Jr. **12**
Gomez-Preston, Cheryl **9**
Harvard, Beverly **11**
Hillard, Terry **25**
Holton, Hugh, Jr. **39**
Hurtt, Harold **46**
Johnson, Norma L. Holloway **17**
Johnson, Robert T. **17**
Keith, Damon J. **16**
McKinnon, Isaiah **9**
Moose, Charles **40**
Napoleon, Benny N. **23**
Noble, Ronald **46**
Oliver, Jerry **37**
Parks, Bernard C. **17**
Ramsey, Charles H. **21**
Schmoke, Kurt **1**
Thomas, Franklin A. **5**
Wainwright, Joscelyn **46**
Williams, Willie L. **4**
Wilson, Jimmy **45**

Lawrence Steele Design
Steele, Lawrence **28**

Lawyers' Committee for Civil Rights Under Law
Arnwine, Barbara **28**
Hubbard, Arnette **38**
McDougall, Gay J. **11**, **43**

LDF
See NAACP Legal Defense and Educational Fund

Leadership Conference on Civil Rights (LCCR)
Henderson, Wade J. **14**

League of Nations
Haile Selassie **7**

League of Women Voters
Meek, Carrie **36**

Leary Group Inc.
Leary, Kathryn D. **10**

"Leave No Child Behind"
Edelman, Marian Wright **5**, **42**

Lee Elder Scholarship Fund
Elder, Lee **6**

Legal Defense Fund
See NAACP Legal Defense and Educational Fund

Les Brown Unlimited, Inc.
Brown, Les **5**

Lexicography
Major, Clarence **9**

Liberian government
Henries, A. Doris Banks **44**

Liberation theology
West, Cornel **5**

Librettist
Chenault, John **40**

Library science
Bontemps, Arna **8**
Franklin, Hardy R. **9**
Harsh, Vivian Gordon **14**
Hutson, Jean Blackwell **16**
Josey, E. J. **10**
Kitt, Sandra **23**
Larsen, Nella **10**
Owens, Major **6**
Rollins, Charlemae Hill **27**
Schomburg, Arthur Alfonso **9**
Smith, Jessie Carney **35**
Spencer, Anne **27**
Wedgeworth, Robert W. **42**
Wesley, Dorothy Porter **19**

Lincoln University
Cuney, William Waring **44**
Randall, Dudley **8**
Sudarkasa, Niara **4**

LISC
See Local Initiative Support Corporation

National Association of Colored Women (NACW)
Bethune, Mary McLeod **4**
Cooper, Margaret J. **46**
Harper, Frances Ellen Watkins **11**
Lampkin, Daisy **19**
Stewart, Ella **39**
Terrell, Mary Church **9**

National Association of Negro Business and Professional Women's Clubs
Vaughns, Cleopatra **46**

National Association of Negro Musicians
Bonds, Margaret **39**
Brown, Uzee **42**

National Association of Regulatory Utility Commissioners
Colter, Cyrus, J. **36**

National Association of Social Workers
McMurray, Georgia L. **36**

National Association of Stock Car Auto Racing
Lester, Bill **42**

National Baptist Convention USA
Jones, E. Edward, Sr. **45**
Lyons, Henry **12**
Shaw, William J. **30**

National Baptist Publishing Board
Boyd, T. B., III **6**

National Baptist Sunday Church School and Baptist Training Union Congress
Boyd, T. B., III **6**

National Bar Association
Alexander, Joyce London **18**
Alexander, Sadie Tanner Mossell **22**
Archer, Dennis **7, 36**
Bailey, Clyde **45**
Hubbard, Arnette **38**
McPhail, Sharon **2**
Robinson, Malcolm S. **44**
Thompson, Larry D. **39**

National Basketball Association (NBA)
Abdul-Jabbar, Kareem **8**
Abdur-Rahim, Shareef **28**
Anthony, Carmelo **46**
Barkley, Charles **5**
Bing, Dave **3**
Bol, Manute **1**
Brandon, Terrell **16**
Bryant, Kobe **15, 31**
Bynoe, Peter C.B. **40**
Carter, Vince **26**
Chamberlain, Wilt **18, 47**
Cheeks, Maurice **47**
Clifton, Nathaniel "Sweetwater" **47**
Cooper, Charles "Chuck" **47**
Drexler, Clyde **4**
Duncan, Tim **20**
Elliott, Sean **26**
Erving, Julius **18, 47**
Ewing, Patrick A. **17**
Garnett, Kevin **14**
Gourdine, Simon **11**
Green, A. C. **32**

Hardaway, Anfernee (Penny) **13**
Hardaway, Tim **35**
Heard, Gar **25**
Hill, Grant **13**
Howard, Juwan **15**
Hunter, Billy **22**
Johnson, Earvin "Magic" **3, 39**
Johnson, Larry **28**
Jordan, Michael **6, 21**
Lanier, Bob **47**
Lucas, John **7**
Mourning, Alonzo **17, 44**
Mutombo, Dikembe **7**
O'Neal, Shaquille **8, 30**
Olajuwon, Hakeem **2**
Parish, Robert **43**
Pippen, Scottie **15**
Rivers, Glenn "Doc" **25**
Robertson, Oscar **26**
Robinson, David **24**
Rodman, Dennis **12, 44**
Russell, Bill **8**
Silas, Paul **24**
Sprewell, Latrell **23**
Thomas, Isiah **7, 26**
Webber, Chris **15, 30**
Wilkens, Lenny **11**

National Basketball Players Association
Erving, Julius **18, 47**
Ewing, Patrick A. **17**
Gourdine, Simon **11**
Hunter, Billy **22**

National Black Arts Festival (NBAF)
Borders, James **9**
Brooks, Avery **9**

National Black Association of Journalist
Pressley, Condace L. **41**

National Black College Hall of Fame
Dortch, Thomas W., Jr. **45**

National Black Farmers Association (NBFA)
Boyd, John W., Jr. **20**

National Black Fine Art Show
Wainwright, Joscelyn **46**

National Black Gay and Lesbian Conference
Wilson, Phill **9**

National Black Gay and Lesbian Leadership Forum (NBGLLF)
Boykin, Keith **14**
Carter, Mandy **11**

National Book Award
Ellison, Ralph **7**
Haley, Alex **4**
Johnson, Charles **1**
Patterson, Orlando **4**

National Broadcasting Company (NBC)
Allen, Byron **3, 24**
Cosby, Bill **7, 26**
Grier, David Alan **28**
Gumbel, Bryant **14**
Hinderas, Natalie **5**
Ifill, Gwen **28**
Johnson, Rodney Van **28**

Jones, Star **10, 27**
Madison, Paula **37**
Rashad, Phylicia **21**
Reuben, Gloria **15**
Roker, Al **12**
Simpson, Carole **6, 30**
Stokes, Carl B. **10**
Thomas-Graham, Pamela **29**
Williams, Montel **4**
Wilson, Flip **21**

National Brotherhood of Skiers (NBS)
Horton, Andre **33**
Horton, Suki **33**

National Center for Neighborhood Enterprise (NCNE)
Woodson, Robert L. **10**

National Coalition of 100 Black Women (NCBW)
Mays, Leslie A. **41**
McCabe, Jewell Jackson **10**

National Coalition to Abolish the Death Penalty (NCADP)
Hawkins, Steven **14**

National Commission for Democracy (Ghana; NCD)
Rawlings, Jerry **9**

National Conference on Black Lawyers (NCBL)
McDougall, Gay J. **11, 43**

National Council of Churches
Howard, M. William, Jr. **26**

National Council of Negro Women (NCNW)
Bethune, Mary McLeod **4**
Blackwell, Unita **17**
Cole, Johnnetta B. **5, 43**
Hamer, Fannie Lou **6**
Height, Dorothy I. **2, 23**
Horne, Lena **5**
Lampkin, Daisy **19**
Sampson, Edith S. **4**
Smith, Jane E. **24**
Staupers, Mabel K. **7**

National Council of Nigeria and the Cameroons (NCNC)
Azikiwe, Nnamdi **13**

National Council of Teachers of Mathematics
Granville, Evelyn Boyd **36**

National Council on the Arts
Robinson, Cleo Parker **38**

National Defence Council (Ghana; NDC)
Rawlings, Jerry **9**

National Democratic Party (Rhodesia)
Mugabe, Robert Gabriel **10**

National Dental Association
Madison, Romell **45**

National Urban League
Brown, Ron **5**
Gordon, Bruce S. **41**
Greely, M. Gasby **27**
Haynes, George Edmund **8**
Jacob, John E. **2**
Jordan, Vernon E. **3, 35**
Price, Hugh B. **9**
Young, Whitney M., Jr. **4**

National War College
Clemmons, Reginal G. **41**

**National Women's Basketball League
(NWBL)**
Catchings, Tamika **43**

National Women's Hall of Fame
Kelly, Leontine **33**

National Women's Political Caucus
Hamer, Fannie Lou **6**

National Youth Administration (NYA)
Bethune, Mary McLeod **4**
Primus, Pearl **6**

Nature Boy Enterprises
Yoba, Malik **11**

Naval Research Laboratory (NRL)
Carruthers, George R. **40**

NBA
See National Basketball Association

NBAF
See National Black Arts Festival

NBC
See National Broadcasting Company

NBGLLF
See National Black Gay and Lesbian
Leadership Forum

NCBL
See National Conference on Black Lawyers

NCBW
See National Coalition of 100 Black
Women

NCCK
See Kenya National Council of
Churches

NCD
See National Commission for Democracy

NCNE
See National Center for Neighborhood
Enterprise

NCNW
See National Council of Negro Women

NDC
See National Defence Council

NEA
See National Endowment for the Arts

Nebula awards
Butler, Octavia **8, 43**
Delany, Samuel R. Jr. **9**

Négritude
Damas, Léon-Gontran **46**

Negro American Labor Council
Randolph, A. Philip **3**

Negro American Political League
Trotter, Monroe **9**

Negro Digest magazine
Johnson, John H. **3**
Fuller, Hoyt **44**

Negro Ensemble Company
Cash, Rosalind **28**
Schultz, Michael A. **6**
Taylor, Susan L. **10**
Ward, Douglas Turner **42**

Negro History Bulletin
Woodson, Carter G. **2**

Negro Leagues
Banks, Ernie **33**
Barnhill, David **30**
Bell, James "Cool Papa" **36**
Brown, Willard **36**
Campanella, Roy **25**
Charleston, Oscar **39**
Dandridge, Ray **36**
Davis, Piper **19**
Day, Leon **39**
Gibson, Josh **22**
Hyde, Cowan F. "Bubba" **47**
Irvin, Monte **31**
Johnson, Mamie "Peanut" **40**
Kaiser, Cecil **42**
Kimbro, Henry A. **25**
Lloyd, John Henry "Pop" **30**
O'Neil, Buck **19**
Paige, Satchel **7**
Pride, Charley **26**
Smith, Hilton **29**
Stearnes, Norman "Turkey" **31**
Stone, Toni **15**

Negro Theater Ensemble
Rolle, Esther **13, 21**

Negro World
Fortune, T. Thomas **6**

NEIC
See National Earthquake Information
Center

Neo-hoodoo
Reed, Ishmael **8**

Nequai Cosmetics
Taylor, Susan L. **10**

NERL
See National Equal Rights League

Netherlands Antilles
Liberia-Peters, Maria Philomena **12**

NetNoir Inc.
CasSelle, Malcolm **11**
Ellington, E. David **11**

Neurosurgery
Black, Keith Lanier **18**
Carson, Benjamin **1, 35**
Canady, Alexa **28**

**Neustadt International Prize for Litera-
ture**
Brathwaite, Kamau **36**

New Birth Missionary Baptist Church
Long, Eddie L. **29**

New Black Muslims
Muhammad, Khallid Abdul **10, 31**

New Black Panther Party
Muhammad, Khallid, Abdul **10, 31**

New Concept Development Center
Madhubuti, Haki R. **7**

New Dance Group
Primus, Pearl **6**

New Jewel Movement
Bishop, Maurice **39**

New Jersey Family Development Act
Bryant, Wayne R. **6**

New Jersey General Assembly
Bryant, Wayne R. **6**

New Jersey Nets
Doby, Lawrence Eugene Sr. **16, 41**

New Jersey Symphony Orchestra
Lewis, Henry **38**

New Life Community Choir
Kee, John P. **43**

New Life Fellowship Church
Kee, John P. **43**

New Orleans city government
Nagin, Ray **42**

New Orleans Saints football team
Brooks, Aaron **33**
Mills, Sam **33**

New Negro movement
See Harlem Renaissance

New York Age
Fortune, T. Thomas **6**

New York City government
Campbell, Mary Schmidt **43**
Crew, Rudolph F. **16**
Dinkins, David **4**
Fields, C. Virginia **25**
Hageman, Hans **36**
Sutton, Percy E. **42**

Thompson, William **35**

New York Daily News
Cose, Ellis **5**

New York Drama Critics Circle Award
Hansberry, Lorraine **6**

New York Freeman
Fortune, T. Thomas **6**

New York Giants baseball team
Dandridge, Ray **36**
Mays, Willie **3**

New York Giants football team
Strahan, Michael **35**
Taylor, Lawrence **25**

New York Globe
Fortune, T. Thomas **6**

New York Hip Hop Theater Festival
Jones, Sarah **39**

New York Institute for Social Therapy and Research
Fulani, Lenora **11**

New York Jets football team
Lott, Ronnie **9**

New York Knicks basketball team
Ewing, Patrick A. **17**
Johnson, Larry **28**
Sprewell, Latrell **23**

New York Mets baseball team
Clendenon, Donn **26**

New York Philharmonic
DePriest, James **37**

New York Public Library
Baker, Augusta **38**
Dodson, Howard, Jr. **7**
Schomburg, Arthur Alfonso **9**

New York Shakespeare Festival
Gunn, Moses **10**
Wolfe, George C. **6, 43**

New York state government
McCall, H. Carl **27**

New York State Senate
McCall, H. Carl **27**
Motley, Constance Baker **10**
Owens, Major **6**

New York State Supreme Court
Wright, Bruce McMarion **3**

New York Stock Exchange
Doley, Harold, Jr. **26**

New York Sun
Fortune, T. Thomas **6**

New York Times
Boyd, Gerald M. **32**
Davis, George **36**

Hunter-Gault, Charlayne **6, 31**
Ifill, Gwen **28**
Price, Hugh B. **9**
Wilkins, Roger **2**

New York University
Brathwaite, Kamau **36**
Campbell, Mary Schmidt **43**

New York Yankees baseball team
Baylor, Don **6**
Bonds, Bobby **43**
Jackson, Reggie **15**
Jeter, Derek **27**
Strawberry, Darryl **22**
Watson, Bob **25**
Winfield, Dave **5**

Newark city government
Gibson, Kenneth Allen **6**
James, Sharpe **23**

Newark Dodgers baseball team
Dandridge, Ray **36**

Newark Eagles baseball team
Dandridge, Ray **36**
Doby, Lawrence Eugene Sr. **16, 41**

Newark Housing Authority
Gibson, Kenneth Allen **6**

The News Hour with Jim Lehrer TV series
Ifill, Gwen **28**

NFL
See National Football League

Nguzo Saba
Karenga, Maulana **10**

NHL
See National Hockey League

Niagara movement
Du Bois, W. E. B. **3**
Hope, John **8**
Trotter, Monroe **9**

Nigerian Armed Forces
Abacha, Sani **11**
Babangida, Ibrahim **4**
Obasanjo, Olusegun **5, 22**

Nigerian Association of Patriotic Writers and Artists
Barrett, Lindsay **43**

Nigerian literature
Achebe, Chinua **6**
Amadi, Elechi **40**
Barrett, Lindsay **43**
Ekwensi, Cyprian **37**
Onwueme, Tess Osonye **23**
Rotimi, Ola **1**
Saro-Wiwa, Kenule **39**
Soyinka, Wole **4**

NIH
See National Institute of Health

NII
See National Information Infrastructure

1960 Masks
Soyinka, Wole **4**

Nobel Peace Prize
Bunche, Ralph J. **5**
King, Martin Luther, Jr. **1**
Luthuli, Albert **13**
Tutu, Desmond Mpilo **6, 44**

Nobel Prize for literature
Soyinka, Wole **4**
Morrison, Toni **2, 15**
Walcott, Derek **5**

Noma Award for Publishing in African
Ba, Mariama **30**

Nonfiction
Abrahams, Peter **39**
Adams-Ender, Clara **40**
Allen, Debbie **13, 42**
Allen, Robert L. **38**
Atkins, Cholly **40**
Ballard, Allen Butler, Jr. **40**
Blassingame, John Wesley **40**
Blockson, Charles L. **42**
Bogle, Donald **34**
Brown, Cecil M. **46**
Brown, Llyod Louis **42**
Buckley, Gail Lumet **39**
Carby, Hazel **27**
Carter, Joye Maureen **41**
Cole, Johnnetta B. **5, 43**
Cook, Mercer **40**
Davis, Arthur P. **41**
Dunnigan, Alice Allison **41**
Edelman, Marian Wright **5, 42**
Elliott, Lorris **37**
Fisher, Antwone **40**
Fletcher, Bill, Jr. **41**
Ford, Clyde W. **40**
Foster, Cecil **32**
Gayle, Addison, Jr. **41**
Gibson, Donald Bernard **40**
Greenwood, Monique **38**
Harrison, Alvin **28**
Harrison, Calvin **28**
Henries, A. Doris Banks **44**
Henriques, Julian **37**
Hercules, Frank **44**
Hill, Errol **40**
Hobson, Julius W. **44**
Horne, Frank **44**
Jakes, Thomas "T.D." **17, 43**
Jolley, Willie **28**
Jordan, Vernon E. **7, 35**
Kayira, Legson **40**
Kennedy, Randall **40**
Knight, Etheridge **37**
Kobia, Rev. Dr. Samuel **43**
Ladner, Joyce A. **42**
Lampley, Oni Faida **43**
Lincoln, C. Eric **38**
Long, Eddie L. **29**
Mabuza-Suttle, Felicia **43**
Malveaux, Julianne **32**
Manley, Ruth **34**
McBride, James **35**
McKenzie, Vashti M. **29**
McWhorter, John **35**
Mossell, Gertrude Bustill **40**

Philanthropy
Brown, Eddie C. 35
Cooper, Evern 40
Cosby, Bill 7, 26
Cosby, Camille 14
Dawson, Matel "Mat," Jr. 39
Golden, Marita 19
Gray, Willie 46
Malone, Annie 13
McCarty, Osceola 16
Millines Dziko, Trish 28
Pleasant, Mary Ellen 9
Reeves, Rachel J. 23
Thomas, Franklin A. 5
Waddles, Charleszetta (Mother) 10
Walker, Madame C. J. 7
White, Reggie 6
Williams, Fannie Barrier 27
Wonder, Stevie 11

Philosophy
Baker, Houston A., Jr. 6
Davis, Angela 5
Toomer, Jean 6
West, Cornel 5

Phoenix Suns basketball team
Barkley, Charles 5
Heard, Gar 25

Photography
Andrews, Bert 13
Barboza, Anthony 10
Cowans, Adger W. 20
DeCarava, Roy 42
Hinton, Milt 30
Jackson, Vera 40
Lester, Julius 9
Moutoussamy-Ashe, Jeanne 7
Parks, Gordon 1, 35
Pinderhughes, John 47
Robeson, Eslanda Goode 13
Serrano, Andres 3
Simpson, Lorna 4, 36
Sleet, Moneta, Jr. 5
Smith, Marvin 46
Smith, Morgan 46
Tanner, Henry Ossawa 1
VanDerZee, James 6
White, John H. 27

Photojournalism
Ashley-Ward, Amelia 23
DeCarava, Roy 42
Jackson, Vera 40
Moutoussamy-Ashe, Jeanne 7
Parks, Gordon 1, 35
Sleet, Moneta, Jr. 5
White, John H. 27

Physical therapy
Elders, Joycelyn 6
Griffin, Bessie Blout 43

Physics
Adkins, Rutherford H. 21
Carruthers, George R. 40
Gates, Sylvester James, Jr. 15
Gourdine, Meredith 33
Imes, Elmer Samuel 39
Jackson, Shirley Ann 12
Massey, Walter E. 5, 45
Tyson, Neil de Grasse 15

Piano
Adams, Leslie 39
Austin, Lovie 40
Basie, Count 23
Bonds, Margaret 39
Brooks, Hadda 40
Cartíer, Xam Wilson 41
Cole, Nat King 17
Cook, Charles "Doc" 44
Donegan, Dorothy 19
Duke, George 21
Ellington, Duke 5
Fats Domino 20
Hancock, Herbie 20
Hardin Armstrong, Lil 39
Hayes, Isaac 20
Hinderas, Natalie 5
Hines, Earl "Fatha" 39
Horn, Shirley 32
Joplin, Scott 6
Keys, Alicia 32
Monk, Thelonious 1
Powell, Bud 24
Pratt, Awadagin 31
Preston, Billy 39
Price, Florence 37
Pritchard, Robert Starling 21
Roberts, Marcus 19
Silver, Horace 26
Simone, Nina 15, 41
Swann, Lynn 28
Sykes, Roosevelt 20
Taylor, Billy 23
Vaughan, Sarah 13
Walker, George 37
Waller, Fats 29
Webster, Katie 29
Williams, Mary Lou 15

Pittsburgh Crawfords
See Indianapolis Crawfords

Pittsburgh Homestead Grays baseball team
Charleston, Oscar 39
Kaiser, Cecil 42

Pittsburgh Pirates baseball team
Bonds, Barry 6, 34
Clendenon, Donn 26
Stargell, Willie 29

Pittsburgh Steelers football team
Dungy, Tony 17, 42
Gilliam, Joe 31
Greene, Joe 10
Perry, Lowell 30
Stargell, Willie 29
Stewart, Kordell 21
Swann, Lynn 28

PLAN
See People's Liberation Army of Namibia

Planet E Communications
Craig, Carl 31

Planned Parenthood Federation of America Inc.
Wattleton, Faye 9

Playboy
Taylor, Karin 34

Playwright
Allen, Debbie 13, 42
Arkadie, Kevin 17
Baldwin, James 1
Barrett, Lindsay 43
Beckham, Barry 41
Branch, William Blackwell 39
Brown, Cecil M. 46
Bullins, Ed 25
Caldwell, Benjamin 46
Carroll, Vinnette 29
Cheadle, Don 19
Chenault, John 40
Childress, Alice 15
Clark-Bekedermo, J. P. 44
Clarke, George 32
Cleage, Pearl 17
Corthron, Kia 43
Cotter, Joseph Seamon, Sr. 40
Dadié, Bernard 34
De Veaux, Alexis 44
Dodson, Owen 38
Elder, Larry III 38
Evans, Mari 26
Farah, Nuruddin 27
Franklin, J.E. 44
Gordone, Charles 15
Hansberry, Lorraine 6
Hayes, Teddy 40
Hill, Errol 40
Hill, Leslie Pinckney 44
Holder, Laurence 34
Hughes, Langston 4
Jean-Baptiste, Marianne 17, 46
Johnson, Georgia Douglas 41
Jones, Sarah 39
Kennedy, Adrienne 11
King, Woodie, Jr. 27
Lampley, Oni Faida 43
Marechera, Dambudzo 39
Milner, Ron 39
Mitchell, Loften 31
Moss, Carlton 17
Mugo, Micere Githae 32
Onwueme, Tess Osonye 23
Orlandersmith, Dael 42
Parks, Suzan-Lori 34
Perry, Tyler 40
Rahman, Aishah 37
Richards, Beah 30
Sanchez, Sonia 17
Schuyler, George Samuel 40
Sebree, Charles 40
Smith, Anna Deavere 6, 44
Talbert, David 34
Taylor, Regina 9, 46
Thurman, Wallace 17
Tolson, Melvin B. 37
Walcott, Derek 5
Ward, Douglas Turner 42
Williams, Samm-Art 21
Wilson, August 7, 33
Wolfe, George C. 6, 43
Youngblood, Shay 32

PNP
See People's National Party (Jamaica)

Podium Records
Patterson, Gilbert Earl 41

Poet laureate (U.S.)
Dove, Rita 6

Voting rights
Clark, Septima **7**
Cary, Mary Ann Shadd **30**
Forman, James **7**
Guinier, Lani **7, 30**
Hamer, Fannie Lou **6**
Harper, Frances Ellen Watkins **11**
Hill, Jessie, Jr. **13**
Johnson, Eddie Bernice **8**
Lampkin, Daisy **19**
Mandela, Nelson **1, 14**
Moore, Harry T. **29**
Moses, Robert Parris **11**
Terrell, Mary Church **9**
Trotter, Monroe **9**
Tubman, Harriet **9**
Wells-Barnett, Ida B. **8**
Williams, Fannie Barrier **27**
Williams, Hosea Lorenzo **15, 31**
Woodard, Alfre **9**

Vulcan Realty and Investment Company
Gaston, Arthur G. **4**

WAAC
See Women's Auxiliary Army Corp

WAC
See Women's Army Corp

Wall Street
Lewis, William M., Jr. **40**

Wall Street Project
Jackson, Jesse **1, 27**

Walter Payton Inc.
Payton, Walter **11, 25**

War Resister's League (WRL)
Carter, Mandy **11**

Washington Capitols basketball team
Lloyd, Earl **26**

Washington Capitols hockey team
Grier, Mike **43**

Washington Color Field group
Thomas, Alma **14**

Washington, D.C., city government
Barry, Marion S. **7, 44**
Cooper Cafritz, Peggy **43**
Dixon, Sharon Pratt **1**
Fauntroy, Walter E. **11**
Hobson, Julius W. **44**
Jarvis, Charlene Drew **21**
Norton, Eleanor Holmes **7**
Washington, Walter **45**
Williams, Anthony **21**

Washington, D.C., Commission on the Arts and Humanities
Neal, Larry **38**

Washington Mystics basketball team
McCray, Nikki **18**

Washington Post
Britt, Donna **28**
Davis, George **36**
Ifill, Gwen **28**

Maynard, Robert C. **7**
McCall, Nathan **8**
Nelson, Jill **6**
Raspberry, William **2**
Wilkins, Roger **2**
Green, Darrell **39**
Monk, Art **38**
Sanders, Deion **4, 31**

Washington State Higher Education Co-ordinating Board
Floyd, Elson S. **41**

***Washington Week in Review* TV Series**
Ifill, Gwen **28**

Washington Wizards basketball team
Bickerstaff, Bernie **21**
Heard, Gar **25**
Howard, Juwan **15**
Lucas, John **7**
Unseld, Wes **23**
Webber, Chris **15, 30**

Watts Repetory Theater Company
Cortez, Jayne **43**

WBA
See World Boxing Association

WBC
See World Boxing Council

WCC
See World Council of Churches

Weather
Brown, Vivian **27**
Christian, Spencer **15**
McEwen, Mark **5**

Welfare reform
Bryant, Wayne R. **6**
Carson, Julia **23**
Williams, Walter E. **4**

Wellspring Gospel
Winans, CeCe **14, 43**

West Indian folklore
Walcott, Derek **5**

West Indian folk songs
Belafonte, Harry **4**

West Indian literature
Coombs, Orde M. **44**
Guy, Rosa **5**
Kincaid, Jamaica **4**
Markham, E.A. **37**
Marshall, Paule **7**
McKay, Claude **6**
Walcott, Derek **5**

West Point
Davis, Benjamin O., Jr. **2, 43**
Flipper, Henry O. **3**

West Side Preparatory School
Collins, Marva **3**

Western Michigan University
Floyd, Elson S. **41**

White House Conference on Civil Rights
Randolph, A. Philip **3**

Whitney Museum of American Art
Golden, Thelma **10**
Simpson, Lorna **4, 36**

WHO
See Women Helping Offenders

"Why Are You on This Planet?"
Yoba, Malik **11**

William Morris Talent Agency
Amos, Wally **9**

WillieWear Ltd.
Smith, Willi **8**

Wilmington 10
Chavis, Benjamin **6**

Wimbledon
Williams, Venus **17, 34**

Winery production
Rideau, Iris **46**

WOMAD
See World of Music, Arts, and Dance

Women Helping Offenders (WHO)
Holland, Endesha Ida Mae **3**

Women's Auxiliary Army Corps
See Women's Army Corp

Women's Army Corps (WAC)
Adams Earley, Charity **13, 34**
Cadoria, Sherian Grace **14**

Women's issues
Allen, Ethel D. **13**
Angelou, Maya **1, 15**
Ba, Mariama **30**
Baker, Ella **5**
Berry, Mary Frances **7**
Brown, Elaine **8**
Campbell, Bebe Moore **6, 24**
Cannon, Katie **10**
Cary, Mary Ann Shadd **30**
Charles, Mary Eugenia **10**
Chinn, May Edward **26**
Christian, Barbara T. **44**
Christian-Green, Donna M. **17**
Clark, Septima **7**
Cole, Johnnetta B. **5, 43**
Cooper, Anna Julia **20**
Cunningham, Evelyn **23**
Dash, Julie **4**
Davis, Angela **5**
Edelman, Marian Wright **5, 42**
Elders, Joycelyn **6**
Fauset, Jessie **7**
Giddings, Paula **11**
Goldberg, Whoopi **4, 33**
Gomez, Jewelle **30**
Grimké, Archibald H. **9**
Guy-Sheftall, Beverly **13**
Hale, Clara **16**
Hale, Lorraine **8**
Hamer, Fannie Lou **6**
Harper, Frances Ellen Watkins **11**

Young Men's Christian Association (YMCA)
Butts, Calvin O., III **9**
Goode, Mal **13**
Hope, John **8**
Mays, Benjamin E. **7**

Young Negroes' Cooperative League
Baker, Ella **5**

Young Women's Christian Association (YWCA)
Baker, Ella **5**
Baker, Gwendolyn Calvert **9**
Clark, Septima **7**
Hedgeman, Anna Arnold **22**
Height, Dorothy I. **2, 23**
Jackson, Alexine Clement **22**
Jenkins, Ella **15**
Sampson, Edith S. **4**
Stewart, Ella **39**

Youth Pride Inc.
Barry, Marion S. **7, 44**

Youth Services Administration
Little, Robert L. **2**

YWCA
See Young Women's Christian Association

ZANLA
See Zimbabwe African National Liberation Army

ZAPU
See Zimbabwe African People's Union

Zimbabwe African National Liberation Army (ZANLA)
Mugabe, Robert Gabriel **10**

Zimbabwe African People's Union (ZAPU)
Mugabe, Robert Gabriel **10**
Nkomo, Joshua **4**

Zimbabwe Congress of Trade Unions (ZCTU)
Tsvangirai, Morgan **26**
Young, Roger Arliner **29**

Zouk music
Lefel, Edith **41**

ZTA
See Zululand Territorial Authority

Zululand Territorial Authority (ZTA)
Buthelezi, Mangosuthu Gatsha **9**

Cumulative Name Index

Volume numbers appear in **bold**

James, Daniel "Chappie", Jr. 1920-1978
16
James, Etta 1938— **13**
James, Juanita (Therese) 1952— **13**
James, LeBron 1984— **46**
James, Sharpe 1936— **23**
James, Skip 1902-1969 **38**
Jamison, Judith 1943— **7**
Jammeh, Yahya 1965— **23**
Jarreau, Al 1940— **21**
Jarret, Vernon D. 1921— **42**
Jarvis, Charlene Drew 1941— **21**
Jasper, Kenji 1976(?)— **39**
Jawara, Sir Dawda Kairaba 1924— **11**
Jay, Jam Master 1965— **31**
Jay-Z 1970— **27**
Jean, Wyclef 1970— **20**
Jean-Baptiste, Marianne 1967— **17, 46**
Jeffers, Eve Jihan
See Eve
Jefferson, William J. 1947— **25**
Jeffries, Leonard 1937— **8**
Jemison, Mae C. 1957— **1, 35**
Jenifer, Franklyn G(reen) 1939— **2**
Jenkins, Beverly 1951— **14**
Jenkins, Ella (Louise) 1924— **15**
Jenkins, Fergie 1943— **46**
Jerkins, Rodney 1978(?)— **31**
Jeter, Derek 1974— **27**
Jimmy Jam 1959— **13**
Joachim, Paulin 1931— **34**
Joe, Yolanda 19(?)(?)— **21**
John, Daymond 1969(?)— **23**
Johns, Vernon 1892-1965 **38**
Johnson, "Magic"
See Johnson, Earvin "Magic"
Johnson, Ben 1961— **1**
Johnson, Beverly 1952— **2**
Johnson, Buddy 1915-1977 **36**
Johnson, Carol Diann
See Carroll, Diahann
Johnson, Caryn E.
See Goldberg, Whoopi
Johnson, Charles 1948— **1**
Johnson, Charles Arthur
See St. Jacques, Raymond
Johnson, Charles Spurgeon 1893-1956
12
Johnson, Dwayne "The Rock" 1972—
29
Johnson, Earvin "Magic" 1959— **3, 39**
Johnson, Eddie Bernice 1935— **8**
Johnson, George E. 1927— **29**
Johnson, Georgia Douglas 1880-1966
41
Johnson, Harvey Jr. 1947(?)— **24**
Johnson, Hazel 1927— **22**
Johnson, J. J. 1924-2001 **37**
Johnson, Jack 1878-1946 **8**
Johnson, James Louis
See Johnson, J. J.
Johnson, James Weldon 1871-1938 **5**
Johnson, James William
See Johnson, James Weldon
Johnson, Jeh Vincent 1931— **44**
Johnson, John Arthur
See Johnson, Jack
Johnson, John H(arold) 1918— **3**
Johnson, Larry 1969— **28**
Johnson, Linton Kwesi 1952— **37**
Johnson, Lonnie G. 1949— **32**
Johnson, Mamie "Peanut" 1932— **40**
Johnson, Marguerite
See Angelou, Maya
Johnson, Mat 1971(?)— **31**

Johnson, Michael (Duane) 1967— **13**
Johnson, Norma L. Holloway 1932—
17
Johnson, R. M. 1968— **36**
Johnson, Rafer 1934— **33**
Johnson, Robert 1911-1938 **2**
Johnson, Robert L. 1946(?)— **3, 39**
Johnson, Robert T. 1948— **17**
Johnson, Rodney Van 19(?)(?)— **28**
Johnson, Shoshana 1973— **47**
Johnson, Taalib
See Musiq
Johnson, Virginia (Alma Fairfax) 1950—
9
Johnson, William Henry 1901-1970 **3**
Johnson, Woodrow Wilson
See Johnson, Buddy
Johnson-Brown, Hazel W.
See, Johnson, Hazel
Jolley, Willie 1956— **28**
Jones, Bill T. 1952— **1, 46**
Jones, Bobby 1939(?)— **20**
Jones, Carl 1955(?)— **7**
Jones, Caroline R. 1942— **29**
Jones, Cobi N'Gai 1970— **18**
Jones, Donell 1973— **29**
Jones, E. Edward, Sr. 1931— **45**
Jones, Ed "Too Tall" 1951— **46**
Jones, Edward P. 1950— **43**
Jones, Elaine R. 1944— **7, 45**
Jones, Elvin 1927— **14**
Jones, Etta 1928-2001 **35**
Jones, Gayl 1949— **37**
Jones, Ingrid Saunders 1945— **18**
Jones, James Earl 1931— **3**
Jones, Jonah 1909-2000 **39**
Jones, Kimberly Denise
See Lil' Kim
Jones, Le Roi
See Baraka, Amiri
Jones, Lillie Mae
See Carter, Betty
Jones, Lois Mailou 1905— **13**
Jones, Marion 1975— **21**
Jones, Merlakia 1973— **34**
Jones, Nasir
See Nas
Jones, Orlando 1968— **30**
Jones, Quincy (Delight) 1933— **8, 30**
Jones, Randy 1969— **35**
Jones, Robert Elliott
See Jones, Jonah
Jones, Roy Jr. 1969— **22**
Jones, Ruth Lee
See Washington, Dinah
Jones, Sarah 1974— **39**
Jones, Sissieretta
See Joyner, Matilda Sissieretta
Jones, Star(let Marie) 1962(?)— **10, 27**
Jones, Thomas W. 1949— **41**
Joplin, Scott 1868-1917 **6**
Jordan, Barbara (Charline) 1936— **4**
Jordan, Eric Benét
See Benét, Eric
Jordan, June 1936— **7, 35**
Jordan, Michael (Jeffrey) 1963— **6, 21**
Jordan, Montell 1968(?)— **23**
Jordan, Ronny 1962— **26**
Jordan, Vernon E(ulion, Jr.) 1935— **3,
35**
Josey, E. J. 1924— **10**
Joyner, Jacqueline
See Joyner-Kersee, Jackie
Joyner, Marjorie Stewart 1896-1994 **26**

Joyner, Matilda Sissieretta 1869(?)-1933
15
Joyner, Tom 1949(?)— **19**
Joyner-Kersee, Jackie 1962— **5**
Julian, Percy Lavon 1899-1975 **6**
Julien, Isaac 1960— **3**
July, William II 19(?(?)— **27**
Just, Ernest Everett 1883-1941 **3**
Justice, David Christopher 1966— **18**
Ka Dinizulu, Israel
See Ka Dinizulu, Mcwayizeni
Ka Dinizulu, Mcwayizeni 1932-1999
29
Kabbah, Ahmad Tejan 1932— **23**
Kabila, Joseph 1968(?)— **30**
Kabila, Laurent 1939— **20**
Kaiser, Cecil 1916— **42**
Kamau, Johnstone
See Kenyatta, Jomo
Kamau, Kwadwo Agymah 1960(?)— **28**
Kani, Karl 1968(?)— **10**
Karenga, Maulana 1941— **10**
Kaunda, Kenneth (David) 1924— **2**
Kay, Jackie 1961— **37**
Kay, Ulysses 1917-1995 **37**
Kayira, Legson 1942— **40**
Kearse, Amalya Lyle 1937— **12**
Kee, John P. 1962— **43**
Keith, Damon Jerome 1922— **16**
Kelly, Leontine 1920— **33**
Kelly, Patrick 1954(?)-1990 **3**
Kelly, R(obert) 1969(?)— **18, 44**
Kelly, Sharon Pratt
See Dixon, Sharon Pratt
Kem 196(?)— **47**
Kendricks, Eddie 1939-1992 **22**
Kennard, William Earl 1957— **18**
Kennedy, Adrienne 1931— **11**
Kennedy, Florynce Rae 1916-2000 **12,
33**
Kennedy, Lelia McWilliams Robinson
1885-1931 **14**
Kennedy, Randall 1954— **40**
Kennedy-Overton, Jayne Harris 1951—
46
Kenoly, Ron 1944— **45**
Kenyatta, Jomo 1891(?)-1978 **5**
Kerekou, Ahmed (Mathieu) 1933— **1**
Kerry, Leon G. 1949(?)— **46**
Keyes, Alan L(ee) 1950— **11**
Keys, Alicia 1981— **32**
Khan, Chaka 1953— **12**
Khanga, Yelena 1962— **6**
Kidd, Mae Street 1904-1995 **39**
Kilpatrick, Carolyn Cheeks 1945— **16**
Kilpatrick, Kwame 1970— **34**
Kimbro, Dennis (Paul) 1950— **10**
Kimbro, Henry A. 1912-1999 **25**
Kincaid, Bernard 1945— **28**
Kincaid, Jamaica 1949— **4**
King, Alonzo 19(?)(?)— **38**
King, B. B. 1925— **7**
King, Barbara 19(?)(?)— **22**
King, Bernice (Albertine) 1963— **4**
King, Coretta Scott 1929— **3**
King, Dexter (Scott) 1961— **10**
King, Don 1931— **14**
King, Gayle 1956— **19**
King, Martin Luther, III 1957— **20**
King, Martin Luther, Jr. 1929-1968 **1**
King, Oona 1967— **27**
King, Preston 1936— **28**
King, Regina 1971— **22, 45**
King, Riley B.
See King, B. B.

Manley, Edna 1900-1987 **26**
Manley, Ruth 1947— **34**
Marable, Manning 1950— **10**
Marchand, Inga
   See Foxy Brown
Marechera, Charles William
   See Marechera, Dambudzo
Marechera, Dambudzo 1952-1987 **39**
Marechera, Tambudzai
   See Marechera, Dambudzo
Mariner, Jonathan 1954(?)— **41**
Marino, Eugene Antonio 1934-2000 **30**
Markham, E(dward) A(rchibald) 1939—
   37
Marley, Bob 1945-1981 **5**
Marley, David
   See Marley, Ziggy
Marley, Rita 1947— **32**
Marley, Robert Nesta
   See Marley, Bob
Marley, Ziggy 1968— **41**
Marrow, Queen Esther 1943(?)— **24**
Marrow, Tracey
   See Ice-T
Marsalis, Branford 1960— **34**
Marsalis, Delfeayo 1965— **41**
Marsalis, Wynton 1961— **16**
Marsh, Henry L., III 1934(?)— **32**
Marshall, Bella 1950— **22**
Marshall, Gloria
   See Sudarkasa, Niara
Marshall, Paule 1929— **7**
Marshall, Thurgood 1908-1993 **1**, **44**
Marshall, Valenza Pauline Burke
   See Marshall, Paule
Martha Jean "The Queen"
   See Steinberg, Martha Jean
Martin, Darnell 1964— **43**
Martin, Helen 1909-2000 **31**
Martin, Jesse L. 19(?)(?)— **31**
Martin, Louis Emanuel 1912-1997 **16**
Martin, Sara 1884-1955 **38**
Marvin X
   See X, Marvin
Mary Mary **34**
Mase 1977(?)— **24**
Masekela, Barbara 1941— **18**
Masekela, Hugh (Ramopolo) 1939— **1**
Masire, Quett (Ketumile Joni) 1925— **5**
Mason, Felicia 1963(?)— **31**
Mason, Ronald 1949— **27**
Massaquoi, Hans J. 1926— **30**
Massenburg, Kedar 1964(?)— **23**
Massey, Brandon 1973— **40**
Massey, Walter E(ugene) 1938— **5**, **45**
Massie, Samuel Proctor, Jr. 1919— **29**
Master P 1970— **21**
Mathabane, Johannes
   See Mathabane, Mark
Mathabane, Mark 1960— **5**
Mathis, Greg 1960— **26**
Mathis, Johnny 1935— **20**
Mauldin, Jermaine Dupri
   See Dupri, Jermaine
Maxey, Randall 1941— **46**
Maxwell 1973— **20**
May, Derrick 1963— **41**
Mayers, Jamal 1974— **39**
Mayfield, Curtis (Lee) 1942-1999 **2**, **43**
Mayhew, Richard 1924— **39**
Maynard, Robert C(lyve) 1937-1993 **7**
Maynor, Dorothy 1910-1996 **19**
Mayo, Whitman 1930-2001 **32**
Mays, Benjamin E(lijah) 1894-1984 **7**
Mays, Leslie A. 19(?)(?)— **41**

Mays, William G. 1946— **34**
Mays, William Howard, Jr.
   See Mays, Willie
Mays, Willie 1931— **3**
Mazrui, Ali Al'Amin 1933— **12**
Mbaye, Mariétou 1948— **31**
Mbeki, Thabo Mvuyelwa 1942— **14**
Mboup, Souleymane 1951— **10**
Mbuende, Kaire Munionganda 1953—
   12
MC Lyte 1971— **34**
McBride, Bryant Scott 1965— **18**
McBride, James C. 1957— **35**
McCabe, Jewell Jackson 1945— **10**
McCall, H. Carl 1938(?)— **27**
McCall, Nathan 1955— **8**
McCann, Renetta 1957(?)— **44**
McCarty, Osceola 1908— **16**
McClurkin, Donnie 1961— **25**
McCoy, Elijah 1844-1929 **8**
McCray, Nikki 1972— **18**
McDaniel, Hattie 1895-1952 **5**
McDaniels, Darryl
   See DMC
McDonald, Audra 1970— **20**
McDonald, Erroll 1954(?)— **1**
McDonald, Gabrielle Kirk 1942— **20**
McDougall, Gay J. 1947— **11**, **43**
McEwen, Mark 1954— **5**
McFadden, Bernice L. 1966— **39**
McGee, Charles 1924— **10**
McGee, James Madison 1940— **46**
McGriff, Fred 1963— **24**
McGruder, Aaron Vincent 1974— **28**
McGruder, Robert 1942— **22**, **35**
McIntosh, Winston Hubert
   See Tosh, Peter
McIntyre, Natalie
   See Gary, Macy
McKay, Claude 1889-1948 **6**
McKay, Festus Claudius
   See McKay, Claude
McKay, Nellie Yvonne 194(?)— **17**
McKee, Lonette 1952— **12**
McKegney, Tony 1958— **3**
McKenzie, Vashti M. 1947— **29**
McKinney, Cynthia Ann 1955— **11**
McKinney, Nina Mae 1912-1967 **40**
McKinney-Whetstone, Diane 1954(?)—
   27
McKinnon, Ike
   See McKinnon, Isaiah
McKinnon, Isaiah 1943— **9**
McKissick, Floyd B(ixler) 1922-1981 **3**
McKnight, Brian 1969— **18**, **34**
McLeod, Gus 1955(?)— **27**
McLeod, Gustavus
   See McLeod, Gus
McMillan, Rosalynn A. 1953— **36**
McMillan, Terry 1951— **4**, **17**
McMurray, Georgia L. 1934-1992 **36**
McNabb, Donovan 1976— **29**
McNair, Steve 1973— **22**, **47**
McNair, Steve 1973— **22**
McNeil, Lori 1964(?)— **1**
McPhail, Sharon 1948— **2**
McPherson, David 1968— **32**
McQueen, Butterfly 1911— **6**
McQueen, Thelma
   See McQueen, Butterfly
McWhorter, John 1965— **35**
Meadows, Tim 1961— **30**
Meek, Carrie (Pittman) 1926— **6**, **36**
Meek, Kendrick 1966— **41**
Meeks, Gregory 1953— **25**

Meles Zenawi 1955(?)— **3**
Memmi, Albert 1920— **37**
Memphis Minnie 1897-1973 **33**
Mercado-Valdes, Frank 1962— **43**
Meredith, James H(oward) 1933— **11**
Merkerson, S. Epatha 1952— **47**
Messenger, The
   See Divine, Father
Metcalfe, Ralph 1910-1978 **26**
Meyer, June
   See Jordan, June
Mfume, Kweisi 1948— **6**, **41**
Micheaux, Oscar (Devereaux) 1884-
   1951 **7**
Michele, Michael 1966— **31**
Mickelbury, Penny 1948— **28**
Milla, Roger 1952— **2**
Millender-McDonald, Juanita 1938—
   21
Miller, Bebe 1950— **3**
Miller, Cheryl 1964— **10**
Miller, Dorie 1919-1943 **29**
Miller, Doris
   See Miller, Dorie
Miller, Maria 1803-1879 **19**
Miller, Percy
   See Master P
Miller, Reggie 1965— **33**
Millines Dziko, Trish 1957— **28**
Mills, Florence 1896-1927 **22**
Mills, Sam 1959— **33**
Mills, Stephanie 1957— **36**
Mills, Steve 1960(?)— **47**
Milner, Ron 1938— **39**
Milton, DeLisha 1974— **31**
Mingo, Frank L. 1939-1989 **32**
Mingus, Charles Jr. 1922-1979 **15**
Minor, DeWayne 1956— **32**
Mitchell, Arthur 1934— **2**, **47**
Mitchell, Brian Stokes 1957— **21**
Mitchell, Corinne 1914-1993 **8**
Mitchell, Leona 1949— **42**
Mitchell, Loften 1919-2001 **31**
Mitchell, Parren J. 1922— **42**
Mitchell, Russ 1960— **21**
Mitchell, Sharon 1962— **36**
Mizell, Jason
   See Jay, Jam Master
Mkapa, Benjamin William 1938— **16**
Mo', Keb' 1952— **36**
Mo'Nique 1967— **35**
Mobutu Sese Seko (Nkuku wa za
   Banga) 1930— **1**
Mobutu, Joseph-Desire
   See Mobutu Sese Seko (Nkuku wa za
   Banga)
Mofolo, Thomas (Mokopu) 1876-1948
   37
Mogae, Festus Gontebanye 1939— **19**
Mohamed, Ali Mahdi
   See Ali Mahdi Mohamed
Mohammed, W. Deen 1933— **27**
Mohammed, Warith Deen
   See Mohammed, W. Deen
Moi, Daniel (Arap) 1924— **1**, **35**
Mollel, Tololwa 1952— **38**
Mongella, Gertrude 1945— **11**
Monica 1980— **21**
Monk, Art 1957— **38**
Monk, Thelonious (Sphere, Jr.) 1917-
   1982 **1**
Monroe, Mary 19(?)(?)— **35**
Montgomery, Tim 1975— **41**
Moody, Ronald 1900-1984 **30**
Moon, (Harold) Warren 1956— **8**

Page, Alan (Cedric) 1945— **7**
Page, Clarence 1947— **4**
Paige, Leroy Robert
　See Paige, Satchel
Paige, Rod 1933— **29**
Paige, Satchel 1906-1982 **7**
Painter, Nell Irvin 1942— **24**
Palmer, Everard 1930— **37**
Parish, Robert 1953— **43**
Parker, (Lawrence) Kris(hna)
　See KRS-One
Parker, Charlie 1920-1955 **20**
Parker, Kellis E. 1942-2000 **30**
Parks, Bernard C. 1943— **17**
Parks, Gordon (Roger Alexander Bucha-
　nan) 1912— **1**, **35**
Parks, Rosa 1913— **1**, **35**
Parks, Suzan-Lori 1964— **34**
Parsons, James Benton 1911-1993 **14**
Parsons, Richard Dean 1948— **11**, **33**
Pascal-Trouillot, Ertha 1943— **3**
Patillo, Melba Joy 1941— **15**
Patrick, Deval Laurdine 1956— **12**
Patterson, Floyd 1935— **19**
Patterson, Frederick Douglass 1901-
　1988 **12**
Patterson, Gilbert Earl 1939— **41**
Patterson, Louise 1901-1999 **25**
Patterson, Orlando 1940— **4**
Patterson, P(ercival) J(ames) 1936(?)—
　6, **20**
Patton, Antwan 1975— **45**
Patton, Antwan "Big Boi" 1975(?)—
　See OutKast
Payne, Allen 1962(?)— **13**
Payne, Donald M(ilford) 1934— **2**
Payne, Ethel L. 1911-1991 **28**
Payne, Ulice 1955— **42**
Payton, Benjamin F. 1932— **23**
Payton, Walter (Jerry) 1954--1999 **11**,
　25
Pearman, Raven-Symone Christina
　See Raven
Peck, Carolyn 1966(?)— **23**
Peck, Raoul 1953— **32**
Peete, Calvin 1943— **11**
Peete, Holly Robinson 1965— **20**
Pelé 1940— **7**
Pendergrass, Teddy 1950— **22**
Penniman, Richard Wayne
　See, Little Richard
Peoples, Dottie 19(?)(?)— **22**
Pereira, Aristides 1923— **30**
Perez, Anna 1951— **1**
Perkins, Anthony 1959?— **24**
Perkins, Edward (Joseph) 1928— **5**
Perkins, Marion 1908-1961 **38**
Perrot, Kim 1967-1999 **23**
Perry, Emmitt, Jr.
　See, Perry, Tyler
Perry, Lee "Scratch" 1936— **19**
Perry, Lincoln
　See Fetchit, Stepin
Perry, Lowell 1931-2001 **30**
Perry, Rainford Hugh
　See Perry, Lee "Scratch"
Perry, Ruth 1936— **19**
Perry, Ruth Sando 1939— **15**
Perry, Tyler 1969— **40**
Person, Waverly (J.) 1927— **9**
Peters, Lenrie 1932— **43**
Peters, Margaret and Matilda **43**
Peters, Maria Philomena 1941— **12**
Petersen, Frank E. 1932— **31**
Peterson, Hannibal

See, Peterson, Marvin "Hannibal"
Peterson, James 1937— **38**
Peterson, Marvin "Hannibal" 1948—
　27
Petry, Ann 1909-1997 **19**
Phifer, Mekhi 1975— **25**
Philip, M. Nourbese
　See Philip, Marlene Nourbese
Philip, Marlene Nourbese 1947— **32**
Phillips, Teresa L. 1958— **42**
Pickett, Bill 1870-1932 **11**
Pickett, Cecil 1945— **39**
Pierre, Andre 1915— **17**
Pierre, Percy Anthony 1939— **46**
Pinchback, P(inckney) B(enton) S(tew-
　art) 1837-1921 **9**
Pinckney, Bill 1935— **42**
Pinderhughes, John 1946— **47**
Pinkett Smith, Jada 1971— **10**, **41**
Pinkett, Jada
　See Pinkett Smith, Jada
Pinkney, Jerry 1939— **15**
Pinkston, W. Randall 1950— **24**
Pippen, Scottie 1965— **15**
Pippin, Horace 1888-1946 **9**
Pitt, David Thomas 1913-1994 **10**
Pitta, (do Nascimento), Celso (Roberto)
　19(?)(?)— **17**
Player, Willa B. 1909-2003 **43**
Pleasant, Mary Ellen 1814-1904 **9**
Plessy, Homer Adolph 1862-1925 **31**
Poitier, Sidney 1927— **11**, **36**
Poole, Elijah
　See Muhammad, Elijah
Porter, Countee Leroy
　See, Cullin, Countee
Porter, James A(mos) 1905-1970 **11**
Potter, Myrtle 1958— **40**
Poussaint, Alvin F(rancis) 1934— **5**
Powell, Adam Clayton, Jr. 1908-1972 **3**
Powell, Bud 1924-1966 **24**
Powell, Colin (Luther) 1937— **1**, **28**
Powell, Debra A. 1964— **23**
Powell, Kevin 1966— **31**
Powell, Maxine 1924— **8**
Powell, Michael Anthony
　See Powell, Mike
Powell, Michael K. 1963— **32**
Powell, Mike 1963— **7**
Powell, Renee 1946— **34**
Pratt Dixon, Sharon
　See Dixon, Sharon Pratt
Pratt, Awadagin 1966— **31**
Pratt, Geronimo 1947— **18**
Premice, Josephine 1926-2001 **41**
Pressley, Condace L. 1964— **41**
Preston, Billy 1946— **39**
Preston, William Everett
　See Preston, Billy
Price, Florence 1887-1953 **37**
Price, Frederick K.C. 1932— **21**
Price, Glenda 1939— **22**
Price, Hugh B. 1941— **9**
Price, Kelly 1973(?)— **23**
Price, Leontyne 1927— **1**
Pride, Charley 1938(?)— **26**
Primus, Pearl 1919— **6**
Prince 1958— **18**
Prince-Bythewood, Gina 1968— **31**
Pritchard, Robert Starling 1927— **21**
Procope, Ernesta 19(?)(?)— **23**
Prophet, Nancy Elizabeth 1890-1960
　42
Prothrow, Deborah Boutin
　See Prothrow-Stith, Deborah

Prothrow-Stith, Deborah 1954— **10**
Pryor, Richard (Franklin Lennox Tho-
　mas) 1940— **3**, **24**
Puckett, Kirby 1961— **4**
Puff Daddy
　See Combs, Sean "Puffy"
Puryear, Martin 1941— **42**
Quarles, Benjamin Arthur 1904-1996
　18
Quarles, Norma 1936— **25**
Quarterman, Lloyd Albert 1918-1982 **4**
Queen Latifah 1970(?)— **1**, **16**
Quirot, Ana (Fidelia) 1963— **13**
Rahman, Aishah 1936— **37**
Raines, Franklin Delano 1949— **14**
Rainey, Ma 1886-1939 **33**
Ralph, Sheryl Lee 1956— **18**
Ramaphosa, (Matamela) Cyril 1952— **3**
Ramphele, Mamphela 1947— **29**
Ramsey, Charles H. 1948— **21**
Rand, A(ddison) Barry 1944— **6**
Randall, Alice 1959— **38**
Randall, Dudley (Felker) 1914— **8**
Randle, Theresa 1967— **16**
Randolph, A(sa) Philip 1889-1979 **3**
Rangel, Charles (Bernard) 1930— **3**
Ras Tafari
　See Haile Selassie
Rashad, Ahmad 1949— **18**
Rashad, Phylicia 1948— **21**
Raspberry, William 1935— **2**
Raven, 1985— **44**
Raven-Symone
　See Raven
Rawlings, Jerry (John) 1947— **9**
Rawls, Lou 1936— **17**
Ray, Gene Anthony 1962-2003 **47**
Raymond, Usher, IV,
　See Usher
Razaf, Andy 1895-1973 **19**
Razafkeriefo, Andreamentania Paul
　See Razaf, Andy
Ready, Stephanie 1975— **33**
Reagon, Bernice Johnson 1942— **7**
Reason, Joseph Paul 1943— **19**
Reddick, Lawrence Dunbar 1910-1995
　20
Redding, J. Saunders 1906-1988 **26**
Redding, Louis L. 1901-1998 **26**
Redding, Otis, Jr. 1941— **16**
Redman, Joshua 1969— **30**
Redmond, Eugene 1937— **23**
Reed, A. C. 1926— **36**
Reed, Ishmael 1938— **8**
Reed, Jimmy 1925-1976 **38**
Reems, Ernestine Cleveland 1932— **27**
Reese, Calvin
　See Reese, Pokey
Reese, Della 1931— **6**, **20**
Reese, Pokey 1973— **28**
Reeves, Dianne 1956— **32**
Reeves, Rachel J. 1950(?)— **23**
Reeves, Triette Lipsey 1963— **27**
Reid, Antonio "L.A." 1958(?)— **28**
Reid, Irvin D. 1941— **20**
Reid, L.A.
　See Reid, Antonio "L.A."
Reid, Vernon 1958— **34**
Reuben, Gloria 19(?)(?)— **15**
Rhames, Ving 1961— **14**
Rhoden, Dwight 1962— **40**
Rhodes, Ray 1950— **14**
Rhone, Sylvia 1952— **2**
Rhymes, Busta 1972— **31**
Ribbs, William Theodore, Jr.

Simmons, Ruth J. 1945-**13**, **38**
Simone, Nina 1933-2003 **15**, **41**
Simpson, Carole 1940— **6**, **30**
Simpson, Lorna 1960— **4**, **36**
Simpson, O. J. 1947— **15**
Simpson, Valerie 1946— **21**
Sims, Lowery Stokes 1949— **27**
Sims, Naomi 1949— **29**
Singletary, Michael
   See Singletary, Mike
Singletary, Mike 1958— **4**
Singleton, John 1968— **2**, **30**
Sinkford, Jeanne C. 1933— **13**
Sisqo 1976— **30**
Sissle, Noble 1889-1975 **29**
Sister Souljah 1964— **11**
Sisulu, Sheila Violet Makate 1948(?)— **24**
Sisulu, Walter 1912-2003 **47**
Sizemore, Barbara A. 1927— **26**
Sklarek, Norma Merrick 1928— **25**
Slater, Rodney Earl 1955— **15**
Sledge, Percy 1940— **39**
Sleet, Moneta (J.), Jr. 1926— **5**
Sly & Robbie **34**
Smaltz, Audrey 1937(?)— **12**
Smiley, Tavis 1964— **20**
Smith, Anjela Lauren 1973— **44**
Smith, Anna Deavere 1950— **6**, **44**
Smith, Arthur Lee,
   See Asante, Molefi Kete
Smith, B(arbara) 1949(?)— **11**
Smith, B.
   See Smith, B(arbara)
Smith, Barbara 1946— **28**
Smith, Bessie 1894-1937 **3**
Smith, Cladys "Jabbo" 1908-1991 **32**
Smith, Clarence O. 1933— **21**
Smith, Danyel 1966(?)— **40**
Smith, Emmitt (III) 1969— **7**
Smith, Greg 1964— **28**
Smith, Hezekiah Leroy Gordon
   See Smith, Stuff
Smith, Hilton 1912-1983 **29**
Smith, Jabbo
   See Smith, Cladys "Jabbo"
Smith, Jane E. 1946— **24**
Smith, Jennifer 1947— **21**
Smith, Jessie Carney 1930— **35**
Smith, John L. 1938— **22**
Smith, Joshua (Isaac) 1941— **10**
Smith, Mamie 1883-1946 **32**
Smith, Marvin 1910-2003 **46**
Smith, Mary Carter 1919— **26**
Smith, Morgan 1910-1993 **46**
Smith, Orlando
   See Smith, Tubby
Smith, Roger Guenveur 1960— **12**
Smith, Stuff 1909-1967 **37**
Smith, Trevor, Jr.
   See Rhymes, Busta
Smith, Trixie 1895-1943 **34**
Smith, Tubby 1951— **18**
Smith, Walker, Jr.
   See Robinson, Sugar Ray
Smith, Will 1968— **8**, **18**
Smith, Willi (Donnell) 1948-1987 **8**
Sneed, Paula A. 1947— **18**
Snipes, Wesley 1962— **3**, **24**
Snoop Dogg 1972— **35**
Soglo, Nicéphore 1935— **15**
Solomon, Jimmie Lee 1947(?)— **38**
Somé, Malidoma Patrice 1956— **10**
Sosa, Sammy 1968— **21**, **44**

Soulchild, Musiq
   See Musiq
Sowande, Fela 1905-1987 **39**
Sowande, Olufela Obafunmilayo
   See Sowande, Fela
Sowell, Thomas 1930— **2**
Soyinka, (Akinwande Olu)Wole 1934— **4**
Spaulding, Charles Clinton 1874-1952 **9**
Spencer, Anne 1882-1975 **27**
Spikes, Dolores Margaret Richard 1936— **18**
Sprewell, Latrell 1970— **23**
St. Jacques, Raymond 1930-1990 **8**
St. John, Kristoff 1966— **25**
St. Julien, Marlon 1972— **29**
Stackhouse, Jerry 1974— **30**
Stallings, George A(ugustus), Jr. 1948— **6**
Stanford, John 1938— **20**
Stanton, Robert 1940— **20**
Staples, "Pops" 1915-2000 **32**
Staples, Brent 1951— **8**
Staples, Roebuck
   See Staples, "Pops"
Stargell, Willie "Pops" 1940(?)-2001 **29**
Staton, Candi 1940(?)— **27**
Staupers, Mabel K(eaton) 1890-1989 **7**
Stearnes, Norman "Turkey" 1901-1979 **31**
Steele, Claude Mason 1946— **13**
Steele, Lawrence 1963— **28**
Steele, Michael 1958— **38**
Steele, Shelby 1946— **13**
Steinberg, Martha Jean 1930(?)-2000 **28**
Stephens, Charlotte Andrews 1854-1951 **14**
Stephens, Myrtle
   See Potter, Myrtle
Stevens, Yvette
   See Khan, Chaka
Steward, David L. 19(?)(?)— **36**
Steward, Emanuel 1944— **18**
Stewart, Alison 1966(?)— **13**
Stewart, Ella 1893-1987 **39**
Stewart, Kordell 1972— **21**
Stewart, Paul Wilbur 1925— **12**
Still, William Grant 1895-1978 **37**
Stokes, Carl B(urton) 1927— **10**
Stokes, Louis 1925— **3**
Stone, Angie 1965(?)— **31**
Stone, Charles Sumner, Jr.
   See Stone, Chuck
Stone, Chuck 1924— **9**
Stone, Toni 1921-1996 **15**
Stout, Juanita Kidd 1919-1998 **24**
Stoute, Steve 1971(?)— **38**
Strahan, Michael 1971— **35**
Strawberry, Darryl 1962— **22**
Strayhorn, Billy 1915-1967 **31**
Street, John F. 1943(?)— **24**
Streeter, Sarah 1953— **45**
Stringer, C. Vivian 1948— **13**
Stringer, Korey 1974-2001 **35**
Studdard, Ruben 1978— **46**
Sudarkasa, Niara 1938— **4**
Sullivan, Leon H(oward) 1922— **3**, **30**
Sullivan, Louis (Wade) 1933— **8**
Sullivan, Maxine 1911-1987 **37**
Summer, Donna 1948— **25**
Supremes, The **33**
Sutton, Percy E. 1920— **42**
Swann, Lynn 1952— **28**
Sweat, Keith 1961(?)— **19**

Swoopes, Sheryl Denise 1971— **12**
Swygert, H. Patrick 1943— **22**
Sykes, Roosevelt 1906-1984 **20**
Tademy, Lalita 1948— **36**
Tafari Makonnen
   See Haile Selassie
Talbert, David 1966(?)— **34**
Tamia 1975— **24**
Tanksley, Ann (Graves) 1934— **37**
Tanner, Henry Ossawa 1859-1937 **1**
Tate, Eleanora E. 1948— **20**
Tate, Larenz 1975— **15**
Tatum, Art 1909-1956 **28**
Tatum, Beverly Daniel 1954— **42**
Taulbert, Clifton Lemoure 1945— **19**
Taylor, Billy 1921— **23**
Taylor, Charles 1948— **20**
Taylor, Helen (Lavon Hollingshed) 1942-2000 **30**
Taylor, John (David Beckett) 1952— **16**
Taylor, Karin 1971— **34**
Taylor, Koko 1935— **40**
Taylor, Kristin Clark 1959— **8**
Taylor, Lawrence 1959— **25**
Taylor, Meshach 1947(?)— **4**
Taylor, Mildred D. 1943— **26**
Taylor, Natalie 1959— **47**
Taylor, Regina 1959(?)— **9**, **46**
Taylor, Ron 1952-2002 **35**
Taylor, Susan L. 1946— **10**
Taylor, Susie King 1848-1912 **13**
Temptations, The **33**
Terrell, Dorothy A. 1945— **24**
Terrell, Mary (Elizabeth) Church 1863-1954 **9**
Terrell, Tammi 1945-1970 **32**
Terry, Clark 1920— **39**
The Artist
   See Prince
The Rock
   See Johnson, Dwayne "The Rock"
Thigpen, Lynne 1948-2003 **17**, **41**
Thomas, Alma Woodsey 1891-1978 **14**
Thomas, Clarence 1948— **2**, **39**
Thomas, Debi 1967— **26**
Thomas, Derrick 1967-2000 **25**
Thomas, Frank Edward, Jr. 1968— **12**
Thomas, Franklin A(ugustine) 1934— **5**
Thomas, Irma 1941— **29**
Thomas, Isiah (Lord III) 1961— **7**, **26**
Thomas, Rozonda "Chilli" 1971—
   See TLC
Thomas, Rufus 1917— **20**
Thomas, Sean Patrick 1970— **35**
Thomas, Vivien (T.) 1910-1985 **9**
Thomas-Graham, Pamela 1963(?)— **29**
Thomason, Marsha 1976— **47**
Thompson, Bennie G. 1948— **26**
Thompson, John W. 1949— **26**
Thompson, Larry D. 1945— **39**
Thompson, Tazewell (Alfred, Jr.) 1954— **13**
Thompson, Tina 1975— **25**
Thompson, William C. 1953(?)— **35**
Thornton, Big Mama 1926-1984 **33**
Thrash, Dox 1893-1965 **35**
Three Mo' Tenors **35**
Thrower, Willie 1930-2002 **35**
Thugwane, Josia 1971— **21**
Thurman, Howard 1900-1981 **3**
Thurman, Wallace Henry 1902-1934 **16**
Till, Emmett (Louis) 1941-1955 **7**
Tillard, Conrad 1964— **47**
Tillis, Frederick 1930— **40**